INTRODUCTION TO

HEALTH BEHAVIOR THEORY

THIRD EDITION

Joanna Hayden, PhD, CHES
Professor Emeritus
Department of Public Health
William Paterson University
Wayne, New Jersey

JONES & BARTLETT
LEARNING

World Headquarters
Jones & Bartlett Learning
5 Wall Street
Burlington, MA 01803
978-443-5000
info@jblearning.com
www.jblearning.com

Jones & Bartlett Learning books and products are available through most bookstores and online booksellers. To contact Jones & Bartlett Learning directly, call 800-832-0034, fax 978-443-8000, or visit our website, www.jblearning.com.

15913-4

Production Credits

VP, Product Management: David D. Cella
Director of Product Management: Michael Brown
Product Specialist: Danielle Bessette
Product Specialist: Carter McAlister
Production Manager: Carolyn Rogers Pershouse
Director of Vendor Management: Amy Rose
Vendor Manager: Juna Abrams
Senior Marketing Manager: Sophie Fleck Teague
Manufacturing and Inventory Control Supervisor: Amy Bacus
Composition: codeMantra U.S. LLC
Project Management: codeMantra U.S. LLC
Cover Design: Scott Moden
Director of Rights & Media: Joanna Gallant
Rights & Media Specialist: Merideth Tumasz
Media Development Editor: Shannon Sheehan
Cover Image (Title Page, Part Opener, Chapter Opener): © ktsdesign/Shutterstock
Printing and Binding: LSC Communications
Cover Printing: LSC Communications

Library of Congress Cataloging-in-Publication Data

Names: Hayden, Joanna, author.
Title: Introduction to health behavior theory / Joanna Hayden.
Description: Third edition. | Burlington, MA: Jones & Bartlett Learning, [2019] | Includes bibliographical references and index.
Identifiers: LCCN 2017038327 | ISBN 9781284125115 (pbk.: alk. paper)
Subjects: | MESH: Health Behavior | Health Promotion | Attitude to Health | Behavioral Research
Classification: LCC RA776.9 | NLM W 85 | DDC 613—dc23
LC record available at https://lccn.loc.gov/2017038327

6048
Printed in the United States of America
21 20 19 18   10 9 8 7 6 5 4 3

Contents

Preface

Theory is the foundation for professional practice and an essential component of professional preparation at any level. However, this does not make the teaching and learning of theory any easier; it just makes it necessary. Theory is often the most difficult for undergraduate students to comprehend. It is difficult because they do not have a reservoir of knowledge from which to draw as they do for, say, math, history, English, or the sciences. This text is written for them.

The purpose of this text is to provide an easy to understand, interesting, and engaging introduction to a topic that is usually perceived as challenging, dry, and boring. The language used and the depth and breadth of the information presented are intentional. It is not meant to be a comprehensive tome on theory, but rather an *introduction* to theory. It is meant to be the headwaters of that reservoir of knowledge.

While written with the undergraduate in mind, this book would also be of value to graduate students or practicing professionals whose own "reservoir" of theory knowledge and understanding could use a refill. It would be an excellent text to use along with others in preparing for certification examinations in which health behavior is included.

The text begins with an explanation of what theory is, how theories are developed, and factors that influence health behavior. Chapters 2–11 cover the more frequently used health behavior theories. New to this edition, each theory chapter begins with a table containing the theory essence sentence (a statement that reflects the essence of the theory in one sentence), its constructs, and brief definitions. This is followed by a more in-depth discussion of the theory concept and constructs using multiple examples from the literature to demonstrate how the theory is used in practice. While some examples are related to college students, many are purposely not, for a few reasons. This book is intended for students in professional preparation programs, so the examples demonstrate how theories are used in a variety of settings, with different populations, addressing an assortment of health issues. Second, because the examples were taken from the literature, students have an extensive reference list at the end of each chapter that contains numerous citations of research studies and programs in which the theory was used.

Each theory chapter ends with a *Theory in Action* section—a full-length, peer-reviewed journal article that provides students a complete picture of the theory used in a practice setting to guide research, develop an intervention, or conduct an evaluation. The *Theory in Action* articles address a variety of health issues in different populations. The articles are also the basis for a class activity included in each chapter. All of the articles in this third edition are new.

Also new to this edition is Chapter 7 on Protection Motivation Theory. This was added in direct response to reviewers' suggestions for additional theories and in particular those deriving from health communication.

The final chapter in the book, Chapter 12, "Choosing a Theory," answers the often-asked question, "How do I know which theory to use?" This chapter provides a framework to help answer that question, a *Theory Chart*. The chart groups the theories by levels and is a compilation of the *Theory Essence Sentence* tables provided at the beginning of each chapter. New to this edition is a table with the construct domains for each theory and suggested techniques for addressing them.

The PowerPoint slide presentations have been revised for this edition to the extent possible in keeping with the publisher's guidelines, as have the examination questions. A new instructor's support is an annotated bibliography with active links to additional journal articles of the theory in practice.

In no way does this book purport to cover all of the theories that could be used to explain health behavior, nor does it claim to provide an in-depth, exhaustive discourse of the theories it does contain. It does, however, provide an introduction to the more commonly used theories in health education and health promotion. It is my hope that students will find this book interesting and engaging enough to read it, and that it will entice them to read further, more deeply filling their theory reservoirs.

Acknowledgments

This book certainly would not have been written if it were not for my former students who struggled to understand theory. They were the reason I stopped trying to find the right book for them and decided to write it myself.

I must give a big "thank you" to my editorial and production staff at Jones & Bartlett Learning for all of their help with this third edition—Lindsey Sousa, Merideth Tumasz, Danielle Bessette, Carter McAlister, and of course my editor, Michael Brown, whose confidence in me allowed this edition to come to fruition. A big thank you also goes to the many reviewers who provided me with wonderful suggestions that guided the writing of this third edition. I hope they see how their recommendations were put into action.

Finally, I'd like to thank my husband Roger for making sure I had a never-ending supply of hot tea during the writing of this edition and our puppy Alfie, for making sure I got away from the computer every few hours for a walk!

© ktsdesign/Shutterstock

CHAPTER 1

Introduction to Theory

The idea of studying theory can be a bit daunting. But, understanding and being able to use theories is essential because they provide the foundation for professional practice. They help us solve problems and formulate interventions to best provide the services we offer. In fact, research tells us that health interventions based on theories are more effective than those without a theoretical base (Bluethmann, Bartholomew, Murphy, & Vernon, 2016; Tebb et al., 2016).

▶ What Is Theory?

So, what is theory? A theory is "a set of statements or principles devised to explain a group of facts or phenomena, especially one that has been repeatedly tested or is widely accepted and can be used to make predictions about natural phenomena" (*American Heritage Dictionary of the English Language*, 2015). "A theory is a set of interrelated concepts, definitions, and propositions that present a systematic view of events or situations by specifying relations among variables in order to *explain* and *predict* events or situations" (Glanz, Rimer, & Viswanath, 2008, p. 26).

From a health promotion and disease prevention perspective, "the term *theory* is used to represent an interrelated set of propositions that serve to explain health behavior or provide a systematic method of guiding health promotion practice" (DiClemente, Crosby, & Kegler, 2002, p. 8). "Theory, then, provides a framework for explaining phenomena and may serve as the basis for further research as well as practice application" (Baumgartner, Strong, & Hansley, 2002, p. 18). Simply put, theories *explain* behavior and thus can suggest ways to achieve behavior change (Glanz et al., 2008). By understanding why people engage in unhealthy behaviors, we can better develop interventions that will enable them to change their behavior and adopt healthier lifestyles, if they choose.

In addition to theories, there are also *models*. A model is a composite, a mixture of ideas or concepts taken from any number of theories and used together. Models help us understand a specific problem in a particular setting (Glanz et al., 2008), which perhaps one theory alone can't do.

Theories and models help us explain, predict, and understand health behavior. Understanding the determinants of health behavior and the process of health behavior change provides the basis upon which interventions can be developed to improve the public's health and their effectiveness evaluated (Noar & Zimmerman, 2005).

Theory is also the driving force behind research. It guides the variables to be studied, how they should be measured, and how they might be combined (Noar & Zimmerman, 2005).

▶ Types of Theories

Theories and models can be separated into three different levels of influence: intrapersonal, interpersonal, and community. Theories at each of these levels attempt to explain behavior by looking at how different factors at these different levels influence what we do and why we do it.

Intrapersonal Theories

At the intrapersonal or individual level, theories focus on factors within the person that influence behavior, such as knowledge, attitudes, beliefs, motivation, self-concept, developmental history, past experience, and skills (National Cancer Institute [NCI], 2005). These theories and models include, among others, the Health Belief Model, Theory of Reasoned Action, Self-Efficacy Theory, Attribution Theory, and the Transtheoretical Model.

Interpersonal Theories

Theories addressing factors at the interpersonal level operate on the assumption that other people influence our behavior. Other people affect behavior by sharing their thoughts, advice, and feelings and by the emotional support and assistance they provide. These other people may be family, friends, peers, healthcare providers, or coworkers (NCI, 2005). Social Cognitive Theory is a very commonly used theory addressing behavior at this level.

Community-Level Theories

Community-level models and theories focus on factors within social systems (communities, organizations, institutions, and public policies), such as rules, regulations, legislation, norms, and policies. These theories and models suggest strategies and initiatives that can be used to change these factors (Cottrell, Girvam, & McKenzie, 2009; NCI, 2005). These are change theories more than explanatory theories. Changing a social system from one that maintains and supports *un*healthy behaviors to one that supports healthy behaviors ultimately supports individual behavior change (McLeroy, Bibeau, Steckler, & Glanz, 1988). A commonly used community-level theory is Diffusion of Innovation. More recent additions to this category are the Social Ecological Model and Social Capital Theory.

In health promotion, theories and models are used to explain why people behave, or don't behave, in certain ways relative to their health. They help us plan interventions to support the public's adoption of healthier behaviors. However, in order to understand how theories explain health behavior and support behavior change, it is important to understand where theories come from in the first place.

▶ Where Do Theories Come From?

Theories are born from the need to solve a problem or find an explanation that would account for some repeatedly observed occurrence. The goal of theory development then, is to identify a few principles that can account for (explain) a large range of phenomena (Bandura, 2005).

> Scientific inquiry is a cyclical process where theory and data can be regarded as either starting points or endpoints. In a spiral-shaped process of research, inductive and deductive phases of inquiry follow each other. The starting points are ideas, hypotheses or conceptual frameworks that guide future research. Endpoints are attained when there is a well-substantiated explanation of a particular facet of reality, based upon empirical evidence.
>
> (Schwarzer, 2014, p. 53)

The development of a theory in this manner begins with inductive reasoning and qualitative methods (Mullen & Iverson, 1982; Thomas, 1992). Inductive reasoning, if you recall, starts with specific observations or evidence and moves to a conclusion. For example, using inductive reasoning we observe that HIV is transmitted through sexual activity and we observe that condoms prevent the transmission of diseases through sexual activity. Therefore, we conclude that condoms prevent the transmission of HIV.

In deductive reasoning we start with the conclusion—condoms prevent the transmission of HIV—and seek the observations to support the conclusion—condoms prevent transmission of diseases through sexual activity. HIV is transmitted through sexual activity.

With this as the basis, let's look at visits to the student health service on campus. Suppose every year it is observed that the number of students needing treatment for alcohol overdose is greater during the month of September than any other time of the academic year. Suppose it is also observed that all of the students needing treatment are freshmen. Through inductive reasoning it might be concluded that risky behavior (drinking) occurs when environmental controls (parents) are absent. This is a reasonable conclusion based on the observations or evidence. However, this may or may not be true, which means the conclusion drawn from the observations needs to be verified, that is, tested to find out how accurate it is in predicting or explaining the behavior. Can risk-taking behavior be explained by the lack of external controls? To further develop this theory, research would be done to determine what happens, why, and under what conditions (Mullen & Iverson, 1982).

Observation, inductive reasoning, and qualitative research methods are what led to the development of the Health Belief Model. The Health Belief Model was developed by researchers at the U.S. Public Health Service in the late 1950s as a means to understand why so few people were being screened for TB. Triggered by the observation of poor screening utilization, possible reasons why people might or might not utilize these screenings were identified and research conducted to determine if the reasons proposed did in fact explain the behavior (Hochbaum, 1958; Rosenstock, 1960). They did explain the behavior and the outcome was the Health Belief Model, one of the most widely used theories in health education and health promotion (Glanz et al., 2008).

Sometimes the starting point of a theory is a problem that sparks a researcher's interest. This is followed by some hunches as to the behavioral causes of the problem, which suggest experiments that might be carried out to test if the hunches are accurate. The results of the experiments lead to refinements of the theory, which leads to more testing and more refinement, and so on. This is a long haul process as human behavior is caused by a number of factors all intricately interwoven and constantly changing (Bandura, 2009).

Sometimes new theories are developed when existing ones are revised, as is the case with the Theory of Reasoned Action. This theory was not very useful in predicting or explaining behaviors that were not under a person's volitional (willful) control. To make the theory more useful for these types of behaviors, the perception of behavioral control (ease or difficulty of doing something) was added and the Theory of Reasoned Action became the Theory of Planned Behavior.

▶ Health Behavior

Health behavior includes all of those things we do that influence our physical, mental, emotional, psychological, and spiritual selves. These behaviors range from brushing our teeth every day to having unprotected sex, from practicing yoga for stress management to smoking for weight management. A myriad of factors influence the types of behaviors we engage in, whether they are helpful or harmful to our health. Some of these factors are socioeconomic status, skills, culture, beliefs, attitude, values, religion, and gender.

Socioeconomic Status

Socioeconomic status (SES) makes a significant contribution to health since it encompasses education, income, and occupation. Education, in particular, affects health because of its relationship to income and occupation. The more education, the better the job, the greater the income. People with more education and money tend to live in safer homes (communities), have better health insurance, and access to healthier foods. These factors are related to less disease risk, especially from chronic illnesses like heart disease, diabetes, and obesity, and more positive health behaviors (Robert Wood Johnson Foundation, 2013).

However, behavior is driven by more than just education. For example, university students know a lot about HIV/AIDS transmission and how to decrease the risk, yet they don't use what they know and continue to engage in risky sexual practices (Ndabarora & Mchunu, 2014). Consider this—if education, and by extension knowledge, was the driving force behind health behavior, then physicians, nurses, dentists, and other healthcare professionals wouldn't smoke. Yet, some do. Why?

Skills

In the grand scheme of things, it's relatively easy to teach people new information, thereby increasing their knowledge. But without the skill or ability to use that knowledge, it's almost useless. So, behavior is influenced by having both knowledge and skill. Going back to the HIV/AIDS example, unless people know how to use condoms, all the knowledge in the world about how to decrease HIV/AIDS transmission risk is not going to make a difference. Another example where knowledge alone is insufficient is with child safety seats. Parents know the importance of using child safety seats. What they don't know is how to use them correctly. In fact, a study conducted by the National Highway Traffic Safety Administration found that 72.6% of them are *not* used correctly (Decina, Lococo, & Block, 2005). An even greater rate of misuse was found among parents of newborns. In this 2015 study, 95% of car seats were used incorrectly (Hoffman, Gallardo, & Carlson, 2015).

Culture

Sometimes, even armed with information and skills, people still don't use what they know and do what they know how to do. That's because behavior is significantly influenced by culture. In every culture there are norms, or expected, accepted practices, values, and beliefs that are the foundation for behavior.

Think about some of the American cultural norms that dictated what you did this morning in preparing for the day. In our culture, people typically shower every day and follow it with a daily application of deodorant. These behaviors are not necessarily based on knowledge because bathing every day is actually not the best thing for our skin, and using deodorant has no health benefit and in fact can cause problems for people who are allergic to the ingredients.

Looking at this scenario, why do we bathe every day? Other cultures bathe much less frequently and don't use deodorant. So, there must be something else that underlies these behaviors—that something else is our culture. Bathing every day and using deodorant is culturally expected if we are mainstream Americans.

Imagine, if you will, that there was a movement underway to change these behaviors to the more health-enhancing ones of bathing less frequently and not using deodorant. Imagine this campaign was based on the factual information that daily bathing is bad for the skin and that deodorants and antiperspirants inhibit a natural bodily process. Would you adopt these new behaviors? Would you simply stop taking that morning shower and stop rolling on that deodorant? Why or why not?

Beliefs

Beliefs are intimately woven with culture. Beliefs are one's own perception of what is true, although they might not be viewed as being true by others. A very common health belief is that going outside with a wet head causes pneumonia. Certainly knowledge, based on our Western medicine, tells us pneumonia has many causes, but a wet head is not one of them. However, if one's belief is that a wet head causes pneumonia, then the behavior it supports is not going out of the house with a wet head. This seems like a very innocuous behavior on the surface. But take it one step further: an elderly woman with this belief would not get a pneumonia vaccine, believing instead that staying indoors until her hair is dry is all that is needed to avoid "catching pneumonia."

Attitude

When there are a series of beliefs, you have an attitude. Add to the previous belief about a wet head causing pneumonia the belief that wet socks also lead to pneumonia, as does "getting a chill." This results in an attitude that pneumonia can be easily avoided by drying your hair, quickly changing your wet socks, and keeping warm.

Values

Along with attitudes are values. Values are what people hold in high regard, things that are important to them, such as nature, truth, honesty, beauty, education, integrity, friendship, and family. What we value influences the types of behaviors we adopt. For example, if someone values nature, she might be more likely to recycle, use organic fertilizers, feed the birds, and plant trees. If someone values health, he might be more likely to exercise, maintain a normal weight, and drink in moderation.

Religion

Values and beliefs are often reflective not only of a culture, but of a religion. So, religion is another enormously important factor in health behavior. Take for example, the practice of male circumcision; there is no question in Judaism that a male infant will be circumcised. In the Muslim faith, followers will fast from sunrise to sunset during Ramadan. Religion dictates diet, as in Hinduism, whose followers adhere to a strict vegan diet, or Orthodox Judaism, whose followers obey strict kosher laws. Religion influences the way we handle stress, such as by prayer or meditation, and our family planning—whether or not we use contraception.

Gender

Gender is another important determinant of health behavior. Research consistently shows that men engage in fewer health-promoting behaviors and have less healthy lifestyles than women. Women are more likely to have an annual physical, attend health education classes, ask for advice from their health provider, and have their blood pressure checked (Deeks, Lomnard, Michelmore, & Teede, 2009), eat the recommend number of fruit and vegetable servings a day, get more exercise, and smoke less (Harvard Medical School, 2010).

▶ Putting It All Together: Concepts, Constructs, and Variables

The factors we have been discussing not only influence health behavior, but are also the concepts of the theories we use to explain behavior. For example, we saw that beliefs influence health behavior. Beliefs form the concept (or idea) of the Self-Efficacy Theory and Health Belief Model, while attitudes are the basis of the Theory of Reasoned Action and the Theory of Planned Behavior. As the concept of a theory develops and evolves, and as it becomes less nebulous and more concrete, constructs emerge. *Constructs* are the ways concepts are used in each specific theory (Kerlinger, 1986).

Each theory, then, has at least one concept at its heart, and a series of constructs that indicate how the concept is used in that theory. To use an analogy, if a theory is a house, the concepts are the bricks and the constructs are the way the bricks are used in the house (see **FIGURE 1.1**). In one house, the bricks are used for the front steps; in another house, the bricks are used for the façade.

A *variable* is the operationalized concept, or how the concept is going to be measured (Glanz et al., 2008). Going back to the house analogy, the bricks can be measured (operationalized) by square footage, number, size, or weight.

▶ Summary

Theories and models help us understand why people behave the way they do. They are based on concepts and take into account the many factors influencing health behavior. They enable us to focus on these factors from three different levels: intrapersonal, interpersonal, and community. In addition to providing an explanation for behavior, theories and models provide direction and justification for health education and health promotion activities.

Although many theories and models are used to explain health behavior, it is beyond the scope of this text to include them all. Rather, this text provides an introduction to the ones most commonly used for health behavior change interventions.

FIGURE 1.1 Theories, concepts, and constructs.

How the concepts (bricks) used in each theory (house) are the constructs (steps, walkway), and how they are measured (number, color, size) are the variables.

▶ Chapter References

American Heritage Dictionary of the English Language. (2015). Retrieved July 11, 2016, from http://ahdictionary.com

Bandura, A. (2005). The evolution of social cognitive theory. In K. G. Smith & M. A. Hitt (Eds.), *Great minds in management: The process of theory development.* New York, NY: Oxford.

Bandura, A. (2009). Science and theory building. *Psychology Review, 14*(4), 2–3.

Baumgartner, T., Strong, C. H., & Hansley, L. D. (2002). *Conducting and reading research in health and human performance.* New York, NY: McGraw-Hill.

Bluethmann, S. M., Bartholomew, L. K., Murphy, C. C., & Vernon, S. W. (2016). Use of theory in behavior change interventions: an analysis of programs to increase physical activity in posttreatment breast cancer survivors. *Health Education and Behavior.* Advanced online publication. doi:10.1177/1090198116647712

Cottrell, R. R., Girvam, J. T., & McKenzie, J. F. (2009). *Principles & foundations of health promotion and education* (4th ed.). San Francisco, CA: Pearson/Benjamin Cummings.

Decina, L. E., Lococo, K. H., & Block, A. W. (2005). *Misuse of Child Restraints: Results of a Workshop to Review Field Data Results* (DOT HS 809 851).

Deeks, A., Lombard, C., Michelmore, J., & Teede, H. (2009). The effects of gender and age on health related behaviors. *BMC Public Health, 9*, 213. doi:10.1186/1471-2458-9-213

DiClemente, R. J., Crosby, R. A., & Kegler, M. C. (2002). *Emerging theories in health promotion practice and research.* San Francisco, CA: Jossey-Bass.

Glanz, K., Rimer, B. K., & Viswanath, K. (Eds.). (2008). *Health behavior and health education* (4th ed.). San Francisco, CA: Jossey-Bass.

Harvard Medical School. (2010). Mars vs. Venus: The gender gap in health. *Harvard Health Publication.* Retrieved July 13, 2016, from http://www.health.harvard.edu/newsletter_article/mars-vs-venus-the-gender-gap-in-health

Hochbaum, G. M. (1958). *Participation in medical screening programs: A socio-psychological study* (Public Health Service Publication No. 572). Washington, DC: U.S. Government Printing Office.

Hoffman, B. D., Gallardo, A. R., & Carlson, K. F. (2015). Unsafe from the start: Serious misuse of car safety seats at newborn discharge. *The Journal of Pediatrics, 171*, 48–54. doi:10.1016/j.eds.2015.11.047Kerlinger, F. N. (1986). *Foundations of behavioral research* (3rd ed.). New York, NY: Holt, Rinehart & Winston.

McLeroy, K. R., Bibeau, D., Steckler, A., & Glanz, K. (1988). An ecological perspective on health promotion programs. *Health Education Quarterly, 15*, 351–377.

Mullen, P. D., & Iverson, D. (1982). Qualitative methods for evaluative research in health education programs. *Health Education, 13*, 11–18.

National Cancer Institute. (2005). *Theory at a glance: A guide for health promotion practice* (2nd ed.). Washington, DC: U.S. Department of Health and Human Services. Retrieved July 15, 2016, from https://www.k4health.org/sites/default/files/NCI%20Theory%20at%20a%20Glance.pdf

Ndabarora, E., & Mchunu, G. (2014). Factors that influence utilization of HIV/AIDS prevention methods among university students residing at a selected university campus. *Journal of Social Aspects of HIV/AIDS Research Alliance, 11*, 202–210.

Noar, S. M., & Zimmerman, R. S. (2005). Health behavior theory and cumulative knowledge regarding health behaviors: Are we moving in the right direction? *Health Education Research, 20*(3), 275–290.

Robert Wood Johnson Foundation. (2013). Why does education matter so much to health? Retrieved July 11, 2016, from http://www.rwjf.org/content/dam/farm/reports/issue_briefs/2012/rwjf403347

Rosenstock, I. M. (1960). What research in motivation suggests for public health. *American Journal of Public Health, 50,* 295–301.

Schwarzer, R. (2014). Life and death of health behavior theories. *Health Psychology, 8*(1), 53–56. doi:10.1080/17437199.2013.810959

Tebb, K. P., Erenrich, R. K., Jasik, C. B., Berna, M. S., Lester, J. C., & Ozer, E. M. (2016). Use of theory in computer-based interventions to reduce alcohol use among adolescents and young adults: A systemic review. *BMC Public Health, 16*(1), 517. doi:10.1186/s12889-016-3183-x

Thomas, B. L. (1992). Theory development. In J. L. Brooking, S. A. Ritter, & B. L. Thomas (Eds.), *Textbook of psychiatric & mental health nursing.* New York, NY: Churchill-Livingstone.

CHAPTER 2

Self-Efficacy Theory

STUDENT LEARNING OUTCOMES

After reading this chapter the student will be able to:

- Explain the concept of Self-Efficacy Theory.
- Define the constructs of Self-Efficacy Theory.
- Explain how vicarious experience influences self-efficacy.
- Describe the influence of mastery experience on self-efficacy.
- Discuss how verbal persuasion impacts self-efficacy.
- Compare how the somatic and emotional states affect self-efficacy.
- Use Self-Efficacy Theory to explain one health behavior.

SELF-EFFICACY THEORY ESSENCE SENTENCE

People will only try to do what they think they can do, and won't try what they think they can't do.

Constructs

Mastery experience: Prior success at having accomplished something that is similar to the new behavior

Vicarious experience: Learning by watching someone similar to ourselves be successful

Verbal persuasion: Encouragement by others

Somatic and emotional states: The physical and emotional states caused by thinking about undertaking the new behavior

▶ In the Beginning

For eons of time, we have been trying to understand and explain why people do what they do. Early on, the theories used to explain behavior were based on psychology and shared three characteristics—behavior is regulated physically at a sub-conscience level; behaviors diverging from the prevailing norm are a symptom of a disease or disorder; and behavior changes as a result of gaining self-insight through analysis with a therapist (Bandura, 2004). These theories formed the foundation of the "lie on the couch" approach of talk therapy thought to be the magic bullet of behavior change. Unfortunately, research on the outcome of talk therapy showed that although people did gain insight into their behavior, their behavior usually didn't change (Bandura, 2004).

In the 1960s, an alternative behaviorist approach to the explanation of human behavior was introduced. This new approach viewed behavior as the result of an interplay between personal, behavioral, and environmental factors rather an unconscious process with psychodynamic roots, and it did not consider deviant behavior a disease symptom (Bandura, 2004).

A shift in treatment also occurred at this time in terms of content, location, and (behavior) change agent. Treatment content became action oriented and focused on changing the actual deviant behavior rather than trying to find the psychological origins of the behavior. Mastery experiences were used to give people the skills and belief in themselves to adopt healthier behavior. Treatment occurred in the settings where the behavior occurred—in homes, schools, workplaces, and communities—rather than in a therapist's office. And this new approach did not limit treatment change agents to only mental health professionals. For example, teachers were trained to assist in reducing problem behaviors in the school setting; peers or role models who had overcome the problem behavior themselves were also used as change agents (Bandura, 2004).

Although both approaches were very different, research done on phobias showed that both were equally as effective. Since both approaches worked, it was apparent there was some underlying mechanism connecting them. It was Albert Bandura in the late 1970s who proposed Self-Efficacy Theory as the unifying mechanism (Bandura, 1977, 2004).

▶ Theory Concept

If you were given the opportunity to fund your college education by swimming 10 laps in a pool, you surely would give it a try, assuming you can swim. Now imagine you were given the same opportunity to raise tuition money, but had to swim the English Channel instead. Would you still go for it? If your swimming ability is like the average person's, there's no way you'd even attempt it. Why the difference? In the first case, you believe you can swim the 10 laps. In the second, you don't believe you can swim the English Channel, and so you won't even try. Think back to your childhood and the book, *The Little Engine That Could*: "I think I can. I think I can." This is the concept of self-efficacy.

Self-efficacy is the belief in one's own ability to successfully accomplish something, achieve a goal. It is a theory by itself, as well as being a construct of Social Cognitive Theory. Self-Efficacy Theory tells us that people generally will only attempt things they believe they can accomplish and won't attempt things they believe they will fail. It makes sense—why would you try doing something you don't think you can do? However, people with a strong sense of efficacy believe they can accomplish even difficult tasks. They see these as challenges to be mastered, rather than threats to be avoided (Bandura, 1994).

Efficacious people set challenging goals and maintain a strong commitment to them. In the face of impending failure, they increase and sustain their efforts to be successful. They approach difficult or threatening situations with confidence that they have control over them. Having this type of outlook reduces stress and lowers the risk of depression (Bandura, 1994).

Conversely, people who doubt their ability to accomplish difficult tasks see them as threats. They avoid them based on their own personal weaknesses or the obstacles preventing them from being successful. They give up quickly in the face of difficulties or failure, and it doesn't take much for them to lose faith in their capabilities. An outlook like this increases stress and the risk of depression (Bandura, 1994).

▶ Theory Constructs

Self-Efficacy Theory introduces the idea that the perception of efficacy is influenced by four factors: mastery experience, vicarious experience, verbal persuasion, and somatic and emotional state (Bandura, 1994, 1997; Pajares, 2002).

Mastery Experience

We all have mastery experiences. These occur when we attempt to do something and are successful; that is, we have mastered something. Mastery experiences are the most effective way to boost self-efficacy, because people are more likely to believe they can do something new if it is similar to something they have already done well (Bandura, 1994).

Perhaps you never thought about this, but babysitting is a significant mastery experience (**FIGURE 2.1**). Babysitting is among the strongest predictors of a new mom's belief in her ability to take care of her own children. Women who have experience taking care of infants prior to becoming mothers themselves are more confident in their maternal abilities, and even more so in completing infant care tasks they did frequently (Froman & Owen, 1989, 1990; Gross, Rocissano, & Roncoli, 1989). So, babysitting as a teenager pays off in many ways.

FIGURE 2.1 Babysitting provides mastery experiences.
© Jamie Wilson/Shutterstock.

Conversely, parents of children with autism usually do not have mastery experiences to support their parenting self-efficacy, even if they had other children prior to the birth of the child with autism. The experiences gained from parenting children without autism are not applicable to parenting a child with autism. Therefore, to provide experiences for mastery of skills necessary for raising a child with special needs, a parent-coaching model is used to give parents opportunities to develop the skills they need to successfully interact with their children (Raj & Kumar, 2010).

Mastery is the basis for preoperative teaching of men undergoing surgery for prostate cancer. Since this type of surgery can result in urinary incontinence, it is important for men to do pelvic exercises postoperatively to restore urine control. If they are taught these exercises before surgery and practice them, their self-efficacy increases and they are more likely to quickly regain urine control after surgery (Maliski, Clerkin, & Litwin, 2004).

Providing opportunities for people to gain mastery is the aim of workshops, training or apprentice programs, internships, and clinical experiences. These are ways people can practice and become proficient at new skills, thereby increasing their self-efficacy. For example, hours in clinical practice areas provide opportunities for student nurses to master nursing skills, and internships afford public health students the chance to master the competencies needed for their professional practice. Increasing self-efficacy through mastery experiences is one way of assisting older adults at risk of falling to gain confidence in safely participating in everyday activities. In a fall prevention program for older adults, providing opportunities for negotiating outdoor activities such as using public transportation, climbing stairs, and crossing streets proved to be among the most effective strategies for increasing participants' fall prevention self-efficacy (Cheal & Clemson, 2001). For personal trainers, mastery experiences are effective ways to support client exercise self-efficacy. Starting with a simple exercise program that can be successfully completed creates a mastery experience that can lead to success with more challenging programs (Jackson, 2010).

It would seem that mastering something new is relatively simple: all you have to do is practice. However, this isn't always the case. If the new tasks are always easy and similar to ones already mastered, and difficult, unfamiliar ones are avoided, then a strong sense of efficacy does *not* develop. To develop a strong sense of efficacy, difficult tasks also need to be attempted, and obstacles worked through (Bandura, 1994). In reality, it is great if you tried to make brownies, were successful, and now make them all the time. But, you can't live on brownies alone. At some point, you need to try making a meal.

Vicarious Experience

Another factor influencing perception of self-efficacy is vicarious experience or the observation of the successes and failures of others (models) who are similar to one's self. Watching someone like yourself successfully accomplish something you would like to attempt increases self-efficacy. Conversely, observing someone like yourself fail detracts or threatens self-efficacy. The extent to which vicarious experiences affect self-efficacy is related to how much like yourself you think the model is (Bandura, 1994). The more one associates with the person being watched, the greater the influence on the belief that one's self can also accomplish the behavior being observed.

This construct can be used to explain how group weight loss programs work. If an obese person sees someone just like himself or herself lose weight and keep it off by following a sensible diet and exercise, then the belief in his or her own ability to also do this is strengthened. Watching friends who have taken a nutrition course choose healthy foods at a fast-food establishment may increase your belief in your ability to also choose healthy foods: "If they can do it, so can I."

Not only do workshops and training sessions increase mastery, they can also provide vicarious experiences as well. Watching others in a training session, a class, or during role playing can provide observational experiences that enhance self-efficacy, especially if the person performing or learning the behavior is similar to the observer. This is what happens when vicarious learning is used to teach medical students how to communicate with patients. As it turns out, medical students learn as much and sometimes more by watching other students practice talking with patients as they do from practicing it themselves (Stegmann, Pilz, Siebeck, & Fischer, 2012).

In the "Sun Protection Is Fun" program (Tripp, Herrmann, Parcel, Chamberlain, & Gritz, 2000) developed to teach children about skin cancer prevention, vicarious learning was used not only with the children, but with the parents and teachers as well. Within the context of the curriculum, children watched their teachers and other students demonstrate how to protect their skin by using sunscreen and wearing protective clothing. Instead of using actors as the role models in the parent and teacher videos developed for this intervention, families and teachers from the intervention schools were used so as to strengthen vicarious learning.

Vicarious learning is at the core of coach/trainer–student/client instruction. The coach or trainer demonstrates the skill, and the student/client then copies. This is also how you learned to tie your shoes, brush your teeth, and eat with a fork. You watched, observed your parents or older siblings, and then copied what they did. Think about all the things you learned by watching others and how successfully accomplishing the skill increased your self-efficacy (**FIGURE 2.2**).

FIGURE 2.2 Learning by watching others.

Verbal Persuasion

The third factor influencing self-efficacy is verbal or social persuasion. When people are verbally persuaded that they can achieve or master a task, it goes a long way in boosting their self-efficacy and making it more likely they will do the task. Coaches frequently use this tactic with their teams. They psyche them up verbally, before a game or a meet (**FIGURE 2.3**). They tell the players they are going to win, that the other team is no match for them, that they are stronger, faster, better prepared, and so on.

If a team performs poorly, the coach's reaction is paramount in the effect the loss has on the players' self-efficacy. For example, the coach saying "We lost the game today because you are all lousy players" doesn't do much for self-efficacy, whereas saying "We lost because we need more practice" does (Brown, Malouff, & Schutte, 2005).

Conversely, when people are told they do not have the skill or ability to do something, they tend to give up quickly (Bandura, 1994). Imagine the same coach telling his team they can't possibly win against the opposition. What would the likely outcome be?

Somatic and Emotional States

The physical and emotional states that occur when someone contemplates doing something provide clues as to the likelihood of success or failure. Stress, anxiety, worry, and fear all negatively affect self-efficacy and can lead to a self-fulfilling prophecy of failure or inability to perform the feared tasks (Pajares, 2002). Stressful situations create emotional arousal, which in turn affects a person's perceived self-efficacy in coping with the situation (Bandura & Adams, 1977).

People new to exercising at a gym, especially if they perceive that others are watching them, may become anxious in anticipation of an exercise session. This

FIGURE 2.3 Coaches use verbal persuasion to psyche up players.
© Doug James/Shutterstock.

is a negative somatic state that may be detrimental to their self-efficacy, and in turn, threaten their continued exercising. The fitness professional in this situation can minimize the negative effects by teaching relaxation techniques and positive self-talk in an effort to reduce anxiety and support self-efficacy (Jackson, 2010).

A classic example of how the emotional state affects self-efficacy and, ultimately, health behavior is fear of the dentist (**FIGURE 2.4**). For millions of people in this country, the mere thought of going to the dentist is associated with intense pain and anxiety. As a result, they cannot bring themselves to make appointments or keep appointments for even routine, preventive dental care. This avoidance behavior results in decayed or missing teeth, a poorer quality of life, the need for more extensive treatment, and the very pain they wanted to avoid (Heidari, Andiappan, Banerjee, & Newton, 2017; Rowe & Moore, 1998).

Being afraid of the dentist is also related to poor daily dental health habits, as a study of over 8000 university students found. Students who reported being very fearful of the dentist brushed their teeth once a day or less and used tobacco, as compared to those less fearful or not fearful at all who brushed their teeth twice a day or more and used tobacco less frequently or not all. As it turned out, the more fearful students were at greater risk of dental problems, which was consistent with their need for frequent dental treatment or treatment at every dental checkup (Pohjola, Rekola, Kuntu, & Virtanen, 2016).

As is evident from this example, emotional arousal affects self-efficacy, and self-efficacy affects the decisions people make. If the emotional state improves—that is, emotional arousal or stress is reduced—a change in self-efficacy can be expected (Bandura & Adams, 1977).

While we tend to think about negative examples of how the emotional state impacts self-efficacy and health behavior, sometimes the emotional state is positive. Think about the effect of the "runner's high" on health behavior. In this case, the emotional state that results is pleasurable, rather than uncomfortable. This would

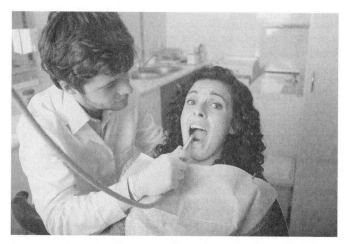

FIGURE 2.4 Fear of the dentist can lead to avoidance behavior.
© Michal Kowalski/Shutterstock.

positively impact self-efficacy and support continued engagement in the behavior that created it.

In summary, according to Self-Efficacy Theory, verbal persuasion, mastery experiences, vicarious experiences, and somatic and emotional states affect our self-efficacy and, therefore, our behavior (**FIGURE 2.5**).

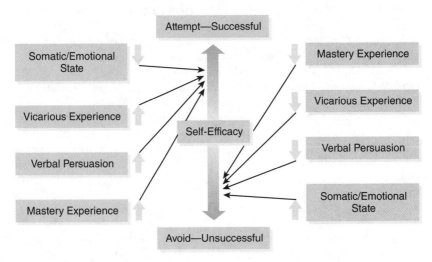

FIGURE 2.5 Self-Efficacy Theory.

THEORY IN ACTION—CLASS ACTIVITY

Exercise is an important aspect of health. Not only does it help with attaining and maintaining a healthy weight, but it also helps with flexibility, balance, and overall muscle strength, the latter of which helps us stay upright and prevents us from falling. While this may not be a big issue for young adults, lack of balance, flexibility, and muscle strength are significant issues for older adults with possible serious consequences. So, engaging older adults in exercise is critical to their wellbeing.

Now, think about your grandparents, another older relative or a close family friend who doesn't exercise at all. Image you are assigned the task of using the constructs of Self-Efficacy Theory to develop a walking program for older adults like them to encourage physical activity.

What might you do relative to:

Mastery experiences
Vicarious experiences
Verbal persuasion
Physical or emotional response

Now, read the following article and answer the questions at the end.

Chapter 2 Article: The feasibility of an intervention combining self-efficacy theory and Wii Fit exergames in assisted living residents: A pilot study[1]

Ying-Yu Chao, RN, MS, PhD(c)*, **Yvonne K. Scherer, RN, EdD,**
Yow-Wu Wu, PhD, Kathleen T. Lucke, RN, PhD,
Carolyn A. Montgomery, PhD, ANP-C, GNP

School of Nursing, University at Buffalo, The State University of New York,
301 Wende Hall, 3435 Main Street, Buffalo, NY 14214-3079, USA

Abstract

The purpose of this study was to examine the feasibility of a self-efficacy based intervention using Wii exergames in assisted living residents. The study was a single-group pre- and post-test design. Seven older adults (aged 80–94 years) were instructed to engage in exergames twice a week for 8 weeks. Physical function (balance, mobility, and walking distance), fear of falling, self-efficacy for exercise, and outcome expectations for exercise were evaluated. All participants had enjoyable experiences and no serious adverse events were reported. Participants had significant improvement on balance. Although not significant, there were trends indicating that participants improved mobility, walking endurance, and decreased fear of falling. The use of Wii exergames was an acceptable, safe, and potentially effective approach to promote physical activity in older adults. Findings provide support for the applications of integrating self-efficacy theory into exergames as a mechanism to encourage older adults to engage in exercise.

Keywords: Exergames, Assisted living residents, Exercise, Physical activity, Self-efficacy theory

▶ Introduction

Effective exercise programs can increase flexibility, leg strength, improve balance, and further reduce the risk of falling of residents in assisted living facilities (ALFs).[1,2] However, ALFs are not mandated to offer specific exercise programs to prevent functional decline. Most activities offered in the ALFs are mainly performed in a

1 Reproduced from Chao, Y., Scherer, Y. K., Wu, Y., Lucke, K. T., & Montgomery, C. A. (2013). The feasibility of an intervention combining self-efficacy theory and WiiFit Exergames in assisted living residents: A pilot study. *Geriatric Nursing, 34,* 377–382. doi: 10.1016/j.gerinurse.2013.05.006. With permission from Elsevier.

* Corresponding author.

seated position (e.g., music, art, and game-oriented activities), rather than physical activity.[3] It is estimated that 30%–50% of ALF residents had a fall over a period of 6 to 12 months. If the possible unreported incidence of falls is included, it may make the estimate even higher by 5%–9%.[4] Older adults who fall or have developed a fear falling are at risk for avoiding activities, resulting in decreased muscle strength and postural control. This activity avoidance could further decrease physical performance and in turn increase risk of falls.[5] Therefore, developing an effective exercise program to prevent functional decline and lower risk of falls is important for residents to delay nursing home placement.

Through recent technological innovation, there has been a rapid growth in the use of the interactive health video games that are particularly designed to encourage people to engage in physical activity. Individuals can practice various activities as they do in the real world. The Nintendo Wii exergames (entertaining video games that combine game play with exercise) is one of the popular health video games and has been broadly used in senior centers and retirement communities.[6] Empirical evidence supports that using Wii exergames as an intervention in older adults can maintain or/and improve physical function, such as balance, mobility, strength, flexibility[7,8] and balance confidence.[9,10] In addition, Wii exergames can make the exercise experience more enjoyable, which motivates older adults to engage in exercise.[11,12]

Self-efficacy theory[13] has been suggested as the most effective theoretical guide to change exercise behavior in older adults.[14] People with higher exercise self-efficacy engage more in physical activity and adhere to an exercise program.[15] Self-efficacy has 2 key concepts: self-efficacy expectations and outcome expectations. Evidence shows that self-efficacy expectations and outcome expectations are both important determinants of exercise behavior in older adults.[16] The interventions based on the 4 approaches (e.g., enactive mastery experiences, vicarious experiences, verbal persuasion, and physiological and affective states) can effectively influence self-efficacy expectations and outcome expectations on exercise behavior in older adults.[17,18]

In ALF residents, only one study was found to investigate the safety and efficacy of the Wii exergames program.[19] Continued research is needed to establish the effects of Wii exergames in this specific older population. In addition, a literature review found no mention of a theoretical framework to guide exergames programs in the older adult population. Therefore, the research investigators designed an intervention incorporating the self-efficacy theoretical-based approach Staying Active, Healthy Aging (SAHA) program by utilizing Wii Fit exergames to encourage ALF residents to engage in exercise. The purpose of this study was to determine the feasibility of a SAHA program to maintain or improve physical function and decrease fear of falling in ALF residents. The specific aims of this pilot study were to (1) evaluate the acceptability, safety and efficacy of the program on physical function and fear of falling; and (2) evaluate how the self-efficacy theoretical-based intervention influenced ALF residents' confidence to continue to exercise and perceived consequence of exercise.

▶ Methodology

Design

This study used a single-group pre-post design. The Staying Active, Healthy Aging (SAHA) program was an 8-week integrated health education and self-efficacy based exercise program. The Wii Fit exergames, which include aerobic, strength, balance, and yoga exercise were used as the exercise device. The study addressed the application of Bandura's self-efficacy theory[13] to improve older adults' exercise behavior and appraise its influence on physical function, fear of falling, cognition, depression, and quality of life. The focus of this article is on physical function and fear of falling. The study was approved by the Health Science Institutional Review Board of the University at Buffalo, the State University of New York.

Sample

Participants were recruited from one 60-bed ALF in a suburb of Buffalo NY. Inclusion criteria for the potential participants were (1) 65 years of age or older; (2) able to ambulate with or without an assistive device; (3) able to speak and read English; (4) able to understand instructions and follow commands (1:1); and (5) medically stable. Participants were excluded if they had contraindications for exercise suggested by the American College of Sports Medicine.[20]

Recruitment flyers were distributed to all residents and an announcement about the program was made at the resident council. A total of 9 residents expressed an interest in joining the study. Two of these individuals did not participate in the study. One did not participate because of failure to obtain the medical clearance approval by the primary care physician, and the other decided not to enroll in the study after being informed of the study procedure. A total of 7 participants (2 male and 5 female) enrolled and all of them completed the study. Participants had an average age of 86 ± 5 years old (range from 80 to 94). All were Caucasian and 6 of them were widowed. Four participants were able to ambulate without an assistive device and required no assistance with the activities of daily living. Three participants had a diagnosis of cognitive deficits; one had stroke; 2 had Parkinson's disease; and one had chronic obstructive pulmonary disease (COPD).

Intervention
Motivational intervention

Methods designed to increase self-efficacy throughout the program including enactive mastery experiences, vicarious experiences, verbal persuasion, and emotional or physical feedback were implemented[13] (**TABLE A.1**). Participants were encouraged to work in pairs since group exercise can serve as a motivator as well as increase social interaction and connections.[21] Prompt encouragements and support were given by partners and researchers supervising the exercise training. In addition, health education was given to participants at each session.

Wii Fit exergames intervention

The design of the exercise program was modified based on the Williams et al. EXercising with Computers in Later Life (EXCELL) program[7] and input from a geriatric nurse practitioner with expertise in designing and promoting physical activity in this population. The SAHA program led by 2 nursing PhD students was conducted twice a week for 8 weeks. The exercise time per session was

TABLE A.1 The self-efficacy-based motivational intervention.

Self-efficacy sources	Methods	Descriptions
Enactive mastery experiences	– Individualized exercise prescription – Goal setting – Evaluation	1. Discussed previous exercise experience and current exercise performance. 2. Discussed specific short- and long-term goals. 3. Exercise prescription was tailored to the needs of each participant. 4. Used diary to monitor progress.
Vicarious experiences	– Self-modeling – Story telling – Role modeling	1. Participants' prior successful performance was used as a reminder to encourage participants themselves and encourage them to share their success with others. 2. Encouraged participants to observe others with comparable degrees of physical impairments successfully perform the tasks. 3. Wii Fit provided a "virtual trainer" to demonstrate the skills of the exercise and educate participants on the ways to improve performance in posture, strength, and balance.
Verbal persuasion	– Education – Support and encouragement	1. Distributed the health education booklets and underscored the benefits of exercise. 2. Displayed a poster in each participant's room as a reminder of exercise benefits. 3. Provided on-going encouragement and positive reinforcement related to goal achievement and adherence to exercise. In addition, participants provided peer support by exchanging successful experiences and encouragement for accomplishments.

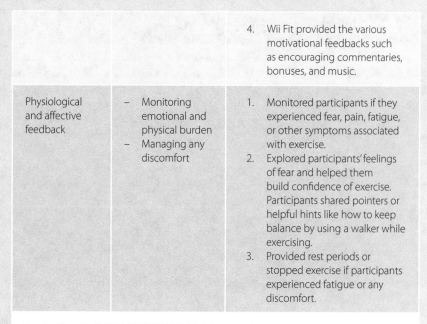

		4. Wii Fit provided the various motivational feedbacks such as encouraging commentaries, bonuses, and music.
Physiological and affective feedback	– Monitoring emotional and physical burden – Managing any discomfort	1. Monitored participants if they experienced fear, pain, fatigue, or other symptoms associated with exercise. 2. Explored participants' feelings of fear and helped them build confidence of exercise. Participants shared pointers or helpful hints like how to keep balance by using a walker while exercising. 3. Provided rest periods or stopped exercise if participants experienced fatigue or any discomfort.

Reproduced from: Chao, Y., Scherer, Y. K., Wu, Y., Lucke, K. T., & Montgomery, C. A.(2013). The feasibility of an intervention combining self-efficacy theory and Wii Fit exergames in assisted living residents: A pilot study. *Geriatric Nursing, 34*, 377–382. doi: 10.1016/j.gerinurse.2013.05.006.

designed for about 30 min per individual. Two participants worked as a team, with a goal of 60 min per session. A walker was placed around the Wii balance board. Participants were allowed to hold the walker for stability while performing any exercise. Exercise floor mats were used to reduce injury from falls. At each session, participants took turns doing gaming activities. Each participant exercised about 30 min and spent the other 30 min encouraging his/her exercise partner to perform the exercise activities. Participants began with range of motion exercise, then they performed an aerobic exercise (jogging), a strength exercise (lunge), 2 balance exercises (penguin slide and table tilt), and 2 yoga exercises (chair and deep breathing). The plan was to increase the amount of time performing strength exercise (lunge) at week 4 and week 7 since strength exercise has the strongest positive effect on improving functional performance, muscle strength, and muscle endurance.[22] The time for doing other gaming activities was decreased in order to accommodate 30 min per exercise session (**TABLES A.2** and **A.3**). However, the actual amount of time spent and progression (game levels) adjusted on each game including the lunge depended on each individual's physical tolerance and performance. Participants were allowed to terminate the session at any point. Additional topics included in the educational portion of the program are presented in Table A.3. The content for each topic was based on the information on exercise and physical activity for older adults located on the National Institutes on Aging websites.[23]

TABLE A.2 Description of Wii Fit exergames.

Exercise	Game	General description	Goals
Aerobic exercise	Jogging	The player walks or jogs along the paths and routes by following the software build-in runner.	Increase mobility, aerobic capacity
Strength exercise	Lunge	The player steps on the balance board and follows the "virtual trainer" to perform lunge exercise on each leg.	Strengthen quadriceps muscles, gluteal muscles, and hamstrings
Balance exercise	Penguin slide	The player steps on balance board and shifts his/her weight side to side to make a penguin catch fish.	Improve balance
	Table tilt	The player steps on the balance board and shifts his/her weight in all directions to direct balls into holes on the shifting platform.	Improve balance
Yoga exercise	Chair	The player steps on the balance board and follows the "virtual trainer" to perform the squat pose.	Strengthen hamstrings, quadriceps, gluteals, and the erector muscles of the back in order to improve balance and stability
	Deep breathing	Participants step on the balance board and follow the "virtual trainer" to breath in sync with the blue circle on the interface.	Improve breathing, metabolism, and circulation

Reproduced from: Chao, Y., Scherer, Y. K., Wu, Y., Lucke, K. T., & Montgomery, C. A.(2013). The feasibility of an intervention combining self-efficacy theory and Wii Fit exergames in assisted living residents: A pilot study. *Geriatric Nursing, 34*, 377–382. doi: 10.1016/j.gerinurse.2013.05.006.

TABLE A.3 Program schedule.		
Week	**Health education topics**	**Wii Fit exergames**
Week 1–3	1. How exercise can help you 2. How to get started exercising 3. Stay safe 4. Preventing injury	Warm-up (5 min) → jogging (5 min) → lunge (4 min) → penguin slide (4 min) → chair (4 min) → table tilt (4 min) → breathing (4 min)
Week 4–6	1. Getting the right shoes 2. How to stay active 3. Four types of exercise (aerobic, strength, balance, and flexibility exercise)	Warm-up (5 min) → jogging (5 min) → lunge (4 min) → penguin slide (4 min) → chair (2 min) → table tilt (4 min) → lunge (4 min) → breathing (2 min)
Week 7–8	1. How to keep going 2. Content review	Warm-up (5 min) → jogging (5 min) → lunge (4 min) → penguin slide (2 min) → chair (2 min) → lunge (4 min) → table tilt (2 min) → lunge (4 min) → breathing (2 min)

Reproduced from: Chao, Y., Scherer, Y. K., Wu, Y., Lucke, K. T., & Montgomery, C. A.(2013). The feasibility of an intervention combining self-efficacy theory and Wii Fit exergames in assisted living residents: A pilot study. *Geriatric Nursing, 34*, 377–382. doi: 10.1016/j.gerinurse.2013.05.006.

▶ Measures

Outcome measures focused on evaluating the acceptability, safety, and the efficacy of the SAHA program. Interview format surveys and functional testing were administered at pre-intervention (week 0) and post-intervention (week 9).

Acceptability outcome

Exergames experience questionnaire

An investigator-designed exergames experience questionnaire[7,11] was used to evaluate the acceptability of using Wii exergmaes in ALF residents. The questionnaire consists of 2 parts. The first part was administered prior to the intervention. Participants were asked about their previous experience with exergames and whether they would consider the Wii exergames as an exercise tool. The second part of the questionnaire was administered after completing the 8-week program. Participants were asked about exercise experience using Wii exergames.

Safety outcome

The safety outcome assessed any intervention-related adverse events during the exercise period, such as falls, injury, or clinical symptoms (e.g., chest pain, dizziness, shortness of breath).[20] Heart rate, blood pressure, and respirations were monitored at each session.

Efficacy outcome

Physical function

Berg balance scale (BBS-14). The BBS-14 is a 14-item scale that was developed to measure both static and dynamic aspects of balance. Each item is rated from 0 to 4, where 0 indicates an inability to complete the task and 4 indicates the highest competence in completing the task. The total score of the BBS is 56.[24] One systematic review shows that the BBS has excellent internal consistency (Cronbach alpha = 0.92–0.98), test-retest reliability (ICC = 0.98), and validity.[25]

Timed up and go test (TUG). TUG is a measure of functional mobility. Participants were instructed to stand up from a chair, walk 3 m, turn around, return to the chair, and sit down. Participants wore regular footwear and used their customary assistive device (cane, walkers, etc.). The time (s) taken to complete this task was recorded.[26] Prior use of the TUG provided support for reliability, internal consistency, and validity.[26]

Six-minute walk test (6MWT). 6MWT is a measure of overall mobility and physical function. Participants were instructed to walk on a straight, flat, non-slippery internal hallway (38.64 m) at the comfortable speed. They were allowed to use their usual assistive devices and walked at their own pace as far as possible. The maximum distance (m) walked in 6 min was measured.[27] Previous studies provided evidence of good reliability (ICC = 0.94–0.96) and validity.[27]

Fear of falling

Falls efficacy scale (FES). The FES is a self-report 10-item measurement that was developed to assess fear of falling. Each item is rated on a 10-point continuum scale from 1 to 10, where 1 represents subjects that have extreme confidence and 10 represents subjects that have no confidence. The total score of the FES is 100.[28] The FES has good test-retest reliability and validity.[28]

Mediating factors for residents

Self-efficacy for exercise scale (SEE). The SEE is a 9-item scale to assess confidence to continue exercising in the face of perceived barriers. The SEE consists of 9 situations that might affect participation in exercise. Items are rated from 0 (not confident) to 10 (very confident). The mean score of numerical ratings from each response indicates the strength of efficacy expectations.[29] The SEE scale has excellent internal consistency (Cronbach alpha = 0.89–0.94) and validity.[29,30]

Outcome expectations for exercise scale (OEE). The OEE is a 9-item measurement to identify perceived consequences of exercise for older adults. Items are rated from 1 (strongly disagree) to 5 (strongly agree) to assess the physical and mental outcomes of exercise. The scale is represented with the mean score of numerical ratings from each response. This OEE scale has good internal consistency (Cronbach alpha = 0.72–0.88) and validity.[30,31]

Data analysis

The statistical software used for the analysis was SPSS version 19.0 (SPSS Inc., Chicago, IL, USA). Descriptive statistics were used for sample characteristics. Since the sample size was small, the non-parametric Wilcoxon signed-rank test was used to compare the values of all the measurement outcomes of the pre-test with the post-test. Significant results were considered if $p < 0.05$. An effect size was calculated for each outcome measure[32] and was interpreted based on the Cohen[33] recommendation.

▶ Results

Acceptability

Prior to the Wii exergames intervention, 4 participants had experienced playing Wii sports, which was held monthly at the facility; however, no one had considered using Wii exergames as an exercise tool. After completing the 8-week program, participants reported using Wii exergames as an enjoyable experience. Five participants had great interest in exercising with Wii exergames again, and would like to recommend exergames to their family and friends. Participants stated they had a closer relationship with their exercise partners by sharing exercise experiences and life stories. All participants reported that "penguin slide" was their favorite game because of the music and visual motion of the presentation.

Safety

All participants were able to complete each exercise session in the time allowed except the one participant with COPD. The participant with COPD experienced mild shortness of breath during exercise training, and required 40–45 min to complete 30 min exercise session. The participants with a diagnosis of stroke and/or Parkinson's disease, although they moved slowly, were able to complete the 30 min exercise session in the time allotted. Overall, participants tolerated the intervention. None of the participants experienced any fall or injury related to the intervention.

Efficacy

TABLE A.4 summarizes the effects of the intervention on the outcomes. The mean score on the balance showed a significant improvement from 40.9 ± 8.5 to 45.1 ± 6.3 following the 8-week program ($p = 0.017$). No significant differences were found between pre- and post-test scores in the other outcome measures. However, there were trends indicating that participants performed better with an average of 3.6 ± 4.8 s in

TABLE A.4 Effects of intervention on the outcomes ($N = 7$).

Outcome	Pre-test (mean ± SD)	Post-test (mean ± SD)	Significance	Effect size
Physical function				
Balance (BBS-14; range: 0–56)	40.9 ± 8.5	45.1 ± 6.3	0.017[a]	0.64
Mobility (s) (TUG)	19.4 ± 5.5	15.8 ± 5.1	0.063	0.50
Walking distance (m) (6MWT)	177.2 ± 42.9			
Fear of falling				
Falls efficacy (FES; range: 0–100)	31.3 ± 15.7			
Self-efficacy for exercise (SEE; range: 0–10)	5.9 ± 1.7	6.0 ± 1.5	0.600	0.14
Outcome expectations for exercise (OEE; range: 1–5)	3.9 ± 0.3	4.1 ± 0.6	0.344	0.25

Note. Cohen's effect sizes (r): 0.10 < small < 0.29; 0.30 < medium < 0.49; large ≥ 0.50; $p < 0.05$. BBS = Berg balance scale; TUG = timed up and go test; 6MWT = six-minute walk test; FES = falls efficacy scale; SEE = self-efficacy for exercise scale; OEE = outcome expectations for exercise scale.
[a] $p < 0.05$.

Reproduced from: Chao, Y., Scherer, Y. K., Wu, Y., Lucke, K. T., & Montgomery, C. A.(2013). The feasibility of an intervention combining self-efficacy theory and Wii Fit exergames in assisted living residents: A pilot study. Geriatric Nursing, 34, 377–382. doi: 10.1016/j.gerinurse.2013.05.006.

mobility ($p = 0.063$) and an average of 68.6 ± 70.1 m in walking distance ($p = 0.063$). Scores also showed higher confidence in performing daily activities without falling ($p = 0.058$). Yet, the mean scores of self-efficacy for exercise and outcome expectations for exercise were comparable between pre- and post-test.

▶ Discussion

Encouraging older adults to engage in exercise over time can be difficult. Boredom is one of the possible reasons for them to quit exercising.[34] Our participants reported playing Wii exergames was an enjoyable experience and expressed the wish to continue to exercise. The results showed that Wii exergames could serve to motivate older adults to continue to engage in exercise. In addition, Wii exergames can be considered as a safe exercise tool since none of participants had falls or injuries during the exercise sessions. Nevertheless, guidance or/and supervision is needed for older adults using exergames in order to provide safety.

Our pilot study found that ALF residents had a significant improvement in balance after exercising twice a week for 8-weeks using the exergames intervention. A similar result was also found in Padala et al.[19] study in which ALF residents showed significant improvement in balance after Wii Fit training 5 days a week over 8 weeks. Although not significant, our participants showed improvements in mobility and walking endurance after the intervention as measured by the TUG and 6MWT. Similar findings were found in previous studies using Wii exergames as an intervention with the exercise prescriptions being varied from 2 to 5 days a week for 8 to 10 weeks with 30 min of exercise per session.[8,19] In addition, our findings showing no significant improvement in fear of falling were consistent with the previous studies.[7,35] Although not significant, the p values of the TUG, 6MWT, and the FES were very close to 0.05. One possible reason for not reaching significance may be due to insufficient power of statistical analyses. A larger sample size may have shown statistically significant results on these outcome measures. However, results showed that there were large effect sizes on mobility, walking distance and fear of falling, which indicated clinical significance in the frail ALF residents. Functional decline is one of the most common reasons for discharge from the ALF to a nursing home.[36] These results support that Wii exergames is a promising intervention to improve ALF residents' physical function thereby delaying and/or avoiding transfer to a nursing home.

Our pilot intervention integrated self-efficacy theory into Wii Fit exergames in order to strengthen an individual's level of confidence to exercise. For example, health education booklets and posters were distributed to each participant. Participants interacted and encouraged each other to exercise (e.g., "You are doing well," "good girl"). Despite the integration of self-efficacy theory, results only showed slight differences on the SEE and OEE. Some participants retained low confidence to perform exercise while having pain (e.g., arthritis pain or neuropathy pain) or feeling tired; while others retained low outcome expectations of exercise due to low scores in the gaming activities. However, McAuley reported that interventions integrating self-efficacy concepts could have a substantial influence on the maintenance of exercise participation in older adults. Self-efficacy has been shown to be a significant predictor of exercise adherence.[37,38] Although our results on the SEE and the OEE did not show significant improvement after the program, most participants expressed that they did experience improvements on balance and mobility for daily activities and they would like to continue to engage in exercise.

Wii exergames provided attractive graphics and audio feedback; however, some games provided negative auditory and visual feedback when participants did not perform well, which may have frustrated the participants. In addition, the Wii balance board was not sensitive enough for certain levels of functional ability and some movements within the games were difficult for participants to control.[39,40] This negative feedback did frustrate the participants who had functional disability or physical intolerance even though they had shown some improvement in the gaming activities. Further research is needed to determine whether the application of self-efficacy theory could effectively boost older adults' confidence to exercise while using Wii exergames.

▶ Limitations

There are some limitations to this pilot study. First, the study utilized a small sample size and a non-controlled design. This limited the generalizability of the findings. Second, the post-test was administered only 1 week following the 8-week exercise program. To more fully determine the effects of Wii exergames, measurements at 6 and 12 months would better determine the long-term effects of this intervention. Third, residents who participated in the study were those who were already more physically active at the facility, perhaps having higher confidence levels in their mobility. Residents who were less physically active or inactive possibly due to pain conditions or other disabilities, may have received more physical and psychosocial benefits, along with greater levels of improvements on the outcome measures from participation in the Wii exergames.

▶ Implications

Promoting physical activity for ALF residents requires the ongoing support from peers, friends, family members, and health care providers working in the facility. The charge nurses or administrative nurses are in an ideal position to support older adults in physical activity engagement. Advanced practice nurses with a specialty in gerontology have the knowledge and skills needed to participate in the design, implementation, and evaluation of such programs. Since there are limited nursing staff resources in the ALF, advanced practice nurses can work with other disciplines and support staff to facilitate the exercise. Selecting 2–3 gaming activities from the currently designed program and having the groups led by activity leaders or the activity trained nursing aides might make the Wii exergames program more translatable to clinical practice. Recommendations for future research include implementing the Wii exergames program in a larger sample size in this population and investigating the effects of different time lengths of Wii exergames program as well as numbers/selections of gaming activities.

▶ Conclusion

Our findings showed that integrating self-efficacy theory into Wii Fit exergames was an acceptable, safe, and potentially effective approach to improve physical function and decrease fear of falling in ALF residents. In addition, the study provides support for the application of self-efficacy theory into exergames as a mechanism to increase ALF residents' confidence to continue to exercise and perceived consequence of exercise, resulting in encouraging older adults to engage in exercise.

▶ Acknowledgment

The authors would like to thank the administrator, staff and all the subjects who participated in the study. The authors would also like to thank the following for assisting with the program implementation and data collection: Anna Jao, MS; Pataraporn Kheaw-wan, RN, MS, PhD(c); and Sunee Suwanpasu, RN, MS, PhD(c). The study was funded by the Sigma Theta Tau International Honor Society of Nursing Gamma Kappa Chapter research grant.

▶ References

1. Hatch J, Lusardi MM. Impact of participation in a wellness program on functional status and falls among aging adults in an assisted living setting. *J Geriatr Phys Ther.* 2010;33(2):71–77.

2. Sung K. The effects of 16-week group exercise program on physical function and mental health of elderly Korean women in long-term assisted living facility. *J Cardiovasc Nurs.* 2009;24(5):344–351.

3. Mihalko SL, Wickley KL. Active living for assisted living: promoting partnerships within a systems framework. *Am J Prev Med.* 2003;25(3 suppl 2):193–203.

4. Resnick B, Galik E, Gruber-Baldini AL, Zimmerman S. Falls and fall-related injuries associated with function-focused care. *Clin Nurs Res.* 2012;21(1):43–63.

5. Delbaere K, Crombez G, Vanderstraeten G, Willems T, Cambier D. Fear-related avoidance of activities, falls and physical frailty. A prospective community-based cohort study. *Age Ageing.* 2004;33(4):368–373.

6. Lange BS, Requejo P, Flynn SM, et al. The potential of virtual reality and gaming to assist successful aging with disability. *Phys Med Rehabil Clin N Am.* 2010;21(2):339–356.

7. Williams MA, Soiza RL, Jenkinson AM, Stewart A. Exercising with computers in later life (EXCELL): pilot and feasibility study of the acceptability of the Nintendo® Wii Fit in community-dwelling fallers. *BMC Res Notes.* 2010;3:238–245.

8. Nitz JC, Kuys S, Isles R, Fu S. Is the Wii Fit a new-generation tool for improving balance, health and well-being? A pilot study. *Climacteric.* 2010;13(5):487–491.

9. Fung V, Ho A, Shaffer J, Chung E, Gomez M. Use of Nintendo Wii Fit™ in the rehabilitation of outpatients following total knee replacement: a preliminary randomised controlled trial. *Physiotherapy.* 2012;98(3):183–188.

10. Rendon AA, Lohman EB, Thorpe D, Johnson EG, Medina E, Bradley B. The effect of virtual reality gaming on dynamic balance in older adults. *Age Ageing.* 2012;41(4):549–552.

11. Joo LY, Yin TS, Xu D, et al. A feasibility study using interactive commercial off-the-shelf computer gaming in upper limb rehabilitation in patients after stroke. *J Rehabil Med.* 2010;42(5):437–441.

12. Wollersheim D, Merkes M, Shields N, et al. Physical and psychosocial effects of Wii video game use among older women. *Int J Emerg Technol Soc.* 2010;8(2):85–98.

13. Bandura A. *Self-efficacy: The Exercise of Control.* New York: W.H. Freeman and Company; 1997.

14. Resnick B, Gruber-Baldini AL, Zimmerman S, et al. Nursing home resident outcomes from the res-care intervention. *J Am Geriatr Soc.* 2009;57(7):1156–1165.

15. Lee LL, Arthur A, Avis M. Evaluating a community-based walking intervention for hypertensive older people in Taiwan: a randomized controlled trial. *Prev Med.* 2007;44(2):160–166.

16. Resnick B. Chapter 3: the theory of self-efficacy. In: Smith MJ, Liehr PR, eds. *Middle Range Theory for Nursing.* 2nd ed. New York: Springer Publishing Company, Inc.; 2003:49e68.

17. Resnick B, Orwig D, D'Adamo C, et al. Factors that influence exercise activity among women post hip fracture participating in the exercise plus program. *Clin Interv Aging.* 2007;2(3):413–427.

18. Resnick B, Luisi D, Vogel A. Testing the senior exercise self-efficacy project (SESEP) for use with urban dwelling minority older adults. *Public Health Nurs.* 2008;25(3):221–234.

19. Padala KP, Padala PR, Malloy TR, et al. Wii-Fit for improving gait and balance in an assisted living facility: a pilot study. *J Aging Res.* 2012;2012:1e6.

20. American College of Sports Medicine. *ACSM's Resource Manual for Guidelines for Exercise Testing and Prescription.* 7th ed. Philadelphia, PA: Lippincott Williams & Wilkins; 2010.

21. Costello E, Kafchinski M, Vrazel J, Sullivan P. Motivators, barriers, and beliefs regarding physical activity in an older adult population. *J Geriatr Phys Ther.* 2011;34(3):138–147.

22. Gu MO, Conn VS. Meta-analysis of the effects of exercise interventions on functional status in older adults. *Res Nurs Health.* 2008;31(6):594–603.

23. National Institute on Aging. Exercise & Physical Activity: Your Everyday Guide from the National Institute on Aging; 2011.

24. Berg KO, Wood-Dauphinee SL, Williams JI, Maki B. Measuring balance in the elderly: validation of an instrument. *Can J Public Health.* 1992;83(suppl 2):S7–S11.

25. Blum L, Korner-Bitensky N. Usefulness of the Berg balance scale in stroke rehabilitation: a systematic review. *Phys Ther*. 2008;88(5):559–566.

26. Podsiadlo D, Richardson S. The timed "up & go": a test of basic functional mobility for frail elderly persons. *J Am Geriatr Soc*. 1991;39(2):142–148.

27. Steffen TM, Hacker TA, Mollinger L. Age- and gender-related test performance in community-dwelling elderly people: six-minute walk test, Berg balance scale, 2002 scale, timed up & go test, and Gait speeds. *Phys Ther*. 2002;82(2):128–137.

28. Tinetti ME, Richman D, Powell L. Falls efficacy as a measure of fear of falling. *J Gerontol*. 1990;45(6):P239–P243.

29. Resnick, Jenkins LS. Testing the reliability and validity of the self-efficacy for exercise scale. *Nurs Res*. 2000;49(3):154–159.

30. Resnick B, Luisi D, Vogel A, Junaleepa P. Reliability and validity of the self-efficacy for exercise and outcome expectations for exercise scales with minority older adults. *J Nurs Meas*. 2004;12(3):235–248.

31. Resnick B, Zimmerman SI, Orwig D, Furstenberg AL, Magaziner J. Outcome expectations for exercise scale: Utility and psychometrics. *J Gerontol B Psychol Sci Soc Sci*. 2000;55(6):S352–S356.

32. Field A. *Chapter 15: Non-parametric Tests. Discovering Statistics Using SPSS*. 3rd ed. Thousand Oaks, CA: SAGE Publications, Inc.; 2009. 539–583.

33. Cohen J. *Statistical Power Analysis for the Behavioral Sciences*. 2nd ed. Hillsdale, NJ: Lawrence Erlbaum Associates; 1988.

34. Resnick B, Spellbring AM. Understanding what motivates older adults to exercise. *J Gerontol Nurs*. 2000;26(3):34–42.

35. Bainbridge E, Bevans S, Keeley B, Oriel K. The effects of the Nintendo Wii Fit on community-dwelling older adults with perceived balance deficits: a pilot study. *Phys Occup Ther Geriatr*. 2011;29(2):126–135.

36. Giuliani CA, Gruber-Baldini AL, Park NS, et al. Physical performance characteristics of assisted living residents and risk for adverse health outcomes. *Gerontologist*. 2008;48(2):203–212.

37. McAuley E. The role of efficacy cognitions in the prediction of exercise behavior in middle-aged adults. *J Behav Med*. 1992;15(1):65–88.

38. McAuley E. Self-efficacy and the maintenance of exercise participation in older adults. *J Behav Med*. 1993;16(1):103–113.

39. Lange B, Flynn S, Rizzo A. Initial usability assessment of off-the-shelf video game consoles for clinical game-based motor rehabilitation. *Phys Ther Rev*. 2009;14(5):355–363.

40. Lange B, Flynn S, Proffitt R, Chang CY, Rizzo AS. Development of an interactive game-based rehabilitation tool for dynamic balance training. *Top Stroke Rehabil*. 2010;17(5):345–352.

THEORY IN ACTION—ARTICLE QUESTIONS

1. How is exercise usually addressed in assisted living facilities?
2. Why is this a problem?
3. How was this problem addressed in the article?
4. How were the constructs of the Self-Efficacy Theory used to guide development of the intervention?
5. How did these compare to the ideas you developed before reading the article?
6. How effective was the intervention in improving exercise confidence, fear of falling, and balance?
7. What might have been done differently?

▶ Chapter References

Bandura, A. (1977). Self-efficacy: Toward a unifying theory of behavioral change. *Psychological Review, 84*(2), 191–215.

Bandura, A. (1994). Self-efficacy. In V. S. Ramachandran (Ed.), *Encyclopedia of human behavior* (Vol. 4, pp. 71–81). New York, NY: Academic Press. (Reprinted from Encyclopedia of mental health, by H. Friedman, Ed., 1998, San Diego, CA: Academic Press)

Bandura, A. (1997). *Self-efficacy: The exercise of control.* New York, NY: Freeman.

Bandura, A. (2004). Swimming against the mainstream: The early years from chilly tributary to transformative mainstream. *Behavior Research and Therapy, 42*, 613–630.

Bandura, A., & Adams, N. (1977). Analysis of self-efficacy theory of behavior change. *Cognitive Therapy and Research, 1*(4), 287–310.

Brown, L. J., Malouff, J. M., & Schutte, N. S. (2005). The effectiveness of a self-efficacy intervention for helping adolescents cope with sport-competition loss. *Journal of Sport Behavior, 28*(2), 136–150.

Cheal, B., & Clemson, L. (2001). Older people enhancing self-efficacy in fall-risk situations. *Australian Occupational Therapy Journal, 48*, 80–91.

Froman, R. D., & Owen, S. V. (1989). Infant care self-efficacy. *Scholarly Inquiry for Nursing Practice: An International Journal, 3*(3), 199–210.

Froman, R. D., & Owen, S. V. (1990). Mothers' and nurses' perceptions of infant care skills. *Research in Nursing and Health, 13*, 247–253.

Gross, D., Rocissano, L., & Roncoli, M. (1989). Maternal confidence during toddlerhood: Comparing preterm and full-term groups. *Research in Nursing and Health, 18*(6), 489–499.

Heidari, E., Andiappan, M., Banerjee, A. & Newton, J. T. (2017). The oral health of individuals with dental phobia. A multivariate analysis of the Adult Dental Survey, 2009. *British Dental Journal, 222*, 595–604. doi:10.1038/sj.bdj.2017.361

Jackson, D. (2010). How personal trainers can use self-efficacy theory to enhance exercise behavior in beginning exercisers. *Strength and Conditioning Journal, 32*(3), 67–71.

Maliski, S. L., Clerkin, B., & Litwin, M. S. (2004). Describing a nurse case manager intervention to empower low-income men with prostate cancer. *Oncology Nursing Forum, 31*(1), 57–63.

Pajares, F. (2002). Overview of social cognitive theory and of self-efficacy. Retrieved March 15, 2013, from http://www.uky.edu/~eushe2/Pajares/eff.html

Pohjola, V., Rekola, A., Kunttu, K., & Virtanen, J. I. (2016). Association between dental fear and oral health habits and treatment need among university students in Finland: a national study. *BMC Oral Health, 16*(26). doi:10.1186/s12903-016-0179-y

Raj, A., & Kumar, K. (2010). Optimizing parent coaches' ability to facilitate mastery experiences of parents of children with autism. *International Journal of Psychosocial Rehabilitation, 14*(2), 4–14.

Rowe, M. M., & Moore, T. A. (1998). Self-report measures of dental fear: Gender difference. *American Journal of Health Behavior, 22*(4), 243–247.

Stegmann, K., Pilz, F., Siebeck, M., & Fischer, F. (2012). Vicarious learning during simulations: Is it more effective than hands-on training. *Medical Education, 46*(10), 1001–1008. doi:10.111/j.1365-2923.2012.04344.x

Tripp, M. K., Herrmann, N. B., Parcel, G. S., Chamberlain, R. M., & Gritz, E. R. (2000). Sun protection is fun! A skin cancer prevention program for pre-schools. *Journal of School Health, 70*(10), 395–401.

CHAPTER 3

Theory of Reasoned Action and Theory of Planned Behavior

STUDENT LEARNING OUTCOMES

After reading this chapter the student will be able to:

- Explain the concept of the Theory of Reasoned Action and the Theory of Planned Behavior.
- Explain how the constructs of attitude, subjective norm, volitional control, and behavioral control influence intention.
- Differentiate between the Theory of Reasoned Action and the Theory of Planned Behavior.
- Use the Theory of Reasoned Action or the Theory of Planned Behavior to explain at least one behavior.

THEORY OF REASONED ACTION/PLANNED BEHAVIOR ESSENCE SENTENCE

Health behavior is influenced by intention.

Constructs

Attitude: A series of beliefs about something that affects the way we think and behave

Subjective norms: The behaviors we perceive important people expect of us and our desire to comply with these expectations

Volitional control: The extent to which we can decide to do something, at will

Behavioral control: The extent of ease or difficulty we believe the performance of a behavior to be

▶ In the Beginning

In the 1960s and 1970s, the prevailing assumption was that attitude and behavior were strongly related in that attitude determined behavior. Even though research repeatedly failed to show a strong relationship between attitude and behavior, there was nonetheless, widespread acceptance of the assumption (Fishbein & Ajzen, 1975).

In 1975, Fishbein and Ajzen (1975) conducted a review of studies done on attitude and behavior and, once again, found little evidence supporting a relationship between the two, further confirming the assumption was false. They argued that although attitude *should* be related to behavior, it is not necessarily so. Instead, they proposed it was the *intention* to perform rather than the attitude toward a behavior that determined behavior; and with this came the conceptual basis for the Theory of Reasoned Action.

As it turned out, the Theory of Reasoned Action (TRA) was useful in explaining behaviors under a person's willful (volitional) control, but not so useful in explaining behaviors *not* under willful control. To address this situation, in 1991 an additional construct was added to the original theory, with the revised identified as the Theory of Planned Behavior (TPB) (Ajzen, 1991, 2002b).

The TRA and the TPB are not presented as behavior change theories. Their utility lie in the ability to predict and explain people's intentions and subsequently, their behavior (Ajzen, 2015).

▶ Theory Concept

The TRA and the TBP propose that behavior is based on the concept of intention. *Intention* is the extent to which someone is ready to engage in a certain behavior or the likelihood that someone will engage in a particular behavior (Ajzen & Fishbein, 1980; Fishbein, 1967). People are more likely to do something if they plan or aim to do it than if they do not.

▶ Theory Constructs

Intention in the TRA/TBP is influenced by attitudes, subjective norms, and, volitional control in the TRA and behavioral control in the TPB.

Attitudes

Attitudes are formed by a series of beliefs and result in a value being placed on the outcome of the behavior (Ajzen, 2002a). If the outcome or result of a behavior is seen as being positive, valuable, beneficial, desirable, advantageous, or a good thing, then a person's attitude will be favorable with a greater likelihood of the person engaging in the behavior. For example, if someone believes eating soy is healthier than eating animal protein, that it's better for the environment, and carries less of a chance of foodborne illness, the individual's attitude toward eating soy products would be favorable. Conversely, an unfavorable attitude toward soy consumption may result from the beliefs that soy products have an unpleasant taste and texture and are too expensive (Rah, Hasler, Painter, & Chapman, 2004). These attitudes would negatively influence the intention to eat soy products.

Another example of how intention to engage in a behavior is impacted by attitude is seen with meditation. When people have a positive attitude toward meditation born from the beliefs that meditating is good, enjoyable, pleasant, and a wise choice, their intention to meditate is greater (Lederer & Middlestadt, 2014).

If a woman believes breastfeeding will protect her baby against infection (Swanson & Power, 2004), is healthier for her, and is more convenient (positive attitude), she is more likely to breastfeed. If she believes breastfeeding is embarrassing (Swanson & Power, 2004), hurts, or restricts her activity (negative attitude), she is more likely to bottle feed.

In another example of how attitude impacts intention and ultimately behavior, parental attitude affects whether they have their children vaccinated. Adolescents whose parents have more positive attitudes toward vaccines are more likely to be vaccinated against the flu than are those whose parents have less positive attitudes (Gargano et al., 2015).

Among college students, attitudes toward tobacco play a role in those who begin smoking at age 18 or older. Smokers have more positive attitude toward having a relationship with a smoker and less positive attitudes toward smoking restrictions on campus and other antismoking policies (Stockdale, Dawson-Owens, & Sagrestano, 2005). Students who have positive attitudes toward hookah smoking, that is, those who believe it is good, pleasant, and a lot of fun, also have strong intentions to smoke hookah (Martinasek, McDermott, & Bryant, 2013).

Subjective Norms

In addition to attitude, intention is influenced by subjective norms. A *subjective norm* is the perceived social pressure to engage or not to engage in a certain behavior. It is determined by normative beliefs. These are the behaviors that *we perceive* important people in our lives expect from us (Ajzen, 2002a). These important people are often family members, friends or peers, religious figures, healthcare providers, or others we hold in high esteem—people we like to please. Subjective norms result from the behaviors we perceive these important people expect from us and our desire to comply with their perceived expectations (**FIGURE 3.1**). Note that these expectations may or may not be based in reality, as they are our *perceptions*.

Continuing with the soy consumption example used previously, if a healthcare provider and family member suggest that an individual eat soy products and if the person wants to make these others happy, there is a greater willingness to comply and a greater likelihood of soy consumption (Rah et al., 2004). On the other hand, if the healthcare provider does not make the suggestion to consume soy and there is limited family support to try this food source, then the likelihood of soy being eaten is greatly diminished.

Just as we have earlier seen how attitudes and beliefs influence infant feeding choice, so too do subjective norms. The decision women make about feeding method for their first baby is influenced by their own mothers, friends, partners, and medical professionals (Swanson & Power, 2004). New moms will choose the method they perceive to be the preference of these important people.

The same is true when we look at condom use among adolescent mothers. The extent of importance given to the parents', peers', and sexual partner's approval or disapproval of condom use influences intention to use it (Koniak-Griffin & Stein, 2006).

FIGURE 3.1 We want to please the important people in our lives.
©ZouZou/Shutterstock

Although one would presume peer group expectations to be strong motivators for other behaviors among college students, parental subjective norms surprisingly are the strong motivators for college students to wear bike helmets. That is, the desire to comply with parental expectations of helmet use is a strong predictor of use. Given this, one approach to ultimately increasing helmet use on campuses is to work with parents of young children to insist that they wear helmets (Ross et al., 2011).

In a study investigating posthumous organ donation in China, subjective norms were the greatest predictor of young adults' intention to discuss this with their families. Since organ donation in China requires the permission of the family, the fact that 88% of the young adults in the study were hesitant to discuss the topic with their parents does not bode well for increasing organ donation rates (Wu, 2008). To affect change in this circumstance, social norms would need to be addressed that make it acceptable to have a conversation with one's parents about donating organs at the time of death.

Volitional Control

Although the TRA tells us behavior is the result of a person's intention to do something, the behavior has to be under volitional control in order for this to happen. A behavior under volitional control is one in which the person is able to decide, at will, to engage in or not (Ajzen, 1991). Eating breakfast in the morning is under volitional control. The type of exercise someone does is under volitional control. Having a dental checkup, going for a mammogram, and giving up red meat are all under volitional control, as is heavy drinking among college students (Colby, Swanton, & Colby, 2012).

In some situations a person may not have complete control over a behavior even though the intention to engage in the behavior is great. For example, a woman may intend to practice safer sex. However, the actual use of the (male) condom is not in her control. Thus, she has limited volitional control over this behavior even though her intention is to use one. Condom use is significantly more likely if, in addition to her intention to use a condom, her male partner also intends to use a condom (DeVisser & Smith, 2004). On the other hand, she can say no to sex without a condom. She does have volitional control over engaging in intercourse (except in the case of rape).

If we look at participating in a team sport, making the team is a good example of a behavior that is not under volitional control. A person may have great intention to join the university lacrosse team, have a really positive attitude toward team sports and exercise, and want to make his parents happy by engaging in a sport in college, but alas, does not make the team. Making the team is not completely under his control because there is no way to affect the skill level of the other people he is competing against (**FIGURE 3.2**).

Behavioral Control

In situations where there is less volitional control, even when intention is great, the TRA is not very useful in predicting or explaining behavior. To address this, the construct of behavioral control was added to the theory; with this, the TPB was born (Ajzen, 1991, 2002b). Therefore, the TPB is nothing more than the TRA with another construct added.

The construct of behavioral control is similar to the concept of Self-Efficacy Theory. However, behavioral control differs from self-efficacy in that self-efficacy is concerned with one's perception of *ability* to perform a behavior, whereas behavioral control is concerned with "perceived *control* over performance of a behavior" (Ajzen, 2002b, p. 4), or how easy or difficult it is to perform the behavior (Ajzen, 1991).

Behavioral control is impacted by a set of control beliefs. These are beliefs the person has that help or hinder performance of the behavior (Ajzen, 2002b); that is, they affect the perception of how easy or difficult it is to carry out the behavior (Ajzen, 1991). For the lacrosse player who didn't make the team, behavioral control influenced his intention to try out. He believed it would be easy for him to make the team. In the condom example, although the woman has limited volitional control, she may believe it is easy to get her partner to use a condom.

FIGURE 3.2 Making the team is not under volitional control.
©Lukiyanova Natalia /frenta/Shutterstock

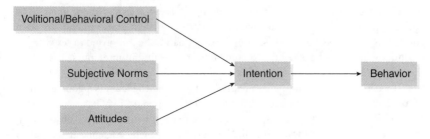

FIGURE 3.3 Theory of reasoned action/planned behavior.

Modified from: Rah, J. H., Hasler, C. M., Painter, J. E., & Chapman-Novakoski, K. M. (2004). Applying the theory of planned behavior to women's behavioral attitudes on and consumption of soy products. *Journal of Nutrition Education, 36*(5), 238–244.

In trying to understand nonsmoking behavior in African-American and Caucasian college students, of all the constructs of the TPB, perceived behavioral control (PBC) emerges as the strongest predictor of nonsmoking intention for both groups of students. In the case of nonsmoking, PBC is the perception of how easy or difficult it is to not smoke (Nehl et al., 2009). If the perception is that refraining from smoking is easy, then the intention to not smoke is greater and the likelihood of smoking is lessened. On the other hand, if the perception is that refraining from smoking is very difficult, then smoking is more likely. The importance of this is in its practical application. Given the importance of PBC in the initiation of smoking among college students, interventions that enhance the sense of control are needed (Wang, 2001) rather than those that focus on the negative health effects of tobacco use.

This was also found to be true with bike helmet use among college students. To increase the positive contribution behavioral control makes to helmet use, hands-on interventions to change the perception of choosing a correct helmet and using it from something that is difficult to something that is easy to do (Ross et al., 2011) is likely to increase use.

In summary, according to the TRA and the TPB attitudes, subjective norms, volitional control, and behavioral control affect intention and, therefore, our behavior (see **FIGURE 3.3**).

THEORY IN ACTION—CLASS ACTIVITY

Female genital mutilation (FGM)—the partial or total removal of the external female genitalia—is a common practice in many countries in Africa, Asia, and the Middle East.

In small groups, share what you each know about FGM, specifically:

How did you come to learn about it?
What do you think accounts for continuation of the practice?
Who do you think is most responsible for its continuation?
What do you think can or should be done to curtail it?
How might you use the constructs of TPB to plan an intervention?

Now read the following article and answer the questions at the end.

Chapter 3 Article: Daughters at Risk of Female Genital Mutilation: Examining the Determinants of Mothers' Intentions to Allow Their Daughters to Undergo Female Genital Mutilation[1]

Tahereh Pashaei[1], Koen Ponnet[2,3,4], Maryam Moeeni[5],
Maryam Khazaee-pool[6], Fereshteh Majlessi[7*]

[1]Department of Public Health, School of Health, Kurdistan University of Medical Sciences, Sanandaj, Iran
[2]Department of Communication Studies, University of Antwerp, Sint-Jacobsstraat 2, 2000, Antwerp, Belgium
[3]Higher Institute for Family Sciences, Odisee, Huart Hamoirlaan 136, 1030, Brussels, Belgium
[4]Faculty of Law, University of Antwerp, Venusstraat 23, 2000, Antwerp, Belgium
[5]Health Management and Economics Research Center, Isfahan University of Medical Sciences, Isfahan, Iran
[6]Department of Health Education and Promotion, School of Health, Zanjan University of Medical Sciences, Zanjan, Iran
[7]Department of Health Education and Promotion, School of Public Health, Tehran University of Medical Sciences, Tehran, Iran

Abstract

Female genital mutilation (FGM) is still a common practice in many countries in Africa and the Middle East. Understanding the determinants of FGM can lead to more active interventions to prevent this harmful practice. The goal of this study is to explore factors associated with FGM behavior among Iranian mothers and their daughters. Based on Ajzen's theory of planned behavior, we examined the predictive value of attitudes, subjective norms, perceived behavioral control and several socio-demographic variables in relation to mothers' intentions to mutilate their daughters. A paper-and-pencil survey was conducted among 300 mothers (*mean age* = 33.20, SD = 9.09) who had at least one daughter and who lived in Ravansar, a county in Kermanshah Province in Iran. Structural equation modeling was used to investigate the relationships among the study variables. Our results indicate that attitude is the strongest predictor of mothers' intentions to allow their daughters to undergo FGM, followed by subjective norms. Compared to younger mothers, older mothers have more positive attitudes toward FGM, perceive themselves as having more control over their behavior and demonstrate a greater intention to allow their daughter to undergo

1 Reproduced from Pashaei, T., Ponnet, K., Moeeni, M., Khazaee-pool, M., Majlessi, F. (2016). Daughters at risk of female genital mutilation: Examining the determinants of mothers' intention to allow their daughter to undergo female genital mutilation. *PLOS ONE, 11*(3), e0151630. DOI: 10.1371/journalpone.0151630

* Corresponding author.

FGM. Furthermore, we found that less educated mothers and mothers living in rural areas had more positive attitudes toward FGM and feel more social pressure to allow FGM. The model accounts for 93 percent of the variance in the mothers' intentions to allow their daughters to undergo FGM. Intervention programs that want to decrease FGM might focus primarily on converting mothers' neutral or positive feelings toward FGM into negative attitudes and on alleviating the perceived social pressure to mutilate one's daughter. Based on our findings, we provide recommendations about how to curtail mothers' intentions to allow their daughters to undergo FGM.

▶ Introduction

The World Health Organization[1] defines female genital mutilation as any procedure that cuts or harms female genitalia without medical indication. As of 2014, there are about 130 million women living in one of the 29 countries of Africa and the Middle East who have experienced female genital mutilation; it is believed that in the next decade, a further 30 million girls, mostly living in Africa and Asia, are in danger of undergoing this harmful practice.[2,3] Although the rate of FGM is slowly diminishing worldwide, the prevalence of FGM in different parts of the world continues at a rate ranging from 0.6% to 98%.[3] FGM can have serious adverse effects on the physical and mental health of women in both the short and long terms, especially since it is often done in unsanitary conditions by relatives, neighbors and elderly women.[4,5] In the short term, severe pain, hemorrhage and abscess from unsterile instruments are the most common problems associated with female genital mutilation. The long term physical effects of FGM include recurrent infections, keloids, fistulas, pain during sexual intercourse, menstrual problems and even infertility.[4,6] Furthermore, FGM is often associated with serious psychological and emotional difficulties including anxiety, depression, stress, insomnia, eating disorders and impaired cognition.[4,7-9] Consequently, FGM has been recognized as a violation of human rights[7,10] and is considered a public health problem.[11] FGM is mainly carried out on young girls under the age of 15 years old who often have little choice in the matter.[7] FGM is often deeply embedded in the culture and traditions of the people, which influence mothers to want to have their daughters undergo this surgery.[12] The main reasons given for the practice of FGM are prevalent social norms,[13,14] the suppression of female sexuality,[2,15-17] aesthetic preferences,[13] social cohesion[18] and religion.[3,16] The attempt to stop FGM is not easy.[19,20] Previous studies on the practices of female genital mutilation have concluded that the development and implementation of legislation as a sole strategy against FGM is not an effective way to reduce its prevalence.[21,22] Although laws signal a country's disapproval of FGM and send a clear message of support to those who abandon the practice,[23] their deterrent effect has not been confirmed.[24] For instance, in a systematic review on practices of FGM in seven different African countries, it was found that only study participants from Burkina Faso mentioned legal prohibition as a reason for not performing FGM. Burkina Faso, however, is the only country in which people who break the law are commonly prosecuted.[25] Participants from nearly all other African countries consistently argued that FGM was simply a cultural tradition and, therefore, must continue.[24] A more effective way to reduce FGM involves community education and awareness. Successful community strategies that have been documented include mutilation-free rite-of-passage ceremonies and collective declarations in which villages pledge not to mutilate their daughters.[25] Furthermore, several studies have argued that educational interventions that emphasize the negative consequences of FGM, that correct faulty knowledge or that provide educational knowledge that is missing can trigger changes in beliefs.[24] In these intervention programs, various people should be targeted, including parents, health workers, religious leaders and other key people.[14,26]

The present study took place in Ravansar, a county in Kermanshah Province in Iran. A recent study conducted by Pashaei[12] found that the prevalence of FGM in the region is approximately 58% and that 96% of the genital mutilations are performed by traditional midwives and old women. Moreover, the same study revealed that FGM is always done based on a mother's request. In other words, mothers allow others to genitally mutilate their daughters. This indicates that FGM is deeply embedded in the culture and traditions of the people, which makes the reduction and elimination of the practice of FGM very challenging.[4] Understanding the factors associated with FGM behavior might help in the designing of appropriate intervention strategies to change this behavior. Therefore, the aim of this study is to test a clinically relevant and theoretical framework to explain and predict mother's intentions to have their daughters undergo FGM; the reason for this approach is that intention is a very strong determinant of actual behavior.[27] One such framework that has proved to be successful is the theory of planned behavior (TPB).[27,28] To date, TPB is one of the most thoroughly tested and robust of the social psychological models for understanding, predicting and changing health-related behaviors.[29–33] To the best of our knowledge, no study has applied this framework to predict mothers' intentions to make their daughters undergo female genital mutilation.

The theory of planned behavior (TPB) proposes that behavior can be predicted by the strength of an individual's intention to behave in a particular way. Behavioral intention is predicted by three variables: attitude toward the behavior, subjective norms and perceived behavioral control over the behavior.[28] Attitude refers to people's positive or negative evaluation of the behavior. A subjective norm is defined as the perceived social pressure to perform or not to perform the behavior. Perceived behavioral control refers to the level of ease or difficulty the individual experiences when attempting to perform the behavior.[27] As a general rule, the more favorable the attitude and the subjective norm and the greater the perceived behavioral control, the stronger is the person's intention to engage in the behavior.[27,28] The stronger the person's intention, the more that person is expected to try, and hence, the greater the likelihood of the person demonstrating the behavior.[34] Except with regard to behaviors that are largely out of the person's behavioral control, the intention to engage in a particular behavior is the strongest predictor of the actual behavior.[28,35] Based on the TPB-literature, we derive three hypotheses (H): There is a positive association between mothers' attitudes (H1), subjective norms (H2) and perceived behavioral control (H3) and their intention to allow their daughters to undergo FGM.

In sum, the present study was conducted in Ravansar, a county in which FGM is still a common practice. The purpose of the study was to gain a better understanding of mothers' intentions to allow their daughters to undergo FGM. We therefore examined the predictive value of attitudes, subjective norms and perceived behavioral control in relation to mothers' intentions to allow their daughter to undergo FGM. The findings of this study may help policy makers design appropriate interventions to prevent the practice of FGM among the new generation of females in Iran.

▶ Material and Method

Procedure and participants

Data were collected with the help of five trained midwives who worked in health centers located in both urban and rural areas of Ravansar, a county in western Iran. Ravansar is a region in Iran in which FGM is practiced fairly commonly.[36] Almost 100% of the population in Ravansar has a Kurdish background (i.e., an ethnic minority in Iran).[36] To identify potential study subjects, the midwives reviewed the existing medical records of mothers who had been referred to the health centers in 2011. In Iran, each family has a medical file at a health center located in the region in which they live. Mothers were eligible if they (a) had experienced female genital mutilation, (b) had at least one daughter younger than seven years old and (c) had no daughter(s) above seven years old. The age criteria were chosen because a recent study[12] found that approximately 54% of the women in Ravansar are mutilated before they are seven years old. All eligible women ($n = 323$) were called by the midwives and were informed about the purpose of the study. All of the contacted women had a medical record at the health center. Therefore, they were asked by phone to come to the health center. In the correspondence with the participants, the Kurdish language was used because it is the ethnic language of Ravansar and is known by all the citizens in the region.

The midwives were trained by the first author in how to contact the mothers. The trained midwives asked the subjects whether they agreed to participate in the study. It was made clear that the respondents were under no obligation to participate and that their responses would be treated anonymously and confidentially. Furthermore, the mothers were assured that their decision to refuse would not deprive them of any health services at the health centers. Mothers who were willing to participate received an introductory letter explaining the purpose and procedure of the survey. Each participant also received a plain-language statement and a written informed-consent form. If women were illiterate, the midwives helped the mothers to fill in the paper-and-pencil questionnaire. No compensation was given to the respondents. The study protocol was approved by the ethics committee of the Tehran University of Medical Sciences.

Measures

Following the recommendations of Ajzen[37] and Francis and colleagues,[38] a self-report questionnaire was developed to assess the constructs of the theory of planned behavior. The questionnaire was built with the aid of health workers (i.e., experienced midwives) who possessed academic knowledge of FGM and were trained to examine mothers and diagnose whether they had ever been mutilated. In order to check if there were any ambiguities or if the respondents had any difficulty in responding to the items, a pilot study was conducted among 30 women who had been referred to the above-mentioned health centers. The final questionnaire included items on attitudes toward female genital mutilation, subjective norms, perceived behavioral control and mothers' intentions to mutilate their daughters (measured using the binary question "Do you intend to make your daughter undergo female genital mutilation?") and the above-mentioned socio-demographic variables. A total of 32.2% ($n = 97$) of surveyed mothers intended to do so.

Attitude. To measure mothers' attitudes toward female genital mutilation, the respondents were asked to answer seven items (e.g., "Female genital mutilation is a good tradition"). The items were scored on a 5-point Likert scale ranging from 1 = strongly disagree to 5 = strongly agree. The reliability of the scale was good ($\alpha = .92$).

Subjective norm. Three items measured the mothers' own estimates of the social pressure to perform the target behavior (e.g., "Family members expect me to mutilate my daughter"). The items were scored on a 5-point Likert scale ranging from 1 = strongly disagree to 5 = strongly agree. The internal consistency of the items was good ($\alpha = .83$).

Perceived behavioral control. One item measured women's confidence that they were capable of preventing their daughters from being genitally mutilated: "Despite the difficulties, I can prevent my daughter from undergoing FGM." The item was scored on a 5-point Likert scale, ranging from 1 = *strongly disagree* to 5 = *strongly agree*.
Descriptions of the variables are presented in **TABLE A.1**.

TABLE A.1 Descriptions of the variables.

	Mean	Standard Deviation (SD)	Skewness	Kurtosis
Attitude				
Att1. Female genital mutilation is a good tradition	2.14	1.27	.64	−.93
Att2. Female genital mutilation is good for controlling female sexuality	2.50	1.04	.49	−.41
Att3. Female genital mutilation is performed for religious reasons	2.10	1.24	.77	−.67
Att4. Female genital mutilation increases women's health	2.13	1.21	.62	−.98
Att5. Female genital mutilation is a violent behavior (reverse scored)	2.47	1.07	.35	−.57

(continues)

TABLE A.1 Descriptions of the variables. (*continued*)

	Mean	Standard Deviation (SD)	Skewness	Kurtosis
Attitude				
Att6. Female genital mutilation should continue	2.34	1.14	.37	−.98
Att7. Female genital mutilation increases the chances of marriage	2.52	1.09	.32	−.51
Subjective norm				
Sn1. Family members expect me to mutilate my daughter	2.66	1.26	.25	−1.02
Sn2. Neighbors put me under pressure to mutilate my daughter	2.94	1.15	.21	−.89
Sn3. My husband wants me to mutilate my daughter	2.89	1.18	.35	−.89
Perceived behavioral control				
Despite the difficulties, I can prevent my daughter from undergoing female genital mutilation	2.33	.81	.60	.28

Reproduced from Pashaei, T., Ponnet, K., Moeeni, M., Khazaee-pool, M., Majlessi, F. (2016). Daughters at risk of female genital mutilation: Examining the determinants of mothers' intention to allow their daughter to undergo female genital mutilation. *PLOS ONE, 11*(3), e0151630. DOI: 10.1371/journalpone.0151630

Analytic strategy

To investigate the relationships among the study variables, structural equation modeling (SEM) was applied to the collected data using M plus 6.[39] The analyses were carried out in the following way. First, we built a measurement model and examined whether the observed variables reliably reflected the hypothesized latent variables in the research model. The latent constructs, i.e., attitudes and subjective norms, were created using the above-mentioned manifest variables. Second, we estimated a structural model with attitudes, subjective norms and perceived behavioral control as predictor variables, and behavioral intention as the endogenous variable. The age and education of the mothers, and whether they lived in an urban or rural area were included as covariates in the model.

Several fit indices were used to evaluate the model fits of the measurement and path models. Given that the χ^2 is almost always significant and not an adequate test of the model fit,[40] we also reported the Comparative Fit Index (CFI), the Root Mean Square Error of Approximation (RMSEA) and the Standardized Root Mean Square Residual (SRMR). The CFI ranges from 0 to 1.00, with a cut-off of .95 or higher indicating that the model provides a good fit and .90 indicating that the model provides an adequate fit.[41] RMSEA values below .05 indicate a good model fit, and values between .06 and .08 indicate an adequate fit.[42,43] An SRMR value below 0.08 indicates a good model fit.[41]

▶ Results

Sample characteristics

In total, 300 mothers who had at least one daughter who was younger than seven years old and with a history of FGM filled out the questionnaire. The mean age of the mothers was 33.20 years (SD = 9.09, skewness = .41). Regarding the place of residence, 49% (n = 147) of the women lived in an urban area, and 51% (n = 153) lived in a rural area. Education was measured according to the highest level of education the mothers had achieved. Within the sample, 43% (n = 129) of the mothers had completed fewer than 6 years of education (primary school), 39.7% (n = 119) had completed secondary or high school education and 17.3% (n = 50) of the women had completed higher education. In the sample, 93.3% of the mothers (n = 280) were married, 3.3% (n = 10) were single and 3.3% (n = 10) were divorced. With regard to employment, 93.7% of the respondents (n = 281) were unemployed, which is comparable to the 90% unemployment rate for women in Kermanshah province.[44] Many mothers (61.7%, n = 185) had experienced acute or chronic complications related to FGM as an infant, child or teenager.

Measurement and structural model

As shown in **FIGURE A.1**, the measurement and structural model provided an adequate fit to the data. All factor loadings of the latent constructs were significant and above .69. Our analyses revealed that the study variables, together with the covariates, explained 93% of the total variance of the mothers' intentions to mutilate their daughters. The attitudes (H1) and subjective norms (H2) were significantly related to the mothers' intentions to mutilate their daughters. Attitudes had the strongest relationship with intention (β = .53, p <. 001), followed by subjective norms (β = .35, p <. 001). Thus mothers with a more favorable attitude and who perceived more social pressure from important others in their lives were more likely to have the intention to mutilate their daughters. Perceived behavioral control (H3) was not significantly related to intention (β = .03, p = .23).

With regard to the covariates, the residence of the mothers was significantly related to attitudes (β = .20, p < .001) and subjective norms (β = .22, p <. 001), suggesting that mothers who live in a rural area had a more positive attitude toward female genital mutilation and perceived more social pressure from important others to mutilate their daughters. Furthermore, the education of the mothers was negatively

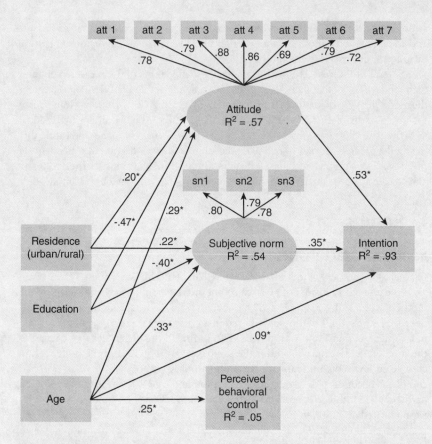

FIG A.1 Structural model for the determinants predicting mothers' intentions to allow their daughters to undergo FGM.

Reproduced from Pashaei, T., Ponnet, K., Moeeni, M., Khazaee-pool, M., Majlessi, F. (2016). Daughters at risk of female genital mutilation: Examining the determinants of mothers' intention to allow their daughter to undergo female genital mutilation. *PLOS ONE, 11*(3), e0151630. DOI: 10.1371/journalpone.0151630

related to attitudes toward female genital mutilation ($\beta = -.47$, $p <. 001$) and subjective norms ($\beta = -.40$, $p <. 001$). This suggests that higher educated mothers had less positive attitudes toward genital mutilation and perceived less social pressure to make their daughters undergo FGM. Finally, the mothers' age was significantly related to attitudes ($\beta = .29$, $p <. 001$), subjective norms ($\beta = .33$, $p < .001$), perceived behavioral control ($\beta = .25$, $p <. 01$) and intention ($\beta = .09$, $p <. 001$). Thus, older mothers had more positive attitudes toward female genital mutilation, felt more social pressure to allow their daughters to undergo FGM, perceived more control over their behavior and had a greater intention to make their daughters undergo FGM.

▶ Discussion

Our descriptive results indicate that 32.2% of the mothers intended to allow their daughters to undergo FGM. This finding is consistent with a study conducted by

Yasin and colleagues in Iraqi Kurdistan, which investigated a sample with the same cultural tradition as our sample and found that 35% of the participants intended to mutilate their daughters.[45] From the relative weights of the structural model paths, we can conclude that mothers' attitudes are the strongest predictor of their intention to allow their daughters to undergo FGM, suggesting that mothers with a more favorable attitude toward FGM are more likely to show the intention of mutilating their daughters. As such, health interventions should focus primarily on changing the attitudes and beliefs of the mothers. To date, in families in which FGM is common, girls who are not genital mutilated are often called rude girls and are believed to be promiscuous.[46] As described by Shell-Duncan and Hernlund,[47] Gambian girls who are not mutilated are even called "Solema," which is a highly derogatory term that refers to being "impolite, immodest, childish, unattractive, guilty and impure." This goes to show that there is a long way to go before people's attitudes are changed for good. It is therefore vital that the opinions and attitudes of mothers who intend to allow their daughters to undergo FGM are heard and understood by health care workers, so that they can adequately inform mothers about the adverse consequences of FGM.

Besides attitudes toward FGM, mothers' subjective norms were strongly associated with respondents' intentions to allow their daughters to undergo FGM. This finding is consistent with a study conducted by UNICEF,[48] which found that the social pressure and moral judgments associated with FGM were key determinants of both the persistence and the rejection of the practice.[48] In Iran, it is the responsibility of health care workers, especially those working in health care centers, to consult mothers and to help them overcome feelings such as stress and fear, which may jeopardize their health or that of their children. Iranian health care workers directly communicate with mothers and their daughters, and most often are the first people to inform mothers of the mental and physical problems associated with FGM. Therefore, Iranian health care workers might be ideally suited to alleviate the social pressure of family members, husbands and neighbors. Unlike traditional midwives, Iranian health care workers are educated in the risks involved with genital mutilation. Although they have grown up in similar conditions to other Iranian men or women, their professional ethics might prevent them from having positive attitudes toward FGM, even when this conflicts with the beliefs or rules prescribed during their youth. Taking this into account, Iranian health care workers can have an important role to play both in the prevention of FGM in girls at risk and in the promotion of health and the treatment of women who have undergone this practice.

Although the findings suggest that mothers care about the perceived expectations of family members, neighbors and their husbands, we did not ask the mothers explicitly which of these people they considered to be most important. The findings of the above-mentioned UNICEF study, however, revealed that it is mothers, grandmothers and older female relatives who influence the decision to perform FGM the most. Mothers also reported that they would be blamed if they did not follow the customs[10,49] and that they feared social sanctions if they neglected the social norms.[48] Furthermore, many mothers believe that FGM can secure their daughters against social and cultural troubles. In other words, they believe that non-mutilated daughters will fall prey to social problems. This belief goes beyond the physical or mental dangers involved with FGM.[8] For practitioners, it might be useful to tell mothers that there are alternative ways to rid themselves of the guilt of not mutilating their daughters. For instance, some mothers already perform female genital mutilation symbolically by cutting a knife through the clothes of the daughter, instead of actually performing the mutilation.[50]

In this study, we found no significant relationship between mothers' perceived behavioral control and intention to allow their daughters to undergo FGM. This is not surprising, considering the fact that women in the selected regions do not enjoy great autonomy and lack empowerment. Ravansar is a region located in Kermanshah province, which is known as an undeveloped and poor province. Most women in Ravansar depend on their family because of their illiteracy and unemployment. Furthermore, women are often expected to obey their husbands, fathers and mothers in law.[12] As suggested by Shell-Duncan and colleagues,[26] being genitally mutilated might serve as a signal to other genitally mutilated women that a girl or woman has been trained to respect the authority of her genitally mutilated elders.[26]

With regard to the covariates, our study demonstrated that older mothers exhibited a greater intention to make their daughters undergo FGM compared to younger respondents. In a way, this finding suggests that FGM will be reduced in the future because the new generations of mothers are less inclined to believe that their daughters should undergo female genital mutilation. Although this might indicate a loosening of the tradition in Iran, it is important to note that Masho and Matthews[4] pointed out that younger woman are still likely to continue the practice. We also found that less educated mothers have more positive attitudes toward FGM, which is consistent with the majority of studies that have investigated the association between education and FGM.[12,20,51,52] The results of our study further indicated that women who resided in an urban region had less positive attitudes toward FGM and felt less social pressure to engage in the behavior. These findings are in line with other studies.[4,52,53] One possible explanation for this finding is that urban residents have more access to the mass media and to education[54] and, as such, might be more aware of the negative consequences of FGM for the mental and physical health of their daughters.

The present study has several limitations. One limitation is sampling bias, which may limit the external validity of the study findings. This study was conducted in Ravansar, a county in western Iran, in which nearly everyone has a Kurdish background. Since the determinants of FGM might differ from region to region and FGM might be related to ethnicity, the generalizability of the findings is limited. Furthermore, we only recruited mothers who had medical records at a health center and had experienced female genital mutilation. Alternative participant recruitment and data collection strategies may be needed to minimize sampling bias in future studies, and corroboration of our findings by data gathered in other regions where FGM is common practice would lend credibility to the findings. Second, the survey data are cross-sectional in nature, which means that inferences with respect to causality should be made with caution. We assume directionality in the relationships between the variables in the model (e.g., the influence of subjective norms on intention), but we acknowledge that causality can only be inferred theoretically. However, the use of theory and prior research that guides this study lends support to the inferences. In future studies, a longitudinal or experimental research design could be deployed to provide further support to the directionality of the observed relationships in our study. Third, the data collection was based on self-report measures. Self-reports may be subject to response distortions (e.g., extreme or central-tendency responding, negative affectivity bias, socially desirable responding), which might inflate the associations between independent and outcome variables.[55,56] In addition, although the midwives were trained to help illiterate mothers fill out the questionnaires, their help might have resulted, to some extent, in social desirability bias. Fourth, we did not investigate how deeply religious the mothers were. In addition, the present study did not capture several background characteristics such as the age of the daughters, the total number of children and the living situation (e.g., living with a mother-in-law). It would be interesting if future research could verify how the degree of religiosity might influence the intention to allow daughters to undergo FGM; this is because it has been demonstrated that some people believe that FGM must be done for religious reasons.[57] It would also be interesting if future research could explore how other background characteristics (e.g., the number of daughters a mother has) might influence the mothers' intentions to allow their daughters to undergo FGM.

▶ Conclusion

Despite the severe negative effects of female genital mutilation (FGM) on the mental and physical health of women, it is still a common practice in Ravansar, a county in western Iran. To prevent this extremely harmful practice, it is essential to understand and change the motivations to practice it, especially those motivations that relate to mothers' intentions to perform the practice. Therefore, the aim of this study was to examine factors that influence mothers' intentions to make their daughters undergo FGM. To investigate the determinants that influence this intention, the current research tested a model based on the theory of planned behavior conducted with a paper-and-pencil survey of 300 mothers living in Ravansar. We found that attitudes, subjective norms and age significantly predicted the intention of mothers to allow their daughters to undergo FGM, and that education, residence and age significantly predicted mothers' attitudes and subjective norms. Evidence has shown that education and health promotion can encourage mothers to stop performing FGM. Therefore, a significant change in factors such as economic development, literacy, education, health promotion and social development might cause a gradual decline in FGM behavior.

▶ Supporting Information

S1 Data.
(SAV)

S1 Questionnaire.
(DOCX)

▶ Acknowledgments

We would like to thank the head of Ravansar's city health center for his contribution to this work. Furthermore, the authors are indebted to all women and personnel at Ravansar's health center.

▶ Author Contributions

Conceived and designed the experiments: TP FM. Performed the experiments: TP MM. Analyzed the data: KP TP. Contributed reagents/materials/analysis tools: KP MK. Wrote the paper: TP MM KP.

▶ References

1. WHO (2008) Eliminating female genital mutilation: an interagency statement UNAIDS, UNDP, UNECA, UNESCO, UNFPA, UNHCHR, UNHCR, UNICEF, UNIFEM, WHO. Geneva, Switzerland. 1–48 p.
2. Mohammed GF, Hassan MM, Eyada MM (2014) Female genital mutilation/cutting: Will it continue? Journal of Sexual Medicine 11: 2756–2763. doi: 10.1111/jsm.12655 PMID: 25123710
3. Mandara M (2004) Female genital mutilation in Nigeria. International Journal of Gynecology & Obstetrics 84: 291–298.
4. Masho S, Matthews L (2009) Factors determining whether Ethiopian women support continuation of female genital mutilation. International Journal of Gynecology & Obstetrics 107: 232–235.
5. Berhane Y, Gossaye Y, Emmelin M, Hogberg U (2001) Women's health in a rural setting in societal transition in Ethiopia. Social Science & Medicine 53: 1525–1539.
6. WHO, UNICEF (1997) Female genital mutilation: a joint WHO/UNICEF/UNFPA statement. Geneva, Switzerland.
7. WHO (2014) Female genital mutilation. Fact sheet N° 241. Geneva, Switzerland. af p.
8. Sundby J (2006) Female genital mutilation. The Lancet 362: s26–s27.
9. Andro A, Cambois E, Lesclingand M (2014) Long-term consequences of female genital mutilation in a European context: Self perceived health of FGM women compared to non-FGM women. Social Science & Medicine 106: 177–184.
10. UNICEF (2013) Female genital mutilation/cutting: A statistical overview and exploration of the dynamics of change. New York: UNICEF. New York. 1–194 p.
11. Chalmers B, Hashi KO (2000) 432 Somali women's birth experiences in Canada after earlier female genital mutilation. Birth 27: 227–234. PMID: 11251507
12. Pashaei T, Rahimi A, Ardalan A, Felah A, Majlessi F (2012) Related factors of female genital mutilation (FGM) in Ravansar (Iran). Journal of Women's Health Care 1: 1–3.
13. Gruenbaum E (2001) The female circumcision controversy: an anthropological perspective: University of Pennsylvania Press.
14. Jones SD, Ehiri J, Anyanwu E (2004) Female genital mutilation in developing countries: an agenda for public health response. European Journal of Obstetrics & Gynecology and Reproductive Biology 116: 144–151.
15. Little CM (2002) Female genital circumcision: medical and cultural considerations. Journal of cultural diversity 10: 30–34.
16. Kluge EH (2009) Female genital mutilation, cultural values and ethics. Journal of Obstetrics & Gynaecology 17: 71–77.
17. El-Defrawi MH, Lotfy G, Dandash KF, Refaat AR, Eyada M (2001) Female genital mutilation and its psychosexual impact. Journal of Sex and Marital Therapy 27: 456–473.
18. Rymer J (2003) Female genital mutilation. Current Obstetrics & Gynaecology 13: 185–190.
19. Abdel-Tawab N, Hegazi S (2000) Critical analysis of interventions against FGC in Egypt. Population Council: Cairo, Egypt.
20. Afifi M (2009) Women's empowerment and the intention to continue the practice of female genital cutting in Egypt. Archives of Iranian medicine 12: 154–160. PMID: 19249886
21. Abolfotouh S, Ebrahim A, Abolfotouh M (2015) Awareness and predictors of female genital mutilation/cutting among young health advocates. International Journal of Women's Health 20: 259–269.

22. Oduro A, Ansah P, Hodgson A, Afful T, Baiden F, Adongo P, et al. (2006) Trends in the prevalence of female genital mutilation and its effect on delivery outcomes in the kassena-nankana district of northern Ghana. Ghana Medical Journal 40: 87–92. PMID: 17299573

23. UNICEF (2005) Changing a harmful social convention: Female genital mutilation/cutting. Florence: UNICEF.

24. Berg R, Denison E (2012) Effectiveness of interventions designed to prevent female genital mutilation/cutting (FGM/C): a systematic review of the best available evidence. Studies in Family Planning 43: 135–146. PMID: 23175952

25. Sipsma H, Chen P, Ofori-Atta A, Ilozumba U, Karfo K, Bradley E (2012) Female genital cutting: current practices and beliefs in western Africa Bulletin of the World Health Organization. 90: 120–127. doi: 10. 2471/BLT.11.090886 PMID: 22423163

26. Shell-Duncan, Wander K, Hernlund Y, Moreau A (2011) Dynamics of change in the practice of female genital cutting in Senegambia: Testing predictions of social convention theory. Social Science & Medicine 73: 1275–1283.

27. Ajzen I (2002) Perceived behavioral control, self-efficacy, locus of control, and the theory of planned behavior. Journal of Applied Social Psychology 32: 665–683.

28. Ajzen I (1991) The theory of planned behavior. Organizational Behavior and Human Decision Processes 50: 179–211.

29. Taylor S (2006) Health Psychology. New York: McGraw-Hill.

30. McEachan R, Conner M, Taylor N, Lawton R (2011) Prospective prediction of health-related behaviours with the Theory of Planned Behaviour: a meta-analysis. Health Psychology Review 5: 97–144.

31. Armitage CJ, Conner M (2001) Efficacy of the theory of planned behaviour: A meta-analytic review. British Journal of Social Psychology 40: 471–499. PMID: 11795063

32. Godin G, Kok G (1996) The theory of planned behavior: A review of its applications to health-related behaviors. American Journal of Health Promotion 11: 87–98. PMID: 10163601

33. Riebl SK, Estabrooks PA, Dunsmore JC, Savla J, Frisard MI, Dietrich AM, et al. (2015) A systematic literature review and meta-analysis: The Theory of Planned Behavior's application to understand and predict nutrition-related behaviors in youth. Eating Behaviors 18: 160–178. doi: 10.1016/j.eatbeh.2015. 05.016 PMID: 26112228

34. Ajzen I, Madden TJ (1986) Prediction of goal-directed behavior: Attitudes, intentions, and perceived behavioral control. Journal of Experimental Social Psychology 22: 453–474.

35. Heirman W, Walrave M, Ponnet K (2013) Predicting Adolescents' Disclosure of Personal Information in Exchange for Commercial Incentives: An Application of an Extended Theory of Planned Behavior. Cyberpsychology Behavior and Social Networking 16: 81–87.

36. Taheri K (2000) Essays on the Archaeology, Geology, Geography, and Culture of Rawansar Area. Kermanshah: Taq-e Bostan Publications.

37. Ajzen I (2011) Constructing a Theory of planned behaviour Questionnaire. http://people.umass.edu/aizen/pdf/tpb.measurement.pdf.

38. Francis J, Eccles MP, Johnston M, Walker AE, Grimshaw JM, Foy R, et al. (2004) Constructing questionnaires based on the theory of planned behaviour: A manual for health services researchers. Newcastle upon Tyne, UK: Centre for Health Services Research.

39. Muthén L, Muthén B (2010) Mplus user's guide. Version 6.0. Los Angeles, CA: Muthén & Muthén.

40. Kline R (2005) Principles and practices of structural equation modeling. New York: The Guilford Press.

41. Hu L, Bentler P (1999) Cutof criteria for fit indexes in covariance structure analysis: Conventional criteria versus new alternatives. Structural Equation Modeling 6: 1–55.

42. Brown T (2006) Confirmatory factor analysis for applied research. New York: The Guilford Press.

43. Ponnet K (2014) Financial Stress, Parent Functioning and Adolescent Problem Behavior: An ActorPartner Interdependence Approach to Family Stress Processes in Low-, Middle-, and High-Income Families. Journal of Youth and Adolescence 43: 1752–1769. doi: 10.1007/s10964-014-0159-y PMID: 25053382

44. Iran SCo (2011) Iranian population and housing census. Available: http://www.amar.org.ir.

45. Yasin BA, Al-Tawil NG, Shabila NP, Al-Hadithi TS (2013) Female genital mutilation among Iraqi Kurdish women: a cross-sectional study from Erbil city. BMC public health 13: 809. doi: 10.1186/1471-2458-13-809 PMID: 24010850

46. Ahanonu EL, Victor O (2014) Mothers' perceptions of female genital mutilation. Health Education Research 29: 683–689. doi: 10.1093/her/cyt118 PMID: 24412809

47. Shell-Duncan B, Herniund Y (2007) Are There "Stages of Change" in the practice of Female Genital Cutting? Qualitative Research Finding from Senegal and the Gambia. African journal of reproductive health 10: 57–71.

48. UNICEF (2010) The Dynamics of Social Change: Towards the abandonment of Female Genital Mutilation/Cutting in five African Countries. New York. 1–68 p.

49. UNICEF (2010) Legislative reform to support the abandonment of female genital mutilation /cutting. New York. 1–61 p.

50. Karimi F (2011) Tragedy of the body violence against of women 1, editor. Tehran: Roshangaran & women studies publishing. 280 p.

51. Dalal K, Lawoko S, Jansson B (2010) Women's attitudes towards discontinuation of female genital mutilation in Egypt. Journal of injury and violence research 2: 41–47. doi: 10.5249/jivr .v2i1.33 PMID: 21483197

52. Tamire M, Molla M (2013) Prevalence and belief in the continuation of female genital cutting among high school girls: a cross-sectional study in Hadiya zone, Southern Ethiopia. BMC public health 13: 1120. doi: 10.1186/1471-2458-13-1120 PMID: 24304497

53. Cook RJ, Dickens B, Fathalla MF (2002) Female genital cutting (mutilation/circumcision): ethical and legal dimensions. International Journal of Gynecology & Obstetrics 79: 281–287.

54. Bekalu MA, Eggermont S (2014) Media use and HIV/AIDS knowledge: a knowledge gap perspective. Health Promotion International 29: 739–750. doi: 10.1093/heapro/dat030 PMID: 23644165

55. Podsakoff P, MacKenzie S, Podsakoff N (2012) Sources of Method Bias in Social Science Research and Recommendations on How to Control It. In: Fiske ST, Schacter DL, Taylor SE, editors. Annual Review of Psychology, Vol 63. pp. 539–569.

56. Ponnet K, Wouters E, Mortelmans D, Pasteels I, De Backer C, Van Leeuwen K, et al. (2013) The Influence of Mothers' and Fathers' Parenting Stress and Depressive Symptoms on Own and Partner's Parent–Child Communication. Family process 52: 312–324. doi: 10.1111 /famp.12001 PMID: 23763689

57. Tag-Eldin MA, Gadallah MA, Al-Tayeb MN, Abdel-Aty M, Mansour E, Sallem M (2008) Prevalence of female genital cutting among Egyptian girls. Bull World Health Organ 86: 269–274. PMID: 18438515

THEORY IN ACTION—ARTICLE QUESTIONS

1. Why is FGM still practiced?
2. What are some of the successful strategies used to curtail the practice?
3. Who should be the focus of interventions?
4. Why were mothers suggested as the most important group to target in an effort to address this issue?
5. How do the constructs of the Theory of Planned Behavior help explain why FGM still occurs?

▶ Chapter References

Ajzen, I. (1991). The theory of planned behavior. *Organizational Behavior and Human Decision Process, 50,* 179–211.

Ajzen, I. (2002a). *Theory of Planned Behavior.* Retrieved October 24, 2004, from http://www-unix.oit.umass.edu/~aizen/index.html

Ajzen, I. (2002b). Perceived behavioral control, self-efficacy, locus of control and the theory of planned behavior. *Journal of Applied Social Psychology, 32,* 1–20.

Ajzen, I. (2015). The theory of planned behavior is alive and well and no ready to retire: A commentary on Sniehotta, Presseau, and Araujo-Soares. *Health Psychology, 9*(2), 131–137. doi:10.1080/17437199.2014.883474.

Ajzen, I., & Fishbein, M. (1980). *Understanding attitudes and predicting social behavior.* Englewood Cliffs, NJ: Prentice-Hall.

Colby, S. M., Swanton, D. N., & Colby, J. J. (2012). College students' evaluation of heavy drinking: the influence of gender, age, and college status. *Journal of College Students Development, 53*(6), 797–810. doi:10.1353/csd.2012.0080.

DeVisser, R. O., & Smith, A. M. A. (2004). Which intention? Whose intention? Condom use and theories of individual decision making. *Psychology, Health & Medicine, 9*(2), 193–204.

Fishbein, M. (1967). *Readings in attitude theory and measurement.* New York, NY: Wiley.

Fishbein, M., & Ajzen, I. (1975). *Belief, attitude, intention and behavior: An introduction to theory and research.* Reading, MA: Addison-Wesley. Retrieved March 15, 2013, from http://people.umass.edu/aizen/f&a1975.html

Gargano, L. M., Underwood, N. I., Sales, J. M., Seib, K., Morfaw, C., Murray, D., … Huges, J. M. (2015). Influence of sources of information about influenza vaccine on parental attitudes an adolescent vaccine receipt. *Human Vaccine and Immunotherapy, 11*(7), 1641–1647. doi:10.1080/21645515.2015.1038445

Koniak-Griffin, D., & Stein, J. A. (2006). Predictors of sexual risk behaviors among adolescent mothers in a human immunodeficiency virus prevention program. *Journal of Adolescent Health, 38,* 297e1–297e11.

Lederer, A. M., & Middlestadt, S. E. (2014). Beliefs about meditating among university students, faculty, and staff: A theory-based salient belief elicitation. *Journal of American College Health, 62*(6), 360–369. doi:10.1080/07448481.2014.907296

Martinasek, M. P., McDermott, R. J., & Bryant, C. A. (2013). Antecedents of university students' hookah smoking intention. *American Journal of Health Behavior, 37*(5), 599–609. doi:10.5993/AJHB.37.5.3

Nehl, E. J., Blanchard, C. M., Peng, C. J., Rhodes, R. E., Kupperman, J., Sparling, P. B., … Baker, F. (2009). Understanding nonsmoking in African American and Caucasian college students: An application of the theory of planned behavior. *Behavioral Medicine, 35,* 23–28.

Rah, J. H., Hasler, C. M., Painter, J. E., & Chapman-Novakofski, K. M. (2004). Applying the theory of planned behavior to women's behavioral attitudes on and consumption of soy products. *Journal of Nutrition Education and Behavior, 36*(5), 238–244.

Ross, L. T., Ross, T. P., Farber, S., Davidson, C., Trevino, M., & Hawkins, A. (2011). The theory of planned behavior and helmet use among college students. *American Journal of Health Behavior, 35*(5), 581–590. doi:10.5993/AJHB.35.5.7

Stockdale, M. S., Dawson-Owens, H. I., & Sagrestano, L. M. (2005). Social, attitudinal, and demographic correlates of adolescents vs college age tobacco initiation. *American Journal of Health Behavior, 29,* 311–323.

Swanson, V., & Power, K. G. (2004). Initiation and continuation of breastfeeding: Theory of planned behavior. *Journal of Advanced Nursing, 50*(3), 272–282.

Wang, M. Q. (2001). Social, environmental influences on adolescents smoking progression. *American Journal of Health Behavior, 25,* 418–425.

Wu, A. M. S. (2008). Discussion of posthumous organ donation in Chinese families. *Psychology, Health & Medicine, 13*(1), 48–54. doi:10.1080/13548500701351992

CHAPTER 4

Health Belief Model

STUDENT LEARNING OUTCOMES

After reading this chapter the student will be able to:

- Explain the concept of the Health Belief Model.
- Discuss how the constructs of perceived seriousness, susceptibility, benefits, and barriers might predict health behavior.
- Analyze the impact of the modifying variables on health behavior.
- Explain how cues to action motivate behavior.
- Use the model to explain at least one behavior.

HEALTH BELIEF MODEL ESSENCE SENTENCE

Personal beliefs influence health behavior.

Constructs

Perceived susceptibility: An individual's assessment of his or her chances of getting a disease

Perceived benefits: An individual's conclusion as to whether the new behavior is better than what he or she is already doing

Perceived barriers: An individual's opinion as to what will stop him or her from adopting the new behavior

Perceived seriousness: An individual's judgment as to the severity of the disease

Modifying variables: An individual's personal factors that affect whether the new behavior is adopted

Cues to action: Factors that start a person on the way to changing behavior

Self-efficacy: Personal belief in one's own ability to successfully do something

▶ In the Beginning

The Health Belief Model (HBM) was developed by researchers at the U.S. Public Health Service in the late 1950s. At the time, a great emphasis was placed on screening programs for disease prevention and early detection. Although public health practitioners were in favor of screenings, the public was not very receptive to being tested for diseases of which they didn't have symptoms. This was particularly true for tuberculosis (TB) (Hochbaum, 1958; Rosenstock, 1960).

Although TB screening programs were attracting some people, they were not attracting the large numbers who were known to be at risk for the disease. Consequently, there was a need to understand both why some people went for the screening and why so many others did not (Hochbaum, 1958; Rosenstock, 1960). To find out, researchers at the U.S. Public Health Service conducted a study to identify the combination of psychological, social, and physical factors (observations) that determined whether a person wanted to be screened for TB, when, and at what type of facility (Hochbaum, 1958).

Because the researchers were all social psychologists, their approach was based on the idea that behavior is the result of how people perceive their environment. That is, individual beliefs or perceptions are what determine behavior. Using this as the foundation, it was reasoned that in order for people to take action to prevent a disease they didn't have, or to be screened/tested for a disease they didn't have symptoms of, certain beliefs or perceptions about the disease needed to exist.

The outcome of the study identified three sets of factors that determined participation in a voluntary screening program: psychological readiness, situational influences, and environmental conditions (Rosenstock, 1958). Factors identified as being indicative of people's psychological readiness to be screened for TB included the belief that they had TB, were at risk of getting TB, or that they would benefit from being tested for TB. Situational influences included having bodily changes thought to be symptoms of TB, other people's opinions of whether they should or shouldn't be screened, and lastly, if environmental conditions provided an opportunity to be screened, and if it was convenient (Rosenstock, 1958). The conclusions drawn from this study formed the basis of the HBM.

▶ Theory Concept

The underlying concept of the HBM is that health behavior is determined by personal beliefs or perceptions about a disease and the strategies available to decrease its occurrence (Hochbaum, 1958). Personal perception is influenced by the whole range of intrapersonal factors affecting health behavior, including, but not limited to: knowledge, attitudes, beliefs, experiences, skills, culture, and religion.

▶ Theory Constructs

The following four perceptions serve as the main constructs of the model: perceived seriousness, perceived susceptibility, perceived benefits, and perceived barriers. Each of these perceptions, individually or in combination, can be used to explain health behavior. Over the years other constructs have been added to the HBM; thus, the model has been expanded to include cues to action, motivating factors, and self-efficacy.

Perceived Seriousness

The construct of perceived seriousness speaks to an individual's belief about the seriousness or severity of a disease. While the perception of seriousness is often based on medical information or knowledge, it may also come from beliefs a person has about the consequences an illness might personally have on him or her. For example, most of us perceive seasonal flu as a relatively minor ailment. We get it, stay home a few days, and get better. However, if you have asthma contracting the flu could land you in the hospital. In this case, your perception of the flu might be that it is a serious disease. Or, if you are self-employed, having the flu might mean a week or more of lost wages. Again, this would influence your perception of the seriousness of this illness.

Perception of seriousness can also be colored by past experience with the illness. No doubt, most people would consider skin cancer a serious disease. However, the perception of serious might be diminished in someone who had a cancerous lesion removed and recovered without much more than a little pain, a Band-Aid for a few days, and a small scar.

Perceived Susceptibility

Perceived susceptibility or personal risk is one of the more powerful perceptions prompting people to adopt healthier behaviors. When an intervention increases the perception of risk, that is, the chances of contacting or developing a disease is believed to be greater, health behavior changes (Sheeran, Harris, & Epton, 2014). The greater the perceived risk, the greater the likelihood of engaging in behaviors to decrease the risk. This is what prompts men who have sex with men to be vaccinated against hepatitis B (de Wit, Vet, Schutten, & van Steenbergen, 2005) and to use condoms in an effort to decrease susceptibility to HIV infection (Belcher, Sternberg, Wolotski, Halkitis, & Hoff, 2005). Perceived susceptibility motivates people to be vaccinated for influenza (Chen, Fox, Cantrell, Stockdale, & Kagawa-Singer, 2007), to have their children vaccinated (Chen et al., 2011), to use sunscreen to prevent skin cancer, and to floss their teeth to prevent gum disease and tooth loss (**FIGURE 4.1**).

It is only logical that when people believe they are at risk for a disease, they are more likely to do something to prevent it from happening. Unfortunately, the opposite also occurs. When people believe they are *not* at risk or have a low risk of susceptibility, unhealthy behaviors tend to result.

This is what researchers found when they investigated the beliefs about pregnancy risk from women seeking abortions. With more than half (52%) of the unplanned pregnancies in the United States occurring in the 11% of women who don't use contraception, studying a sample of this population yielded interesting results—the women didn't believe they were at risk of pregnancy, and/or believed their risk of getting pregnant was low (Frohwirth, Moore, & Maniaci, 2013).

Not believing they are at risk of contracting HIV is why many older adults don't practice safer sex (Adekeye, Heiman, Onyeabor, & Hyacinth 2012; Maes & Louis, 2003; Rose, 1995). Early in the HIV epidemic, Asian-American college students believed the same thing. They tended to view the epidemic as a non-Asian problem; thus, their perception of susceptibility to HIV infection was low, as was practicing safer sex behaviors (Yep, 1993).

Unfortunately, this lack of perceived susceptibility to sexually transmitted infections (STIs) is still alive and well on campuses, albeit not necessarily because

FIGURE 4.1 Risk avoidance is a powerful motivator for change.
© Michael D Brown/Shutterstock

of ethnicity as seen in the previous example. Rather, students underestimate their risk of contracting infections from their partners, because they underestimate their partners susceptibility. (They ignore the old adage that you are sleeping with everyone your partner has ever slept with.) Consequently, they do not protect themselves against STIs, especially when sexual activity is restricted to oral sex. This is particularly evident if they attend schools in a geographic area with a low incidence of HIV/AIDS (Downing-Matibag & Geisinger, 2009).

Underestimation of risk not only influences risk reducing behaviors, it also influences screening behavior. A study of 16- to 18-year-olds in the Netherlands found that although they considered sexually transmitted infections STIs to be severe, they underestimated their STI risk and consequently didn't see the need to go for testing (Wolfers, deZwart, & Kok, 2011). As it turns out, this underestimation of risk, or unrealistic optimism, is fairly common (Ferrer & Klein, 2015).

When the perception of susceptibility is combined with seriousness, it results in perceived threat (Stretcher & Rosenstock, 1997). If the perception of threat is to a serious disease for which there is a real risk or susceptibility, behavior is likely to change. This is what happened in Germany in 2001 after an outbreak of bovine spongiform encephalitis (BSE), better known as mad cow disease. Although mad cow disease does not occur in people, research suggests that eating cattle with the disease can cause a human version of it called variant Creutzfeldt–Jakob disease (CJD). CJD, like BSE, causes tiny holes in the brain giving it a spongelike appearance. Both diseases are untreatable and fatal (National Institute of Neurological Disorders and Stroke, 2007). The perception of threat of contracting this disease through eating beef was one factor related to declining meat consumption in Germany (Weitkunat et al., 2003). People changed their behavior based on the perception of threat of a fatal disease.

Another example in which perception of threat is linked to behavior change is found in colon cancer survivors. Colorectal cancer is a very serious disease with a high risk of recurrence. It is the perception of the threat of recurrence that increases the likelihood of behavior change in people previously treated for this disease. In particular, changes occur in their diets, exercise, and weight (Mullens, McCaul, Erickson, & Sandgren, 2003).

Just as perception of increased susceptibility doesn't always lead to behavior change, nor does a perception of increased threat. When the skin cancer prevention behaviors of landscapers in Mississippi were studied, the results showed that even though they perceived skin cancer to be serious and they saw themselves as being at greater risk of developing it, they still didn't practice preventative behaviors such as using sunscreen, wearing a wide brimmed hat, or wearing long sleeves and long pants (Nahar et al., 2013).

The same results were found in a study of female smokers who had cardiac catheterization testing for coronary artery disease. As with the landscapers, although the women had realistic perceptions of their increased threat of heart disease and heart attack because of their smoking, most of them continued to smoke anyway (Moore et al., 2013).

Perceived Benefits

The construct of perceived benefits is a person's opinion of the value or usefulness of a new behavior in decreasing the risk of developing a disease. In order for a new behavior to be adopted, the perceived benefits of the new behavior have to be are seen as outweighing the consequences of continuing the old behavior (Centers for Disease Control and Prevention, 2004), and that the new behavior will decrease the chance of developing a disease. Would people strive to exercise if they didn't believe it was beneficial? Would people quit smoking if they didn't believe it was better for their health? Would people use sunscreen if they didn't believe it worked? Probably not.

A prime example of this is seen among parents who either do not have their children vaccinated for vaccine-preventable diseases (VPDs), or delay having them vaccinated. Children whose parents do not see a benefit in vaccination—that is, are more likely to agree vaccines may have serious side effects and that too many vaccines overwhelm the immune system—tend not to have their children vaccinated. Conversely, parents who see a benefit to vaccination—that is, agree vaccines are effective in preventing diseases and are safe and necessary to protect the health of the child—are more likely to have their children vaccinated (Smith et al., 2011).

Another example of how perceived benefits influence behavior is among older adults at risk of health consequences from summertime heat. Extreme heat is a serious situation for older adults, especially those with chronic heart and lung problems. For some it can be fatal. The best primary prevention measure is air conditioning. If people believe using an air conditioner has benefits—for example, they believe they'll sleep better, be able to do their daily activities, or avoid respiratory problems—it's likely they'll use it (Richard, Kosatsk, & Renouf, 2011).

Sometimes the perceived benefits are not apparent at the onset of an intervention, as was the case for a year-long yoga program for high school students. At the beginning of the program there was questionable perception of benefits. At the end of the year, student perception of benefits included increased self-esteem, academic performance, stress reduction, mindfulness, self-control, and physical conditioning (Wang & Hagins, 2016).

Perceived benefits play an important role in the adoption of secondary prevention behaviors as well. A good example of this is screening for colon cancer. One of the screening tests for colon cancer is a colonoscopy. It requires a few days of preparation prior to the procedure to completely cleanse the colon: a diet restricted to clear liquids followed by cathartics. The procedure involves the insertion of a very long, flexible tube instrument with a camera on the end into the rectum to view the length of the colon. The procedure itself is done under anesthesia, so it is not uncomfortable, but it does take time afterward to recover, and the preparation is time consuming. Regardless of the inconvenience, presently this is the best method for early detection of colon cancer, which is the third leading cause of cancer deaths in the United States. When colon cancer is found early, it has a 90% cure rate. However, only 36% of people over age 50 (who are most at risk) have this screening done (New York-Presbyterian Hospital, 2006). What makes some people undergo screening and others not? Among women, those who perceive a benefit from colonoscopy (early detection) are more likely to undergo screening than those who do not see the screening as having a benefit (Frank, Swedmark, & Grubbs, 2004).

Perceived Barriers

Since change is not something that comes easily to most people, the last construct of the HBM addresses the issue of perceived barriers to change. Perceived barriers are the most significant construct in behavior change (Janz & Becker, 1984). These are an individual's perception of the obstacles in the way of adopting a new behavior (**FIGURE 4.2**).

Even though there is much education on college campuses about HIV/AIDS risk reduction, and even though students demonstrate they are knowledgeable about HIV/AIDS, condom use among college students remains inconsistent (Fehr, Vidoreck, & King, 2014; Ndabarora & Mchunu, 2014) leaving them exposed to a greater risk of infection. There is obviously something else at play here. Using the HBM to explain what that something else might be reveals perceived barriers as a possible contributing factor. Among the barriers are: relationship dynamics, how long the relationship has existed, romance, and risk perception. Relationship dynamics has to do with who in the relationship has the power and makes the decisions (Fehr et al., 2014). This might be an important barrier since HIV/AIDS prevention education often focuses on empowering women to negotiate safer sex rather than addressing it as a shared responsibility (Winfield & Whaley, 2002). The length of a relationship might also be a barrier since those in long-term monogamous relationships are less likely to use condoms. And then there is the issue of reduced romance. Condom use is often viewed as less romantic, which may be more important to a college population than is safer sex (Fehr et al., 2014).

Barriers are also contributing factors in fruit and vegetable consumption. As it turned out, people who can't cook are less likely to eat the recommended servings of fruits and vegetables, a barrier that can be overcome by cooking classes or instructions on how to prepare raw foods. However, another barrier to healthy eating is disliking the taste of fruits and vegetables; this barrier isn't as easy to address

FIGURE 4.2 Barriers can be overcome.
© iQoncept/Shutterstock

(McMorrow, Ludbrook, Macdiamid, & Olajide, 2016). However, this barrier might be the result of not knowing how to prepare vegetables in tasty ways, which would make sense if you can't cook. Or it could be lack of exposure to a wide variety of fresh fruits.

Not surprising, some barriers are easier to address than others. For example, college students' fear of being disconnected from friends for even a short time is a significant barrier to the prevention of texting while driving. If a friend texts, it can't be ignored even if you're driving (Watters & Beck, 2016). While overcoming this barrier is much more difficult and entails changing social norms, knowing that this is the barrier means prevention programs focused on the serious consequences of texting while driving may not be effective because they don't address the underlying barrier—missing your friends.

Modifying Variables

Modifying variables are factors that alter or affect a person's perceived benefit of a prevention behavior. They are grouped into three categories: demographic, such as age, gender, marital status, and ethnicity; sociopsychological, such as peer group, social class, and personality; and structural, such as knowledge and past experience (Rosenstock, 1974).

In Northern Malawi, for instance, ethnicity and culture play a large role in modifying the perceived benefits of HIV prevention. In this region, ones ancestors are thought to be the cause of disease (Munthali, 2006; Sano et al., 2016). Consequently, there is no benefit in adopting the HIV/AIDS prevention behaviors of abstinence, being faithful, and condom use (ABC). Among some ethnic groups in Kenya and Ghana, HIV is thought to be contracted by touching an infected person or through a mosquito bite (Bernardi, 2002; Tenkorang, 2013) negating the benefits of ABC as useful for preventing HIV infection.

We also see ethnicity and culture as modifying variables in U.S. populations. Hispanics are less likely to believe they can lower their risk of getting cancer by changing their behaviors than are African-Americans and whites. This is because when compared to whites, Hispanics believe they're generally at a lower risk of getting cancer (Davis, Buchanan, & Green, 2013). Given this, think about how the effectiveness of interventions, such as smoking cessation, pap smears, sunscreen use, or mammograms, aimed at risk reduction are impacted.

Among women in Iran, age and marital status are modifying variables for breast self-exam (BSE) with older married women performing BSE more than younger women (Noroozi, Jomand, & Tahmasebi, 2011). Similarly, age is a modifying variable for mammogram screening in Canadian women, with older women (60–69 years) more likely to have had a screening than those 10 years younger (Sun et al., 2010). Among Hispanic women in the United States, age, marital status, income level, and access to a regular source of health care influence perception about cervical cancer and benefits of pap smears. Those with higher incomes and regular health care are more likely to have cervical cancer screening (Moore de Peralta & Holaday, 2015).

Past experience with noise exposure at work is a modifying variable for the use of hearing protection devices among firefighters. Volunteer firefighters who experienced more frequent exposure to loud noise at their regular jobs use hearing protection devices more often than those whose jobs infrequently expose them to loud noise (Hong, Chin, & Ronis, 2013).

In personal health classes on many campuses, students are required to complete a behavior change project. They choose an unhealthy behavior and develop a plan to change it and adopt a more healthy behavior. The modifying variable behind this is motivation. The motivation is a grade.

Cues to Action

In addition to the four beliefs or perceptions and modifying variables, the HBM suggests that behavior is also influenced by cues to action. Cues to action are events, people, or things that move people to change their behavior. Examples include illness of a family member or friend; newspaper, magazine, or online articles; reminder emails or mailings from a healthcare provider; or health warning labels on a product (**FIGURE 4.3**).

For some women, developing gestational diabetes is a cue to action for behavior change to decrease the risk of developing type 2 diabetes (Tang et al., 2015). For others, it might be having an overweight friend diagnosed with type 2 diabetes, or a healthcare provider's warning.

With between 71% and 85% of deaths from flu occurring in people 65 and older, vaccination is key for prevention in this age group (Centers for Disease Control, 2017). For older adults in nine different countries, the most important cues to action for flu vaccination are recommendations from medical personnel, family members, friends, and neighbors; information about flu vaccination from mass media; and public health education (Kwong, Pang, Choi, & Wong, 2010).

Cues to action for children to brush their teeth are pictures of "perfect teeth" in the media (Walker, Steinfort, & Keyler, 2015). A cue to action for kids to eat more

FIGURE 4.3 Cue to action—don't drink and drive.
© Wendy M. Simmons/Shutterstock

fruits, might be having fruit on the kitchen counter (instead of it being hidden in the refrigerator).

Physical health problems, mental or emotional health concerns, word of mouth from friends and family, and mass media are all cues to action for starting a yoga practice (Atkinson & Permuth-Levine, 2009). Having difficulty walking the dog, bending over, and not being able to fit into last summer's clothes might be cues to action for starting an exercise program and changing ones food intake.

A common cue to action used on college campuses to prevent drinking and driving is a display of cars involved in fatal crashes from drunk driving. Another is a drunk driving simulator or drunk simulation goggles.

Self-Efficacy

In 1988, self-efficacy was added to the original four beliefs of the HBM (Rosenstock, Strecher, & Becker, 1988). Self-efficacy is the belief in one's own ability to do something (Bandura, 1977). People generally do not try to do something new unless they think they can do it. If someone believes a new behavior is useful (perceived benefit), but does not think he or she is capable of doing it (perceived barrier), chances are it will not be tried.

In a study aimed at identifying parental factors associated with children's intake of sweetened beverages, self-efficacy was found to be the only parental associated factor. The less able parents believed they were to limit their child's intake of sugar laden beverages, the greater the chances were that their kids drank these drinks (Nickelson, Lawerence, Parton, Knowlden, & McDermott, 2014). Given this, one approach to decreasing children's consumption of these types of beverages is to strengthen parents' ability to restrict them.

Self-efficacy also impacts oral health, specifically dental cavities and tooth brushing behavior. People with strong beliefs in their ability to brush twice a day brush more frequently and therefore, have better oral health (Anagnostopoulos, Buchanan, Frousiounioti, Niakas, & Potamianos, 2011).

Another example of how self-efficacy impacts health behavior is with medication adherence. It seems only logical that people who believe they can take their medication as directed are more likely to do so. For people taking medication to control their high blood pressure, greater self-efficacy, along with higher levels of perceived susceptibility (to the complications of uncontrolled high blood pressure) and cues to action, is significantly associated with better medication adherence (Yue, Li, Weilin, & Bin, 2015).

Self-efficacy is also associated with the desire to control elevated cholesterol. In this situation, the greater perceived seriousness of high cholesterol coupled with greater self-efficacy to take action to control cholesterol are predictive of a greater desire to control cholesterol (Zullig et al., 2016).

Self-efficacy is not only useful as a predictor of behavior but can also be the target of education to change behavior, which is how it was used in an intervention aimed at reducing second hand smoke exposure among pregnant woman in Taiwan. The need to strengthen self-efficacy was identified through focus groups and interviews with pregnant women. It was during these data gathering sessions that the women shared their sense of powerlessness in getting people around them to not smoke (Chi et al., 2015).

Based on the information gathered, an intervention was developed aimed at strengthening their self-efficacy in confronting members of their households and coworkers who smoked. It included five strategies—the importance of speaking up; using a nonaggressive approach; emphasizing that the smoker does not have to quit smoking, just not smoke in the presence of the pregnant woman; reminding male smokers of their role as protector of the family and that not smoking contributed to the health of the mother and baby, an honorable action; and lastly, that the mom-to-be always had the option of leaving the smoke-filled environment. As a result, self-efficacy improved which led to a significant drop in exposure to second-hand smoke (Chi et al., 2015).

In summary, according to the HBM, modifying variables, cues to action, and self-efficacy affects our perception of susceptibility, seriousness, benefits, and barriers and, therefore, our behavior (**FIGURE 4.4**).

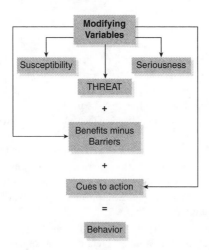

FIGURE 4.4 Health belief model.

Modified from Stretcher, V., & Rosenstock, I. M. (1997). The health belief model. In K. Glanz, F. M. Lewis, & B. K. Rimer (Eds.), *Health behavior and health education: Theory, research and practice* (2nd ed.). San Francisco, CA: Jossey-Bass

THEORY IN ACTION—CLASS ACTIVITY

Obesity is a leading public health issue in the United States with more than 36% of the U.S. population falling into this category. However, the prevalence is even greater among African-American women with 57% of female adults over age 20 obese (National Center for Health Statistics, 2015). The desire to lose weight is obvious by the 60 billion dollar weight loss industry in this country. Unfortunately, dieting rarely, if ever, results in sustained weight loss. There are many reasons for this; among them is the generic, one-size-fits all nature of weight loss interventions that ignore the many factors that affect a person's weight.

For this activity, imagine you are given the task of developing a weight loss intervention for people of your predominate cultural/ethnic heritage.

1. Make a list of the specific factors you would need to take into consideration.
2. Group the factors on your list according to the HBM constructs they would fall under. For example, if in your culture, being "big" means you are healthy, this would fall under "perceived seriousness or severity"—as it would contribute to the perception of the seriousness of obesity.
3. Based on the results from the previous question, suggest how the factors you identified might be used as the basis of a culturally appropriate weight management intervention.

Then read the following article and answer the questions at the end.

Chapter 4 Article: Using the Health Belief Model to Develop Culturally Appropriate Weight-Management Materials for African-American Women[1]

Delores C.S. James*, PhD, RD, LD/N; Joseph W. Pobee, MS; D'lauren Oxidine; Latonya Brown; Gungeet Joshi, MS

D. C. S. James is an associate professor and J. W. Pobee, D. Oxidine, L. Brown, and G. Joshi are students, all in the Department of Health Education and Behavior, University of Florida, Gainesville.

Address correspondence to: Delores C. S. James, PhD, RD, LD/N, Department of Health Science Education, PO Box 118210, Room 5 Florida Gym, University of Florida, Gainesville, FL 32611-2034. E-mail: djames@hhp.ufl.edu

1 Reproduced from James, D.C.S., Pobee, J.W., Oxidine, D., Brown, L., & Joshi, G. (2012). Using the health belief model to develop culturally appropriate weight-management materials for African-American women. *Journal of the Academy of Nutrition and Dietetics, 112,* 664–670, doi: 10.1016/j.jand.2012.02.003. With permission from Elsevier.

* Corresponding author.

Abstract

African-American women have the highest prevalence of adult obesity in the United States. They are less likely to participate in weight-loss programs and tend to have a low success rate when they do so. The goal of this project was to explore the use of the Health Belief Model in developing culturally appropriate weight-management programs for African-American women. Seven focus groups were conducted with 50 African-American women. The Health Belief Model was used as the study's theoretical framework. Participants made a clear delineation between the terms *healthy weight, overweight,* and *obese*. Sexy, flirtatious words, such as *thick, stacked,* and *curvy* were often used to describe their extra weight. Participants accurately described the health risks of obesity. Most believed that culture and genetics made them more susceptible to obesity. The perceived benefits of losing weight included reduced risk for health problems, improved physical appearance, and living life to the fullest. Perceived barriers included a lack of motivation, reliable dieting information, and social support. Motivators to lose weight included being diagnosed with a health problem, physical appearance, and saving money on clothes. Self-efficacy was primarily affected by a frustrated history of dieting. The data themes suggest areas that should be addressed when developing culturally appropriate weight-loss messages, programs, and materials for African-American women.

Keywords: African-Americans, Health belief model, Obesity, Weight management

The health burdens of obesity are severe, especially among African-American women who experience lower life expectancy and higher rates of chronic diseases than the general population. Furthermore, losing weight continues to be a major challenge for African-American women, who are less likely to participate in weight-loss programs and tend to have a low success rate when they do.[1,2] The reason for lack of success is largely unknown, but many believe that most weight-loss programs are very generic and ignore culturally influenced factors, such as body image, beauty, and traditions.[3-5] In addition, they do not consider the stigma, prejudice, and discrimination that obese individuals experience because of their weight.[6]

Perceptions about weight and knowledge, attitudes, and beliefs about obesity and weight management cannot be effectively measured and quantified solely with surveys.[7-9] Therefore, this qualitative study used focus groups to explore these issues. Focus groups allow participants to critique, comment, explain, and share their experiences, opinions, and attitudes on the issues in question. The results from focus groups can be used to plan, develop, and implement specific messages and programs.[10]

The Health Belief Model (HBM) was used as the theoretical framework for this study. The framework is often used to explain why individuals change or maintain specific health behaviors. It also can be used to guide development of culturally appropriate weight-loss materials and intervention strategies for weight loss.[11-14] HBM contains the following constructs: perceived susceptibility, perceived severity/seriousness, perceived benefits, perceived barriers, cues to action, and self-efficacy.[14-17] **FIGURE A.1** depicts the HBM framework using the example of obesity and weight management. Few studies have applied all of the HBM constructs in studying weight management. The goal of this project was to explore the use of the HBM in developing culturally appropriate weight-management programs for African-American women.

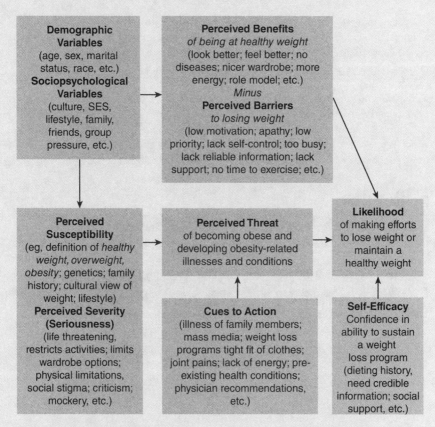

FIG A.1 Health Belief Model theoretical framework applied to weight management. SES=socioeconomic status.

Reproduced from: James, D.C.S., Pobee, J.W., Oxidine, D., Brown, L., & Joshi, G. (2012). Using the health belief model to develop culturally appropriate weight-management materials for African-American women. *Journal of the Academy of Nutrition and Dietetics, 112,* 664–670, doi: 10.1016/j.jand.2012.02.003. With permission from Elsevier.

▶ Methods

The project was approved by the Institutional Review Board at the researchers' institution. Seven focus groups were conducted with a convenience sample of African-American women who were overweight or obese and who were interested in losing weight. Fifty women were recruited from beauty salons, churches, sororities, a college campus, and a low-income housing community. Three community liaisons recruited participants and located convenient venues for the focus groups. The liaisons asked each woman her height and weight and used a body mass index (BMI; calculated as kg/m^2) chart to determine if they met the study's criteria for being overweight or obese.

Each group consisted of six to nine women who provided written consent to participate in the study. Each group was homogeneous with respect to ethnicity and socio-economic status, but with sufficient variation in life experience to allow for contrasting opinions.[6–10,18] A reminder phone call was made 2 days before each focus group. The lead author moderated the discussions. The focus groups were digitally recorded and transcribed. A research assistant also took hand notes. Each focus group lasted an average of 1.5 hours. The liaisons and participants were given a $25 gift card for their participation.

The moderator's guide consisted of 13 questions with relevant probe questions. Major topics included perception of a healthy weight, overweight, and obesity; perceived consequences of obesity; barriers and motivators to weight loss; information needed to lose weight; and sources of dieting information. Thematic analysis was used to identify the data for common themes and patterns in the data.[7-10] The transcripts were hand coded by four members of the research team. Coders conducted in-depth reviews and re-reviews of the transcripts based on established data themes from the codebook.[19,20] Inter-coder reliability was 0.90 and was based on percent agreement, which is one of the most popular coefficients used.[21] Select verbatim quotes that captured participants' sentiments, views, and opinions are included in the text.

▶ Results

Sociodemographic characteristics of the participants are listed in the Table. Data themes were organized based on the HBM constructs and are listed in **FIGURE A.2**.

HBM construct	Major data themes	Select quotes
Perceived susceptibility	Clear distinction made about weight categories *Obesity* is a dirty word African-Americans more susceptible to obesity Culture affects weight perception	Healthy weight: "When your jeans fit right." "Not feeling sluggish." Overweight: "Just a few pounds over where you want to be." Obesity: "... when you're like 300 pounds and even 600 pounds." "You can't take a shower or tie your shoelaces." "It's an insult. Why would you call people names like that?" "It runs in our family." "It is in our genes." "I think that as black women, we have been brought up to think that big is beautiful."
Perceived severity (seriousness)	Obesity is life threatening Obesity is life restricting	"You're getting ready to have a heart attack or stroke. Your health is at risk and you need medical treatment." "It limits what you can and can't do." "You can't move around like you want to."
Perceived benefits	Personal health benefits Physical appearance Live life more fully (e.g., try new activities, travel more) Role model for children	"I just want to do it for health reasons. My weight is a sign of me being healthy." "I am tired of having to worry about a whole new wardrobe." "I want to wear the cute stuff." "There are things that I want to try like horseback riding, sky diving, skiing. And I know they require me to have more energy and be a whole lot smaller." "I also want to be around to enjoy my kids and learn new things with them."

Perceived barriers	Lack of motivation/apathy No time to exercise Lack of reliable information Lack of social support	"I am very lazy. I just don't want to make the effort.""I have to work two jobs and I just can't fit it in." "When I see new stuff advertised on TV, I go online and order it. I am ashamed to admit some of the nonsense I've tried." "My family eats a lot of junk food. It's everywhere. That's the reason I am so damn fat."
Cues to action	Personal diagnosis with a health problem Family/friend diagnosed with health problem Tight-fitting clothes Physical appearance	"I started focusing on my weight when I was diagnosed with high blood pressure." "I don't want to end up like my mom. She lost a leg to diabetes." "All of my clothes are tight. I spend so much money on clothes and then they are too tight." "I hate to see how I look in the mirror. The only thing I can see is gut and more gut."
Self-efficacy	Dieting history Need credible information Dieting buddy/partner	"I need help. I've tried everything, but nothing works." "I am barely in my 20s and I am obese. It seems that I have been on a diet all of my life." "I eat lots of health stuff, but I don't know how much I should eat.""I bought the exercise video and equipment that say you can lose weight in just 10 minutes a day. It's not working." "I walk with the women at work during my breaks and it really helps. We just don't do it often enough."

FIG A.2 Major data themes and select quotes from 50 African-American women focus-group participants based on the Health Belief Model (HBM) constructs.

Reproduced from: James, D.C.S., Pobee, J.W., Oxidine, D., Brown, L., & Joshi, G. (2012). Using the health belief model to develop culturally appropriate weight-management materials for African-American women. *Journal of the Academy of Nutrition and Dietetics, 112*, 664–670, doi: 10.1016/j.jand.2012.02.003. With permission from Elsevier.

TABLE A.1 Demographic characteristics of 50 African-American women in seven focus groups used to explore the Health Belief Model constructs

	n	%
Marital status		
Married	19	38
Single	41	62

(continues)

TABLE A.1 Demographic characteristics of 50 African-American women in seven focus groups used to explore the Health Belief Model constructs (*continued*)

	n	%
Age, y		
18–24	12	24
25–34	11	22
35–44	15	30
45–54	10	20
55–64	2	4
Highest education level		
Did not finish high school	5	10
High school graduate	18	36
Some college	10	20
Bachelor of Science degree	7	14
Graduate or professional degree	10	20
Household income, $		
<25,000	19	38
25,000–50,000	25	50
>$51,000	6	12
BMI[a]		
<18.5	0	0
18.5–24.9	0	0
25–29.9	32	64

[a]BMI = body mass index; calculated as kg/m^2.

Reproduced from: James, D.C.S., Pobee, J.W., Oxidine, D., Brown, L., & Joshi, G. (2012). Using the health belief model to develop culturally appropriate weight-management materials for African-American women. *Journal of the Academy of Nutrition and Dietetics, 112,* 664–670, doi: 10.1016/j.jand.2012.02.003. With permission from Elsevier.

Perceived Susceptibility to Obesity and Obesity-Related Illnesses

Understanding how African-American women define concepts such as "healthy weight," "overweight," and "obesity" is important because it affects their perception of their weight, body image, and likelihood of developing obesity. The women often used sexy, flirtatious words like *thick, stacked, brick house, curvy,* and *big boned* to describe their bodies.

Clear Distinctions Made about Weight Categories. Most participants made a clear delineation between the terms *healthy weight, overweight,* and *obese*. Being at a healthy weight was defined as "when your jeans fit right" and "not feeling sluggish." Overweight was considered to be "just a few pounds over where you want to be." "When you are overweight you can lose weight if you want to." A few women expressed extreme views of obesity. "Obesity is when you're like 300 pounds and even 600 pounds." "You can't take a shower or tie your shoelaces." One woman pointed out that obese people had the "jiggly" kind of fat rather than the "solid" kind of fat when one is overweight.

Obesity Is a Dirty Word. "It's an insult. Why would you call people names like that?" None of the women referred to themselves as "obese." Instead, they used words like "extremely overweight" and "really big."

We Are Very Susceptible to Obesity. A few stated that African-American women were naturally more susceptible to being obese than white women because it "runs in our family" and it is "in our genes." "They [white women] are naturally skinny and we gain weight more than they do."

Culture Affects Perception of Weight. Many believed their communities protect women from the media pressure to be thin. "I think that as black women, we have been brought up to think that big is beautiful." Another added, "Yes, most of us want some kind of thickness." "We don't want to be skin and bones like them [white women]. For them, a size 8 means they are fat, but for us it means that we look good." "They have the luxury of going to the gym. We have to work two jobs."

Perceived Severity of Obesity

Understanding how women view the health and social consequences of obesity is important because women who perceive the threat to be serious might be more inclined to get their weight under control.

Obesity Is Life Threatening. Obesity was viewed as a life threatening, debilitating condition. "You're getting ready to have a heart attack or stroke. Your health is at risk and you need medical treatment." "You can get diabetes." Other health consequences mentioned were arthritis, high cholesterol, depression, and cancer.

Obesity Is Life Restricting. Several respondents said obesity limited enjoying life. "It limits what you can and can't do." "You can't move around like you want to." "I have pains in my knees when I go for long walks." Obesity also limits wardrobe options. "You can't buy the really nice clothes." "You're limited to stretch pants that show your dimples." A few women said that people often laughed at and mocked them.

Perceived Benefits to Losing Weight

The health and social benefits of losing weight can be strong motivators to change eating habits, physical activity levels, and the response to environmental influences. Many women personalized the benefits of losing weight.

I Want to Be Healthy. "I just want to do it for health reasons. My weight is a sign of me being healthy." "When I am at a good weight I have more energy, my self-esteem is high, and I am confident." Avoiding illness was also mentioned. "I want to lose weight because I've got high blood pressure, and I don't want to have other problems to make it worse." "Diabetes runs in my family. Yes that's a big one."

I Want to Look Good. Improved personal appearance was cited as another benefit. "I want to get back into short shorts." [Laughter.] "I am tired of having to worry about a whole new wardrobe." One woman summed it up, "It affects my self-image, you know. I want to feel like I look good to myself, nobody else." [Nods of agreement.]

I Want to Enjoy Life. Some participants believed that losing weight would add to their enjoyment of life. "There are things that I want to try like horseback riding, sky diving, skiing. And I know they require me to have more energy and be a whole lot smaller." "I think I would take more risks." "I also want to be around to enjoy my kids and learn new things with them."

Perceived Barriers to Weight Loss

External circumstances and negative beliefs often prevent women from trying to lose weight. They might understand the benefits of weight loss, but the tradeoffs can seem overwhelming or unrealistic.

No Motivation. Lack of motivation was the major reason for not taking action. "I am very lazy. I just don't want to make the effort." Another cited lack of control. "What's really stopping me from losing weight is all the good food that is around. I've got to have it all."

Lack of Reliable Information. Access to credible information was a major barrier. Many relied on television shows, such as Oprah and The Biggest Loser for dieting information. They also got dieting tips from other women. One participant used the Internet extensively to order diet pills and supplements. "When I see new stuff advertised on TV, I go online and order it. I am ashamed to admit some of the nonsense I've tried." Another stated, "I don't know what to do. I don't know what works. I need somebody there every second telling me what to do."

No Time to Exercise. Lack of time to exercise was also a barrier. "We cook, clean, take care of the kids, and then it's time for bed. There's no time to do anything else." "I have to work two jobs and I just can't fit it in."

Lack of Support. Friends and relatives were not always supportive. In fact, they were often enablers. "Your surroundings have a lot to do with it. They always have food around." "My family eats a lot of junk food. It's everywhere. That's the reason I am so damn fat." However, they also acknowledged the value of a nurturing environment. "It has to do with the people around you. As long as you have more people helping you, then you're going to be all right. It's all about your surroundings."

Cues to Action

Women are motivated to lose weight for different reasons. For some, one cue might be enough to motivate her to lose weight, but for others a series of cues might be needed.

Diagnosed with Health Problems. Health problems were frequently cited as a motivator to change. "I went to my doctor thinking everything was all right. He told me I was 50 pounds overweight and had high blood pressure. I went in OK and I came out obese. I got to get this weight off." "I don't want to end up like my mom. She lost a leg to diabetes." "I started focusing on my weight when I was diagnosed with high blood pressure."

Appearance. Physical appearance and a limited wardrobe were common cues to action. "All of my clothes are tight. I spend so much money on clothes and then they are too tight." "I hate to see how I look in the mirror. The only thing I can see is gut and more gut." "You can't wear the cute stuff you see in the store."

Self-Efficacy

Women with high levels of self-efficacy are likely to take the necessary actions to manage their weight. Prior dieting experiences, access to credible information, and having adequate resources appear to affect the women's self-efficacy.

Dieting History. Most women had a frustrating history of dieting. "I need help. I've tried everything, but nothing works." One young woman remarked, "I am barely in my 20s and I am obese. It seems that I have been on a diet all of my life. I don't know what else to do. Nothing I do works." "I feel helpless and hopeless."

Need Basic Information. Access to credible information can build a woman's self-efficacy. Women said they needed information on portion control, quick healthy meals, and exercises that worked. "I eat lots of health stuff, but I don't know how much I should eat." "I bought the exercise video and equipment that say you can lose weight in just 10 minutes a day. It's not working."

Dieting/Exercise Buddy. A few women felt that they could stay on their diet longer if they had a diet or exercise buddy. "I would stick with my diet if I had someone doing it with me and cheering me on." "I walk with the women at work during my breaks and it really helps. We just don't do it often enough."

▶ Discussion

Despite the abundance and variety of weight-loss programs that are available to the public, 80% of African-American women are still overweight or obese.[22] The women's narrative from this study revealed a struggle between accepting themselves and their bodies "as is" and being motivated to make substantial lifestyle changes to manage their weight and decrease their health risks.

The decision to lose weight is heavily based on the perception of one's weight.[23] Participants made distinctions between "healthy weight," "overweight," and "obese." Weight perception differs by culture, with African-American women half as likely to consider themselves overweight or obese compared to their white counterparts.[24] African-American women need help in assessing their weight in the context of their health risks. In addition to using BMI, health risks should also be assessed with waist circumference, waist-to-hip ratio, and biochemical indicators.[25]

Practitioners should also remember that obesity is a medical diagnosis and not a personal characteristic. Describing someone as obese is often perceived as an insult.[26] It is more accurate and sensitive to tell a client that they have been diagnosed with obesity rather than saying "you are obese."

Most women believed culture and genetics made them susceptible to obesity. African-American culture appears to have a cocoon effect that prevents many women from buying into the popular notion that "thin is beautiful."[27] Dietetics practitioners walk a fine line when addressing weight within a cultural context. It might be helpful to emphasize that obesity is a health threat for all Americans, regardless of ethnicity, income, and sex.

▶ Research

Participants accurately described the health and social risks of obesity. They listed several benefits of losing weight, especially avoiding diabetes and hypertension. The benefits of being at a healthy weight and even losing just a few pounds should be stressed.[28-30] Several women said their weight limited them from living life to the fullest, made them embarrassed to shop for clothes, and made them the subject of jokes. It is important to show empathy when clients describe their negative social experiences with their weight. Obese women experience high levels of frustration, body dissatisfaction, weight ideation, stigma, and discrimination because of their weight.[6] They also express feelings of constant hunger and deprivation, shame, and body hatred.[31] Some women will be motivated to change solely for appearance and this can be used as a starting place for change with clients.

Regular physical activity is necessary for long-term weight management and studies consistently show that African-Americans do not meet the national recommendations.[32] Lack of time was cited as a major barrier. Working mothers can feel especially guilty about taking time for themselves because they also experience social pressure to devote their spare time to their families.[33,34] Given the importance of physical activity, emphasis needs to placed on setting realistic goals, participating in family-centered activities, and exercising with a buddy.[3] Frequent, short intervals of activity are recommended for heavy women and those starting an exercise program.[32,35]

Because many individuals are motivated to make lifestyle changes only when they or a family member are diagnosed with a health problem,[4,36] it is important to discuss other indicators of an unhealthy weight, such as lack of energy, fatigue, and tight-fitting clothes. Tying these indicators to a family history of diabetes, hypertension, and heart disease can provide added motivation to get to a healthy weight.

Self-efficacy is integral to weight-management success. Dietetics practitioners can help foster self-efficacy through positive reinforcement and acknowledging small behavior changes. They can also encourage clients to join a support group, sign a health contract, and use positive thinking and daily affirmations.[37] A depression questionnaire can also help to identify clients who might need referral to a therapist.[38] A culturally tailored program can also increase self-efficacy. Tailored program are usually effective because clients are more likely to scrutinize and personalize the information, thereby increasing the likelihood of change.[38]

▶ Conclusions

The HBM provided a good fit for the data and allowed the researchers to use the themes generated from each theoretical construct to develop weight-management materials for African-American women. However, one must remember that qualitative data are not generalizable to other groups, but the exploratory nature of focus groups is useful in assessing the needs of the target group and developing relevant programs.[7,10] The researchers encourage food and nutrition practitioners to consider the HBM constructs when developing weight-loss messages and programs for African-American women. Specifically, programs and messages should:

- focus on lifestyle management;
- define healthy weight, overweight, and obesity;
- emphasize the health benefits of losing weight, even just a few pounds;
- address ways to overcome barriers, manage stress, and increase self-efficacy;
- use ways other than BMI to assess weight status and health risk;
- acknowledge that it is okay to be motivated by appearance;
- emphasize the relationship between weight and chronic diseases;
- emphasize the importance of physical activity and suggest ways to increase physical activity throughout the day; and
- emphasize the importance of maintaining a healthy weight, not just losing weight.

▶ References

1. Kumanyika SK. Cultural differences as influences in obesity treatment. In: Bray, GA, Bouchar, C, eds. *Handbook of Obesity: Clinical Applications,* Vol. 1. 3rd ed. New York, NY: Informa Health Care; 2008:55–80.
2. Kumanyika SK, Obarzanek E, Stevens VJ, et al. Weight-loss experience of black and white participants in NHLBI-sponsored clinical trials. *Am J Clin Nutr.* 1991;53 (6 Suppl):1631S–1638S.
3. James DCS. Gender differences in weight perception, body satisfaction, and obesity status among African Americans. *Health Educ.* 2007; 36(2):8–14.
4. James DCS. Improving the diets of African-Americans: Challenges and opportunities. *ESG Monograph Ser.* 1998;30(1):29–37.
5. Diaz VA, Mainous AG, Pope C. Cultural conflicts in the weight loss experience of overweight Latinos. *Int J Obes.* 2007; 31(2):328–333.
6. Puhl RM, Heuer CA. The stigma of obesity: A review and update. *Obesity.* 2009;17(5):941–964.
7. Morse JM, Field PA. *Qualitative Research Methods for Health Professionals.* 2nd ed. Thousand Oaks, CA: Sage Publications; 1995.
8. Kreuger RA, Morgan D. *The Focus Group Kit.* 1st ed. Newbury Park, CA: Sage Publications; 1997.
9. Kreuger RA. *Focus Groups: A Practical Guide for Applied Research.* 2nd ed. Newbury Park, CA: Sage Publications; 1994.
10. Morgan DL. *Focus Groups as Qualitative Research.* 1st ed. Newbury Park, CA: Sage Publications; 1988.
11. Daddario DK. A review of the use of the health belief model for weight management. *Med Surg Nurs.* 2007;16(6):363–366.

12. Kelly KT. The behavior and psychology of weight management. *JAAPA*. 2004;17(4):29–32.
13. Lambert L, Raidl M, Safaii S, et al. Perceived benefits and barriers related to postpartum weight loss of overweight/obese postpartum WIC participants. *Top Clin Nutr*. 2005;20(1):16–27.
14. Hochbaum G, Kegels S, Rosenstock I. *Health Belief Model*. 1st ed. Washington, DC: US Public Health Service; 1952.
15. Rosenstock IM, Strecher VJ, Becker MH. Social learning theory and the health belief model. *Health Educ Behav*. 1988;15(2):175–183.
16. Champion VL, Celette SS. The Health Belief Model. In: Glanz K, Rimer B, Viswamath K, eds. *Health Behavior and Health Education: Theory, Research, and Practice*. 4th ed. San Francisco, CA: Jossey-Bass; 2008:45–62.
17. Bandura A. Self-efficacy human mechanism in human agency. *Am Psychol*. 1982;37(2):122–147.
18. Stewart DW, Shamdasani PN. *Focus Groups: Theory and Practice*. 2nd ed. Newbury Park, CA: Sage Publications; 1990.
19. Guba EG. Toward a methodology of naturalistic Inquiry in educational evaluation. *CSE Monograph Series in Evaluation*. No. 8. Los Angeles, CA: University of California; 1978.
20. Patton MQ. *Qualitative Research and Evaluation Methods*. 3rd ed. Thousand Oaks, CA: Sage; 2002.
21. Neuendorf KA. *The Content Analysis Guidebook*.1st ed. Thousand Oaks, CA: Sage; 2002.
22. Flegal KM, Carroll MD, Ogden CL, Curtin LR. Prevalence and trends in obesity among US adults, 1999–2008. *JAMA*. 2010;303(3):235–241.
23. Miller EC, Schulz MR, Bibeau DL, et al. Factors associated with misperception of weight in the stroke belt. *J Gen Intern Med*. 2008;23(3):323–328.
24. Stevens J, Kumanyika SK, Keil JE. Attitudes toward body size and dieting: Differences between elderly black and white women. *Am J Public Health*. 1994;84(8):1322–1325.
25. National Heart Lung and Blood Institute, National Institutes of Health. Clinical Guidelines on the Identifications, Evaluation and Treatment of Overweight and Obesity in Adults. http://www.nhlbi.nih. gov/guidelines/obesity/ob_gdlns.pdf. Accessed June 24, 2010.
26. Thomas JL, Stewart DW, Lynam I M, et al. Support needs of overweight African American women for weight loss. *Am J Health Behav*. 2009; 33(4):339–352.
27. Molloy BL, Herzberger SD. Body image and self-esteem: A comparison of African-American and Caucasian women. *Sex Roles*. 1998;38(7–8):631–643.
28. US Department of Health and Human Services. *Healthy People 2020: The Road Ahead*. http://www.health.gov/healthypeople/url/. Accessed May, 2, 2011.
29. Surgeon General. The Surgeon General's vision for a fit and healthy nation. 2010. http://www.surgeongeneral.gov/library/obesityvision/ obesityvision2010.pdf. Accessed May 24, 2011.
30. US Department of Agriculture. Dietary Guidelines for Americans, 2010. http://www.cnpp.usda.gov/dietaryguidelines.htm. Accessed May 24, 2010.
31. Ikeda JP, Lyons P, Schwartzman F, Mitchell RA. Self-reported dieting experiences of women with body mass indexes of 30 or more. *J Am Diet Assoc*. 2004;104(6):972–974.
32. US Department of Health and Human Services. 2008 Physical Activity Guidelines for Americans. http://www.health.gov/paguidelines/pdf/ paguide.pdf. Accessed March, 10, 2011.
33. Fallon EA, Wilcox S, Ainsworth BE. Correlates of self-efficacy for physical activity in African American women. *Women Health*. 2005;41(3):47–62.
34. Baturka N, Hornsby PP, Schorling JB. Clinical implications of body image among rural African-American women. *J Gen Intern Med*. 2000; 15(4):235–241.
35. Jeffery RW, Wing RR, Sherwood NE, Tate DF. Physical activity and weight loss: Does prescribing higher physical activity goals improve outcome? *Am J Clin Nutr*. 2003;78(4):684–689.
36. Befort CA, Thomas JL, Daley CM, Ahluwalia JS. Perceptions and beliefs about body size, weight, and weight loss among obese African American women: A qualitative inquiry. *Health Educ Behab*. 2008;35(3):410–426.
37. Foreyt JP. Need for lifestyle intervention: How to begin. *Am J Cardiol*. 2005;96(4):11E–14E.
38. Steer RA, Cavalieri TA, Leonard DM, Beck AT. Use of the Beck Depression Inventory for primary care to screen for major depression disorders. *Gen Hosp Psychiatry*. 1999;21(2):106–111.

1. What reasons are proposed for the lack of success of African-American women in weight loss programs?
2. What factors were found to affect perceived susceptibility to obesity?
3. What factors were found to affect perceived severity?
4. What were the perceived benefits to weight loss?
5. What factors were identified as barriers?
6. What were the cues to action?
7. What factors influenced self-efficacy?
8. How could factors influencing the constructs be used to develop more appropriate interventions for African-American women?
9. Discuss the similarities and differences between your suggestions for your culture and those in the article.

▶ Chapter References

Anagnostopoulos, F., Buchanan, H., Frousiounioti, S., Niakas, N., & Potamianos, G. (2011). Self-efficacy and oral hygiene beliefs about tooth brushing in dental patients: A model-guided study. *Behavioral Medicine, 32*, 132–139. doi:10.1080/08964289.2011.636770

Atkinson, N. L., & Permuth-Levine, R. (2009). Benefits, barriers, and cues to action of yoga practice: A focus group approach. *American Journal of Health Behavior, 33*(1), 3–14.

Belcher, L., Sternberg, M. R., Wolotski, R. J., Halkitis, P., & Hoff, C. (2005). Condom use and perceived risk of HIV transmission among sexually active HIV positive men who have sex with men. *AIDS Education and Prevention, 17*(1), 79–89.

Bernardi, L. (2002). Determinants of individual AIDS risk perception: Knowledge, behavioral control, and social influence. *African Journal of AIDS Research, 1*, 111–124.

Centers for Disease Control and Prevention. (2017). What you should know and do this flu season if you are 65 years and older. Retrieved April 10, 2017, from https://www.cdc.gov/flu/about/disease/65over.htm

Chen, J. K., Fox, S. A., Cantrell, C. H., Stockdale, S. E., & Kagawa-Singer, M. (2007). Health disparities and prevention: Racial/ethnic barriers to flu vaccinations. *Journal of Community Health, 32*(1), 5–20.

Chen, M., Wang, R., Schneider, J. K., Tsai, C. Jiang, D. D., Hung, M., & Lin, L. (2011). Using the health belief model to understand caregiver factors influencing childhood influenza vaccinations. *Journal of Community Health Nursing, 28*(1), 29–40. doi:10.1080/07370016.2011.539087

Chi, Y. C., Wu, C. L., Chen, C. Y., Lyu, S. Y., Lo, F. E., & Morisky, D. E. (2015). Randomized trial of secondhand smoke exposure reduction intervention among hospital-based pregnant women. *Addictive Behaviors, 41*, 117–123. doi:10.1016/addbeh.2014.10.001

Davis, J. L., Buchanan, K. L., & Green, B. L. (2013). Racial/ethnic differences in cancer prevention beliefs: Applying the health belief model framework. *American Journal of Health Promotion, 27*(6), 384–389. doi:10.4278/ajhp.120113-QUAN-15

de Wit, J. B. F., Vet, R., Schutten, M., & van Steenbergen, J. (2005). Social-cognitive determinants of vaccination behavior against hepatitis B: An assessment among men who have sex with men. *Preventive Medicine, 40*(6), 795–802.

Downing-Matibag, T. M., & Geisinger, B. (2009). Hooking up and sexual risktaking among college students: A Health Belief Model perspective. *Qualitative Health Research, 19*(9), 1196–1209.

Fehr, S. K., Vidourek, R. A., & King, K. A. (2014). Intra- and inter-personal barriers to condom use among college students: A review of the literature. *Sexuality & Culture, 19*(1), 103–121. doi:10:1007/s12119-014-9249-y

Ferrer, R. A., & Klein, W. M. P. (2015). Risk perceptions and health behavior. *Current Opinion in Psychology, 5*, 85–89. doi:10.1016/j.copsyc.2015.03.012

Frank, D., Swedmark, J., & Grubbs, L. (2004). Colon cancer screening in AfricanAmerican women. *ABNF Journal, 15*(4), 67–70.

Frohwirth, L., Moore, A. M., & Maniaci, R. (2013). Perceptions of susceptibility to pregnancy among U.S. women obtaining abortions. *Journal of Social Science & Medicine, 99*, 18–26. doi:10.1016/j.socscimed.2013.10.010

Hochbaum, G. M. (1958). *Public participation in medical screening programs: A socio-psychological study* (Public Health Service Publication No. 572). Washington, DC: Government Printing Office.

Hong, O., Chin, D. L., & Ronis, D. L. (2013). Predictors of hearing protection behavior among firefighters in the United States. *International Journal of Behavioral Medicine, 20*, 121–130. doi:10.1007/s12529-011-9207-0

Janz, N. K., & Becker, M. H. (1984). The health belief model: A decade later. *Health Education Quarterly, 11*(1), 1–47.

Kwong, E. W., Pang, S. M., Choi, P., & Wong, T. K. (2010). Influenza vaccine preference and uptake among older people in nine countries. *Journal of Advanced Nursing, 66*(10), 2297–2308. doi:10.1111/j.1365-1648.2010.05397

Maes, C. A., & Louis, M. (2003). Knowledge of AIDS, perceived risk of AIDS, and at-risk sexual behaviors of older adults. *The Journal of the American Academy of Nurse Practitioners, 15*(11), 509–516.

McMorrow, L., Ludbrook, A., Macdiarmid, J. I., & Olajide, D. (2016). Perceived barriers toward healthy eating and their associations with fruit and vegetable consumption. *Journal of Public Health.* Published online on May 24, 2016. doi:10.1093/pubmed/fwd038

Moore, L. C., Clark, P. C., Lee, S. Y., Eriksen, M., Evans, K., & Smith, C. H. (2013). Smoking cessation in women at the time of an invasive cardiovascular procedure and 3 months later. *Journal of Cardiovascular Nursing, 28*(6), 524–533. doi:10.1097/JCN.0b013e31826620d4

Moore de Peralta, A., & Holaday, B. (2015). Factors affecting Hispanic women's participation in screening for cervical cancer. *Journal of Immigrant Minority Health, 17*, 684–695. doi:10.1007/s10903-014-9997-7

Mullens, A. B., McCaul, K. D., Erickson, S. C., & Sandgren, A. K. (2003). Coping after cancer: Risk perceptions, worry, and health behaviors among colorectal cancer survivors. *Psycho-oncology, 13*, 367–376.

Nahar, V. K., Ford, M. A., Hallam, J. S., Bass, M. A., Hutcheson, A., & Vice, M. A. (2013). Skin cancer knowledge, beliefs, self-efficacy, and preventative behaviors among North Mississippi landscapers. *Dermatology, Research and Practice, 2013*, 1–7. doi:10.1155/2013/496913

National Center for Health Statistics. (2015). Prevalence of obesity among adults and youth: United States 2011–2014. Retrieved May 29, 2017, from https://www.cdc.gov/nchs/data/databriefs/db219.pdf

National Institute of Neurological Disorders and Stroke. (2007). Transmissible spongiform encephalopathies information page. Retrieved March 29, 2007, from http://www.ninds.nih.gov/disorders/tse/tse.htm

Ndabarora, E., & Mchunu, G. (2014). Factors that influence utilization of HIV/AIDS prevention methods among university students residing at a selected university campus. *Journal of Social Aspects of HIV/AIDS Research Alliance, 11*, 202–210. doi:10.1080/17290376.2014.986517

New York-Presbyterian Hospital. (2006). Colonoscopy promoted during colorectalcancer awareness month. Retrieved April 22, 2007, from http://www.nyp.org/news/health/060322.html

Nickelson, J., Lawrence, J. C., Parton, J. M., Knowlden, A. P., & McDermott, R. J. (2014). What proportion of pre-school aged children consume sweetened beverages? *Journal of School Health, 84*(3), 185–194, doi:10.1111/josh.12136

Noroozi, A., Jomand, T., & Tahmasebi, R. (2011). Determinants of breast self-exam performance among Iranian women: An application of the health belief model. *Journal of Cancer Education, 26*, 365–374. doi:10.1007/s13187-010-0158-y

Richard, L., Kosatsky, T., & Renouf, A. (2011). Correlates of hot day air-conditioning use among middle aged and older adults with chronic heart and lung diseases: The role of health beliefs and cues to action. *Health Education Research, 26*(1), 77–88. doi:10.1093/her/cyq072

Rose, M. A. (1995). Knowledge of human immunodeficiency virus and acquired immunodeficiency syndrome, perception of risk, and behaviors among older adults. *Holistic Nursing Practice, 10*(1), 10–17.

Rosenstock, I. (1974). Historical origins of the health belief model. *Health Education Monographs, 2*(4), 328–335.

Rosenstock, I. M. (1960). What research in motivation suggests for public health. *American Journal of Public Health, 50*(3), 295–302.

Rosenstock, I. M., Strecher, V. J., & Becker, M. H. (1988). Social learning theory and the health belief model. *Health Education Quarterly, 15*(2), 175–183.

Sano, Y., Antabe, R., Atuoye, K. N., Hussey, L. K., Bayne, J., Galaa, S. Z., … Luginaah, I. (2016). Persistent misconceptions about HIV transmission among males and females in Malawi. *BMC International Health and Human Rights, 16*, 16. doi:10.1186/s12914-016-0089-8

Sheeran, P., Harris, P. R., & Epton, T. (2014). Does heightening risk appraisals change people's intentions and behavior? A meta-analysis of experimental studies. *Psychology Bulletin, 140*, 511.

Smith, P. J., Humiston, S. G., Marguse, E. K., Zhao, Z., Dorell, C. G., Howes, C., & Hibbs, B. (2011). Parental delay or refusal of vaccine doses, childhood vaccination coverage at 24 months of age, and the health belief model. *Public Health Reports, 126*(Supp 2), 135–146.

Stretcher, V., & Rosenstock, I. M. (1997). The health belief model. In K. Glanz, F. M. Lewis, & B. K. Rimer (Eds.), *Health behavior and health education: Theory, research and practice* (2nd ed.). San Francisco, CA: Jossey-Bass.

Sun, A., Xiong, H., Kearney, A., Zhang, J., Liu, W., & Huang, G. (2010). Breast cancer screening among Asian immigrant women in Canada. *Cancer Epidemiology, 34*, 73–78. doi:10.1016/j.canep.2009.12.001

Tang, J., Foster, K., Pumarino, J., Ackermann, R., Peaeman, A., & Cameron, K. (2015). Perspectives on prevention of type 2 diabetes after gestational diabetes: A qualitative study of Hispanic, African-American and white women. *Maternal & Child Health Journal, 19*(7), 1526–1534. doi:10.1007/s10995-014-1657-y

Tenkorang, E. Y. (2013). Myths and misconceptions about HIV transmission in Ghana: What are the drivers? *Culture, Health & Sex, 15*, 296–310. doi:10.1080/13691058.2012.752107

Walker, K. K., Steinfort, E. L., & Keyler, M. J. (2015). Cues to action as motivators for children's brushing. *Health Communication, 30*(9), 911–921. doi:10.1080/10410236.2014.904030

Wang, D., & Hagins, M. (2016). Perceived benefits of yoga among urban school students: A qualitative analysis. *Evidence-Based Complementary and Alternative Medicine, 2016*(2016). doi:10.1155/2016/8725654

Watters, S. E., & Beck, K. H. (2016). A qualitative study of college students' perception of risky driving and social influence. *Traffic Injury Prevention, 17*(2), 122–127. doi:10.1080/15389588.20151045063

Weitkunat, R., Pottgieber, C., Meyer, N., Crispin, A., Fischer, R., Schotten, K., … Uberia, K. (2003). Perceived risk of bovine spongiform encephalopathy and dietary behavior. *Journal of Health Psychology, 8*(3), 373–382.

Winfield, E. B., & Whaley, A. I. (2002). A comprehensive test of the health belief model in predicting condom use among African American college students. *Journal of Black Psychology, 28*(4), 330–346.

Wolfers, M., deZwart, O., & Kok, G. (2011). Adolescents in The Netherlands underestimate risk for sexually transmitted infections and deny need for sexually transmitted infection testing. *AIDS Patient Care and STDs, 25*(5), 311–319. doi:10.1089/apc.2010.0186

Yep, G. A. (1993). HIV prevention among Asian American college students: Does the health belief model work? *Journal of American College Health, 41*(5), 199–205.

Yue, Z., Li, C., Weilin, Q., & Bin, W. (2015). Application of the health belief model to improve the understanding of antihypertensive medication adherence among Chinese patients. *Patient Education and Counseling, 98*, 669–673. doi:10.1016/j.pec.2015.02.007

Zullig, L. L., Sanders, L. L., Thomas, S., Brown, J. N., Danus, S., McCant, F., & Bosworth, H. B. (2016). Health beliefs and desire to improve cholesterol levels among patients with hyperlipidemia. *Patient Education and Counseling, 99*, 830–835. doi:10.1016/j.pec.2015.11.025

CHAPTER 5
Attribution Theory

STUDENT LEARNING OUTCOMES

After reading this chapter the student will be able to:

- Explain the concept of Attribution Theory.
- Discuss the constructs of internal and external locus of control.
- Explain the construct of stability.
- Use the theory to explain at least one behavior.

ATTRIBUTION THEORY ESSENCE SENTENCE

There is a cause or explanation for things that happen.

Constructs

Locus of control: The extent to which a person believes he/she has control over life events

Stability: The extent to which a cause of an event is permanent or temporary

Controllability: The extent to which a person can willfully change a cause of an event

▶ In the Beginning

Attribution Theory grew out of a desire to identify an overarching theory to explain what motivates people (Weiner, 2010). Much of the research leading up to the development of this theory focused on perceived attributional causes of achievement or the behaviors and other factors that influenced success or failure.

It was Heider (1944, 1958) in the 1940s and 1950s who originally proposed that achievement (success and failure) could be explained by the formula "Can × Try" where "Can" represents the relationship between ability and task difficulty, multiplied by "Try" which is the effort put forth by the person (Weiner, 2010). So success or failure is the result of how difficult a task is and the person's ability to do it, multiplied by how much effort the person puts into trying to do it.

Simply put, this theory explains why people "attribute" or assign cause to what happens to them. Think of it this way—when you work really hard in a difficult course and get a good grade, what do you attribute the grade too? Perhaps you attribute your good grade to the long hours you spent reading and studying, or working with a tutor, or the way the professor taught the course. This theory explains *why* you attribute those things to your success.

Attributions are separated into two categories: personal and environmental. Personal attributions include ability, personality, and other factors internal to the person. Environmental attributions or factors are external to the person (Strickland, 2006; Kearsely, 2006; Weiner, 1985).

To further explain what motivates people, the concept of locus of control was added to the mix (Rotter, 1966). Since locus of control is the perception of the extent to which one has control over life events, it seemed logical that it might be a significant determinant of success or failure. People with a high need for achievement would view life events as being in their control—things happen because of what I do (internal controls). People with low achievement needs would view life events as not being in their control, but instead the result of luck or some other external force (external controls) (Weiner, 2010). In 1971, Weiner combined the four characteristics related to success and failure—ability, effort, difficulty of task, and locus of control—and added causal stability and control to develop the framework of Attribution Theory (Weiner, 2010).

▶ Theory Concept

In 1982, there was a football team in Los Angeles—the Los Angeles Rams—that had a really bad season. "Here it is Thanksgiving week, and the Los Angeles Rams are looking like the biggest turkeys in town. Coach Ray Malavasi has eliminated bad luck, biorhythms, and 'sunspots' as the reason for his team's poor performance" (Robert, 1982). Clearly, poor Coach Malavasi was trying to attribute his team's lousy game (failure) to some external cause in order to explain why they played (behaved) so poorly.

Why is it so important for us to attribute a cause to an outcome? Well, sometimes we assign causation just for the sake of having an explanation. Other times, we need to attribute a cause because it helps us psychologically deal with a specific event (Weiner, 1985). Then there are times when it's important for us to understand why a certain event happened because we want to have it happen again (repeated success), or if it was something negative (failure), we want to change what we did so it won't happen again (Weiner, 1985).

As the saying goes, "If you keep doing the same thing, you'll keep getting the same results." That's fine, if the results are what you want. But if they aren't, then knowing the cause will enable you to change what you are doing so you won't keep getting the same undesirable outcome.

▶ Theory Constructs

Since causality is the basis for this theory, understanding more about causes helps us better understand why people behave in certain ways. To this end, three aspects of a cause, or causal dimensions, have been identified in this theory: locus, stability, and controllability (Weiner, 1985).

Locus of Control

The causal dimension of locus is really referring to the idea of locus of control (Rotter, 1966). Locus of control has to do with the extent to which people believe they have control over events in their lives. Locus of control comes in two flavors: internal and external. A person with an internal locus of control believes events happen as a result of something within himself or herself (e.g., skill, intelligence, desire, commitment, work ethic, values, or beliefs), attributes over which the person has control.

A person with an external locus of control believes events happen because of things outside the realm of personal control or because of things in the environment. External causes are divided into those attributed to fate, luck, or chance and those attributed to powerful others. These powerful others can be significant in health because they are often physicians, dentists, therapists, and other health or medical personnel (Levenson, 1974; Wiegmann & Berven, 1998).

Whether someone attributes internal or external causes to a given situation varies from situation to situation (Rotter, 1993). This is typically seen in students. If a student fails a course, the cause for the poor grade is inevitably external and often a powerful other—the professor (she is a tough grader, he didn't like me, his tests are too hard, or she didn't teach us anything). However, if a student does really well in a course, then the cause for the good grade is attributed to attending class, taking notes, and studying—internal conditions over which the student has control. It is a rare student who will assign the cause of failure to internal conditions over which he or she had control. How many students do you know fail a course and say, "She was a great professor, but I just didn't care if I learned the information," or "I should have bought the book and read it, taken notes in class, handed in all of the assignments, and not partied as much" (**FIGURE 5.1**).

FIGURE 5.1 Internal cause for failing a course—sleeping on your notes.
© Sergey Dubrov/Shutterstock

Locus of control can and does impact health. When applied to health behavior, it is referred to as *health locus of control*. For example, when people with multiple medical problems are more external, they believe they have little control over their situation, making it unlikely they will do what they should to manage their conditions (Henninger, Whitson, Cohen, & Ariely, 2012). After all, they are not personally responsible for their health or illness and nothing they do will change the situation since they attribute their illness to bad luck, chance, fate, or family predisposition (genetics).

This is exactly what was found in a study done on a South Asian population with type 2 diabetes living in the United Kingdom. The predominate locus of control was external with a strong religious belief that lead to acceptance of their diabetes as something they were helpless to do anything about, and a relegation of illness management to their healthcare practitioners. They saw little need to do anything more than take their medications. This meant they were not inclined to make any of the lifestyle changes necessary for diabetes control; that is adjust their diets, exercise, and lose weight. In contrast, those few with an internal locus of control were of the mindset that there was something they could do to manage their diabetes and so they made the necessary lifestyle changes (Macaden & Clarke, 2010). This is consistent with other research on older adults that found those with an internal locus of control more likely to have healthier lifestyles that included getting enough sleep, eating a nutritious diet, exercising, and having regular dental check-ups (Stewart, Chipperfield, Perry, & Weiner, 2012).

Locus of control has also been used to explain violence behavior. Young people who believe they are in control of the outcomes of their behavior, that is, having an internal locus of control, are *less* likely to engage in violent behavior. Youth who attribute the consequences of their behavior to luck (good or bad) or fate are more likely to engage in violence (Ahlin, 2014).

Heavy workload, long hours, job insecurity, and interpersonal relationships/ conflict are all examples of workplace stressors (National Institute for Occupational Health and Safety, 2014). Everyone pretty much agrees that job stress results from the interaction between an employee and the work conditions when the two don't mesh. Interestingly, interpersonal conflict is one of the workplace stressors where locus of control makes a difference. "Internals" have less stress from interpersonal conflict than do "externals." When confronted with a workplace conflict, internals use a problem solving approach to manage the situation. Managing conflict this way turns out to be a buffer against stress (Dijkstra, Beersma, & Evers, 2011).

An internal locus of control isn't always associated with positive or successful outcomes, nor is an external locus always associated with negative outcomes or failures. A case in point is depression. In this example, people with an external locus of control are less likely to develop depression because when things don't work out the way they had hoped, it had nothing to do with them—it was fate, luck, or the draw of the cards. When opportunities don't pan out in a successful way for people with an internal locus, they see the failure as something they had control over (Yu & Fan, 2016), which results in greater likelihood of depression.

Stability

Another attributional cause of behavior is stability, or the extent to which a cause fluctuates or remains constant. Ability or aptitude, for example, is viewed as a constant or stable cause, whereas effort or mood is unstable because it can vary or fluctuate from moment to moment or situation to situation (Weiner, 1985). A stable cause of behavior is something that doesn't change; it remains the same.

It would be logical to assume that internal causes of behavior—intelligence, work ethic, innate ability, and values—are more stable or consistent, meaning they don't vary from day to day. Athletic ability is one example. It's pretty stable or consistent and it doesn't fluctuate from day to day. If it wasn't stable, can you imagine what a professional football game would be like?

However some internal causes, such as mood, desire, drive, and effort do vary. Although these are internal causes, they are not stable, permanent, or consistent (Weiner, 1985). They can change from day to day, from situation to situation.

External causes work the same way. Summer following spring every year is an external, stable cause of behavior. It is consistent, and it doesn't vary. Summer doesn't follow winter one year and autumn the next. And people behave differently in the summer than they do in the other seasons. They tend to be outdoors more, are more active, go on family vacations, and have picnics. However, temperature and humidity on any given summer day are unstable external causes of behavior. If the temperature is in the 90s with high humidity, chances are people will seek refuge in air conditioning. If it's in the low 80s with little humidity, we're more likely to be outside.

Another example of an unstable external cause of behavior is luck. Luck varies. It's inconsistent and certainly not permanent. Sometimes you have it, and unfortunately, sometimes you don't (**FIGURE 5.2**) (Weiner, 1985).

The idea of cause stability has implications when we are trying to explain health behavior using the Attribution Theory. For instance, when an alcoholic relapses, he or she is more likely to attribute this negative behavior to an external, unstable cause (Seneviratne & Saunders, 2000): "When I wasn't looking, someone switched my soda with champagne, and since everyone was expected to join in the toast, I drank it. I won't ever take my eye off my soda again." The external cause was "someone," and the unstable aspect was that this was a temporary situation that won't happen again. Ah, the devil made me do it!

When teachers view learning disabilities as a stable cause of failure, it affects the way they interact with students. They are less frustrated, more sympathetic and give more positive feedback when students with learning disabilities and low ability

FIGURE 5.2 Luck—sometimes you have it and sometimes you don't.
© iQoncept/Shutterstock

put forth great effort and still fail. Conversely, they are more frustrated, show less sympathy, and give more negative feedback to students without learning disabilities who have high ability but put forth little effort (Woodcock & Vialle, 2011).

When the cause of an outcome is thought be biological and, therefore, stable or not able to be changed, more helping behaviors result. When the cause is believed to be behavioral, that is unstable or changeable, it can trigger anger, hostility (Vishwanath, 2014), and less sympathy, as seen in the example above of the highly able student who puts forth little effort.

One of the problems with assigning causation as stable or unstable is that accurate information needs to be the foundation. This seems to be the issue fostering the negative perception of type 1 or juvenile diabetes. Type 1 diabetes is an autoimmune disorder that most often occurs in children and young adults as a result of immune system destruction of insulin producing cells in the pancreas (Center for Disease Control [CDC], 2015).This is not the same as type 2 diabetes which is associated with obesity. However, because public understanding of type 1 diabetes seems to be based on misinformation and confusion with type 2 the perception is that it happens to children who don't eat right, are lazy, overweight, and that it *can* be cured (Vishwanath, 2014) when in reality, it is a stable, permanent cause that cannot be changed or cured.

Misperception or misattribution of causation stability by the public also occurs with brain injury (McClure, 2011). Because the actual injury to the brain is invisible, people react to the behaviors that result from the injury which are often common behaviors such as fatigue and aggression. So when an adolescent with brain injury is tired and aggressive, it's attributed to a life stage, adolescence (Hastings, Remington, & Hopper, 1995), which is an unstable cause rather than to the brain injury which may be more stable. This misattribution of cause to something that is unstable (adolescence doesn't last forever) becomes problematic because it can lead to frustration, unrealistic hopes for recovery, incorrect legal decisions about the effects of the injury on the person, and inappropriate rehabilitation (Guilmette & Paglia, 2004; McClure, 2011).

A study done in 2015 with nurses found that their perception of causal stability of distress in their patients affected how much effort they put into helping them cope with their illnesses. When nurses perceived patient distress to be from unstable causes, that is, something changeable, they invested more emotional energy in trying to help them as they believed it might lead to a positive outcome. They interacted with them in a more "authentic" way. Conversely, when the cause of patient distress was seen as being stable and therefore unchangeable, nurses expended less of their emotional energy. They were less authentic in their interactions because the investment of their energy would not reduce patient distress (Golfenshtein & Drach-Zahavy, 2015).

It's interesting to see how stability affects the way we explain other people's behavior (as in the previous brain injury example) and the way we interact with other people (as in the case of the nurses). But stability also explains why we behave the way we do in regard to our own health issues. For example, people with fatigue who attribute its cause to stable factors they can't change rate their fatigue more severely than those who attribute it to unstable causes that can be changed (Wells, Thorsteinsson, & Brown, 2012).

Another example of how the stability of a cause affects outcome is seen in women living in poverty. When poor women attribute the cause of their poverty to less stable causes such as having children and their romantic relationships, they tend to see their situation as temporary rather than permanent. When the children grow up and leave the house, and when the relationship ends, they will rise out of poverty. Conversely, women who attribute their poverty to more stable causes such as a fatalistic life view or individual characteristics believe their situation will either remain the same or get worse over time (Mickelson & Hazlett, 2014).

Controllability

According to Weiner (1985), causal controllability is the extent to which a person can willfully change or has volitional control over a cause. This is particularly important because it's strongly linked to blame, stigmas, or stereotypes. In general, we attribute negative conditions in other peoples' lives to controllable causes; that is, we blame them for their problems because we think they have control over them.

A prime example of this is obesity. Obesity is seen as the result of a whole host of controllable causes such as lack of willpower, overeating, laziness, inactivity, lack of motivation and self-discipline, incompetence, noncompliance, and sloppiness (Puhl & Brownwell, 2001, 2003).

Since the "causes" of obesity are seen as controllable, obese people are held responsible for their weight and are stigmatized because of it (Pearl & Lebowitz, 2014), with obese children most at risk of stigmatization (Sikorski, Luppa, Brahler, Konig, & Ridel-Heller, 2012). Obesity stigmatization has real effects on health. For example, obese women tend to delay or don't go for breast and cervical cancer screenings (Puhl & Heuer, 2009) because of the negative attitudes and unsolicited advice about weight loss from healthcare providers, exam tables, gowns and other equipment that is too small, and embarrassment about their weight (Amy, Aalborg, Lyons, & Keranen, 2006). Couple this with a culture that associates thinness with being "good" and fatness with being "bad" (Puhl & Brownell, 2003), we end up with an increased likelihood of depression and suicidal attempts in the obese (Carpenter, Hasin, Allison, & Faith, 2000) at one extreme and eating disorders and their health consequences at the other.

Stigmas based on public perception of controllability are certainly not limited to obesity. When we assign a controllable behavioral cause to a disease, we get angry, hostile and are less empathetic toward the person with the disease. In contrast, when we perceive the cause of a disease to be biological, or uncontrollable, we are more likely to help the person (Vishwanath, 2014). In the case of type 1 diabetes (as opposed to type 2) even though it has a biological cause, public perception is that unhealthy behaviors cause it (Vishwanath, 2014). In this situation, there is a misattribution of causality—behavioral rather than biological—which results in public stigmatization. Public stigma or shame is a concern because it leads to isolation and withdrawal (Puhl & Brownell, 2003). Given that type 1 diabetes occurs most often during puberty and young adulthood (and can occur earlier in childhood), has no cure, no preventative measures, and affects all aspects of a person's life from childhood on (Vishwanath, 2014) adding public stigmatization from misattribution of causation into the mix does not support positive health outcomes.

Attitudes toward homosexual orientation and same-sex parenting is another example of how causal control affects behavior. When people attribute homosexual orientation to a genetic cause, meaning it is uncontrollable, they are more supportive of gay/lesbian marriage and parenting as compared to those who assign a controllable (learned) cause to a homosexual orientation (Frias-Navarro, Monterde-i-Bort, Pascual-Soler, & Badenes-Ribera, 2015).

Another example of when perceived controllability leads to blame is with children who stutter. In an attempt to understand speech therapists' perceptions of children who stutter and casual control, it turned out that perceived controllability of stuttering was linked to blaming the child for his/her communication problem, less willingness to help, less sympathy toward the child, and greater likelihood of agreement with negative stereotypes of people who stutter (Boyle, 2014).

How teens perceive the cause of depression in a peer can explain why some depressed teens are accepted by their peers while others are excluded. If the depressed teen is perceived as having little control over the cause of his/her depression, and is not personally responsibility for the depression, the peer group is more sympathetic and there is a greater likelihood of social acceptance (Dolphin & Hennessy, 2014).

Interestingly, the peer group response differs for males and females when the cause of the depression is considered controllable. When a male is depressed and his peers believe he is responsible for his depression, they are more likely to be angry. Conversely, when a female is depressed, her peers are more likely to react with social acceptance (Dolphin & Hennessy, 2014).

Believing that we have control over a situation sometimes makes it more likely for us to rise above the problem. Look at loneliness in older adults. Lonely older adults who believe the feeling of loneliness is in their control are more hopeful that the situation can be changed by changing their behavior (Newall, Chipperfield, Clifton, Perry, & Swift, 2009). For example, they might join a community social group, take a vacation with a tour group, volunteer at an agency or local food kitchen, or take a course at the local adult school. This is a good example of the influence perceived causal controllability has over peoples' lives. For older adults, believing they have control over their loneliness means they can be less lonely if they choose to do something about their situation. The opposite would be true for those who perceive loneliness as not being in their control, or having an uncontrollable causality. If being lonely is not in their control, then there is nothing they can personally do to change the situation.

Although not all health behaviors can be explained or changed on the basis of causal attribution, it can be a starting point. Assigning causation may not only help explain the behavior, but also identify the type of intervention needed to achieve behavior change.

In summary, according to Attribution Theory, internal factors, external situations, locus of control, stability, and controllability explain behavior (**FIGURE 5.3**).

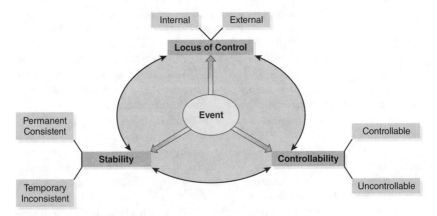

FIGURE 5.3 Attribution flowchart.

THEORY IN ACTION—CLASS ACTIVITY

1. In small groups, identify the causes attributed to obesity.
2. Identify possible effects of stigmatization resulting from inaccurate controllability beliefs.
3. Next, identify ways weight/obesity stigmatization might be reduced.

Now, read the following article and answer the questions at the end.

Chapter 5 Article: Weight Stigma Reduction and Genetic Determinism[1]

Anja Hilbert*

Integrated Research and Treatment Center Adiposity Diseases, Department of Medical Psychology and Medical Sociology, University of Leipzig Medical Center, Leipzig, Germany

Abstract

One major approach to weight stigma reduction consists of decreasing beliefs about the personal controllability of—and responsibility for—obesity by educating about its biogenetic causes. Evidence on the efficacy of this approach is mixed, and it remains unclear whether this would create a deterministic view, potentially leading to detrimental side-effects. Two independent studies from Germany using randomized designs with delayed-intervention control groups served to (1) develop and pilot a brief, interactive stigma reduction intervention to educate N = 128 university students on gene × environment interactions in the etiology of obesity; and to (2) evaluate this intervention in the general population (N = 128) and determine mechanisms of change. The results showed (1) decreased weight stigma and controllability beliefs two weeks post-intervention in a student sample; and (2) decreased internal attributions and increased genetic attributions, knowledge, and deterministic beliefs four weeks post-intervention in a population sample. Lower weight stigma was longitudinally predicted by a decrease in controllability beliefs and an increase in the belief in genetic determinism, especially in women. The results underline the usefulness of a brief, interactive intervention promoting an interactionist view of obesity to reduce weight stigma, at least in the short term, lending support to the mechanisms of change derived from attribution theory. The increase in genetic

1 Reproduced from Hilbert, A. (2016). Weigh stigma reduction and genetic determinism. *PLOS One, 11*(19), e0162993. doi: 10.1371/journalpone.0162993

* Corresponding author. E-mail: anja.hilbert@medizin.uni-leipzig.de

determinism that occurred despite the intervention's gene × environment focus had no detrimental side-effect on weight stigma, but instead contributed to its reduction. Further research is warranted on the effects of how biogenetic causal information influences weight management behavior of individuals with obesity.

▶ Introduction

People with obesity are pervasively stigmatized and exposed to weight-related discrimination in many domains of life.[1] Posing a threat for mental and physical health and well-being,[2-4] interventions to reduce weight stigma are being developed. One major approach consists of decreasing beliefs about the personal controllability of body weight by educating about the biogenetic causes of obesity; however, this has been inconsistently efficacious.[5] In addition, it remains unclear whether focusing on biogenetic causes promotes a deterministic view of individuals with obesity as being genetically and thus, fundamentally and inevitably different,[6] potentially exacerbating stigma as a side-effect.

Stigmatizing attitudes towards individuals with obesity emerge in the context of beliefs about the controllability of and responsibility for the excess body weight.[7-10] As predicted by the prominent attribution theory,[11] the more a stigma such as weight stigma is attributed to internal, controllable causes, and, thus, responsibility is perceived, the greater are one's negative reactions to it, including, for example, negative emotions, stigmatizing attitudes, and behavioral discrimination. In line with these predictions, attributions to uncontrollable causes, such as biogenetic causes, have been shown to co-occur with lower stigmatizing attitudes in most,[12,14,16,17] but not all studies on weight stigma.[13,15]

Providing information on the biogenetic causes of obesity has shown mixed effects on stigmatizing attitudes.[18] Some experimental studies that briefly informed adult participants in student and community-based samples about the biogenetic causes of obesity found reduced stigmatizing attitudes,[7,19-22] while others did not.[13,17,23,24] Interpreting results is complicated by methodological shortcomings (e.g., lack of adequate control groups, no pre-post design), so that causality in some studies cannot clearly be determined. In contrast to these brief experimental manipulations, more comprehensive, multi-component interventions that were designed to reduce stigmatizing attitudes by using education on genetic factors, among other interventions (e.g., information on the sociocultural background), led to decreased explicit stigmatizing attitudes over several weeks of follow-up in students.[25-29] One comprehensive, multi-component intervention in a student sample even reduced implicit, unconscious stigmatizing attitudes,[27] as assessed by the Implicit Association Test (IAT).[30] In contrast, an anti-stigma film[28] and a brief experimental manipulation of biogenetic causes[24] did not reduce implicit stigmatizing attitudes in students.

Despite the increasing evidence based on the stigma-reducing potential of providing information on the biogenetic causes of obesity, little research has been conducted on the potential mechanisms and side-effects of interventions.[31] Some studies documented a specific decrease in controllability beliefs,[21,25,27,28] as would be predicted by attribution theory.[11] It has not been consistently demonstrated whether interventions increased biogenetic causal attributions,[23,27,29] or had no impact on these attributions.[13,20] It further remains unclear whether internal causal attributions to an individual's behavior decreased, whether knowledge of obesity and its etiology increased, and whether the belief of obesity to be genetically determined, involving the view of people with obesity as fundamentally different, was heightened.

While most of the aforementioned experimental manipulations presented an essentialist, deterministic view of obesity according to which genes form the basis of individuals and determine his/her behavior or body weight, thereby limiting personal control and responsibility, multi-component studies sought to provide a more complex, multi-factorial view of obesity in order to reduce weight stigma. For any provision of genetic causal information, it has been argued that the reference to genetic factors could be misinterpreted in an essentialist way: Genetic essentialism,[32] because of its potential to promote perceptions of fundamental genetic differentness, could lead to increased stigma as a side-effect.[6,31,33] Indeed, a meta-analysis on the stigma of mental illness found that a stronger consideration of biogenetic causes was associated with less blame, but views of mental illness as more dangerous.[34] While in the obesity field none of the aforementioned experimental or multi-component stigma reduction studies documented increased weight stigma after providing genetic causal information, Persky and Eccleston[20] found that information on the genetic causes of obesity was associated with a reduced readiness of medical students to recommend weight loss, exercise, and diet to patients with obesity in a virtual treatment setting. Thus, more research is warranted on potential mechanisms and side-effects, including causal attributions, genetic determinism, and knowledge.

Two independent studies were designed (1) to develop and pilot a brief, inter-active multicomponent intervention on weight stigma reduction with a focus on providing a gene × environment model of obesity etiology in a student sample; and (2) to evaluate effects of this intervention in the general population over a pro-longed follow-up. It was hypothesized that the intervention would reduce explicit stigmatizing attitudes (primary outcome) and controllability beliefs; leave implicit stigmatizing attitudes unchanged—based on the aforementioned inconsistent find-ings on the variability of implicit stigmatizing attitudes; and increase knowledge, genetic causal attributions, and genetic determinism, but decrease internal causal attributions (secondary outcomes).

▶ Study 1: Development of a Brief, Interactive Intervention for Weight Stigma Reduction Providing Gene × Environment Causal Information

Materials and Methods

Participants and procedure. Participants were 128 university students (79 women, 49 men) recruited for the study at Philipps University of Marburg, Germany. Partici-pants were on average 23.01 ± 3.24 years old and had a mean body mass index (BMI, kg/m²) of 22.41 ± 3.00 kg/m² that was calculated based on self-reported height and weight. Using the guidelines by the World Health Organization,[35] overweight or obe-sity were identified in 21 (16.4%) participants (BMI 2: 25.00 kg/m²).

Of the 128 participants, 64 individuals were randomly assigned to the exper-imental group to receive the intervention, and 64 individuals were assigned to a delayed-intervention control group that was offered the intervention after the post-intervention assessment. A delayed intervention control group is an appropriate control condition in the early stage of intervention development. The two groups did not differ significantly in the distribution of gender, [$\chi^2(1, N = 128) = 1.62$], age [$F(1, 126) = 0.45$], BMI [$F(1, 126) = 3.34$], or weight status [underweight/normal weight vs. overweight/obese; $\chi^2(1, N = 128) = 2.79$; all $p > .05$].

Participants were seen individually in the laboratory suite. Prior to all study procedures, they were informed about the study in a verbal and written format, and written informed consent was obtained. Consent forms and personal information collected therein were archived at the University in a locked facility and locked cabinet, so that only study personnel had access to them. When the study was conducted from 01/2006–04/2007, it was not mandatory to seek approval by an Institutional Review Board for studies in non-clinical participants in Germany. There was no Institutional Review Board in place for non-clinical studies from the Psychology Department of Philipps University of Marburg at that time.

For the baseline assessment, participants completed the measures described below. Participants of the experimental group then received the computerized intervention. Participants of both groups were given an appointment for the post-intervention assessment 10 to 16 days after the initial appointment in order to complete the same measures as at baseline. Participants of the control group were offered the intervention at this time point. All participants were offered two hours of research participation credits as incentive.

Measures. The Antifat Attitudes Test (AFAT)[19] was used to assess the primary outcome of explicit stigmatizing attitudes. The AFAT includes 47 statements to be rated on a 5-point Likert rating scale ranging from 1 = Definitely disagree to 5 = Definitely agree (e.g., "Fat people have no will power"). A total mean score was calculated, with higher scores indicating greater explicit stigmatizing attitudes. The German version, controlled by a retranslation procedure, demonstrated an excellent internal consistency of the total mean score (Cronbach α's = .96) in this study's sample that was comparable to the original AFAT's internal consistency.[19]

Regarding secondary outcomes, the Beliefs About Obese Persons Scale (BAOP)36 was used to measure explicit beliefs about diverse personal and biological causes of obesity and the controllability of body weight of individuals with obesity. Participants are asked to rate eight statements about the causes of obesity on a 6-point Likert scale ranging from -3 = I strongly disagree to $+3$ = I strongly agree (e.g., "Obesity is usually caused by overeating"). Higher sum scores (with a maximum value of 24) indicate a stronger belief that obesity is not under personal control. The German translation of the BAOP was controlled by a retranslation procedure. Internal consistency of the BAOP in this study's sample was adequate (Cronbach α = .77) and comparable to that reported for the original version.[36]

Further, a test of knowledge was constructed to measure the participants' knowledge about the etiology of obesity, weight stigma, and modifiability of body weight through weight loss interventions. This test included 10 items offering four response options each, one of which was correct (e.g., "In family and twin studies, how much is body weight influenced by genetic factors?" 10–20%, 20–50%, 30–70% [correct response], 70–100%). Correct answers were summed up, with a possible range of 0 = No knowledge about obesity to 10 = Very knowledgeable about obesity.

To measure implicit stigmatizing attitudes, a computerized version of the IAT[30] was used to determine the relative strength of associations between a pair of opposing attribute and target categories. In weight stigma IATs, probands classify target stimuli (e.g., skinny, plump) into a thin or fat category, and attribute stimuli (e.g., smart, stupid) into a positive or negative category. Responses are typically more correct or faster for compatible (e.g., fat and negative) than for incompatible (e.g., fat and positive) pairings.[37,38] The weight stigma IAT in this study used culturally adapted items from Teachman and Brownell[38] and followed the structure recommended by Nosek, Greenwald, and Banaji.[39] As the dependent variable, the D score was calculated by dividing the mean differences of reaction times by standard deviations of all reaction times of the trials presenting compatible and incompatible antifat pairings.[40] Higher D scores are indicative of a stronger association between fat and negative, and thus of stronger implicit stigmatizing attitudes.

Intervention. The stigma reduction intervention sought to make participants reflect about their view on the controllability and responsibility of individuals with obesity regarding their excess weight. The intervention was delivered through an interactive audio-visual slide show (55 slides), presented via Microsoft Power-Point (Microsoft Corporation, Redmond, Washington State, USA), and took about 60 minutes to complete. In order to involve participants in the reflection about their own thoughts and attitudes about overweight people, the intervention used psycho-education, guided discovery, and mental imagery techniques. Additional material was provided that the participants were asked to work through during the intervention (e.g., comparison of current and desired body size).

To introduce the topic, participants were asked in a guided imagery task to imagine encountering an overweight woman in a public place, and were instructed to observe their reactions using a behavior analytic framework of the emotional, cognitive, behavioral, and perceptual levels. In Module 1, participants received general information on the definition, prevalence, risk factors, and treatment of obesity. The emphasis was on the etiological relevance of genetic factors in interaction with environmental factors and on the limited modifiability of body weight through weight loss treatment. Module 2 addressed weight stigma in the context of the current societal pressure to be slim. Using body image interventions,[41] relativity of the beauty ideal was addressed by showing paintings of women at different sizes from different eras. In addition, participants were made aware of their own beauty ideal and current body size using Stunkard's Standard Figural Stimuli.[42] Module 3 addressed prejudice against people with obesity. Current research was presented on the origin of weight stigma, forms of weight related stigmatization and discrimination, and the consequences for people with obesity. A reflection task was designed to make participants aware of their own prejudice against individuals with obesity. The presentation was concluded by summarizing take-home messages.

Data analytic plan. Post-intervention group differences on the primary and secondary outcome variables were analyzed using univariate analyses of variance with baseline values as covariates (ANCOVAs). Change over time was analyzed by conducting repeated measures ANOVAs of Group (experimental, control group; between-subjects) $\times$ Time (baseline, post-intervention; within-subjects). In order to determine influences by participants' body weight, weight status (underweight/normal weight vs. overweight/obesity) was entered as a covariate in an additional step in the analyses outlined above; the results were reported only if changed. Partial η^2, describing the proportion of total variability attributable to a factor, was displayed to estimate effect size (η^2, small: 2: 0.01, medium: 2: 0.06, large: 2: 0.14).[43] A two-tailed α of .05 was applied to all tests. Analyses were performed using SPSS 22.0 (SPSS Inc., Chicago, Illinois, USA). The sample size of N = 128 provided 80% power to detect a medium effect size for a Group $\times$ Treatment effect of $\eta^2 = 0.06$. Data are made available in the Supporting Information (S1 Data).

Results

As summarized in **TABLE A.1**, post-intervention ANCOVAs showed significantly less explicit stigmatizing attitudes (AFAT) in the experimental than in the control group (p < .01; medium effect). In addition, less controllability beliefs (BAOP), and greater knowledge of obesity were found (both p < .001; large effects). Implicit stigmatizing attitudes (IAT) did not differ between groups (p > .05).

Repeated measures ANOVAs revealed significant Group $\times$ Time effects for explicit stigmatizing attitudes (p < .05; small effect), and for controllability beliefs and knowledge of obesity (both p < .001; medium-to-large effects). Post-hoc analyses showed that explicit stigmatizing attitudes decreased significantly and knowledge increased significantly in the experimental group (both p < .01; $\eta^2 = 0.11, 0.47$), while in the control group both variables remained unchanged (both p > .05; $\eta^2 = 0.03, 0.04$). In addition, both groups showed a large-size decrease in controllability beliefs post-intervention when compared to baseline, but the effect size was more than twice as high in the experimental group than in the control group (all p < .05; $\eta^2 = 0.44$ vs. 0.17). Implicit stigmatizing attitudes did not show any significant effect in the Group $\times$ Time analysis (both p > .05).

Discussion

The results demonstrated that the brief interactive intervention for weight stigma reduction yielded a significant but small reduction in explicit stigmatizing attitudes two weeks after the intervention. In addition, the intervention led to medium-to-large decreases in controllability beliefs and increases in knowledge, as predicted. In contrast, the control group showed unchanged scores in knowledge and slightly decreased scores in controllability beliefs, which may result from participating in the study, possibly stimulating a reflection about attitudes towards people with obesity. Overall, the results confirm previous evidence on the destigmatizing potential of multi-component programs,[25-29] even with the brief time commitment of the intervention (60 minutes).

In contrast to the significant effects on explicit measures, no effects emerged for implicit stigmatizing attitudes, as expected, which reflects some previous research on relatively brief interventions,[24,28] but is not consistent with the results from a more comprehensive health curriculum.[27] Although the interactive intervention was designed to activate implicit stigmatizing attitudes (e.g., by guided imagery), the intervention may not have been potent enough to substantially change them.

Based on these results, further evidence was deemed necessary to determine whether this intervention would: be useful in a population-based sample; show maintenance of effects over a prolonged follow-up; modify causal attributions and increase genetic knowledge of obesity; and increase the belief in genetic determinism even if it was based on a gene $\times$ environment model.

TABLE A.1 Study 1: Effects of a brief interactive stigma reduction intervention over two weeks in a student sample (N = 128).

M	Experimental group				Control group					Group[a]		Group × Time[b]		Time[b]	
	Baseline		Post-Intervention		Baseline		Post-Intervention		F(1, 125)	F(1, 126)	η^2	F(1, 126)	η^2	F(1, 126)	η^2
	M	SD	M	SD	M	SD	M	SD							
Explicit measures															
Stigmatizing attitudes (AFAT)	1.98	0.47	1.85	0.41	2.25	0.65	2.22	0.65	0.69	7.36**	0.06	4.23*	0.03	9.42***	0.07
Controllability beliefs (BAOP)	18.00	7.70	25.27	6.66	16.52	6.85	18.30	7.47	7.47	36.06***	0.22	22.76***	0.15	61.94***	0.33
Knowledge of obesity	3.70	1.58	5.80	1.90	3.53	1.41	3.78	1.41	1.33	50.72***	0.29	33.48***	0.21	54.10***	0.30
Implicit measure															
Stigmatizing attitudes (IAT-D)	0.56	0.37	0.57	0.43	0.63	0.38	0.63	0.42	0.42	0.05	0.00	0.01	0.00	0.09	0.00

AFAT indicates Antifat Attitudes Test (1–5); BAOP, Beliefs About Obese Persons Scale (0–48); Knowledge of obesity (0–10); IAT, Implicit Association Test; D, mean differences of reaction times divided by standard deviations of all reaction times when presenting compatible and incompatible anti-fat pairings.

[a]Univariate analysis of variance by Group (EG, CG; between-subjects) with baseline values as covariates.

[b]Repeated measures analysis of variance of Group (EG, CG; between-subjects) × Time (baseline, post-intervention; within-subjects).

*p < .05

**p < .01

***p < .001

Reproduced from Hilbert, A. (2016). Weight stigma reduction and genetic determinism. *PLOS One, 11*(19), e0162993. doi: 10.1371/journal.pone.0162993

▶ Study 2: Effects of a Brief, Interactive Weight Stigma Reduction Intervention on Stigmatizing Attitudes and Genetic Knowledge, Attributions, and Determinism

Materials and Methods

Participants and procedure. A total of 128 individuals (79 women, 49 men) were recruited from the community for the study in the region of Marburg, Germany, using flyers, public notices, and newspaper announcements. Participants were on average 35.31 ± 12.54 years old and had a mean BMI of 25.64 ± 5.64 kg/m² (calculated based on self-reported height and weight), with overweight or obesity identified in 54 (42.2%) participants (BMI 2: 25.00 kg/m²). Of the 128 participants, 63 individuals were randomly assigned to the experimental group to receive the intervention, and 65 individuals were assigned to a delayed-intervention control group. The two groups did not differ significantly in the distribution of gender [$\chi^2(1, N = 128) = 1.10$], age [$F(1, 126) = 1.27$], BMI [$F(1, 126) = 0.04$], or weight status [underweight/normal weight vs. overweight/obesity; $\chi^2(1, N = 128) = 0.02$; all p > .05]. However, significantly more participants in the experimental group than in the control group had a lower level of education [< 13 years vs. 2: 13 years of school education; experimental group: 39, 61.9%, control group: 26, 40.0%; $\chi^2(1, N = 128) = 6.14$, p < .05].

The procedure, including informed consent, followed that in Study 1. As opposed to Study 1, participants were seen four weeks instead of two weeks after baseline for their post-intervention assessment. The study was conducted from 09/2008–12/2009. Participants were offered 25 EUR as an incentive.

Measures. As in Study 1, the AFAT was used as the primary outcome measure, and the BAOP and the computerized IAT were used as secondary outcome measures to assess explicit stigmatizing attitudes, controllability beliefs, and implicit stigmatizing attitudes. The following additional secondary outcome measures were assessed.

A test on the genetic knowledge of obesity was created in order to evaluate interventional effects on the specific knowledge about genetic factors of obesity. Eight items offered three to five response options, one of which was correct (e.g., "Only maternal genes predispose for the development of obesity." This is right, this is wrong [correct response], I don't know). Correct answers were summed with a range of 0 = No knowledge about obesity genetics to 8 = Very knowledgeable about obesity genetics.

To assess causal attributions of obesity, the 11-item Causal Attributions of Obesity Questionnaire (CAOQ) was used.[12] This questionnaire includes three subscales on the perceived risk factors of obesity: Behavior (or internal attributions), which encompassed eating and activity behavior likely leading to a positive energy balance (e.g., "Binge eating," "Lack of physical activity;" 5 items); Environment (or external attributions), which referred to the obesogenic food and activity environment (e.g., "Healthy food is too expensive," "Lack of facilities for outside physical activity;" 5 items); and Heredity (genetic attributions; "Obesity is something that is inherited from the parents;" 1 item). All scales were derived from principal components analysis.[44] Items were given five-point rating scales (1 = Disagree completely to 5 = Agree completely) and subscale means were used for the analysis.

An adapted version of the Belief in Genetic Determinism Scale (BGDS)[45] was used for this study to measure how much participants believed that obesity is determined by genetics. Of the original 18 items, 10 items with the highest explanation of variance of the total mean score were selected for this study and adapted to obesity (e.g., "The fate of each person lies in his or her genes."). Items, averaged to a mean score, were supplied with 7-point rating scales ranging from 1 = Not at all true to 7 = Completely true. The adapted scale revealed an adequate internal consistency in this study's sample (Cronbach α's = .73), comparable to that reported for the original version.[45]

Control variable. The Social Desirability Scale-17 (SDS-17)[46] was used to control for the effect of social desirability in how participants answered in the outcome measures. The SDS-17 consists of 17 items to be answered with right or wrong. To analyze, socially desirable answers were summed (e.g., "During arguments I always stay objective and matter-of-fact"). Stöber[46] reported adequate retest-reliability (r^{tt} = .82).

Intervention. The intervention developed and piloted in Study 1 was applied, with minor modifications (e.g., reduced difficulty level of scientific content).

Data analytic plan. The same data analytic strategy as in Study 1 was used, with three adaptations: (1) The dependent variables included causal attributions subscale scores, genetic knowledge of obesity sum score, BGDS total score, beyond AFAT total score, BAOP sum score, and IAT-D score. (2) Education was used as a covariate in the analyses. (3) In order to determine effects of participants' social desirability, the SDS-17 sum score was entered as a covariate in an additional step in the analyses; the results were reported only if changed. In addition to these analyses, a stepwise multiple linear regression analysis was conducted, controlling for sociodemographic variables in step 1, in order to identify predictors of explicit stigmatizing attitudes (effect size evaluation: small: R^2 2: .02, medium: 2: .15, large: 2: .35). To select predictors, zero-order associations with post-intervention AFAT total score were determined using Pearson's r or Spearman's rho correlation coefficients for the following continuous or ordinal variables: group status, gender, age, weight status, education, baseline AFAT total score, and baseline and change scores (post-intervention minus baseline) of all secondary outcome variables. The variables showing at least small-effect associations with the post-intervention AFAT total score were retained for regression analysis (small: r 2: .10, medium: 2: .30, large: 2: 0.50). A two-tailed α of .05 was applied to all tests. Analyses were performed using SPSS 22.0 (SPSS Inc., Chicago, Illinois, USA). Data are made available in the Supporting Information (S2 Data).

Results

Change by group and time. As summarized in **TABLE A.2**, ANCOVAs did not show any group difference in post-intervention explicit stigmatizing attitudes (AFAT), controlling for baseline values and education (p > .05). Likewise, there were no significant

TABLE A.2 Study 2: Effects of a brief interactive stigma reduction intervention over four weeks in a general population sample (N = 128).

| | Experimental group | | | | | | Control group | | | | | | | |
| | Baseline | | Post-Intervention | | | | Baseline | | Post-Intervention | | | | | |
	M	SD	M	SD	$F_{(1, 125)}$	η^2	M	SD	M	SD	$F_{(1, 125)}$	η^2	$F_{(1, 125)}$	η^2
Explicit measures														
Stigmatizing attitudes (AFAT)	2.10	0.53	2.15	0.50	0.00	0.00	2.08	0.51	2.12	0.49	0.01	0.00	1.92	0.02
Controllability beliefs (BAOP)	18.42	7.92	20.44	7.51	0.71	0.01	17.64	5.93	19.06	7.05	0.29	0.00	0.81	0.01
Genetic knowledge of obesity	2.40	1.53	3.54	1.54	28.37***	0.19	2.52	1.50	2.54	1.56	23.72***	0.16	0.13	0.00
Genetic attributions (CAOQ)	2.92	0.89	3.41	0.94	10.20**	0.08	2.85	1.00	2.89	1.03	6.07*	0.05	0.27	0.00

Measure														
Internal attributions (CAOQ)	3.98	0.56	3.79	0.74	3.99	0.49	3.87	0.53	0.09	0.06	0.06	0.00	7.51**	0.06
External attributions (CAOQ)	3.16	0.64	3.06	0.60	3.21	0.60	3.12	0.64	0.00	0.00	0.02	0.00	2.80	0.02
Genetic determinism (BGDS)	4.10	0.73	4.67	0.90	4.05	0.88	4.15	0.91	13.33***	0.10	10.97**	0.08	3.78	0.03
Implicit measure														
Stigmatizing attitudes (IAT-D)	0.51	0.31	0.45	0.25	0.47	0.32	0.41	0.34	0.06	0.00	0.00	0.00	0.48	0.00

AFAT indicates Antifat Attitudes Test (1–5); BAOP, Beliefs About Obese Persons Scale (0–48); Genetic Knowledge of Obesity (0–8); CAOQ, Causal Attributions of Obesity Questionnaire (1–5); BGDS, Belief in Genetic Determinism Scale (1–7); IAT, Implicit Association Test, D, mean differences of reaction times divided by standard deviations of all reaction times when presenting compatible and incompatible anti-fat pairings.

a Univariate analysis of variance by Group (EG, CG; between-subjects) with baseline values and education as covariates.

b Repeated measures analysis of variance of Group (EG, CG; between-subjects) × Time (baseline, post-intervention; within-subjects) with education as covariate.

$*p < .05$

$**p < .01$

$***p < .001$

effects for controllability beliefs (BAOP), internal attributions (CAOQ), or implicit stigmatizing attitudes (IAT; all p > .05). In contrast, genetic knowledge of obesity, genetic causal attributions (CAOQ), and belief in genetic determinism (BGDS) were greater in the experimental group than in the control group (medium to large effects; p < .01).

Repeated measures ANCOVAs did not reveal any significant effect on explicit stigmatizing attitudes, controllability beliefs, or implicit stigmatizing attitudes (all p > .05; Table A.2). However, significant Group × Time effects for genetic knowledge of obesity, genetic causal attributions, and belief in genetic determinism emerged (small to large effects; all p < .05), but not on internal attributions (p > .05). Post-hoc analyses showed that genetic knowledge about obesity, genetic attributions, and the belief in genetic determinism increased significantly and at large effect sizes in the experimental group (all p < .001; $\eta^2 = 0.17, 0.37, 0.32$), while in the control group these variables remained unchanged (all p > .05; $\eta^2 = 0.00, 0.00, 0.02$). In addition, a significant main effect of time was found for internal attributions that decreased across both study groups (p < .05; medium effect). This effect was no longer significant when weight status or social desirability were included in the model as additional covariates (p > .05).

Prediction of post-intervention explicit stigmatizing attitudes. To select predictor variables in the multiple linear regression analysis, correlational analyses showed that lower post-intervention explicit stigmatizing attitudes had at least small-size correlations with: lower baseline explicit stigmatizing attitudes (r = .86) and controllability beliefs (−.35), and more genetic causal attributions, less internal and external causal attributions, and greater belief in genetic determinism (−.28 ≤ r ≤ .36). In addition, post-intervention explicit stigmatizing attitudes were lower the greater the increase in genetic determinism beliefs and the greater the decrease in controllability beliefs (−.19 ≤ r ≤ −.11). From the sociodemographic variables, female gender, higher age, and overweight/obesity revealed small-size associations with lower post-intervention explicit stigmatizing attitudes (−.11 ≤ r ≤ .19).

When entering these variables into a stepwise multiple linear regression analysis (**TABLE A.3**), lower baseline stigmatizing attitudes (large effect), greater decrease in controllability beliefs, greater increase in genetic determinism beliefs, and female gender (small effects) showed significant prediction effects for lower post-intervention explicit stigmatizing attitudes (all p < .05). The final model including these predictors was significant [F(4, 123) = 113.96, p < .001] and explained 78% of the variance.

Additional analyses. Because of the differences between the experimental and the control group in educational level, additional analyses stratified by educational level were conducted (< 13 years or 2: 13 years of school education). In the ANOVAs of Group (experimental, control group; between-subjects) × Time (baseline, post-intervention; within-subjects), in participants with high educational level only, controllability beliefs increased [F(1, 61) = 4.27, p < .05, $\eta^2 = 0.07$] and implicit stigmatizing attitudes decreased over time [F (1, 61) = 4.70, p < .05, $\eta^2 = 0.07$] in both the experimental and the control group, while genetic causal attributions increased over time specifically in the experimental group [F(1, 61) = 4.00, p < .01, $\eta^2 = 0.12$]. In contrast, internal causal attributions decreased over time in participants with low educational level only [F(1, 63) = 10.82, p < .01, $\eta^2 = 0.15$]. As reported for the total sample (see above), in both participants with high and low

TABLE A.3 Study 2: Multiple linear regression analysis: Prediction of explicit stigmatizing attitudes towards obesity (N = 128).

	B	SE	Beta	t test	R^2	R^2 change
Gender	0.09	0.04	0.09	2.13*	.03	.03
Baseline explicit stigmatizing attitudes (AFAT)	0.81	0.04	0.85	20.30***	.74	.71
Change controllability beliefs (BAOP)	−0.01	0.00	−0.16	−3.74***	.77	.03
Change genetic determinism (BGDS)	−0.07	0.03	−0.11	−2.51*	.78	.01
Constant	0.37	0.10				

Outcome variable: Stigmatizing attitudes towards obesity 4 weeks post-intervention (AFAT, Antifat Attitudes Test, 1–5).
B indicates unstandardized regression coefficient; SE, standard error; Beta, standardized regression coefficient; R2, adjusted multiple R2 (cumulative); R2 change, adjusted multiple R2 (by predictor). Gender (female = 1, male = 2); BAOP, Beliefs About Obese Persons Scale (0–48); BGDS, Belief in Genetic Determinism Scale (1–7). Excluded predictor variables: age, baseline: controllability beliefs (BAOP); genetic, internal, and external causal attributions (CAOQ); genetic determinism (BGDS).
*p < .05
**p < .01
***p < .001
Reproduced from Hilbert, A. (2016). Weight stigma reduction and genetic determinism. *PLOS One, 11*(19), e0162993. doi: 10.1371/journalpone.0162993

educational level, genetic knowledge and the belief in genetic determinism increased specifically in the experimental group (all p < .05).

In the regression analysis of participants with high educational level, lower baseline explicit stigmatizing attitudes (0.83), greater decrease in controllability beliefs (−0.16), greater increase in genetic determinism beliefs (−0.17), and greater genetic causal attributions (−0.13) significantly predicted lower post-intervention explicit stigmatizing attitudes (all p < .05). The final model including these predictors was significant [F(4, 62) = 67.86, p < .001] and explained 81% of the variance. In participants with low educational level, only lower baseline stigmatizing attitudes (0.85) and greater decrease in controllability beliefs (−0.18) were significant predictors (all p < .05). The final model including these predictors was significant [F(2, 64) = 96.62, p < .001] and explained 75% of the variance.

Discussion

As opposed to Study 1, the brief interactive intervention to reduce weight stigma did not show any significant effect on explicit stigmatizing attitudes in a general population sample over a prolonged follow-up of four weeks. Neither were beliefs about the personal controllability of one's overweight attenuated. Stratification of the analyses by educational level, however, showed a decrease in controllability beliefs and implicit stigmatizing attitudes in participants with higher educational level only, which applied to both the experimental and the control group. These results are consistent with meta-analytical results suggesting almost zero effects for weight stigma interventions that were conducted in individuals from the general population, while interventions in higher educated student samples tended to yield greater reductions in stigmatizing attitudes.[18] Beyond the population-based sample, the extended time frame of four weeks in this study may have attenuated effects that were found to be small after two weeks in Study 1. Further, older age was significantly associated with lower stigmatizing attitudes, so that age differences between studies are unlikely to be accountable. Overall, the results in this study were stable when weight status or social desirability were controlled.

Regarding mechanisms of change, the brief interactive intervention increased specific knowledge on obesity genetics and fostered genetic causal attributions as hypothesized, with the latter especially pronounced in individuals with high educational level. In contrast, unexpectedly, causal attributions to internal factors (e.g., overeating, lack of physical activity) decreased in both study groups, thus indicating that this reduction was not related to the intervention, but presumably to participating in the study provoking a reflection about the responsibility of the onset of obesity. This effect was not stable when controlled for covariates, and especially applied to individuals with low educational level. As hypothesized, the belief in genetic determinism was increased in the intervention group only, although the program's focus was on gene $\times$ environment interactions. Thus, the reference to gene $\times$ environment interactions may have been misunderstood in a deterministic way. However, four weeks after the intervention, the participants still scored—with low variability—close to the BGDS mean ($M = 4.67$, $SD = 0.90$ vs. scale $M = 4$); thus, they were unlikely to perceive obesity as fully genetically determined. Unlike preliminary results on potential negative side-effects of genetic causal information on students' weight loss recommendations or overeating behavior,[16,20] deterministic beliefs were not shown to have detrimental effects on stigmatizing attitudes. Rather, together with a greater decrease in controllability beliefs, a greater increase in deterministic views of obesity contributed to the prediction of decreased stigmatizing attitudes four weeks post-intervention, with small effect size. This was true especially for women, who revealed in some previous investigations lower stigmatizing attitudes than men,[12,14] and for individuals with high educational level.

▶ Conclusions

Based on two well-controlled, adequately powered studies, the newly developed brief, interactive intervention educating about gene $\times$ environment interactions in the etiology of obesity was found to be useful to decrease weight stigma, at least in the short term and in individuals with high educational level. In a comprehensive investigation of mechanisms of change and potential side-effects, the results further lended some support to the prediction of attribution theory,[11] in that a focus on uncontrollable—genetic—factors (moderated by environmental influences that are at least partly controllable) can attenuate controllability beliefs (Study 1), which predicts lesser weight stigma (Study 2). Beyond fostering genetic causal attributions and knowledge, the intervention further led to an increase in beliefs in genetic determinism that was not found to be harmful, as previously cautioned,[6,31,33] but contributed to decreased stigmatizing attitudes. Nevertheless, future research should rule-out any harmful effects of biogenetic causal information on individuals with obesity themselves. One study from the obesity field showed that providing genetic information did not have any effect on weight stigma internalization of individuals with overweight or obesity,[47] a variable highly correlated with mental and physical health.[48]

Limitations of this study include the use of different follow-up periods (2 versus 4 weeks) and types of samples (student versus population sample), making the differences in results of Study 1 and Study 2 difficult to interpret. An assessment of the mechanisms of change at time points prior to the primary endpoint would be desirable in order to examine mediational effects. Related to the brevity of the intervention, it was not possible to discern effects of specific components. Further, stigmatizing attitudes may have been reduced via other mechanisms than studied here. For example, empathy has been found to be inversely associated with biogenetic attributions,[49] and the intervention's guided imagery task may have increased empathy). While this study addressed the development and initial evaluation of a new stigma reduction intervention, in future studies effects could be compared to other control conditions, for example, providing genetic information, or providing gene × environment information without other intervention components, in order to further dismantle intervention effects. Using a sample more representative of the population than the relatively young sample in Study 2 (mean population age 43.9 years)[50] would bolster generalizability of findings. Moreover, it would be desirable to examine effects on additional outcomes, including body image, self-efficacy, depression, eating behavior, or physical activity, and behavioral outcomes (e.g., social distance). Further, more work on the assessment of the belief in genetic determinism would be desirable, for example, clarifying its nature as a categorical or continuous concept.[51]

Given that potent weight stigma reduction programs with sustainable success are widely lacking,[5,18] more research is warranted to develop efficacious interventions targeting both explicit and implicit stigmatizing attitudes in individuals from all educational backgrounds. Regarding the challenge to develop interventions to improve implicit stigmatizing attitudes,[52] this can most likely be achieved by intensive multi-component interventions.[27] Other approaches that could be tested are, for example, evaluative conditioning or attentional bias modification.[52] Once safety and efficacy are further confirmed, interventions like the one described could be one low-cost and highly disseminable component, albeit with limited sustainability, in the societal challenge of reducing weight stigma. Because of the substantial individual and societal stigma-related burden,[2,53] interventions to reduce weight stigma should become part of public health strategies, for example, within larger efforts towards health promotion or prevention of obesity and eating disorders.

▶ Supporting Information

S1 Data. Study 1 Data.
(SAV)

S2 Data. Study 2 Data.
(SAV)

▶ Acknowledgments

I am grateful to M.Sc. candidates Natalie Altmann, Charlotte Fischer, Bianca Hucke, Anna Nitsche, and Judith Ritter for their impact on the realization of this study. I am also grateful to Jamie L. Manwaring, Ph.D. and Lisa Opitz, B.Sc. for their editing of the current paper.

▶ Author Contributions

Conceptualization: AH. Data curation: AH. Formal analysis: AH. Methodology: AH. Project administration: AH.
Resources: AH. Supervision: AH. Validation: AH. Visualization: AH.
Writing – original draft: AH.
Writing – review & editing: AH.

▶ References

1. Puhl RM, Heuer CA. The stigma of obesity: a review and update. Obesity. 2009; 17: 941–964. doi: 10. 1038/oby.2008.636 PMID: 19165161

2. Brewis AA. Stigma and the perpetuation of obesity. Soc Sci Med. 2014; 118: 152–158. doi: 10.1016/j. socscimed.2014.08.003 PMID: 25124079

3. Papadopoulos S, Brennan L. Correlates of weight stigma in adults with overweight and obesity: a systematic literature review. Obesity. 2015; 23: 1743–1760. doi: 10.1002/oby.21187 PMID: 26260279

4. Puhl RM, King KM. Weight discrimination and bullying. Best Pract Res Clin Endocrinol Metab. 2013; 27: 117–127. doi: 10.1016/j.beem.2012.12.002 PMID: 23731874

5. Daníelsdóttir S, O'Brien KS, Ciao A. Anti-fat prejudice reduction: a review of published studies. Obes Facts. 2010; 3: 47–58. doi: 10.1159/000277067 PMID: 20215795

6. Dar-Nimrod I, Heine SJ. Genetic essentialism: on the deceptive determinism of DNA. Psychol Bull. 2011; 137: 800–818. doi: 10.1037/a0021860 PMID: 21142350

7. Crandall CS. Prejudice against fat people: ideology and self-interest. J Pers Soc Psychol. 1994; 66:882–894. doi: 10.1037/0022-3514.66.5.882 PMID: 8014833

8. Crandall CS, D'Anello S, Sakalli N, Lazarus E, Nejtardt GW, Feather NT. An attribution-value model of prejudice: anti-fat attitudes in six nations. Pers Soc Psychol Bull. 2001; 27: 30–37. doi: 10.1177/0146167201271003

9. Crandall CS, Martinez R. Culture, ideology, and antifat attitudes. Pers Soc Psychol Bull. 1996; 22:1165–1176. doi: 10.1177/01461672962211007

10. Crandall CS, Moriarty D. Physical illness stigma and social rejection. Br J Soc Psychol. 1995; 34: 67–83. doi: 10.1111/j.2044-8309.1995.tb01049.x PMID: 7735733

11. Weiner B. An attributional theory of motivation and emotion. New York: Springer; 1986.

12. Hilbert A, Rief W, Braehler E. Stigmatizing attitudes toward obesity in a representative populationbased sample. Obesity. 2008; 16: 1529–1534. doi: 10.1038/oby.2008.263 PMID: 18464749

13. Lippa NC, Sanderson SC. Impact of information about obesity genomics on the stigmatization of overweight individuals: an experimental study. Obesity. 2012; 20: 2367–2376. doi: 10.1038/oby.2012.144 PMID: 22673191

14. Puhl RM, Latner JD, O'Brien K, Luedicke J, Danielsdottir S, Forhan M. A multinational examination of weight bias: predictors of anti-fat attitudes across four countries. Int J Obes. 2015; 39: 1166–1173. doi: 10.1038/ijo.2015.32

15. Sikorski C, Luppa M, Braehler E, Koenig HH, Riedel-Heller SG. Obese children, adults and senior citizens in the eyes of the general public: results of a representative study on stigma and causation of obesity. PLoS One. 2012; 7: e46924. doi: 10.1371/journal.pone.0046924 PMID: 23071664

16. Dar-Nimrod I, Cheung BY, Ruby MB, Heine SJ. Can merely learning about obesity genes affect eating behavior? Appetite. 2014; 81: 269–276. doi: 10.1016/j.appet.2014.06.109 PMID: 24997408

17. Pearl RL, Lebowitz MS. Beyond personal responsibility: effects of causal attributions for overweight and obesity on weight-related beliefs, stigma, and policy support. Psychol Health. 2014; 29: 1176–91. doi: 10.1080/08870446.2014.916807 PMID: 24754230

18. Lee M, Ata RN, Brannick MT. Malleability of weight-biased attitudes and beliefs: a meta-analysis of weight bias reduction interventions. Body Image. 2014; 11: 251–259. doi: 10.1016/j.bodyim.2014.03.003 PMID: 24958660

19. Lewis RJ, Cash TF, Bubb-Lewis C. Prejudice toward fat people: the development and validation of the antifat attitudes test. Obes Res. 1997; 5: 297–307. doi: 10.1002/j.1550-8528.1997.tb00555.x PMID: 9285835

20. Persky S, Eccleston CP. Impact of genetic causal information on medical students' clinical encounters with an obese virtual patient: health promotion and social stigma. Ann Behav Med. 2011; 41: 363–372. doi: 10.1007/s12160-010-9242-0 PMID: 21136226

21. Puhl RM, Schwartz MB, Brownell KD. Impact of perceived consensus on stereotypes about obese people: a new approach for reducing bias. Health Psychol. 2005; 24: 517–525. doi: 10.1037/0278-6133.24. 5.517 PMID: 16162046

22. Weiner B, Perry RP, Magnusson J. An attributional analysis of reactions to stigmas. J Pers Soc Psychol. 1988; 55: 738–748. doi: 10.1037/0022-3514.55.5.738 PMID: 2974883

23. Bannon KL, Hunter-Reel D, Wilson GT, Karlin RA. The effects of causal beliefs and binge eating on the stigmatization of obesity. Int J Eat Disord. 2009; 42: 118–124. doi: 10.1002/eat.20588 PMID: 18798228

24. Teachman BA, Gapinski KD, Brownell KD, Rawlins M, Jeyaram S. Demonstrations of implicit anti-fat bias: the impact of providing causal information and evoking empathy. Health Psychol. 2003; 22: 68–78. doi: 10.1037/0278-6133.22.1.68 PMID: 12558204

25. Diedrichs PC, Barlow FK. How to lose weight bias fast! Evaluating a brief anti-weight bias intervention. Br J Health Psychol. 2011; 16: 846–861. doi: 10.1111/j.2044-8287.2011.02022.x PMID: 21988068

26. Hague AL, White AA. Web-based intervention for changing attitudes of obesity among current and future teachers. J Nutr Educ Behav. 2005; 37: 58–66. doi: 10.1016/S1499-4046(06)60017-1 PMID: 15882481

27. O'Brien KS, Puhl RM, Latner JD, Mir AS, Hunter JA. Reducing anti-fat prejudice in preservice health students: a randomized trial. Obesity. 2010; 18: 2138–2144. doi: 10.1038/oby.2010.79 PMID: 20395952

28. Swift JA, Tischler V, Markham S, Gunning I, Glazebrook C, Beer C, et al. Are anti-stigma films a useful strategy for reducing weight bias among trainee healthcare professionals? Results of a pilot randomized control trial. Obes Facts. 2013; 6: 91–102. doi: 10.1159/000348714 PMID: 23466551

29. Wiese HJ, Wilson JF, Jones RA, Neises M. Obesity stigma reduction in medical students. Int J Obes Relat Metab Disord. 1992; 16: 859–868. PMID: 1337340

30. Greenwald AG, McGhee DE, Schwartz JL. Measuring individual differences in implicit cognition: the implicit association test. J Pers Soc Psychol. 1998; 74: 1464–1480. PMID: 9654756

31. Hoyt CL, Burnette JL, Auster-Gussman L, Blodorn A, Major B. The obesity stigma asymmetry model: The indirect and divergent effects of blame and changeability beliefs on antifat prejudice. Stigma and Health. 2016, June 2. Advance online publication. doi: 10.1037/sah0000026

32. Nelkin D, Lindee MS. The DNA mystique: the gene as a cultural icon. Ann Arbor: University of Michigan; 2004.

33. Phelan JC. Geneticization of deviant behavior and consequences for stigma: the case of mental illness. J Health Soc Behav. 2005; 46: 307–322. doi: 10.1177/002214650504600401 PMID: 16433278

34. Kvaale EP, Haslam N, Gottdiener WH. The 'side effects' of medicalization: a meta-analytic review of how biogenetic explanations affect stigma. Clin Psychol Rev. 2013; 33: 782–794. doi: 10.1016/j.cpr. 2013.06.002 PMID: 23831861

35. World Health Organization. Obesity: preventing and managing the global epidemic (WHO Technical Report Series 894). Geneva; 2000.

36. Allison DB, Basile VC, Yuker HE. The measurement of attitudes toward and beliefs about obese persons. Int J Eat Disord. 1991; 10: 599–607.

37. Brauhardt A, Rudolph A, Hilbert A. Implicit cognitive processes in binge-eating disorder and obesity. J Behav Ther Exp Psychiatry. 2014; 45: 285–290. doi: 10.1016/j.jbtep.2014.01.001 PMID: 24480398

38. Teachman BA, Brownell KD. Implicit anti-fat bias among health professionals: is anyone immune? Int J Obes. 2001; 25: 1525–1531. doi: 10.1038/sj.ijo.0801745

39. Nosek BA, Greenwald AG, Banaji MR. Understanding and using the Implicit Association Test: II. Method variables and construct validity. Pers Soc Psychol Bull. 2005; 31: 166–180. doi: 10.1177/ 0146167204271418 PMID: 15619590

40. Greenwald AG, Nosek BA, Banaji MR. Understanding and using the Implicit Association Test: I. An improved scoring algorithm. J Pers Soc Psychol. 2003; 85: 197–216. doi: 10.1037/0022-3514.85.2.197 PMID: 12916565

41. Hilbert A, Tuschen-Caffier B. Essanfälle und Adipositas: Ein Manual zur kognitiv-behavioralen Therapie der Binge-Eating-Störung [Binge eating and obesity. A cognitive-behavioral therapy manual for binge eating disorder]. Göttingen: Hogrefe; 2010.

42. Stunkard AJ, Sørensen T, Schulsinger F. Use of the Danish adoption register for the study of obesity and thinness. Res Publ Assoc Res Nerv Ment Dis. 1983; 60: 115–120. PMID: 6823524

43. Cohen J. Statistical power analysis for the behavioral sciences. Hillsdale, NJ: Erlbaum; 1988.

44. Hilbert A, Rief W, Braehler E. What determines public support of obesity prevention? J Epidemiol Community Health. 2007; 61: 585–590. PMID: 17568049

45. Keller J. In genes we trust: the biological component of psychological essentialism and its relationship to mechanisms of motivated social cognition. J Pers Soc Psychol. 2005; 88: 686–702. doi: 10.1037/ 0022-3514.88.4.686 PMID: 15796668

46. Stöber J. Die Soziale-Erwünschtheits-Skala-17 (SES-17): Entwicklung und erste Befunde zu Reliabilität und Validität [The Social Desirability Scale-17 (SDS-17): Development and first findings on reliability and validity]. Diagnostica. 1999; 45: 173–177.

47. Lippa NC, Sanderson SC. Impact of informing overweight individuals about the role of genetics in obesity: an online experimental study. Hum Hered. 2013; 75: 186–203. doi: 10.1159/000353712 PMID: 24081234

48. Hilbert A, Braehler E, Haeuser W, Zenger M. Weight bias internalization, core self-evaluation, and health in overweight and obese persons. Obesity. 2014; 22: 79–85. doi: 10.1002/oby.20561 PMID: 23836723

49. Lebowitz MS, Ahn WK. Effects of biological explanations for mental disorders on clinicians' empathy. Proc Natl Acad Sci U S A. 2014; 111: 17786–90. doi: 10.1073/pnas.1414058111 PMID: 25453068

50. Bundesamt Statistisches. Zensus 2011 [Census 2011]. Available: https://www.destatis.de/DE /ZahlenFakten/GesellschaftStaat/Bevoelkerung/Bevoelkerung.html.

51. Sheeran P, Gollwitzer PM, Bargh JA. Nonconscious processes and health. Health Psychol. 2013; 32: 460–473. doi: 10.1037/a0029203 PMID: 22888816

52. Ruscio J, Ruscio AM, Carney LM. Performing taxometric analysis to distinguish categorical and dimensional variables. J Exp Psychopathol. 2011; 2: 170–196. doi: 10.5127/jep.010910 PMID: 23946883

53. Puhl RM, Heuer CA. Obesity stigma: important considerations for public health. Am J Public Health. 2010; 100: 1019–1028. doi: 10.2105/AJPH.2009.159491 PMID: 20075322

▶ Chapter References

Ahlin, E. M. (2014). Locus of control redux: Adolescents' choice to refrain from violence. *Journal of Interpersonal Violence, 29*(14), 2695–2717. doi:10.1177/0886260513520505

Amy, N. K., Aalborg, A., Lyons, P., & Keranen, L. (2006). Barriers to routine gynecological cancer screening for White and African-American obese women. *International Journal of Obesity, 30*, 147–155. doi:10.1038/sj.ijo.0803105

Boyle, M. P. (2014). Understanding perceptions of stuttering among school-based speech-language pathologists: An application of attribution theory. *Journal of Communication Disorders, 52*, 143–155. doi:http://dx.doi.org/10.1016/j.jcomdis.2014.06.003

Carpenter, K. M., Hasin, D. S., Allsion, D. B., & Faith, M. S. (2000). Relationships between obesity and DSM-IV major depressive disorder, suicide ideation, and suicide attempts: Results from a general population study. *American Journal of Public Health, 90*(2), 251–257.

Centers for Disease Control. (2015). *Basics about diabetes.* Retrieved September 28, 2016, from http://www.cdc.gov/diabetes/basics/diabetes.html

Dijkstra, M. T. M., Beersma, B., & Evers, A. (2011). Reducing conflict related employee strain: The benefits of an internal locus of control and a problem-solving conflict management strategy. *Work & Stress, 25*(2), 167–184.

Dolphin, L., & Hennessy, E. (2014). Adolescents perceptions of peer depression: An attributional analysis. *Psychiatry Research, 218*, 295–302. doi:10.1016/j.psychres.2014.04.051Frais-Navarro, D., Monterde-i-Bort, H., Pascual-Soler, M., & Badenes-Ribera, L. (2015). Etiology of homosexuality and attitudes towards same-sex parenting: A randomized study. *Journal of Sex Research, 52*(2), 151–161. doi:10.1080./00224499.2013.802757

Golfenshtein, N., & Drach-Zahavy, A. (2015). An attribution theory perspective on emotional labour in nurse-patient encounters: A nested cross-sectional study in paediatric settings. *Journal of Advanced Nursing, 71*(5), 1123–1134. doi:10.1111/jan.12612

Guilmette, T. J., & Paglia, M. F. (2004). The public's misconception about traumatic brain injury: A follow up survey. *Archives of Clinical Neuropsychology, 19*(2), 183–189. doi:10.1016/S0887-6177(03)00025-8

Hastings, R. P., Remington, B., & Hopper, G. M. (1995). Experienced and inexperienced health care workers' beliefs about challenging behaviours. *Journal of Intellectual Disabilities Research, 39*(6), 474–483. doi:10.1111/j.1365-2788.1995.tb00567.x

Henninger, D. E., Whitson, H. E., Cohen, H. J., & Ariely, D. (2012). Higher medical morbidity burden is associated with external locus of control. *Journal of the American Geriatrics Society, 60*, 751–755. doi:10.1111/j.1532.5415.2012.03904.x

Levenson, H. (1974). Activism and powerful others: Distinctions within the concept of internal-external control. *Journal of Personality Assessment, 38*, 377–383.

Macaden, L., & Clarke, C. L. (2010). The influence of locus of control on risk perception in older South Asian people with type 2 diabetes in the U.K. *Journal of Healthcare of Chronic Illness, 2*(2), 144–152. doi:10.1111/j.1752-9824.2010.01054.x

McClure, J. (2011). The role of causal attributions in public misconceptions about brain injury. *Rehabilitation Psychology, 56*(2), 85–93. doi:10.1037/a0023354

Mickelson, K. D., & Hazlett, E. (2014). Why me?: Low income women's poverty attributions, mental health and social class perceptions. *Sex Roles, 71*, 319–332. doi:10.1007/s11199-014-0414-4

National Institute for Occupational Safety and Health. (2014). *Stress at work.* Retrieved September 28, 2016, from http://www.cdc.gov/niosh/docs/99-101/pdfs/99-101.pdf

Newall, N. E., Chipperfield, J. G., Clifton, R. A., Perry, R. P., & Swift, A. U. (2009). Causal beliefs, social participation, and loneliness among older adults: A longitudinal study. *Journal of Social and Personal Relationships, 26*(2–3), 273–290.

Pearl, R. L., & Lebowitz, M. S. (2014). Beyond personal responsibility: Effects of causal attributions for overweight and obesity on weight-related beliefs, stigmas, and policy support. *Psychology & Health, 29*(10), 1176–1191. doi:10.1080/08870446.2014.916807

Puhl, R. M., & Brownell, K. D. (2001). Obesity, bias and discrimination. *Obesity Research, 9*, 788–805.

Puhl, R. M., & Brownell, K. D. (2003). Psychosocial origins of obesity stigma: Toward changing a powerful and pervasive bias. *Obesity Reviews, 4*, 213–227.

Puhl, R. M., & Heuer, C. A. (2009). The stigma of obesity: A review and update. *Obesity, 17*(5), 941–964. doi:10.1038/oby.2008.636

Robert, R. (1982, November 24). Malavasi questions character of some, says coaching is tough. *Los Angeles Times*, Pt. 3, 3.

Rotter, J. B. (1966). Generalized expectancies for internal versus external control of reinforcement. *Psychological Monograph, 80*, 1–28.

Rotter, J. B. (1993). Expectancies. In C. E. Walker (Ed.), *The history of clinical psychology in autobiography* (Vol. II, pp. 273–284). Pacific Grove, CA: Brooks/Cole.

Seneviratne, H., & Saunders, B. (2000). An investigation of alcohol dependent respondents' attributions for their own and "others" relapses. *Addiction Research, 8*(5), 439–453.

Sikorski, C., Luppa, M., Brahler, E., Konig, H. H., & Riedel-Heller, S. G. (2012). Obese children, adults and senior citizens in the eyes of the general public: Results of a representative study on stigma and causation of obesity. *PLOS ONE, 7*(10), e46924. doi:10.1371/journal.pone.0046924

Stewart, T. L., Chipperfield, J. G., Perry, R. P., & Weiner, B. (2012). Attributing illness to 'old age:' Consequences of a self-directed stereotype for health and mortality. *Psychology and Health, 27*(8), 881–897. doi:10.1080/08870446.2011.630735

Strickland, B. R. (Ed.). (2006). Fritz Heider. In *Encyclopedia of psychology* (2nd ed.). Retrieved December 7, 2007, from http://www.enotes.com/gale-psychology-encyclopedia/fritz-heider

Vishwanath, A. (2014). Negative perceptions of juvenile diabetics: Applying attribution theory to understand the public's stigmatizing views. *Health Communication, 29*, 516–526. doi:10.1080/10410236.2013.777685

Weiner, B. (1985). An attributional theory of achievement motivation and emotion. *Psychological Review, 92*(4), 548–573.

Weiner, B. (2010). The development of an attribution-based theory of motivation: A history of ideas. *Educational Psychologist, 45*(1), 28–36.

Wells, L., Thorsteinsson, E. B., & Brown, R. F. (2012). Control cognitions and causal attributions as predictors of fatigue severity in a community sample. *The Journal of Social Psychology, 152*(2), 185–198. doi:10.1088/00224545.2011.586655

Wiegmann, S. M., & Berven, N. L. (1998). Health locus-of-control beliefs and improvement in physical functioning in a work-hardening, return-to-work program. *Rehabilitation Psychology, 43*(2), 83–100.

Woodcock, S., & Vialle, W. (2011). Are we exacerbating students' learning disabilities? An investigation of preservice teachers' attributions of the educational outcomes of students with learning disabilities. *Annals of Dyslexia, 61*, 223–241. doi:101007/s11881-011-0058-9

Yu, X., & Fan, G. (2016). Direct and indirect relationship between locus of control and depression. *Journal of Health Psychology, 21*(7), 1293–1298. doi:10.1177/1359105314551624

CHAPTER 6

Transtheoretical Model— Stages of Change

STUDENT LEARNING OUTCOMES

At the end of this chapter the student will be able to:

- Explain the conceptual basis of the Transtheoretical Model.
- Describe the five different stages of change.
- Explain the 10 processes of change.
- Analyze decisional balance.
- Use the theory to explain the adoption of a common health behavior.

TRANSTHEORETICAL MODEL ESSENCE SENTENCE

Behavior change is a process that occurs in stages.

Constructs

Stages of change: When progress toward change happens
Decisional balance: Weighing the pros and cons of change
Processes of change: How progress toward change happens
Self-efficacy: One's belief in one's own ability to do something

▶ In the Beginning

The Transtheoretical Model (TTM) was developed in the early 1980s as a way to understand *how* people change behaviors; in particular, addictive behaviors such as smoking, drug use, and alcohol abuse. Although research consistently showed that behavior change occurred both with and without psychotherapy (self-change), it did not explain *how* the change took place in either of these approaches (Prochaska, DiClemente, & Norcross, 1992). Consequently, the Transtheoretical Model/Stages of

111

Change sought to answer the following question: "…are there basic common principles that can reveal the structure of change occurring with and without psychotherapy?" (Prochaska et al., 1992, p. 1102).

The Transtheoretical Model answered this with a resounding "yes,"; there were commonalities in how people changed, regardless of the behavior being changed or the method used. In fact, there were 10 processes that explained how change occurred as people progressed through the different stages of change (Prochaska et al., 1992).

▶ Theory Concept

The TTM proposes that behavior change is a process that occurs in stages. As people attempt to change their behavior, they move through different stages using a variety of processes to help them get from one stage to the next until the desired behavior is attained. Thus, the theory is also known as Stages of Change.

▶ Theory Constructs

The constructs of the theory include not only the stages of change but also the processes of change and self-efficacy. Analyzing behavior change from these perspectives is helpful when trying to understand why some people are successful at changing behavior and others are not.

Stages of Change

There are five stages of change: pre-contemplation, contemplation, preparation, action, and maintenance. Each has its own distinct characteristics and time frame, and builds upon the preceding stage.

Pre-contemplation

The first stage of change is pre-contemplation. People are in this stage from 6 months before they start thinking about changing a behavior to the point when they do start thinking about it. During this "pre-thinking" stage, they either don't recognize they have a behavior that needs to be changed because they don't know it's unhealthy, that is, they are uninformed or under-informed about the health consequences, or they just aren't ready to change a behavior they know they should (Prochaska et al., 1992).

You might be in this "pre-thinking" stage yourself right now. There may be a behavior you are not giving any thought to changing at this moment, because you don't know anything about the health consequences of what you are doing. In this case, you would be uninformed.

Let's look at sun exposure, for example. If you didn't know that sun exposure increased your risk of skin cancer, you probably wouldn't use sunscreen, stay in the shade, or wear sun protective clothing. Once you found out that lying in the sun for hours at the beach and burning increased your chances of skin cancer, that is, once you became aware, you were no longer *un*informed. This doesn't mean people change their behavior just because they learn something; clearly this is not the case.

But until people are informed or aware of the negative health consequences of their behaviors, they are not likely to begin thinking about changing them.

You may also be in pre-contemplation because you don't know enough about the effects of a behavior to make a decision to change. In this case you would be under-informed either about the negative consequences of what you're doing or about the benefits of changing (Cancer Prevention Research Center, n.d.; Velicer, Prochaska, Fava, Norman, & Redding, 1998). We see this with older adults and exercise. Although older adults know exercise is healthy, they view it as something for young people and believe it is not good for people with certain health conditions (Lach, Everard, Highstein, & Brownson, 2004). This is a case where being under-informed explains why change to a healthy behavior such as exercise is avoided. A change in this behavior will not begin until the under-informed are informed that exercise is beneficial at any age and is not restricted by most health conditions.

You might be in pre-contemplation because you've had an unsuccessful past attempt at trying to change an unhealthy behavior and are not thinking about trying again.

This is often the case with cigarette smokers who say, "Quitting is easy, I've done it a million times before," or with people who have lost weight and regained it, plus more.

People are also in pre-contemplation when they don't or won't recognize they have a problem, or aren't ready to admit it to themselves. We see this with depression (Levit, Cismaru, & Zederayko, 2016), alcoholism, and when an older person isn't ready to admit he/she can't drive anymore and has no intention of giving up his/her car keys.

Knowing why people might be in the pre-contemplation stage is useful when trying to understand why unhealthy behaviors are not changed. The goal is to take this information and use it to help move them from not thinking about changing their behavior to thinking about or contemplating a change.

Contemplation

When people move from pre-contemplation to contemplation, it means they recognize there is a problem and have started thinking about making a change. A myriad of things can get people to start thinking about changing their behavior, for example, newspapers or magazine articles, TV, Internet, Twitter, Facebook, news reports, family, friends, healthcare professionals, and so on.

Once people start thinking about changing an unhealthy behavior, the goal is for them to make a decision to move ahead with making the change. Thinking about doing something, and deciding to do something are two different things. This is *decisional balance*, the process of weighing the perceived pros and cons or costs and benefits of the new behavior against the old (Prochaska, 1994) and then making a decision. What we see in childhood obesity is parents who are aware of the pros or benefits of physical activity for their children, but whose barriers (cons)—unsafe neighborhoods, parental work schedules, or higher regard for academic pursuits rather than physical activity—hinder them from limiting screen time (computer, phone, and TV) and ensuring time is set aside each day for physical activity (Giannisi et al., 2014).

Decisional balance affects family planning and contraception use in sub-Sahara African families where husbands are usually the decisions makers in this matter and are expected to have large families (Berhane, Biadgilign, Berhane, & Memiah, 2015). Unfortunately, men in these families lack access to family planning information and services, which weighs against their use and is a barrier that affects the reproductive health of the women (Federal Ministry of Health [FMOH], 2006). Barriers for the women which weigh against use (cons) include misinformation or lack of information about different types of family planning methods, fear of side effects and infertility after use, and religious prohibition (Ayele, Tesfaye, Gebreyes, & Gebreselassie, 2013). In this situation, tipping the scale of pro and con toward the pro side and the decision to use family planning might be influenced by increased accessibility to accurate information for the husband and wife.

In looking at the decisional balance of college students in regard to human papillomavirus (HPV) vaccination, the pros include protection from HPV, protection from certain cancers and genital warts and other STIs, and decreased likelihood of transmitting HPV to a partner. The cons include needing to get three shots which they may feel take too much time, embarrassment in talking about it with parents or doctor, partner disapproval, and having parents know that they are sexually active. Since the barriers or cons carry more weight in the decisional balance than do the pros, interventions aimed at increasing vaccination rates among this population should focus on removing the barriers rather than emphasizing benefit (Lipschitz et al., 2013).

In contrast, decisional balance in condom use for HIV/STI prevention among college students more strongly relates to the pros or benefits, that is, the pros of condom use outweigh the cons. Unfortunately though, many campus programs focus on the negative consequences of not using condoms rather than the benefits of using them (Prat, Planes, Gras, & Sullman, 2011), which may be more effective.

The weight given to pros and cons changes as people go through the different stages. Cons outweigh the pros in pre-contemplation. This makes sense, since the person in this stage is not thinking about making a change. As people move into the contemplation stage, the pros or benefits of changing start to increase and in the next stages, the pros outweigh the cons (DiNoia & Prochaska, 2010).

In the case of domestic abuse, the cons of leaving can be stronger than the pros and result in a woman deciding to remain in an abusive situation (Burke, Denison, Gielen, McDonnell, & O'Campo, 2004). The cons, or reasons for not leaving, may include not wanting to lose the relationship (even though it is abusive), financial dependency, emotional need, or low self-esteem. Often, it is only after the safety of her children is factored in as a reason for leaving (pro) that the woman decides to and is able to leave (Burke et al., 2004).

Typically, we want to explain how people change behavior from one that hinders health to one that enhances health, for example, from smoking to quitting smoking, from not exercising to exercising, from not practicing safer sex to using condoms correctly and consistently. Unfortunately, though, not all health behavior change is a change to a healthier behavior. For example, the same stages of change and decisional balance can be applied to the behavior change that results in androgenic-anabolic steroid use. The decisional balance here is to weigh the pros of *using* androgenic-anabolic steroids against the cons of using them. The pros of using them might be increased strength, power, and self-confidence (Leone, Gray, Rossi, & Colandreo, 2008). The cons of using them might be side effects, cost, and illegality.

Usually once people start thinking about changing their behavior, they make a decision and plan to change within 6 months. However, this does not hold true for everyone in all situations. Some people get stuck in "thinking" mode for extended periods of time—some for years—without making the decision to change their behavior or not (DiClemente, Schlundt, & Gemmell, 2004; Prochaska et al., 1992). When it takes more than 6 months to make a decision, this is behavioral procrastination or chronic contemplation (CPRC, n.d.; Velicer et al., 1998).

Preparation

The preparation stage begins once the decision to change is made. Preparation is a short stage, lasting only about one month, since once people decide to change a behavior, they are anxious to get started. This preparation time is used to make a plan, obtain any tools they might need, learn new skills (CPRC, n.d.; Velicer et al., 1998), acquire resources of money or support, housing, and whatever else is necessary for the change to occur.

In the case of a smoker, preparation may mean setting a quit date, obtaining a prescription for a nicotine patch, or signing up for a smoking cessation program (**FIGURE 6.1**). For the woman who never had a Pap smear, preparation is finding a healthcare provider and making an appointment. For someone who decides to begin exercising, preparation might mean joining a gym, buying new sneakers, or developing an exercise plan or maybe it means signing up for a yoga class, getting a mat and some comfortable clothes. For the student who wants to eat healthier, it may mean finding easy recipes online, developing a weekly menu, and going grocery shopping.

The preparation stage for the athlete who decides to use anabolic steroids includes talking to others who already take steroids (to find a source of steroids [a dealer]), getting supplies (Leone et al., 2008), and if they are injectable, learning how to administer them.

The preparation stage of change can be particularly important when the issue is domestic partner abuse. It may entail seeking counseling or therapy, legal advice, police protection, changing a place of employment (Reisenhofer & Taft, 2013) or finding employment so as to be financially independent, and possibly relocating.

FIGURE 6.1 Preparation includes setting a quit date.
© Christy Thompson/Shutterstock

Action

Once preparation is complete, the next 6 months are spent implementing the plan or putting the plan into action to change the behavior. Keep in mind that action and change are not the same thing. Just because someone is working the plan, it does not necessarily mean there will be a permanent change in behavior. Action is when people are in the active process of modifying their behavior to address the problem they identified in earlier stages. Behavior change is the goal of action.

In order to know if the action taken is successful, behavior has to change as measured against criteria previously determined to reduce the risk of disease. For example, in the case of the smoker, the change that needs to be accomplished is quitting; switching to a low-tar cigarette or cutting down by half is not enough (CPRC, n.d.; Prochaska et al., 1992). For college students whose sexual behavior puts them at risk of STIs and pregnancy, a criteria that indicates successful change is carrying and using condoms correctly and consistently. Carrying them is a key preparatory action for their use (Arden & Armitage, 2008). If students don't have them, they can't use them. In domestic partner abuse, the change action needs to be that the victim leaves or ends the relationship. This is a particularly difficult action to engage in and one that usually causes stress, depression, and a concern for physical safety (Reisenhofer & Taft, 2013), all of which should be addressed in the previous planning/preparation stage.

Maintenance

Maintenance is the final stage of change. During this stage, people work (and sometimes struggle) to prevent relapsing to the old behavior. In general, maintenance begins after 6 months of being in the active stage of changing and continues for at least another 6 months. With some behavior changes, maintenance goes on for years (Prochaska et al., 1992), as is the case with recovering alcoholics or other substance abusers.

For some behaviors, such as diet and exercise, maintaining changes is extremely difficult. Although most people who participate in a weight loss program are successful in losing weight (i.e., they make it through the action), only about 20% keep the weight off for a year (Wing & Phelan, 2005); the remaining 80% or so relapse to their old diet and sedentary behaviors. Although the initial change may occur, permanently incorporating the new behavior into one's lifestyle, or maintaining the change, can be the most difficult part.

This is also true among people who quit smoking. Data collected from 2001 to 2010 from the National Health Interview Surveys (Centers for Disease Control, 2011) showed that although almost 70% of smokers wanted to quit, and about 52% tried, only about 6% of them actually quit. Results from research on smoking relapse after 1 year of quitting found it to be about 10% (Hughes, Peters, & Naud, 2008). Quitting isn't the difficult part—on average people quit 30 times before they have success (Chaiton et al., 2016). It's staying "quit" and maintaining the change that is the challenge.

Self-Efficacy

The second construct of the TTM is self-efficacy. Remember that self-efficacy is one's confidence in one's own ability to do something. It plays a major role in not only how successful people are in changing their behavior, that is moving from pre-contemplation to maintenance, but also in maintaining the change. In the context of maintaining a behavior change, it has to do with one's confidence in coping with situations in which there is a high risk of relapse. For example, an ex-smoker would need a great deal of self-efficacy to avoid relapsing to smoking in social situations where alcohol is served or when under financial stress (Borland, 1990; Dijkstra & Borland, 2003; Siahpush & Carlin, 2006). For a disabled person who wants to maintain a change to an active lifestyle, self-efficacy means having confidence in the ability to overcome barriers to physical activity (Kosma, Gardner, Cardinal, Bauer, & McCubbin, 2006), which may include negotiating public transportation to an exercise facility or park, for example, or wheelchair-inaccessible dressing rooms. For older women wanting to remain physically active, self-efficacy may mean having confidence in their ability to overcome a lack of energy, motivation, or discomfort with body image (Aubertin-Leheudre, Rousseau, Melancon, Chaput, & Dionne, 2005).

Self-efficacy was a key factor in an effort to have men in Northern Ethiopia involved in family planning. Their self-efficacy levels increased as they moved through the stages of change, going from the lowest level in pre-contemplation to the highest in maintenance. Self-efficacy addressed in the earlier stages of change helped move them through the stages (Berhane et al., 2015) and helped them avoid relapsing.

The same increase in self-efficacy from pre-contemplation to maintenance was seen in Latina women and cervical cancer screening. To support maintenance of regular Pap testing, strengthening self-efficacy (and decreasing barriers) was more effective than focusing on promoting the benefits of screening (Tung, Smith-Gagen, Lu, & Warfield, 2016).

So, self-efficacy supports behavior change in two ways. It helps people move through the stages of change and it helps them resist relapse in high risk situations once they have made the change.

Processes of Change

While the stages of change help us understand *when* people change their behavior, the processes of change help us understand *how* change occurs (Prochaska & DiClemente, 1982). There are 10 processes of change: consciousness raising, dramatic relief or emotional arousal, environmental reevaluation, social liberation, self-reevaluation, stimulus control, helping relationships, counter conditioning, reinforcement management, and self-liberation (Prochaska & DiClemente, 1983; Prochaska, Velicer, DiClemente, & Fava, 1988; Velicer et al., 1998).

The 10 processes are divided into two groups: cognitive or experiential processes and behavioral processes. Consciousness raising, dramatic relief, self-reevaluation, environmental reevaluation, and social liberation are cognitive processes and stimulus control, helping relationships, counter conditioning, reinforcement management, and self-liberation are behavioral processes (Prochaska et al., 1988).

Consciousness Raising

Obviously, before people can begin to think about making a behavior change, they have to recognize they have a behavior that needs to be changed. That's where

consciousness raising comes in. Consciousness raising is the process whereby people obtain information about themselves and the problem behavior. It is how people
become aware of the problem, its causes, consequences, and what can be done about
it (Prochaska et al., 1992; Velicer et al., 1998). Using fast food as an example, consciousness raising might be evidenced by a person saying, "I didn't realize fast food
was so bad for me until I saw *Super Size Me* and *Fast Food Nation*." This awareness
may help move a person from pre-contemplation to contemplation. Or, it may have
been the nutrition course a student took that provided new insight into his/her poor
eating habits.

Recalling information about ways to quit smoking (Velicer et al., 1998), seeing
a friend's post on Facebook about the Great American Smoke Out, and doing a
health risk appraisal that recommends quitting are all ways people might become
more aware of the consequences of their smoking and what they can do about it.
This is the impetus behind the warnings on tobacco products—providing people
with information about the health effects of their behavior they might not have
known.

The first step for women in abusive situations is to realize that they are in an
abusive relationship. Having cognitive recognition that there is something wrong
and gathering information about abusive relationships and safe options (Reisenhofer
& Taft, 2013) are examples of consciousness raising—ways women might gain better
understanding of their problem and how it might be changed.

Dramatic Relief

Dramatic relief, also referred to as emotional arousal, is expressing feelings
about or reacting emotionally to the behavior in question (Prochaska et al., 1992;
Velicer et al., 1998) and the possible solutions (Cancer Prevention Research
Center, n.d.).

For the smoker trying to quit, this process may mean talking about how much
one loathes quitting (Andersen & Keller, 2002); for the person who eats fast food, it
might be feeling disgusted when viewing fast-food commercials on TV.

In domestic violence situations, dramatic relief is telling other people about
the abuse and feeling validated and supported (Reisenhofer & Taft, 2013). In skin
cancer, it is being upset by seeing other people whose skin has been damaged by the
sun due to sun tanning or sunburns (Yusufov et al., 2016).

Dramatic relief in substance abuse is a trigger than can get people to recognize
their problem and how it affects people around them. Admitting that their drug
use will hurt people they care about, feeling indebted to the people who are trying to help them, self-loathing, fear, guilt, and hope are some of the emotions that
help people move from pre-contemplation to contemplation (Conner, Longshore, &
Anglin, 2008).

Environmental Reevaluation

The process of environmental reevaluation is looking at the behavior being
changed (old behavior) in light of its impact or effect on the physical and social
environments (Prochaska et al., 1992; Velicer et al., 1998). Examples of this process
for the smoker who wants to quit is understanding the environmental effects of

secondhand smoke (Andersen & Keller, 2002); for the conventional farmer who wants to change to organic farm practices, it's the environmental damage caused by continued pesticide use; or for the college student who drinks water from plastic bottles but wants to change to a refillable bottle, it is the environmental impact of plastic. In the case of domestic violence, environmental reevaluation may mean recognizing the deleterious effects of living in an abusive situation has on the children (Reisenhofer & Taft, 2013) or that the abuser's behavior is affecting friends and neighbors.

Environmental reevaluation may be very helpful in moving people along with adopting more altruistic behaviors. For example, in an effort to increase blood donation among blacks, where rates are significantly lower than whites, environmental reevaluation may take the form of thinking about how donating blood would help the larger community or how it might save a life (Amoyal et al., 2013).

Social Liberation

Social liberation is the process whereby options or alternatives are sought that support the new behavior (Prochaska et al., 1992; Velicer et al., 1998). People look for opportunities that allow them to engage in their new behavior. These opportunities might always have been there, but they didn't use them before. For the person who regularly ate fast food and stopped, it would mean ordering a salad with the dressing on the side and an unsweetened ice tea, instead of a double cheeseburger with fries and a milk shake; for the former couch potato, it might be planning a vacation hiking along the Appalachian Tail. It might be looking to move to a neighborhood or community that has a park for someone who is focused on becoming more active, or joining an organic food co-op food for the person who wants to eat healthier. In the case of behavior change for stress management, social liberation might be noticing that it is becoming a greater societal concern (Horiuchi, Tsuda, Prochaska, Kobayashi, & Mihara, 2012) which makes it easier for the person to admit the need for change (dramatic relief).

Self-Reevaluation

Self-reevaluation is the process in which people look at themselves with and without the problem behavior and assess the differences in their self-esteem (Prochaska et al., 1992; Velicer et al., 1998). For example, a woman in an abusive relationship would think about what it would be like to not live with her violent partner and how it would make her feel about herself (Reisenhoefer & Taft, 2013).

Realizing you'd be happier and feel healthier if you chose to eat fruits and vegetables (DiNoia & Thompson, 2012) rather than junk food is self-reevaluation. The same is true for people who want to cut down or cut out drinking. Self-reevaluation is knowing they'd feel good about themselves the morning after a party because they didn't over indulge the night before. When people donate blood it makes them feel good about themselves (Amoyal et al., 2013) because they are contributing to the betterment of the community. Sunscreen use takes the worry away about getting skin cancer (Yusufov et al., 2016) which may make people proud of themselves for doing something healthy, just as using healthy strategies to manage stress does (Horiuchi et al., 2012). A smoker may feel disappointed because of his/her dependency on cigarettes (Velicer et al., 1998) but can imagine the pride when he/she quits.

Stimulus Control

Stimulus control is when people remove the cues or triggers for the problem behavior from their environment (Prochaska et al., 1992; Velicer et al., 1998). The person who eats fast food might drive to work on back roads rather than the highway in order to avoid passing fast-food restaurants (**FIGURE 6.2**). For someone else, it might be hunger on the way home from work that triggers stopping for fast food. In this case, the stimulus control would be to eat something before leaving work, or bringing healthier food to eat on the way home. The smoker might avoid drinking coffee after dinner and switch to drinking tea, since coffee is a trigger for many smokers; or maybe she has to stop drinking alcohol for a while, since it too often triggers smoking.

The overeater might stop buying the half-gallon carton of ice cream and switch to the pint-size fruit sorbet instead. Replacing candy and cookies with fruit on the kitchen counter would be an example of stimulus control for someone who wants to eat healthier (DiNoia & Thompson, 2012). Removing all of the alcohol in the house would go a long way in helping someone whose behavior change is to quit drinking.

Helping Relationships

Helping relationships are relationships with people who act as a support system for changing the unwanted, unhealthy behavior (Prochaska et al., 1992; Velicer et al., 1998). This might be the roommate who agrees to keep only fruit to snack on in

FIGURE 6.2 Stimulus control may mean avoiding the dessert table at a buffet.
© Christine Langer-Pueschel/Shutterstock

the room, or the sponsor in a 12-step program who is there whenever the urge for a drink hits. It can be a neighbor who calls another neighbor at 7 A.M. to confirm they are meeting for their morning walk.

Sometimes these relationships are with professionals, in the case of a therapist or counselor working with a woman to help her leave an unsafe relationship (Reisenhofer & Taft, 2013) or an advisor helping a student with time management.

Counter Conditioning

In counter conditioning, a healthier behavior is substituted for the unhealthy one (Prochaska et al., 1992; Velicer et al., 1998). Using this process, the person trying to change fast-food consumption might bring fruit to eat in the car on the way home from campus, instead of stopping for fries and a soda. The smoker might doodle when talking on the phone rather than smoke a cigarette. The person wanting to add more activity to his/her daily routine might use the stairs rather than the elevator whenever possible. Learning how to meditate instead of drinking to relax, shutting down the computer an hour before bed and reading instead to encourage healthier sleep hygiene, drinking water instead of soda to manage weight are all examples of counter conditioning.

Reinforcement Management

The process of reinforcement management has to do with rewards and punishments. Although unwanted behavior can be changed through the fear of punishment or negative consequences (as any child will tell you), rewards for engaging in the targeted behavior are more natural. The reward can be from the person to himself/herself, or from someone else (Prochaska et al., 1992; Velicer et al., 1998). For example, a reward for not eating fast food during the week might be dinner at a nice restaurant with friends. For the woman who quits smoking, a reward from a significant other might be a bouquet of fresh flowers at the end of every week she doesn't smoke. For the exerciser, it might be a new exercise outfit or sneakers. For someone who has lost weight and is trying to keep it off, it might be buying new clothes in a smaller size.

Self-Liberation

When using the process of self-liberation, people choose to change their behavior, believe they can, and commit to making the change (Andersen & Keller, 2002; Burke et al., 2004; Prochaska et al., 1992). In self-liberation, people free themselves from a behavior in which they no longer choose to engage.

This process is what enables women in abusive relationships to do something about changing their situation. The behavior they choose to change is remaining in an abusive relationship. The commitment they make is to a different lifestyle, one that does not rely on violence as an expression of love (Burke et al., 2004; Reisenhofer & Taft, 2013). For the person with chronic obstructive pulmonary disease, self-liberation is frequently used to change from being inactive to exercising (walking) (Yang & Chen, 2005). For a college student, self-liberation might mean choosing not to drink every night, or committing to reducing sun exposure (Yusufov et al., 2016), eating less red meat, or using condoms correctly and consistently.

Stages of Change and Processes of Change

The processes of change help people move through the stages of change. Thus, different processes are used during different stages (**FIGURE 6.3**). The research to identify the processes used in each stage was originally conducted on smokers and may or may not hold true for all behavior changes (DiClemente et al., 1991; Fava, Velicer, & Prochaska, 1995; Prochaska et al., 1992) (**TABLE 6.1**).

People in pre-contemplation use processes of change the least as they move from pre-contemplation to contemplation (DiClemente et al., 1991). When processes of change are used, consciousness raising, dramatic relief, and environmental reevaluation (Prochaska et al., 1992), social liberation (Andersen & Keller, 2002; Marcus, Ross, Selby, Niaura, & Abrams, 1992), and counter conditioning (Andersen & Keller, 2002) are used more than the others. These processes increase awareness of a behavior as being a problem, including talking about the behavior as a problem and looking at how the behavior affects others in the environment.

All of the processes are used as people move through contemplation to preparation, although helping relationships, self-reevaluation, social liberation, and dramatic relief are the ones most associated with this stage (Andersen & Keller, 2002; DiClemente et al., 1991). Using these processes helps people talk with others and express feelings about the change, to look at themselves with respect to the problem

FIGURE 6.3 Processes and stages of change.

TABLE 6.1 Processes and Strategies for Moving Through the Stages of Change

Moving from Pre-Contemplation to Contemplation

Process of Change	Strategies for Change
Consciousness raising Seeking new information and gaining an understanding of the problem behavior	Media campaigns, print materials, online resources, educational programs
Dramatic relief Expressing feelings about the problem behavior and potential solutions	Role playing, personal testimonials, media campaigns, motivational interviews, psychodrama, grieving losses
Environmental reevaluation Considering how the problem behavior affects the physical and social environment	Empathy training, developing or showing documentaries, family interventions

Moving from Contemplation to Planning

Process of Change	Strategies for Change
Self-reevaluation Reappraising personal values with respect to the problem behavior and seeing one's self with and without the problem behavior	Conducting value clarification exercises, using imagery, identifying role models
Social liberation Accepting the problem-free lifestyle	Developing advocacy, polices, empowerment activities
Helping relationships Accepting the support of caring others while changing the problem behavior	Rapport building, counselor calls, buddy system
Dramatic relief Expressing feelings about the problem behavior and potential solutions	Role playing, personal testimonials, media campaigns, motivational interviews, psychodrama, grieving losses

Moving from Preparation to Action

Process	Strategies
Self-liberation Committing to changing the problem behavior, and believing in the ability to change	New Year's resolutions, public testimonies, developing behavior change plans, setting goals, signing contracts

(continues)

TABLE 6.1 Processes and Strategies for Moving Through the Stages of Change (*continued*)

Moving from Action/Maintenance	
Process	**Strategies**
Counter conditioning Substituting alternative behaviors for the problem behavior	Relaxation strategies (for stress), assertiveness training (for peer pressure), nicotine replacement (for cigarette smoking) use of positive self-statements, desensitization activities
Helping relationships Accepting the support of caring others while changing the problem behavior	Rapport building, counselor calls, buddy system
Reinforcement management Rewarding oneself or being rewarded by others for making changes	Contingency agreements, positive self-talk, group recognition, identifying meaningful rewards
Stimulus control Controlling situations and other causes which trigger the problem behavior	Establish self-help groups, avoidance training, environmental restructuring to support the new behavior and diminish the old triggers

Data from: Prochaska, J. O. & Velicer, W. F. (1997). The transtheoretical model of health behavior change. *American Journal of Health Promotion, 12*(1), 38–48. Conner, B. T., Longshore, D., & Anglin, M. D. (2008). Modeling attitude towards drug treatment: The role of internal motivation, external pressure and dramatic relief. *Journal of Behavioral Health Services & Research, 36* (2), 150–158. doi: 10.1007/s11414-008-9119-1.

behavior, and to look at or evaluate the types of support they have available in their social environments.

In moving from preparation to action, self-liberation is the most important process (Andersen & Keller, 2002; DiClemente et al., 1991; Marcus et al., 1992). Self-liberation makes sense in this stage because this is the point at which people are ready to actually do something about changing their behavior. Logically, they need to make a commitment to act before they take action.

In maintenance, the processes of counter conditioning, helping relationships, reinforcement management, and stimulus control are used most often (DiClemente et al., 1991). These enable people to sustain the new behaviors, have supportive people available, avoid triggers for the problem behavior that may cause relapse, and be rewarded for changing.

In summary, according to the TTM, behavior change occurs in stages with specific processes moving the change along.

THEORY IN ACTION—CLASS ACTIVITY

Don't move—sit perfectly still without changing or adjusting your position, and take note of how you are sitting. Are you slouching in your seat? Are your legs crossed? Are you hunched over? Are you holding your head up with your hands? Once you became aware of your position, what did you do? Congratulations, you just moved from *pre-contemplation* to *contemplation* using the process of consciousness raising.

In small groups, brainstorm how the processes of change could be used to move you from contemplation to action in adopting correct sitting body posture:

Feet on the floor
Uncrossed legs
Buttocks touching back of chair
Back with all three curves present

Now, read the following article and answer the questions at the end.

Chapter 6 Article: Effect of an Ergonomics-Based Educational Intervention Based on Transtheoretical Model in Adopting Correct Body Posture Among Operating Room Nurses[1]

Zeinab Moazzami[1], Tahere Dehdari[2], Mohammad Hosein Taghdise[2] & Alireza Soltanian[3]

[1] School of Health. Tehran University of Medical Sciences. Tehran. Iran
[2] School of Health. Iran University of Medical Sciences, Tehran. Iran
[3] School of Health. Hamadan University of Medical Sciences, Hamadan, Iran

Abstract

Background: One of the preventive strategies for chronic low back pain among operating room nurses is instructing proper body mechanics and postural behavior, for which the use of the Transtheoretical Model (TTM) has been recommended.

Methods: Eighty two nurses who were in the contemplation and preparation stages for adopting correct body posture were randomly selected (control group = 40, intervention group = 42). TTM variables and body posture were measured at

---

1 Reproduced from Moazzami, Z., Dehdari, T., Taghdisi, M.H.,& Soltanian, A. (2016). Effect of ergonomics-based educational intervention based on transtheoretical model in adopting correct body posture among operating room nurses. *Global Journal of Health Science, 8*(7), 26–34.doi: 10.5539/gjhs.v8n7p26.

baseline and again after 1 and 6 months after the intervention. A four-week ergonomics educational intervention based on TTM variables was designed and conducted for the nurses in the intervention group.

Results: Following the intervention, a higher proportion of nurses in the intervention group moved into the action stage ($p < 0.05$). Mean scores of self-efficacy, pros, experimental processes and correct body posture were also significantly higher in the intervention group ($p < 0.05$). No significant differences were found in the cons and behavioral processes, except for self-liberation, between the two groups ($p > 0.05$) after the intervention.

Conclusions: The TTM provides a suitable framework for developing stage-based ergonomics interventions for postural behavior.

Keywords: body posture, ergonomics, nurse, operating room, transtheoretical model

▶ 1. Introduction

Work-related musculoskeletal disorders (WMSD), especially lower back pain are common among operating room nurses (Sheikhzadeh, Gore, Zuckennan, & Nordin, 2009). Awkward posture, prolonged standing and fixed postures, holding and managing equipment such as retractors during surgical procedures and pulling/pushing or lifting patients, heavy instruments and equipment sets are the major contributing factors in WMSD development in this group (Meijsen & Knibbe, 2007).

One of the preventive strategies for chronic low back pain is instructing proper body mechanics and posture (Owen, Keene & Olson, 2002). Studies showed that ergonomics training for maintaining an adequate body posture while at work reduces the prevalence of WMSD among nurses (Sheikhzacleh et al., 2009: Owen et al., 2002).

It is worth mentioning that individuals are in different stages of readiness to adopt the appropriate body posture, any educational approach should identify these differences and accordingly design and provide interventions tailored to an individual's current stage of change (Keller, Herda, Ridder, & Basler. 2001).

The Transtheoretical Model (TTM), one of the stage models, postulates that people differ in their readiness to adopt a new behavior. According to the TTM individuals adopting a new behavior go through six stages of change: (a) precontemplation—no intention of changing behavior within the next 6 months; (b) contemplation—intends to make a change behavior within the next 6 months; (c) preparation—intends to make a change behavior within the next 30 days and have a plan of action; (d) action—have made overt behavior change within the past 6 months; (e) maintenance—have maintained the overt change in behavior for over six months; and (f) relapse—returning to older behavior (Adams & White, 2005). TTM assumes that progressive movement from stage to stage is also linked to differences in perceived self-efficacy (refers to the degree of confidence an individual has about his/her ability to perform a specific behavior), decisional balance (reflects the weighting of the perceived pros (advantages) and cons (costs or barriers) of behavior change). The processes of change are covert and overt activities people use to advance through their stages of change; the ten processes include five experimental and five behavioral processes: the five experimental processes include awareness-raising, dramatic relief, environmental re-evaluation, self-reevaluation and social liberation. The five behavioral processes consist of counter conditioning, stimulus control, helping relations, self-liberation and reinforcement management (Patten, Vollman, & Thurston, 2000: Prochaska, Di Clemente, & Norcross, 1992; Rodgers, Courneya, & Bayduza, 2001; Prochaska, Velicer, DiClemente, & Fava. 1988: Shanna & Romas, 2008; Grimley, Prochaska, & Prochaska, 1997). Although, use of TTM has been recommended for postural behavior (Keller et al., 2001), few studies have used this model for developing ergonomics-based educational interventions (T. Mohammacli Zeidi, Morshedi, & B. Mohammadi Zeidi, 2011). Given the importance of ergonomics training in adopting good body posture for nurses in the operating room environment (Owen et al., 2002) and the clear need for developing stage-based interventions in this field, the present study was designed to determine the effect of a TTM-based ergonomics educational intervention in adopting correct body posture among operating room nurses working in hospitals.

▶ 2. Material and Methods

2.1 Design and Samples

This quasi-randomized controlled trial study was conducted from April 2011 to July 2012. A convenience sample of 84 nurses in the contemplation and preparation stages in terms of body posture with more than 6 months of job experience in the operating room and without any history of chronic lower back pain or previous lower back surgery were randomly chosen from the four hospitals of Hamadan (21 nurses from each hospital). Nurses from two hospitals were assigned into the intervention group, while those from the two remaining hospitals were assigned to the control group. Two nurses in the control group refused to take part in the study and finally, 42 nurses participated in the intervention group and 40 in the control group. The study was approved by the ethics committee of Tehran University of Medical Sciences and written informed consent was obtained from all the nurses.

2.2 Study Instrument and Measures

Demographic characteristics and TTM items were measured by a self-administered questionnaire, the completion of which took 20 to 25 minutes. Work-related posture for the prevention of lower back pain in the operating room was measured using the observational checklist that was completed by observers before the intervention. To develop the TTM items, we reviewed the related literature (Sheikhzadeh et al., 2009; Karahan & Bayraktar, 2004; Choobineh, Movahed, Tabatabaie, & Kumashiro, 2010). Also, to develop the observational checklist, an ergonomist was observed nursing movements and body mechanisms in the operating room for a duration of one month, following which, fifteen types of movements were identified. The questionnaires were given on 10 nurses, who did not form part of any study group. A briefing session was held to give participants a chance to comment on the clarity, simplicity and readability of the items. Finally, based on their comments, minor syntax errors were corrected and any ambiguous items were clarified and edited. Content validity of the instrument items was estimated quantitatively. For this purpose, the scale was reviewed by an expert panel of twenty specialists in health education, nursing and ergonomics. The panel was asked to judge the necessity and relevance of the items in order to calculate the content validity ratio (CVR) and content validity index

(CVI). Finally, items having CVI less than 0.80 or CVR less than 0.62 were deleted from the scale. Internal consistency and reliability of the TTM sub-scales were estimated using Cronbach's α and the test-retest correlation coefficients, and an estimate of $\alpha \geq 0.70$ and correlation coefficient ≥ 0.61 were considered an acceptable value (Dehdari, Rahimi, Atyaeian, Gohari, & Esfeh, 2014); the inter-rater reliability was measured for the checklist, simultaneously by the two ergonomists, who then independently filled in the checklist. Kappa values 0.6 were considered satisfactory (Nathan et al., 2015). Both groups completed the questionnaires prior to intervention. The checklist was completed by observers before the intervention. Based on pre-test results of both groups, an educational intervention was developed for nurses in the intervention group, while the control group received no intervention. Finally, the two groups were followed up one and six months after the intervention.

2.2.1 Instruments for Assessing TTM Variables

2.2.1.1 Decisional Balance Scale. Eight items described the perceived pros for good body posture (e.g., "If I maintain correct body posture, I can prevent low back pain"); five items described the perceived cons (e.g., "I would have less time for my work if I adopt correct body posture"). These items were measured on a Likert scale ranging from 1 = "completely disagree" to 5 = "completely agree."

2.2.1.2 Self-Efficacy Scale. Six items were used to measure self-efficacy (e.g., "Even if I am tired, I can adopt correct body posture in the operating room"); these items were measured on a Likert scale ranging from 1 = "completely unconfident" to 5 = "completely confident."

2.2.1.3 TTM Processes of Change Scale. In this study, four experimental and three behavioral processes were used to move nurses in the intervention group into the action stage. The experimental processes of change scale was an 11-item measure with four sub-scales including: (1) awareness-raising (three items; e.g., "I always search for instructional materials that can enhance my awareness regarding correct body posture"); (2) environmental reevaluation (two items; e.g., "If my colleagues and I maintain correct posture, our work place will be safe"); (3) self-reevaluation (three items; e.g., "I think if I do not observe correct posture, how would my fitness be in the future") and (4) social liberation (three items; e.g., "there are facilities in operating room that nurses can use for adopting correct body posture"). All the above items were measured on a Likert scale ranging from 1 = "never" to 5 = "very often."

The behavioral processes of change scale was a 7-item measure with three sub-scales including: (1) self-liberation (two items; e.g., "I promise myself to consider adopting correct body posture as part of my occupational life"); (2) reinforcement management (two items; e.g., "I praise myself when adopting correct body posture"); and (3) counter conditioning (three items; e.g., "in my shifts, I can do stretching moves instead of wasting time"). These items were measured on a Likert scale ranging from 1 = "never" to 5 = "very often." Higher scores on these two scales indicate that participants use the experimental and behavioral processes of change more frequently.

2.2.1.4 Staging Algorithm for Adopting Correct Body Posture. Stage of change for adopting correct body posture was measured by a 5-item algorithm, a short staging algorithm, which is useful and valid for various behaviors (Prochaska & Velicer, 1997).

According to this algorithm, nurses were categorized into one of the five stages of readiness to change based on the following answers to this question: "Do you engage in behaviors for correct body posture in the operating room?" (1) No. and I do not intend to adopt correct body posture in the next 6 months (pre-contemplation); (2) No, but I intend to adopt correct body posture within the next 6 months (contemplation); (3) No, but I intend to adopt correct body posture within the next 30 days (preparation); (4) Yes, I have adopted a correct body posture, but for 6 months or less (action); (5) Yes, I have adopted a correct body posture for more than 6 months (maintenance).

2.2.2 Observational Checklist for Body Posture Practices

Fifteen items were used to measure work-related body posture in the operating room, including: standing, bending, twisting, body mechanics and body posture while handling trays and instruments, lifting, pulling, pushing, posture during work (e.g., remaining in wanted posture during a long surgery), using comfortable chairs when doing nursing procedures, wearing suitable shoes during work, extending, carrying, lifting patients, transferring patients, and positioning a patient. The checklist developed included items such as movements (Yes/No/Not Observed), and was completed by the observers at baseline and 1 month and 6 months after the intervention.

2.3 Developed Educational Intervention

The instructional intervention was designed based on the analysis of the findings of the two groups' pre-tests, which showed that only half of the nurses agreed with the advantages of adopting correct body posture, advantages such as preventing body spasms, improved flexibility of the body and the joints, relaxed sleeping at night and fitness. A low percentage of the nurses believed that they could correctly manage body posture despite boredom, stress and the busy operating room. Based on the nurses' opinions the main barriers for adopting correct body posture included their shyness, the lack of adequate and safe equipment (e.g., suitable seat to sit during intervals between surgeries or non-standard trolleys), being arrogant and putting themselves before their work, instead of doing their job; only half of the nurses said that they sought educational sources to become aware of adopting correct body posture and only a small percentage contemplated on the pros and cons of correct body posture. With regard to environmental reevaluation, a limited percentage of the nurses believed that adopting correct body posture would improve the quality of task performance in the operating room, making it a healthy working environment; moreover, a low percentage of the nurses reported that they felt good about adopting correct body posture and most of the time they wondered whether their fitness in the future would be affected if they did not observe correct body posture (self-reevaluation). Most of the nurses reported that there were insufficient sources of information/data on adopting correct body posture in the operating room and that there are many nurses, who do not maintain correct body posture (social liberation). Less than half of the nurses praised themselves after adopting correct body posture and encouraged themselves for adopting it. About half of them expected that following adopting body posture they should be praised by others (reinforcement management). A small percentage of the nurses stated that they availed of every opportunity to rest during the operation, by doing movements and deep breathing (counter conditioning). A small group of nurses said that they mostly told themselves that they could observe correct body posture and make it as part of their work routine (self-liberation).

The ergonomics educational intervention involved four 60-minute sessions implemented during a four week period for the nurses in the intervention group and one instructional session for the head nurses. During the educational sessions, the nurses were divided into small groups and received appropriate instructions for adopting correct body posture through lectures, group discussions and question-and-answer sessions. Moreover, before the instructional sessions for the nurses, in a session with the head nurses, the importance of having a more appropriate operating room environment regarding positioning of the instruments (for the effects on the posture of nurses using the instruments) was emphasized; during this session with the head nurses, they were encouraged to contact and coordinate with the hospital managers to provide up-to-date equipment and discard timeworn instruments which could negatively affect the body posture of the nurses in the intervention group. Finally, it was decided to encourage those nurses who tried more and made more effort to adopt correct body posture. The first training session (for the nurses) was an introduction to the importance of occupational low back pain, the most important risk factors, the importance of adopting correct body posture in the operating room and its advantages were explained; at the end of this session, an instructional pamphlet on the issue was given to the nurses. In the second session, using a multi-media CD which included several clips/movies about body posture; correct body posture in the operating room was taught to the nurses and they were encouraged to learn and adopt appropriate correct posture in the operating room. In the third session, by posing some open-ended questions, the nurses were asked to relate/express their experiences and positive or negative feelings upon adopting correct body posture and its perceived advantages/disadvantages. They were asked to imagine themselves after adopting the correct body posture and tell the group members about it. In this session, the nurses were assured that they could adopt correct body posture in the operating room. In addition, they were asked to develop commitment to adopting and maintaining correct body posture in the operating room, in a way that it becomes a habit for them. They were also instructed to encourage other nurses to adopt correct body posture in the operating room. Moreover, three posters illustrating the dangers of incorrect body posture and related slogans were hung in the operating room. In the fourth session, besides nurses discussing the positive experiences of correct body posture, they were also instructed on ways of reducing stress and trying to avoid rushing through their tasks; they were also trained in doing stretching movements during any free time in the operating room; an audio CD about gradual body relaxation was distributed among the nurses as well.

2.4 Data Analysis

Data were analyzed using the SPSS statistical software package (SPSS Inc., Chicago, IL, USA). The homogeneity of baseline data in demographic characteristics, TTM variables and body posture of the two groups were analyzed by x^2 and independent-samples t tests. Normality of the data was also examined and continued by the Kolmogorov-Smirnov test. Differences between the baseline and the one month assessments and those documented six months after the intervention in each group were tested using one-way repeated measurement analysis. Differences in TTM variables (except for the stages of change) and body posture between the groups were also tested using mixed model repeated measurement. Whitney U-test was used to identify significant differences in stages of change between the groups and Friedman test to identify significant differences in stages of change in each group before and one and six months after the intervention; p values < 0.05 were considered significant.

▶ 3. Results

3.1 Reliability of the Sub-Scales of Developed Instrument

The correlation coefficients, Cronbach's alpha and Kappa values of the sub-scales of developed instrument were presented in **TABLE A.1**.

TABLE A.1 The Cronbach's Alpha, test-retest correlation coefficient and kappa values of the sub-scales of the instrument

Sub-scales	Cronbach's alpha	Test–retest correlation coefficient	Kappa values
Perceived pros	0.85		
Perceived cons	0.86		
Self-efficacy	0.78		
Awareness-raising	0.88		
Self-reevaluation	0.84		
Environmental reevaluation	0.85		
Social liberation	0.80		
Self-liberation	0.80		
Reinforcement management	0.99		
Counter conditioning	0.78		
Stage of change		P = 0.01, r = 0.81	
Adopting correct body posture			0.80

Reproduced from Moazzami, Z., Dehdari, T., Taghdisi, M.H.,& Soltanian, A. (2016). Effect of ergonomics-based educational intervention based on transtheoretical model in adopting correct body posture among operating room nurses. *Global Journal of Health Science, 8*(7), 26–34.doi: 10.5539/gjhs.v8n7p26.

3.2 Demographic Characteristics of the Participants

The mean age (SD) of the nurses in the intervention (70% women) and control (62.5% women) groups was 31 (5.8) and 32 (6.7) years respectively. Nurses in the intervention and control groups had an average of 2.7 (SD = 7) and 2.9 (SD = 6.6) years of working experience in the operating room, respectively. Also, prior to the implementation of the intervention, no significant differences were found between any of the demographic characteristics of the two groups (p < .05).

3.3 Individuals' Readiness Stages for Change at Baseline and Follow-Up

As shown in **TABLE A.2**, at baseline, all of the nurses in both groups were in the contemplation and preparation stages. Results showed that after the intervention, significantly more nurses in the intervention group moved into the action stage (61.9% at post-test 1 and 50% at post-test 2) compared to the control group (0% at post-test 1 and 10% at post-test 2) (p < 0.05); however, significantly fewer nurses in the intervention group were in the contemplation and preparation stages following the intervention (see Table A.2).

3.4 Comparison of Differences in TTM Variables and Adopting Correct Body Posture at Baseline and Follow-Up

No significant differences were found between the two groups for any TTM variables and adopting correct body posture (p < 0.05) before the interventions. As shown in **TABLE A.3**, results showed that following the intervention, the intervention group had higher total mean scores on self-efficacy, pros of correct body posture, self-reevaluation, environmental reevaluation, social liberation, experimental processes, self-liberation and correct body posture (p < 0.05) compared with the control group. In addition, one and six months after the intervention, no significant differences (p < 0.05) were found for the perceived cons, awareness-raising, reinforcement management, counter conditioning and total scores of behavioral processes between the two groups (see Table A.3).

▶ 4. Discussion

Results of the present study showed that one month and six months after the intervention, considerable progress occurred in terms of nurses' stages of change in the intervention group, compared to the controls. Based on TTM, adopting correct body posture score should increase accordingly as individuals progress through the stages. The findings of this study indicate that the mean score of adopting correct body posture score among nurses in the intervention group could be improved through the educational program conducted. This finding was consistent with Munchaona (2003) and Woods et al. (2002). In agreement with findings of similar studies (Molaison & Yadrick, 2003; Kim & Cardinal, 2009; Shirazi et al., 2007), results of the present study showed that stage-matched educational intervention could move the individuals to later stages of readiness to change.

TABLE A.2 Distribution of nurses according to TTM stages of readiness to change for adopting correct body posture in the before and one-month and six-months after educational intervention in the intervention (n = 42) and the control group (n = 40)

	Pre-intervention		One month after intervention		Six months after intervention	
	Intervention group	Control group	Intervention group	Control group	Intervention group	Control group
Precontemplation	0 (0.0)	0 (0.0)	0 (0.0)	1 (2.5)	0 (0.0)	3 (7.5)
Contemplation	19(452)	21 (52 5)	1 (2.4)	24 (60)	1 (2.4)	27 (67.5)
Preparation	23 (54 8)	19 (475)	15 (35.7)	15 (37.5)	20 (47.6)	6 (15)
Action	(0.0) 0	0 (00)	26 (61.9)*†	0 (0.0)	21 (50)*†	4 (10)
Maintenance	0 (0.0)	0 (00)	0 (0.0)	0 (0.0)	0 (0.0)	0 (0.0)

1. Result of Mann Whitney U-test; P^* < 0.05 compared to the control group.
2. Result of Friedman test; $P^†$ < 0.05 compared to pre-intervention values.
3. † Stages with 0 cells were not included in the analysis.

Reproduced from Moazzami, Z., Dehdari, T., Taghdisi, M.H., & Soltanian, A. (2016). Effect of ergonomics-based educational intervention based on transtheoretical model in adopting correct body posture among operating room nurses. *Global Journal of Health Science, 8*(7), 26–34. doi: 10.5539/gjhs.v8n7p26.

TABLE A.3 Comparison of TTM variables and adopting correct body posture in the before and one-month and six-months after educational intervention in the intervention (n = 42) and the control group (n = 40)

	Pre-intervention		One month after intervention		Six months after intervention	
	Intervention group	Control group	Intervention group	Control group	Intervention group	Control group
Pros of correct body posture	33.55±7.27	32.25±3.63	34.02±3.19	31.73±3.50	34.26±3.11†	31.20±3.09
Cons of correct body posture	24.19±3.83	23.32±4.3	22±3.97	23.75±4.03	21.48±3.91*	23.60±3.84
Self-efficacy	12.62±4.51	11.88±4.82	15.26±4.13	11.80±4.61	14.74±3.88†	11.93±4.71
Awareness-raising	8.83±2.46	8.98±2.54	9.74±2.39	10.08±2.18	9.79±2.50*	10.18±2.09
Environmental reevaluation	6.74±2.20	7.28±1.31	7.21±1.94	7.18±1.68	7.48±1.84*†	7.28±1.74
Self-reevaluation	10.79±2	10.58±2.14	11.40±1.84	10.45±2.06	11.48±1.49*†	10.68±1.72
Social liberation	7.52±1.78	7.15±1.30	8.40±1.68	7.08±1.79	8.83±1.65*†	7.23±1.48

Total score of experimental processes	33.88±5.16	33.97±4.58	36.76±4.80	34.78±3.51	33.98±4.93*†	34.90±3.63
Counter conditioning	7.74±2.21	7.33±1.80	8.50±2.13	7.30±1.79	8.67±1.88*†	7.68±1.65
Reinforcement management	5.48±1.56	5.40±1.74	6.02±1.40	5.33±1.61	6.31±1.11*	5.70±1.38
Self-liberation	6.69±1.44	6.23±1.98	7.31±1.39	6.08±1.77	7.21±1.44*†	6.08±1.54
Total score of behavioral processes	19.90±3.30	18.95±3.61	21.83±3.10	18.70±3.38	21.76±2.94*	18.75±3.45
Adopting correct body posture	19.5±3.81	18.2±4	25.41±4	19.45±4.15	30.33±4.02*†	19.7±4.21

1. Values are Mean ± SD
2. Result of one-way repeated measurement analysis; $P^* < 0.05$ compared to pre intervention.
3. Result of mixed model repeated measurement; $P^\dagger < 0.05$ compared to the control

Reproduced from Moazzami, Z., Dehdari, T., Taghdisi, M.H.,& Soltanian, A. (2016). Effect of ergonomics-based educational intervention based on transtheoretical model in adopting correct body posture among operating room nurses. *Global Journal of Health Science, 8*(7), 26–34.doi: 10.5539/gjhs.v8n7p26.

In addition, results showed that the mean score of self-efficacy among nurses in the intervention group increased significantly following the intervention. The findings were also consistent with those of similar studies (Gorely & Bruce, 2000: Lubans & Sylva, 2006; Sol, Graaf, Petersen, & Visseren, 2011). Progressively moving individuals into the later stages of readiness to change, increases their self-efficacy, as reported by Keller et al. (2001), who showed that the self-efficacy scores of a German administration unit with regard to adopting correct body posture differed in the five different stages of change and those who were in later stages of change were found to be more self-confident (Keller et al., 2001). In our study, more nurses in the intervention group advanced to the action stage, demonstrating a significant difference between the groups following the intervention. Given the importance of self-efficacy to adopt correct body posture among nurses, researchers should focus on developing ergonomics-oriented educational interventions aimed at increasing self-efficacy among them.

We also found that the intervention considerably increased perceived pros in the intervention group compared to the control group 1 month and 6 months following the intervention. Mohammadi Zeidi et al. (2011) showed that developing a TTM-based ergonomics educational program can considerably enhance the advantages of adopting good body posture among computer users (Mohammadi Zeidi et al., 2011). Numerous studies have also shown that individuals in the later stages of change had more perceived pros than those in the earlier stages (Shirazi et al., 2007; Sarkin, Johnson, Prochaska, & Prochaska, 2001). Both the above-mentioned data and our findings affirm that by designing ergonomics educational interventions to progressively move nurses into the later stages of change (e.g., action and maintenance), the advantages of adopting correct body posture can be appropriately instructed.

While the results of this study indicate the effectiveness of the educational intervention on the perceived pros of correct body posture, the mean scores of cons among the nurses in the intervention group, did not show any significant decrease compared to the control group, findings that are consistent with TTM assumptions. The balance between benefits (pros) and costs (cons) of changing a health behavior for progression within stages is important. Participants whose perceived pros outweigh their perceived cons are more motivated to adopt recommended behavior (Prochaska & Velicer, 1997). In this study, the pros of correct body posture outweighed the cons before and following the intervention among the nurses; this finding was supported with Gorely and Bruce (2000), but was contradicted with Mohammadi Zeidi et al. (2011), who reported that educational interventions could have significantly decreased the perceived cons of computer users for adopting correct body posture, a paradox, which may be explained by the sample of the study (Mohammadi Zeidi et al., 2011). Since nurses are considered healthcare staff, it goes without saying that compared with other non-health care occupations, they are more aware of the advantages of the correct body posture.

Overall, the present study showed that while there was no significant difference in behavioral processes of change (except for self-liberation) between the two groups. Total mean scores of all experimental processes (including environmental reevaluation, self-reevaluation, social liberation and counter conditioning variables) were higher in the intervention group than the controls following the intervention. In other words, use of these processes of change caused the nurses to advance into the action stage, which was supported with Kirk et al. (2010) (Kirk, MacMillan, & Webster, 2010). The TTM assumes that the behavioral processes are most often used in the later stages (i.e., maintenance and action) whereas the cognitive processes are most often used in the early stages of change (i.e., pre-contemplation, contemplation and preparation) (Prochaska & Marcus, 1994). Since nurses in the current study were in the contemplation and preparation stages, they mainly used the experimental processes of change for moving through the earlier stages.

4.1 Implication for Future Research

Despite high prevalence of low back pain among operating room nurses and the importance of ergonomics education to reducing their WMSD, to the best of our knowledge, no educational intervention has been developed on this issue. Current educational programs regarding this issue for nurses will never be sufficient. Further theory-based education efforts should be established for operating room staff about measures that should be taken to prevent low back pain in-service training. It is recommended that further similar researches be designed and conducted for nurses in other hospital wards.

▶ 5. Conclusion

Results of the present study showed that the educational ergonomics intervention based on TTM can progressively facilitate significant change in movement of nurses from the contemplation and preparation stages to the action stage of adopting correct body posture in the operating room.

▶ Acknowledgements

This article was funded through grant 13751 from the Occupational Health Research Center, Tehran University of Medical Sciences as part of a dissertation project in the School of Health.

▶ References

1. Adams, J., & White, M. (2005). Why don't stage-based activity promotion interventions work? *Health Education Research, 20*(2). 237–243. http://dx.doi.org/10.1093/her/cyg105
2. Choobineh, A., Movahed, M., Tabatabaie, S. H., & Kumashiro, M. (2010). Perceived Demands and Musculoskeletal Disorders in Operating room nurses of Shiraz city hospitals. *Industrial Health,* 48. 74–84. http://dx.doi.org/10.2486/indhealth.48.74
3. Dehdari, T., Rahimi. T., Atyaeian, N., Gohari, M. R., & Esfeh. J. M. (2013). Developing and testing a measurement tool for assessing predictors of breakfast consumption based on a health promotion model. *Journal of Nutrition Education and Behavior, 46*(4), 250–258. http://dx.doi.org/10.1016/j.jneb.2013.12.007
4. Gorely, T., & Bruce. D. (2000). A 6-month investigation of exercise adoption from the contemplation stage of the transtheoretical model. *Psychology of Sport and Exercise, 1*(2). 89-10I. http://dx.doi.org/10.1016/S1469-0292(00)00012-1

5. Grimley. D. M., Prochaska. G. E., & Prochaska. J. 0. (1997). Condom use adoption and continuation: A transtheoretical approach. *Health Education Research, 12.* 61-75. http://dx.doi.org/10.1093/her/12.1.61

6. Karahan, A., & Bayraktar, N. (2004). Determination of the usage of body mechanics in clinical settings and the occurrence of low back pain in nurses. *International Journal of Nursing Studies, 41,* 67–75. http://dx.doi.org/10.1016/50020-7489(03)00083-X

7. Keller, S., Herda, C. H., Ridder, K., & Basler, H. D. (2001). Readiness to adopt adequate postural habits: An application of the Transtheoretical Model in the context of back pain Prevention. *Patient Education Counseling, 42,* 175–184. http://dx.doi.org/10.1016/S0738-3991(00)00103-8

8. Kim, Y. H., & Cardinal, B. J. (2009). Effects of a transtheoretical model-based stage-matched intervention to promote physical activity among Korean adults. *International Journal of Clinical and Health Psychology, 9*(2), 259–273.

9. Kirk, A., MacMillan, F., & Webster, N. (2010). Application of the Transtheoretical model to physical activity in older adults with Type 2 diabetes and/or cardiovascular disease. *Psychology of Sport and Exercise, 11*(4), 320–324. http://dx.doi.org/10.1016/j.psychsp01t.2010.03.001

10. Lubans, D., & Sylva, K. (2006). Controlled evaluation of physical activity intervention for senior school students: effect of the lifetime activity program. *Journal of Sport & Exercise Psychology, 28*(3), 252–268.

11. Meijsen, P., & Knibbe, H. J. J. (2007). Work-related musculoskeletal disorders of perioperative personnel in the Netherlands. *Association of Operating Room Nurses Journal, 86*(2), 193–208. http://dx.doi.org/10.1016/j.aom.2007.07.011

12. Mohammadi Zeidi, I., Morshedi, H., & Mohammadi Zeidi, B. (2011). The effect of interventions based on Transtheoretical Model on computer operators' postural habits. *Clinical Chiropractic, 14*(1), 17–28. http://dx.doi.org/10.1016/j.clch.2010.07.001

13. Molaison, E. F., & Yadrick, M. K. (2003). Stage of change and fluid intake in dialysis patients. *Patient Education and Counseling, 49*(1), 5–12. http://dx.doi.org/l0.1016/50738-3991(02)00036-8

14. Munchaona, S. (2003). *Application of Transtheoretical Model on Muscle Pain Prevention of Industrial Sewing Machine Operators* (Master's thesis. Mahidol University, Thailand). Retrieved from http://www.thaithesis.org/detail.php?id=l202546000502

15. Nathan, A. M., Zaki, R., Rozario, R., Dhania, K. Mohd Hamirudin, S. N. S., Kah Peng, Eg., … Bruyne, J. D. (2015). Cross cultural translation, adaptation and reliability of the Malay version of the Canadian Acute Respiratory Illness and Flu Scale (CARIFS). *Health and Quality of Life Outcomes, 13,* 139–142. http://dx.doi.org/ 10.1186/s12955-015-0336-z

16. Owen, B. D., Keene, K., & Olson, S. (2002). An ergonomic approach to reducing back/shoulder stress in hospital nursing Personnel: A five year follows up. *International Journal of Nursing Studies, 39*(5). 295–302. http://dx.doi.org/10.1016/S0020-7489(01)00023-2

17. Patten, S., Vollman, A., & Thurston, W. (2000). The utility of the Trans theoretical model of behavior change for HIV risk reduction in injection drug users. *The Journal of the Association of Nurses in AIDS Care, 11*(1), 57–66. http://dx.doi.org/l0.1016/S1055-3290(06)60422-6

18. Prochaska, J. O., Diclemente, C. C., & Norcross, J. C. (1992). In search of how people change, applications to addictive behaviors. *The American Psychologist, 47*(9), 1102–1114. http://dx.doi.org/10.1037/0003-066X.47.9.1102

19. Prochaska, J. O., & Marcus, B. H. (1994). The Transtheoretical model: applications to exercise. In: Dishman, R. K. (Ed.), *Advances in Exercise Adherence.* Human Kinetics. Champaign. IL; pp. 161–180.

20. Prochaska, J. O., & Velicer, W. F. (1997). The Transtheoretical Model of behavior change. *American Journal of Health Promotion, 12*(1). 38–48. http://dx.doi.org/l 0.4278/0890-1171-12.1.38

21. Prochaska, J. O., Velicer, W. F., Diclemente, C. C., & Fava, J. (1988). Measuring processes of change: Applications to the cessation of smoking. *Journal of Consulting and Clinical Psychology, 56*(4). 520-528. http://dx.doi.org/10.1037/0022-006X.56.4.520

22. Rodgers, W. M., Courneya, K. S., & Bayduza, A. L. (2001). Examination of the Transtheoretical model and exercise in 3 populations. *American Journal of Health Behavior, 25*(1), 33–41. http://dx.doi.org/10.5993/AJHB.25.1.4

23. Sarkin, J. A., Johnson, S. S., Prochaska, J. O., & Prochaska, J. M. (2001). Applying the Transtheoretical Model to Regular Moderate Exercise in an Overweight Population: Validation of a stages of change measure. *Preventive Medicine, 33*(5), 462–469. http://dx.doi.org/10.1006/pmed.2001.0916

24. Sharma, M., & Romas, J. A. (2008). Theoretical foundations of health education and promotion (2nd ed., pp. 98–103). Jones and Bartlett Publishers, Sudbury, MA.

25. Sheikhzadeh, A., Gore, Ch., Zuckennan, J. D., & Nordin, M. (2009). Perioperating nurses and technicians' perceptions of ergonomic risk factors in the surgical environment. *Applied Ergonomics, 40*, 833–839. http://dx.doi.org/10.1016/j.apergo.2008.09.012

26. Shirazi, K. K., Wallace, L. M., Niknami, S., Hidamia, A., Torkaman, G., Gilchrist, M., & Faghihzadeh, S. (2007). A home-based, transtheoretical change model designed strength training intervention to increase exercise to prevent osteoporosis in Iranian women aged 40–65 years: A randomized controlled trial. *Health Education Research, 22*(3), 305–317. http://dx.doi.org/10.1093/her/cyl067

27. Sol, B. G., Graaf, V. D., Petersen, R. V., & Visseren, F. L. (2011). The Effect of self-efficacy on cardiovascular lifestyle. *European Journal of Cardiovascular Nursing, 10*(3), 180–186. http://dx.doi.org/10.1016/j.ejcnurse.2010.06.005

28. Woods, C., Mutrie, N., & Scott, M. (2002). Physical Activity intervention: A transtheoretical model-based intervention designed to help sedentary young adults become active. *Health Education Research, 17*(4). 451–460. http://dx.doi.org/10.1093/her/17.4.451

THEORY IN ACTION—ARTICLE QUESTIONS

1. What factors contributed to the need for the intervention?
2. How would the process of environmental reevaluation contribute to moving some nurses from contemplation/preparation to contemplation?
3. How was the process of social liberation hindered?
4. What were the pros and cons of the decisional balance?
5. How did the process of self-reevaluation contribute to moving nurses from contemplation/ preparation to action?
6. How did the process of counter conditioning contribute to moving the nurses from contemplation/preparation to action?
7. How did the nurses use the process of self-liberation?
8. What was addressed during each intervention session and what process did it address that helped move the nurses from contemplation to action?
9. What effect did the intervention have in moving the nurses from the contemplation/preparation stages pre-intervention to action 1 month post intervention?
10. Look back at your group's brainstorming results and identify any similarities in what you would do relative to using the processes to move yourselves to taking action on sitting properly.

▶ **Chapter References**

Amoyal, N., Robbins, A., Pavia, A. L., Burditt, C., Kessler, D., & Shaz, B. H. (2013). Measuring the processes of change for increasing blood donation in black adults. *Transfusion, 53*, 1280–1290. doi:10.1111/j.1537-2995.2012.03864.x

Andersen, S., & Keller, C. (2002). Examination of the transtheoretical model in current smokers. *Western Journal of Nursing Research, 24*(3), 282–294.

Aubertin-Leheudre, M., Rousseau, S., Melancon, M. O., Chaput, J., & Dionne, I. J. (2005). Barriers to physical activity participation in North American elderly women: A literature review. *American Journal of Recreation Therapy, 4*(1), 21–30.

Arden, M. A., & Armitage, C. J. (2008). Predicting and explaining transtheoretical model stage transition in relation to condom carrying behavior. *British Journal of Health Psychology, 13*, 719–735. doi:10.1348/135910707x249589

Ayele, W., Tesfaye, H., Gebreyes, R., & Gebreselassie, T. (2013). *Trends and determinants of unmet need for family planning and programme options, Ethiopia*. Federal Ministry of Health, Ethiopia. Retrieved October 17, 2016, from http://dhsprogram.com/pubs/pdf/FA81/FA81.pdf

Berhane, A., Biadgilign, S., Berhane, A., & Memiah, P. (2015). Male involvement in family planning program in Northern Ethiopia: An application of the transtheoretical model. *Patient Education and Counseling, 98*, 469–475. doi:10.1016/j.pec.2014.12.012

Borland, R. (1990). Slip-ups, and relapse in attempts to quit smoking. *Addictive Behavior, 15*(3), 235–245. doi 10.1016/0306-4603(90)90066-7

Burke, J. G., Denison, J. A., Gielen, A. C., McDonnell, K. A., & O'Campo, P. (2004). Ending intimate partner violence: An application of the transtheoretical model. *American Journal of Health Behavior, 28*(2), 122–133.

Cancer Prevention Research Center (n.d.). Transtheoretical model. Retrieved March 24, 2017, from http://web.uri.edu/cprc/transtheoretical-model/

Centers for Disease Control and Prevention (CDC). (2011, November). Quitting smoking among adults—United States, 2001–2010. *Morbidity Mortality Weekly Reports (MMWR)*. Retrieved October 17, 2016, from www.cdc.gov/mmwr/index

Chaiton, M., Diemert, L., Cohen, J. E., Bondy, S. J., Selbby, P., Philipneri, A., & Schwartz, R. (2016). Estimating the number of quit attempts it takes to quit smoking successfully in a longitudinal cohort of smokers. *British Medical Journal Open, 6*, e011045. doi:10.1136/bmjopen-2016-011045

Conner, B. T., Longshore, D., & Anglin, M. D. (2008). Modeling attitude towards drug treatment: The role of internal motivation, external pressure and dramatic relief. *Journal of Behavioral Health Services & Research, 36*(2), 150–158. doi:10.1007/s11414-008-9119-1

DiClemente, C. C., Prochaska, J. O., Fairhurst, S. K., Velicer, W. F., Velasquez, M. M., & Rossi, J. S. (1991). The process of smoking cessation: An analysis of pre-contemplation, contemplation, and preparation stages of change. *Journal of Consulting and Clinical Psychology, 59*(2), 295–304.

DiClemente, C. C., Schlundt, D., & Gemmell, L. (2004). Readiness and stages of change in addiction treatment. *American Journal of Addiction, 13*, 103–119.

Dijkstra, A., & Borland, R. (2003). Residual outcome expectations and relapse in ex-smokers. *Health Psychology, 23*(4), 340–346.

DiNoia, J., & Prochaska, J. O. (2010). Dietary stages of change and decisional balance: A meta-analytic review. *American Journal of Health Promotion, 34*(5), 618–632.

DiNoia, J., & Thompson, D. (2012). Processes of change for increasing fruit and vegetable consumption among economically disadvantaged African American adolescents. *Eating Disorders, 13*, 58–61. doi:10.1016/j.eabeh.2011.10.001

Fava, J. L., Velicer, W. F., & Prochaska, J. O. (1995). Applying the transtheoretical model to a representative sample of smokers. *Addictive Behaviors, 20*(2), 189–201.

Federal Ministry of Health (FMOH). (2006). National adolescent and youth reproductive health strategy in Ethiopia, 2007–2015. Retrieved October 17, 2016, from www.countryoffice.unfpa .org/filemanager/files/Ethopia/ayrh_strategy.pdf

Giannisi, F., Pervandiou, P., Michalaki, E., Papanikolaou, K., Chrousos, G., & Yannakoulia, M. (2013). Parental readiness to implement life-style behavior changes in relation to children's excess weight. *Journal of Paediatrics and Child Health, 50*, 476–481. doi:10.1111/jpc.12500

Horiuchi, S., Tsuda, A., Prochaska, J. M., Kobayashi, H., & Mihara, K. (2012). Relationship between stages and processes of change for effective stress management in Japanese college students. *Psychology, 3*(6), 494–499. doi:org/10.4236/psych.2012.36070

Hughes, J. R., Peters, E. N., & Naud, S. (2008). Relapse to smoking after 1 year of abstinence: A meta-analysis. *Addictive Behavior, 33*(12), 1516–1520. doi:10.1016/j.addbeh.2008.05.012

Kosma, M., Gardner, R. E., Cardinal, B. J., Bauer, J. J., & McCubbin, J. A. (2006). Psychosocial determinants of stages of change and physical activity among adults with physical disabilities. *Adapted Physical Activity Quarterly, 23*, 49–64.

Lach, H. W., Everard, K. M., Highstein, G., & Brownson, C. A. (2004). Application of the transtheoretical model to health education for older adults. *Health Promotion Practice, 5*(1), 88–93.

Leone, J. E., Gray, K. A., Rossi, J. M., & Colandreo, R. M. (2008). Using the transtheoretical model to explain androgenic-anabolic steroid use in adolescents, and young adults: Part one. *Strength and Conditioning Journal, 30*(6), 47–54.

Levit, T., Cismaru, M., & Zederayko, A. (2016). Application of the transtheoretical model and social marketing to antidepression campaign websites. *Social Marketing Quarterly, 22*(1), 54–77. doi:10.1177/1524500415620138.

Lipschitz, J. M., Fernandez, A. C., Larson, E., Blaney, C. L., Meier, K. S., Redding, C. A., ... Paiva, A. L. (2013). Validation of decisional balance and self-efficacy measures for HPV vaccination in college women. *American Journal of Health Promotion, 27*(5), 299–307. doi:10.4278/ajhp .110606-QUAN-240

Marcus, H., Ross, J., Selby, V., Niaura, R., & Abrams, D. (1992). The stages and processes of exercise adoption and maintenance in a worksite sample. *Health Psychology, 11*(6), 386–395.

Prat, F., Planes, M., Gras, M. E., & Sullman, M. J. M. (2011). Stages of change and decisional balance for condom use with a romantic partner. *Journal of Health Psychology, 17*(8), 1193–1202. doi:10.1177/1359105311433911

Prochaska, J. O. (1994). Strong and weak principles for progressing from precontemplation to action on the basis of twelve problem behaviors. *Health Psychology, 13*, 47–51.

Prochaska, J. O., & DiClemente, C. C. (1982). Transtheoretical therapy: Toward a more integrative model of change. *Psychotherapy: Theory, Research and Practice, 20*, 161–173.

Prochaska, J. O., & DiClemente, C. C. (1983). Stages and processes of self-change of smoking: Toward an integrative model of change. *Journal of Consulting and Clinical Psychology, 51*, 390–395.

Prochaska, J. O., DiClemente, C. C., & Norcross, J. C. (1992). In search of how people change: Applications to addictive behaviors. *American Psychologist, 47*(9), 1102–1114.

Prochaska, J. O., & Velicer, W. F. (1997). The transtheoretical model of health behavior change. *American Journal of Health Promotion, 12*(1), 38–48.

Prochaska, J. O., Velicer, W. F., DiClemente, C. C., & Fava, J. L. (1988). Measuring the processes of change: Applications to the cessation of smoking. *Journal of Consulting and Clinical Psychology, 56*, 520–528.

Reisenhofer, S., & Taft, A. (2013). Women's journey to safety—The transtheoretical model in clinical practice when working with women experiencing intimate partner violence: A scientific review and clinical guidance. *Patient Education and Counseling, 93*, 536–548. doi:10.1016 /jpec.2013.08.004

Siahpush, M., & Carlin, J. B. (2006). Financial stress, smoking cessation and relapse: Results from a prospective study of an Australian national sample. *Addiction, 101*(1), 121–127. doi:10.1111/j.1360-0443.2005.01292.x

Tung, W. C., Smith-Gagen, J., Lu, M., & Warfield, M. (2016). Application of the transtheoretical model to cervical cancer screening in Latina women. *Journal of Immigrant Minority Health, 18*, 1168–1174. doi:10.10IA07/s10903-015-0183-3

Velicer, W. F., Prochaska, J. O., Fava, J. L., Norman, G. J., & Redding, C. A. (1998). Smoking cessation and stress management: Applications of the transtheoretical model of behavior change. *Homeostasis, 38*, 216–233.

Wing, R. R., & Phelan, S. (2005). Long term weight loss maintenance. *American Journal of Clinical Nutrition, 82*(1), 222S–225S. Retrieved October 17, 2016, from www.AJCN.nutrition.org /content/82/1/222S.full.pdf+html

Yang, P. S., & Chen, C. H. (2005). Exercise and process of change in patients with chronic obstructive pulmonary disease. *Journal of Nursing Research, 13*(2), 97–104. doi:10.1097/01 .JNR.0000387531.30266.75

Yusufov, M., Rossi, J. S., Redding, C. A., Yin, H. Q., Paiva, A. L., Velicer, W. F., … Prochaska, J. O. (2016). Transtheoretical model constructs' longitudinal prediction of sun protection over 24 months. *International Journal of Behavioral Medicine, 23*, 71–83. doi:10.1007/s12529-015-9498-7

© ktsdesign/Shutterstock

CHAPTER 7
Protection Motivation Theory

PROTECTION MOTIVATION THEORY ESSENCE SENTENCE

Fear motivates people to change attitudes and behaviors.

Constructs

Threat appraisal: Assessing personal vulnerability to and seriousness of a threat

Coping appraisal: Assessing recommended action effectiveness, personal ability to carry out, and cost

▶ In the Beginning

Protection Motivation Theory (PMT) has its roots in health communication and the fear appeal. Fear, remember, is an emotional state that protects us from danger. When we're afraid of something, we tend to avoid it or do something to counter the possible feared outcome. Fear appeals are based on this. They change attitude, intention, or behaviors through the threat of impending harm (Rogers, 1975). They are

FIGURE 7.1 Fear leads to protective behaviors.
© Patrik Slezak/Shutterstock

intended to cause fear in order to motivate people to take protective action against the threat (Rogers & Deckner, 1975) (**FIGURE 7.1**).

Fear appeals expose people to two types of information. One type presents some threat as a way to raise fear about something the person may find serious and be vulnerable or susceptible to. The other information has to do with health-protective actions or recommendations the person can adopt to avert the threat. Fear appeals have worked to change attitudes and behaviors for a whole host of health issues, including, but not limited to, smoking, heart disease, cancer, injuries, food safety, environmental hazards, asthma, and diabetes (Floyd, Prentice-Dunn, & Rogers, 2000; Ruiter, Kessels, Peters, & Kok, 2014).

Although fear appeals changed behavior, it was generally accepted that factors other than the fear itself played a role in the behavior or attitude changes that occurred, and that these other factors influenced the level of fear aroused. However, little research had been done to identify the other factors that acted as stimulants for arousing fear or the associated thought processes used to assess the threat causing the fear (Rogers, 1975).

Rogers (1975) attempted to rectify this situation with the introduction of PMT in 1975, grounding it in a well-established category of theories that have expectancy and value constructs, with Social Cognitive Theory as one such example. Expectancy-value theories explain expectancy as the consequence of performing a behavior and value as the worth or importance the consequence has to the person. For example, using condoms (behavior) will decrease the risk of sexually transmitted infections (consequence), which is a desirable outcome (value).

What Rogers (1975) proposed in PMT was a limited set of factors, or "stimulus variables"; the thought processes people used that led to their adoption of the recommended behaviors proposed in the fear appeal. Initially, he identified three such variables. The first was appraisal of the threat severity or how awful or terrible the person believed the threat to be. The second was expectancy of exposure to the threat, or

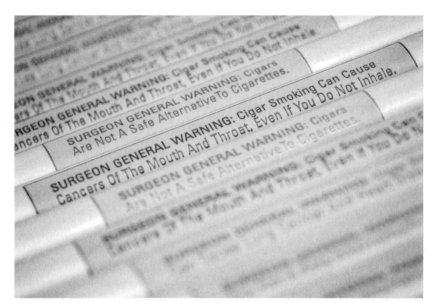

FIGURE 7.2 Threat—tobacco smoking causes cancer.
© Paul Velgos/Shutterstock

the probability or likelihood of the threatened outcome happening to the person. Lastly was response efficacy or how effective the person believed the recommended response was in eliminating or minimizing the feared outcome (Rogers, 1975).

Think about this in the context of tobacco smoking. The warning labels on cigarettes packs and cigar tubes are based on fear. Smoking causes cancer—that's the threat and it's pretty severe. If you smoke, you will get cancer—that's the probability of the threat happening. Quit smoking and your chances of cancer from smoking will be reduced or eliminated—that's the recommended response and it is very effective (**FIGURE 7.2**).

In a 1983 revision of the theory, a fourth process was added—self-efficacy expectancy. Self-efficacy expectancy is a person's belief in his or her own ability to perform a given behavior (Maddux & Rogers, 1983). In relation to fear appeals and PMT, the given behavior is the one recommended to thwart the feared outcome.

These four thought or cognitive processes are responsible for triggering the motivation to protect oneself from a threat (i.e., protection motivation). Protection motivation has the typical characteristics of any behavioral motivation; it arouses, sustains, and directs some activity. Based on this, Rogers proposed that the motivation to protect oneself—to adopt the recommendations in the appeal—does not come from fear itself, but rather from the cognitive processes use to appraise the feared outcome (Rogers, 1975).

▶ Theory Concept

The underlying concept or basis of PMT is that fear triggers a set of thought processes that motivate us to protect ourselves from the threat and feared outcome by adopting recommended health-protective actions. The concept involves any threat for which there is an effective recommended response the person can carry out (Floyd et al., 2000). The degree of our motivation to protect ourselves results from the extent to which we assess threat severity, probability of the threatened outcome occurring, effectiveness of the recommendations to avert or lessen the threat, and the ability to perform those recommendations (Maddux & Rogers, 1983).

▶ Theory Constructs

The constructs of the PMT are the cognitive processes that motivate us to adopt the health-protective recommendations (adaptive response). They are divided into two categories: threat appraisal and coping appraisal (Floyd et al., 2000).

Threat Appraisal

Threat appraisal consists of two processes: the perception of threat severity and threat probability or vulnerability. The more severe or serious we believe a threat is and the more we believe we are at risk of it happening to us, the greater the likelihood of us adopting an adaptive response or the behaviors recommended to reduce the feared outcome.

As an example, the National Institutes on Alcohol Abuse and Alcoholism (2006) used the threat appraisal constructs in a brochure aimed at reducing drinking during pregnancy. The brochure informs pregnant women that:

> "everything you eat and drink while you are pregnant affects your baby. If you drink alcohol, it can hurt your baby's growth. Your baby can have physical and behavioral problems that can last for the rest of his or her life."

This information conveys the severity of drinking while pregnant and suggests the probability of the negative consequence happening (Cismaru, Deshpande, Thurmeier, Lavack, & Agrey, 2010).

The next time you read the warning label on a package of acetaminophen, think about this theory. It is well documented that acetaminophen is in more than 600 different prescription and nonprescription medications (U.S. Department of Health and Human Services, 2016). Consequently, the warning on the label informs consumers that if more than the prescribed amount is taken (a total of 4000 mg in 24 hours from all sources (Johnson & Johnson, 2016)), the drug can cause severe liver damage. Armed with this information, consumers appraise the threat and make a determination as to its severity, that is, "Do I think liver damage is severe or serious?" Next, they determine the extent to which they think they are at risk of developing liver damage from taking this medication. As it turns out, people who think liver damage is a severe or serious outcome (threat) or who believe they are vulnerable to liver damage if they take too much, are more likely to follow recommended guidelines for safely taking acetaminophen (Sawant et al., 2016).

Perception of threat severity and personal vulnerability also influence vaccination decisions. During the 2009 H1N1 influenza pandemic, people who believed they were vulnerable to catching the flu and that it was severe and could have long-term effects were more likely to be vaccinated. On the flip side, people who perceived themselves to be at low risk or no risk of contracting swine flu—that is not vulnerable—or who believed it was a mild disease that too much fuss was being made about, were less likely to be vaccinated (Bish, Yardley, Nicoll, & Michie, 2011).

Unfortunately threat appraisal, specifically severity, does not always support adoption of the health-protective recommendations. This is particularly true in the case of skin protection behaviors aimed at reducing risk of cancer.

While it may seem logical to highlight the severity of skin cancer, especially malignant melanoma, in an attempt to increase skin protective behaviors, this does not work with adolescents. A possible explanation is that adolescents are generally less afraid of skin cancer and its consequences than are those in an older population. The difference may be due to personal experience with skin cancer either in themselves, a relative, or friend and consequently, a better understanding of the potential negative outcomes. What is more effective in increasing protective behaviors in adolescents is personal risk of skin cancer (Ch'ng & Glendon, 2014). The important point here is that relying on the severity of a threat to result in adoption of the recommended behavior does not always lead to the wanted outcomes. Sometimes, even when the threat is severe it's personal risk that makes the difference (**FIGURE 7.3**).

A good example of how severity and vulnerability influence behavior differently occurred in the process of trying to increase adherence to the North American Guidelines for Children's Agriculture Tasks (NAGCAT). NAGCAT was developed as a way to reduce childhood agricultural injuries. It provides guidelines to farm parents in assigning appropriate chores to children. In an effort to maximize parental acceptance of and adherence to the guidelines, it was important to understand what the parental motivators might be (Ashida, Heaney, Kmet, & Wilkins, 2011).

As it turned out, parents generally believed farm related accidents could be serious, so there was no need to focus on threat severity as a motivator. It wouldn't be useful. But, perceived risk or vulnerability was an issue. While parents acknowledged

FIGURE 7.3 Personal risk assessment influences adoption of health-protective response.
© Yeexin Richelle/Shutterstock

farm work could be dangerous for children, they did not necessarily connect the risk of injury with their own children. Since risk of an accident was something that *would* motivate the parents, it was used as the basis for an educational intervention aimed at increasing guideline compliance (Ashida et al., 2011).

Threat appraisal also includes evaluation of the rewards we get from engaging in a maladaptive response—a risky, dangerous, or harmful behavior. These rewards, both internal and external, inhibit adoption of the adaptive response or the health-protective recommendation. Rewards for maladaptive responses increase the likelihood of us continuing them rather than adopting the recommended adaptive alternative (Floyd et al., 2000; Maddux & Rogers, 1983).

Speeding is a good example of a maladaptive response (risky, dangerous behavior) where the reward—enjoyment—negatively impacts adoption of the adaptive response—driving within the speed limit (Glendon & Walker, 2013). Trying to encourage driving within the speed limit by using messages to counter the rewards of speeding sometimes backfires. For example, the message "Speed—the thrill that kills" could be interpreted as a challenge to those who like the feeling they get from speeding rather than it being effective at reducing speeding (Cathcart & Glendon, 2016). (Think about how effective this message proposed by the Iowa Department of Transportation might be: "Speeding is for the birds; slow the flock down." While this did not make it on to a street sign, this message did—"Get your head out of your apps. Drive safely." (Munson, 2015).)

Using skin protection is another example of when rewards for the maladaptive behavior—in this case tanning—offset the serious threat—skin cancer. Tanning has many rewards for adolescents and young adults including enjoyment, social acceptance (Ch'ng & Glendon, 2014), fashion, positive mood, physical and emotional health, attractiveness, and personal image, among others.

To move people from the maladaptive behavior of tanning to skin-protective ones, focusing on threat perception might be a worthwhile approach. Another approach might be to focus on changing attitudes toward the rewards in that "while it might feel good to look good, it will not do you good" (Calder & Aitken, 2008, p. 584).

In working with American Indian adolescents on an intervention to reduce risky sexual behavior, the intrinsic rewards of not using condoms included belonging, pride, curiosity, and, interestingly, pregnancy. The risk of having a child was not a deterrent to unprotected sex and was in fact viewed by females as a way to solidify a relationship; a way to always have the boy there for her (Chambers et al., 2016).

An extrinsic reward of not using condoms (or any other birth control method, for that matter) was the reduced risk of parents finding the birth control method. For males, another extrinsic reward of risky sexual behavior was gaining the reputation of having sex with multiple partners and bragging about it (Chambers et al., 2016).

Coping Appraisal

Coping appraisal is how the recommended action is assessed in terms of effectiveness, personal ability to carry out the action, and cost. It entails two cognitive processes: coping response efficacy (Rogers, 1975) and self-efficacy expectancy (Maddux & Rogers, 1983) or response self-efficacy, in addition to response costs (Floyd et al., 2000). Coping response efficacy is the belief that the recommended course of action will indeed prevent or reduce the threat or harm (Rogers, 1975). Self-efficacy expectancy or (response self-efficacy) is an individual's personal belief in his or her ability to perform the recommended action (Maddux & Rogers, 1983). Response costs include any cost or expenditure associated with adopting the recommendation whether it be monetary, personal time, personnel (Floyd et al., 2000), equipment, or space.

When people believe the coping response or recommended action is effective and they believe in their own ability to carry out it out, the probability of adoption increases. However, high response costs tend to decease the probability of adoption (Floyd et al., 2000). What does that tell you about the importance of designing interventions with minimal costs in all of its permutations to achieve success with the intervention?

Let's look at PMT in relation to reducing the incidence of foodborne illness. First, people do a threat appraisal—they determine if they believe food poisoning is serious and if they are susceptible to it. Next, they do a coping appraisal and determine if the adaptive response being proposed, in this case safe food handling, which includes reducing cross-contamination, cooking food properly, maintaining correct temperatures, and avoiding unsafe foods—works to protect them from illness (response efficacy) and if they are capable of doing it (response self-efficacy) (Mullan, Allom, Sainsbury, & Monds, 2016). As it turns out, in this example response self-efficacy is the most important factor in adopting safe food handling practices. Why do you think that may be so?

Another example where coping appraisal impacts either intention to adopt or actual adoption of the adaptive response is with farmers and drought. Drought is a disastrous consequence of climate change causing significant disruption in the natural environment's ability to produce food and water. One way to mitigate this situation is for farmers to adopt pro-environmental practices, which include rotational grazing, reducing herd size, reducing water usage for nonessential purposes, and fertilizer and pesticide management. If farmers believe that the pro-environmental changes can help them control the extent of drought impact on their farms and they believe they can institute them, then there is a greater chance of them adopting the protective measures. However, the response cost—time needed to implement these practices and the associated financial costs—are significant barriers (Keshavarz & Karami, 2016) (**FIGURE 7.4**).

Coping response efficacy and response self-efficacy also plays a role in parental use of safety gates in the house. Having a gate at the top and bottom of staircases is an effective action to prevent unintentional injuries among preschoolers. Parental belief in the effectiveness of a stair gate to prevent accidents (coping response efficacy) and in their ability to install and use the gate (response self-efficacy) are associated with or predictive of gate use. This information could be used to develop interventions to increasing gate use by focusing on their effectiveness in preventing injury. To increase parental self-efficacy, parents already using gates might share their experiences with parents who don't use them (Beirens et al., 2008).

Coping response efficacy and response self-efficacy for condom use may be important constructs in the decision to adopt safer sex behaviors, as is the case with American Indian adolescents. Their limited knowledge about effectiveness and how different birth control methods work coupled with low condom use self-efficacy (Chambers et al., 2016) hinders intention to use or adopt the adaptive response (safer sex).

Consequently, these PMT constructs provided the framework for the development of *Respecting the Circle of Life: Mind, Body and Soul,* an intervention aimed at providing information and skills to increase condoms use and decrease

FIGURE 7.4 Response cost can be a barrier to change.
© Sarawut Aiemsinuk/Shutterstock

unprotected sex among American Indian adolescents. Specifically, the internal and external rewards of unprotected sex (maladaptive coping response appraisal) were balanced against the risk of HIV. The ability to use a condom (response self-efficacy) and its effectiveness in preventing HIV (response efficacy) were balanced with the costs of using a condom. As a result, youth participating in the intervention had greater condom use intention, which is a predictor of actual use (Tingey et al., 2017) (**FIGURE 7.5**).

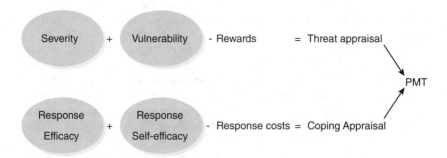

FIGURE 7.5 Protection motivation theory.
Modified from: Floyd, D.L., Prentice-Dunn, S. & Rogers, R. (2000). A meta-analysis of research on protection motivation theory. *Journal of Applied Social Psychology, 30*(2), 407–429.

THEORY IN ACTION—CLASS ACTIVITY

Take a moment and think about your own skin cancer prevention behavior relative to sun exposure.

1. Do you use sunscreen?
2. Do you wear a hat to protect your face from the sun and clothing to protect other areas of your body?
3. Do you avoid the sun between 10 A.M.–2 P.M. when the rays are the strongest?
4. Based on the Protection Motivation Construct of threat appraisal, explain why do or do not use skin protective behaviors? That is, how do the processes of threat appraisal, perception of severity, and vulnerability affect your behavior?
5. If you do *not* engage in skin protective behaviors, what are your intrinsic and extrinsic rewards for not doing so?
6. How do the processes of coping appraisal (response appraisal, self-efficacy, and cost) contribute to your behavior?
7. Based on what you learned about your own skin protection behaviors, do you need to change those behaviors; if so, what would get you to make the changes?

Now, read the following article and answer the questions posed at the end.

Chapter 7 Article: Determinants of Skin Cancer Preventive Behaviors Among Rural Farmers in Iran: an Application of Protection Motivation Theory[1]

Towhid Babazadeh[1]* & Haidar Nadrian[1] & Morteza Banayejeddi[2] & Baratali Rezapour[3]

[1]Department of Health Education and Promotion, Tabriz University of Medical Sciences, Tabriz, Iran
[2]Department of Disease Control and Prevention, Chalderan Health Care Center, Urmia University of Medical Sciences, Urmia, Iran
[3]Department of Public Health, Urmia University of Medical Sciences, Urmia, Iran

1 Reproduced from Babazadeh, T., Nardrian, H., Nanayejeddi, M., & Rezapour, B. (2016). Determinants of skin cancer prevention behaviors among rural farmers in Iran: An application of protection motivation theory. *Journal of Cancer Education*, online. doi: 10.1007/s13187-016-1004-7

* Corresponding author.

Abstract

Skin cancer is one of the most prevalent cancers, worldwide, which happens more among those with more sunlight exposure like farmers. The aim of this study was to explore the determinants of skin cancer preventive behaviors (SCPBs) among rural farmers using Protection Motivation Theory (PMT). In this cross-sectional study, multistage random sampling was employed to enroll 238 farmers referring to rural health houses (HH) in Chaldoran County, Iran. A valid and reliable instrument based on PMT variables was used. Significant correlations were found between all PMT variables with SCPBs ($p < 0.05$). Hierarchical multiple linear regressions were performed with Protection Motivation and SCPBs as outcome variables. Predictors for these two outcome variables were classified in two different blocks according to their natures. Demographic characteristics ($p > 0.05$) and PMT constructs ($p < 0.001$) explained 3 and 63.6% of the observed variance in Protection Motivation, respectively. Also, no significant effect was found on SCPBs by demographic variables, in the first block ($\Delta R^2 = 0.025$); however, in the second block, Perceived Susceptibility ($p = 0.000$), Rewards ($p = 0.022$), Self-efficacy ($p = 0.000$), and Response Cost ($p = 0.001$) were significant predictors of SCPBs ($\Delta R^2 = 0.432$). Healthcare providers may consider PMT as a framework for developing educational interventions aiming at improving SCPBs among rural farmers.

Keywords: Skin cancer prevention, Protection Motivation Theory, Rural farmers

▶ Introduction

Cancers have the highest mortality rate after cardiovascular diseases throughout the world and are the third leading cause of death.[1, 2] Skin cancer is an increasing problem for public health, worldwide.[3] Based on the statistics reported by World Health Organization (WHO), between 2 to 3 million non-melanoma skin cancers and 132,000 melanoma skin cancers occur, annually, throughout the world.[4] In the Middle East, skin cancer is the most common cancer.[5] In terms of prevalence, it is the most prevalent kind of cancer among men.[1] According to Iran Cancer Registry Reports in 2008, skin cancer had been the most common cancer among men with 14.8 cases per 100,000 people.[6]

The main reason for skin cancer is constant exposure with sunlight.[7] In addition, some other risk factors include family history, having a weak immune system,[8] and exposure to ultraviolet radiation.[9] Ultraviolet radiation is the main cause of basal cell carcinoma[10] which is more prevalent among people with excess exposure to sunlight.[11] The effects of UV ray on the skin are divided into two categories: short term and long term. The short-term effects include tanning, sunburn, heatstroke, and redness, and the long-term effects include rapid skin aging, melanoma, and basal cell carcinoma.[12]

A systematic review on worldwide incidence of skin cancer urged the need for prevention studies in this area.[3] With simple changes in everyday sun-protective behaviors such as wearing thick clothing when encountering to sunlight, applying a sunscreen with an appropriate SPF, and avoiding artificial sources of ultraviolet ray, the detrimental effects of UV ray may be prevented.[13] As preventing constant sunlight exposure is considered as a priority in skin cancer prevention, promoting sunlight protective behaviors among those with high exposure (like rural areas inhabitants) should be one of the focuses for skin cancer prevention interventions.

Despite the efforts to provide more health care services for rural areas and, thus, to decrease inequalities between rural and urban areas, rural inhabitants are dealt with more diverse health care problems and challenges.[14-16] From the most important and fundamental problems in rural areas are lack of cognitive abilities (e.g., health knowledge, attitude, and self-efficacy) and healthy behaviors,[17] as well. Therefore, investigation on health-related behaviors and their determinants in such communities has a great importance, considering that such studies may provide evidence to design more sophisticated health educational interventions in efforts to address unhealthy behaviors.

Because of the nature of rural living, sunlight exposure is more prevalent among men farmers in rural areas, and thus they are at greater risk for developing skin cancer in proportion to the other people. The issue is getting worse when it is estimated that residency in a rural area put people in a disadvantaged situation in terms of skin cancer survival.[18] Ahmadi et al.,[18] in a study conducted in Kurdistan Province, Iran, found that 44% of skin cancer patients living in the urban areas had been diagnosed in stage 1 or 2, while this amount for rural residents was 27%, showing that the patients in rural areas tended to be diagnosed at a later stage of the disease. This disparity highlights the importance of skin cancer prevention as one of the best strategies in rural areas. Therefore, educational intervention as a strategy to promote sun-protective behaviors aiming at rural farmers sounds to be critical.

Theory-based interventions are more effective in influencing health-related behaviors compared to non-theoretical approaches, as they provide a reasonable framework to develop interventions and a guide for their evaluation.[19] To do so, health researchers have used lots of theories in order to create positive changes in health-related behaviors. Protection Motivation Theory (PMT) is one of those theories used frequently as a framework for educational interventions. This theory was introduced by Rajers in 1975 and since then has been accepted, extensively, as a framework to predict health-related behaviors and design health educational interventions.[20, 21] PMT is one of social cognitive theories that are helpful in assessing the cognitive mediation process of behavioral changes in terms of threat and coping appraisal.[22]

In PMT model (**FIGURE A.1**), threat appraisal component includes (1) perceived severity (a person's estimation of the severity of a disease), (2) perceived

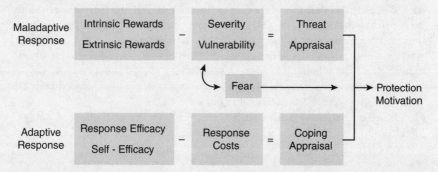

FIG. A.1 Cognitive mediating processes of Protection Motivation Theory (Rogers and Prentice-Dunn, 1997).[23]

Reproduced from Babazadeh, T., Nardrian, H., Nanayejeddi, M., & Rezapour, B. (2016). Determinants of skin cancer prevention behaviors among rural farmers in Iran: An application of protection motivation theory. *Journal of Cancer Education*, online. doi: 10.1007/s13187-016-1004-7

vulnerability (a person's estimation of the probability of constructing a disease), and (3) intrinsic and extrinsic rewards (get rewards from the implementation of a behavior). Also, coping appraisal includes (1) the response efficacy (an individual's expectancy that implementing the recommendations can remove a threat), (2) self-efficacy (belief in one's ability to carry out a recommended plan of action successfully), and (3) the response cost (beliefs about how costly performing the recommended response will be to the individual).[20, 24] Previous studies have shown that PMT may be useful in predicting health-related intentions and behaviors like breast cancer screening, dietary behaviors, and smoking cessation.[21, 24] McClendon et al. conducted a study to reduce skin cancer risk factors applying PMT and concluded that PMT may be useful as a guide on how to use specific techniques in changing inconsistent attitudes toward SCPBs and, also, reforming behavioral risk factors for skin cancer.[25]

This study was conducted to examine the determinants of Skin Cancer Preventive Behaviors (SCPBs) among rural area farmers utilizing PMT model. Identifying skin cancer influential factors in such studies may be helpful in designing interventional efforts aiming at skin cancer prevention. The questions that guided the study were as follows:

1. What is the pattern of performing skin cancer preventive behaviors among farmers in a rural area?
2. To what extent do the threat and coping appraisals and protection motivation predict SCPBs among rural area farmers?
3. May PMT model be applied as a framework for designing interventional programs aiming at skin cancer prevention among rural area farmers?

▶ Methods

Participants

The present cross-sectional study was conducted in Chaldoran, a mountainous county in West Azerbaijan, the northwestern part of Iran. The majority of rural men residents in this county are farmers working in their own farms from sunrise to sunset, and thus their exposure to the sunlight is high. This 3-month study took place from August to July 2015. Multistage random sampling was employed to recruit 248 rural farmers in the study. Almost all rural farmers in this area are men, and the number of women farmers is scarce. Most of women are doing livestock and household works at home. Therefore, it was decided to focus on men as farmers in the present study. Ten farmers refused to participate in the study, and finally 238 questionnaires were collected (response rate = 95.9%).

Based on National Health Care System (NHCS) in Iran, Chaldoran County is divided into four rural areas which are covered by independent rural health care centers (RHCCs). Every RHCC, in turn, covers some health houses (HHs) in proportion to its population. HH is the first level of contact with rural population in the NHCS, which delivers primary health care services (such as health education, maternal and child health, health nutrition education, and so on) to these populations. These centers cover one (as the main village within which HH is situated) and/or some other villages (as satellite villages) depending on the population of the villages, geographical situations, and the communication facilities and channels, as well. In this study, two HHs were randomly selected from every four HCCs (eight HHs). As the health information of all rural areas' inhabitants is recorded in the HHs, the respondents were randomly selected based on their health records existed in the HHs in order to be invited to participate in the study.

The literate respondents completed the self-administered PMT-based questionnaire. As official educational language in Iran is Persian, all literate people were dominant to the Persian self-administered questionnaire. Also, interview method was used to collect data from the illiterates. All the interviews with illiterates/those with elementary education were conducted by the first author. The local languages in this area are Kurdish and Azeri. As the first author was dominant to these languages as well as Persian, there was no problem in documenting the answers in Kurdish/Azeri languages into the Persian questionnaire.

Inclusion criteria for this study included male gender, working as a farmer in spring and summer, and with no history of skin cancer in the family. Exclusion criterion was as follows: refusal for participation in study. Before providing the participants with the questionnaire, the purpose of the study was explained and all those accepted the participation signed consent form. Those who refused to participate were excluded from the study.

▶ Measures

In order to collect data, a valid and reliable instrument[7] was used. In 2013, Tazval et al.[9] developed this questionnaire aiming to assess PMT constructs among rural farmers in Ilam—another Iranian province. As this instrument was developed, in Persian, to be used among farmers in rural settings, no prior specific change was needed. An expert panel (including three health educationist, one psychologist, and one community health nurse with specific experience in skin cancer prevention) confirmed its validity. In order to assess the reliability, a pilot study conducted on 35 rural farmers who did not included in the final sample. The Cronbach α of the scales found in the pilot and main studies are presented in Table A.2. A brief description of the questionnaire is as follows: Demographic Data Form included four questions and was developed by researchers to obtain data related to the participants' age, education, economic status, and family size (the number of household members living together). In order to assess economic status, in a single item, the respondents were asked to rate their own economic status as good, fair, or weak.

PMT Questionnaire included seven constructs: Perceived Susceptibility, Perceived Severity Towards Skin Cancer, and Internal and External Rewards from Performing SCPBs, as well as Self-efficacy, Response Efficacy and Response Cost. Perceived Susceptibility, Perceived Severity, and Rewards from Performing SCPBs comprised 5, 8, and 12 items, respectively. Also, Self-efficacy, Response Efficacy, and Response Cost comprised 5, 7, and 13 items, respectively. For all six constructs, the items were rated on a five-point Likert-type scale ranged from 1 to 5 (1 = totally disagree through 5 = totally agree). The higher the scores, the more susceptibility and severity toward skin cancer, and the more the rewards from performing SCPBs were concluded. Also, the higher the scores, the more self-efficacy, response efficacy, and response cost toward conducting SCPBs were concluded.

Protection Motivation comprised four items rated on a five-point Likert-type scale ranged from 1 to 5 (1 = totally disagree through 5 = totally agree). The higher the score, the higher motivation for performing SCPBs was concluded.

Finally, SCPBs included four items in a five-point Likert scale ranging from "never" (1) to "always" (5). The items consisted activities to avoid the sunlight including wearing long sleeve shirt and wide-brimmed hat, applying sunscreen, and avoiding the sun at middays.

▶ Statistics

Data were coded numerically and entered into Statistical Package for Social Sciences (SPSS) software, version 20.0 for Windows. Summary statistics and frequency distributions were used to describe and interpret the meaning of data. An additional calculation was performed on the mean score of the variables. As the minimum possible score for no variable was 0, presenting their mean and standard deviations alone does not seem to provide a clear understanding about their level among the respondents. Therefore, mean percent was calculated applying this formula: ((mean score-minimum score) ÷ (maximum score-minimum score)) × 100. The differences between PMT constructs by demographic variables were analyzed using one-way ANOVA. Pearson correlation coefficient was applied to indicate the associations between PMT structures and SCPBs. Moreover, multiple linear regression analysis with Enter method was applied to illustrate the variations in SCPBs and Protection Motivation scores on the basis of PMT constructs. A p value less than 0.05 was considered significant at the priori.

▶ Findings

A total of 238 individuals agreed to participate in the study. The demographic characteristics of the participants as well as their associations with SCPBs and Protection Motivation are displayed in **TABLE A.1**. The mean age of participants was 35.5 ± 8.79, and the majority was in the range of 30–39 years old. The minimum, maximum, and the median of the respondents' age were 20, 59, and 35.5, respectively. No significant difference was found in SCPBs and Protection Motivation by demographic characteristics (Table A.1). The only exception was for Protection Motivation, which had a statistically significant difference among the respondents by income status.

Mean, standard deviation, mean percent, number of items along with possible range, and Cronbach α in the pilot and main study for every PMT variable and SCPBs are presented in **TABLE A.2**. The Cronbach α for all PMT constructs in the main study was 0.7 and more showing an acceptable to excellent internal consistency for the constructs. The level of scores for almost all variables was less than 36%, which means that the respondents acquired less than 36% out of the maximum possible score in almost all variables. The lowest scores were found to be for Perceived Susceptibility (15.45%), Response Cost (19.57%), Protection Motivation (21.56%), and SCPBs (21.68%).

The least and the most frequent behaviors reported by the study participants were "avoiding the sun at middays" and "applying sunscreen," respectively. The differences between SCPB items by demographic variables were assessed. Although data are not

TABLE A.1 Demographic characteristics and their associations with outcome variables among the participants

Variable		N (%)	SCPBs		PM	
			Mean (SD)	p value[a]	Mean (SD)	p value[b]
Age	20–29	65(27.3)	7.30(1.99)	0.849	7.70(2.46)	0.700
	30–39	95(39.9)	7.52(1.73)		7.37(1.84)	
	40–49	65(27.3)	7.53(1.75)		7.30(1.95)	
	≤ 50	13(5.5)	7.61(1.38)		7.53(2.58)	
Level of education	Illiterate/primary level (1–5 years)	77(32.4)	7.45(1.45)	0.992	7.37(1.94)	0.797
	Middle level (6–9 years)	90(37.8)	7.48(1.84)		7.55(2.09)	
	Secondary level (10–12 years) and diploma	71(29.8)	7.47(2.05)		7.46(2.21)	
Income status	Good					
	Fair	110(46.2)	7.6(1.81)			7.21(1.76)
	Weak	35(14.7)	7.40(2.04)			7.05(1.78)
Family size	Less than 3	196(82.4)	7.30(1.99)	0.980		7.50(2.09)
	4 through 5	22(9.2)	7.50(2.09)			7.22(2.06)
	More than 6	20(8.4)	7.22(2.06)		7.30(1.97)	

SCPBs Skin cancer preventive behaviors, *PM* protection motivation
[a] Significance level for PM by demographic variables
[b] Significance level for SCPBs by demographic variables

Reproduced from Babazadeh, T., Nardrian, H., Nanayejeddi, M., & Rezapour, B. (2016). Determinants of skin cancer prevention behaviors among rural farmers in Iran: An application of protection motivation theory. *Journal of Cancer Education*, online. doi: 10.1007/s13187-016-1004-7

TABLE A.2 Descriptive statistics for PMT variables and SCPBs

PMT constructs	Mean (SD)	Mean percent	Number of items	Possible range	Cronbach α in the pilot study	Cronbach α in the main study
Perceived susceptibility	8.09 (2.23)	15.45	5	5–25	0.91	0.93
Perceived severity	19.75 (2.56)	36.71	8	8–40	0.61	0.72
Rewards	27.47 (3.70)	32.22	12	12–60	0.81	0.82
Response efficacy	15.13 (1.84)	29.03	7	7–35	0.93	0.92
Response cost	23.18 (3.23)	19.57	13	13–65	0.93	0.89
Self-efficacy	9.63 (0.95)	23.15	5	5–25	0.76	0.72
Protection motivation	7.45 (2.07)	21.45	4	4–20	0.70	0.70
Skin Cancer Preventive Behaviors	7.47 (1.78)	21.68	4	4–20	0.81	0.81

Reproduced from Babazadeh, T., Nardrian, H., Nanayejeddi, M., & Rezapour, B. (2016). Determinants of skin cancer prevention behaviors among rural farmers in Iran: An application of protection motivation theory. *Journal of Cancer Education*, online. doi: 10.1007/s13187-016-1004-7

presented, the most significant differences were found in "applying sunscreen" and "wearing wide-brimmed hat" by respondents' income status ($p = 0.026$) and education level ($p = 0.038$), respectively. More concisely, farmers with a good self-reported income status applied sunscreen more than the other two groups. Also, illiterates /those with elementary level of education used hat less than the other two groups.

As the least commonly Perceived Susceptibility and Severity items, 88.2 and 94.1% of the respondents disagreed/totally disagreed to "I am susceptible to skin cancer because of my job" and "Skin cancer makes the patient's face ugly and scary," respectively. Also, as the most commonly negative Perceived Reward item, 88.7% agreed /totally agreed to "I can do my daily farming practices, more effectively, when I do not use any cover on my head." Moreover, as the least commonly Perceived Response

Efficacy and the most commonly Perceived Cost Efficacy items, 67.6 and 31.5% of the respondents agreed/totally agreed to "Using sunscreen has no effect on skin cancer prevention" and "If I use sunscreen, my relatives around will mock me," respectively. Also, as the most commonly negative Perceived Self-efficacy item, only 30.7% agreed /totally agreed to "I believe that I can use sun protective cloths without any problem."

TABLE A.3 presents bivariate correlations for PMT constructs and SCPBs. Applying Pearson correlation coefficient test, it was found that SCPBs had statistically significant positive correlations with all PMT constructs except for Response Cost that was negatively associated with SCPBs ($r = -0.240$).

According to PMT, Perceived Susceptibility, Rewards, Response Cost, and Self-efficacy may influence on SCPBs. Also, Perceived Susceptibility and Response Cost may influence on Protection Motivation. Considering that there were two outcome variables (SCPBs and Protection Motivation) in this study, separate hierarchical multiple linear regressions were performed in two blocks to assess the efficiency of PMT constructs over the influence of other parameters. Predictors for the two outcome variables were classified in two different blocks according to their natures:

TABLE A.3 Bivariate correlations of PMT variables and skin cancer preventive behaviors (SCPBs)

Constructs	1	2	3	4	5	6	7	8
1 = Perceived susceptibility	1							
2 = Perceived severity	0.512*	1						
3 = Rewards	−0.418*	0.004	1					
4 = Response efficacy	0.327*	0.219*	0.448*	1				
5 = Response cost	−0.030	−0.107	−0.363*	−0.313*	1			
6 = Self-efficacy	−0.030	0.130*	−0.022	0.210*	−0.001	1		
7 = Protection motivation	0.782*	0.406*	0.331*	0.210*	−0.085	0.017	1	
8 = SCPBs	0.534*	0.294*	0.460*	0.354*	−0.240*	0.210*	0.445*	1

*Correlation is significant at the 0.05 level (two-tailed)

Reproduced from Babazadeh, T., Nardrian, H., Nanayejeddi, M., & Rezapour, B. (2016). Determinants of skin cancer prevention behaviors among rural farmers in Iran: An application of protection motivation theory. *Journal of Cancer Education*, online. doi: 10.1007/s13187-016-1004-7

1. Demographic characteristics block: age, level of education, income status, and family size.
2. PMT block: This block comprised the seven different constructs of PMT.

For both analyses (**TABLE A.4**), the variables classified in block 1 were the same, but for the analysis in which was Protection Motivation considered as outcome variable, the Protection Motivation construct was excluded from the list of predictors (Table A.4).

Hierarchical multiple linear regressions were performed with Protection Motivation and SCPBs (Table A.4) as outcome variables. As shown in Table A.4, demographic characteristics of the respondents explained only 3% of the observed variance in Protection Motivation which was not statistically significant at 0.05 level. However, PMT constructs were responsible for 63.6% change in observed variance which was statistically significant ($p < 0.001$). The other hierarchical multiple linear regressions were performed with SCPBs (Table A.4), and no significant effect was found on SCPBs by demographic variables, in the first block ($\Delta R^2 = 0.025$); however, in the second block, Perceived Susceptibility ($p = 0.000$), Rewards ($p = 0.022$), Self-efficacy ($p = 0.000$), and Response Cost ($p = 0.001$) were significant predictors of SCPBs ($\Delta R^2 = 0.432$). Perceived Susceptibility, Rewards, and Self-efficacy were, in order, the strongest and the most positive predictors, and Response Cost was a significant negative predictor of SCPBs.

TABLE A.4 Hierarchical regression analysis to predict Protection Motivation and SCPBs

Step/variable	B (Step 1)	B (Step 2)
Outcome variable: protection motivation		
(1) Age	−0.056	−0.009
Level of education	0.005	0.036
Income status	0.160	0.072
Family size	−0.041	0.002
(2) Perceived susceptibility		0.728
Perceived severity	0.041	
Rewards	0.105	
Response efficacy	−0.059	

Self-efficacy	0.054	
Response cost	−0.162	
ΔR2	0.030	0.636
Cumulative ΔR2	0.030	0.666
p value	0.121	0.001
Outcome variable: SCPBs		
(1) Age	0.055	0.076
Level of education	0.061	−0.022
Income status	0.131	0.024
Family size	0.002	0.032
(2) Perceived susceptibility		0.347
Perceived severity	0.040	
Rewards	0.225	
Response efficacy	0.021	
Self-efficacy	0.212	
Response cost	−0.146	
Protection motivation	0.090	
ΔR2	0.025	0.432
Cumulative ΔR2	0.025	0.457
p value	0.205	0.001

▶ Discussion

This research was conducted aiming at examining the determinants of SCPBs among rural area farmers using PMT in Chaldoran County, Iran. Having a good knowledge on SCPBs and identifying their influential factors may be helpful in addressing those factors through educational interventions.

The results of the present study showed that the mean scores for all PMT constructs and SCPBs were significantly low. The level of SCPBs was about 22% which means that less than one fourth of the rural farmers apply SCPBs in their daily farming practices. This finding is quite similar with those found by Carley et al.[26] who reported that only about 23% of outdoor workers used SCPBs. Gould et al.,[27] also, found that performing sunlight protective behaviors among adolescents was low. In another study, Morowatisharifabad et al.[28] reported that sunlight protective behaviors were higher than moderate among Kazerooni farmers in Iran, which is somewhat inconsistent with those found in the present study. A reason for this dissimilarity may be the different residency of the respondents included in the two studies, as they studied both urban and rural farmers, but we studied rural farmers, only. Another reason may be the difference in the place of studies; the first was conducted in Kazeroon, a semi-desert city, and the latter in Chaldoran, a mountainous county. So, there is a possibility that the rural farmers in this study consider themselves less susceptible to skin cancer.

Our findings showed that "avoiding the sun at middays" and "applying sunscreen" had the lowest scores among preventive behaviors. Further analysis showed significant difference in "applying sunscreen" by respondents' income status, in a way that farmers with a better income status applied sunscreen more. On the other hand, a significant difference was found in Protection Motivation by farmers' income status. It can be concluded that having a better economic situation may lead to less perceived barrier among farmers to perform economy-related preventive behaviors and therefore may be an influential factor in motivating rural farmers to conduct such protective behaviors while exposing sunlight as a health hazard.

Similar with those found in the present study, Zare Sakhvidi et al.[29] found no difference in cancer preventive behaviors by education level of industrial workers. They noted the availability of health care services and their good quality as well as the high level of education level among the workers as possible reasons for this indifference. But, none of above-mentioned reasons does apply in the present study. Unlike with their reasoning, a possible reason for this finding may be the very low level of education among these rural farmers, considering that about three fourths of them had a guidance education level and lower. Further analysis in our study showed that rural farmers with a lower level of education were less likely to use hat while on their daily farming practices. Therefore, conducting educational interventions aiming at health literacy promotion among these rural farmers is recommended.

The findings of the current study revealed significant associations between all PMT constructs with SCPBs. The strongest association was found between Perceived Susceptibility ($r = 0.534$) and Rewards ($r = 0.460$) with SCPBs, suggesting that if a farmer considers himself more vulnerable toward skin cancer and if he receives more rewards for performing SCPBs, then he may perform more SCPBs.

Increasing the knowledge of rural farmers regarding susceptibility toward skin cancer and its influential consequences on family and individual health may lead to increase in their perceived threat toward the disease and thus improve in their performance in SCPBs.

Statistically significant positive associations were found between intrinsic and extrinsic rewards ($r = 0.460$) and protection motivation ($r = 0.445$) with SCPBs. This finding suggests that when a farmer receives more rewards from performing SCPBs, he will be more motivated to comply more with SCPBs. Tazval et al.[7] found that farmers participated in their study believed that wearing hat while working decreases their concentration. These findings suggest that the farmers do not consider themselves susceptible to skin cancer and solar radiation complications. Thus, it is recommended to consider perceived susceptibility as a priority while designing educational intervention aiming at this population.

Similar with those found in previous studies,[29-31] statistically significant positive correlations were found between Self-efficacy and Response Efficacy with SCPBs. In agreement with Zare Sakhvidi et al.,[29] workers with a higher self-efficacy believe that they have the ability to overcome a given problem and, therefore, they tend to perform healthy behavior while exposed in hazardous situations. Several studies have shown that promoting self-efficacy may improve preventive behaviors among different populations.[32-35] Considering self-efficacy promotion as a main strategy while designing skin cancer educational programs may promote SCPBs among rural farmers.

The findings of the present study showed a significant negative correlation between response costs and sun-protective behaviors. In other words, if a farmer perceives that responding costs to a sun-protective behavior is higher, he may less likely perform that behavior. Further analysis showed that the most commonly perceived cost efficacy noted by the farmers was "If I use sunscreen, my relatives around will mock me." In another study, Buller et al.[36] found that the most commonly perceived cost noted by construction outdoor workers was "warm clothing and perspiration." In order to alleviate such complains among workers, several measures may be conducted. Basically, a social health campaign aiming at skin cancer prevention in rural areas is recommended. Moreover, as an example, it should be recommended to the farmers, construction workers, and work employers to provide their workers with cool uniforms made from specific material like cotton-made uniforms. As another recommendation, health care centers along with agricultural organizations may sign contract with sun-protective manufacturers to provide such sun-protective equipment for farmers with some discount or may design subsidy plan to provide farmers with those equipment.

Based on our results, no significant effect was found on SCPBs by demographic variables, in the first block; however, in the second block, PMT constructs explained 43.2% of the variance for SCPBs. In the study conducted by Morowatisharifabad et al., among drivers, PMT explained 36.5% of the variance for risky driving behaviors.[37] Moreover, Baghianimoghaddam et al. reported that the strength of PMT on SCPBs among students was 54%, and perceived susceptibility and self-efficacy were the most powerful predictors for SCPBs and Protection Motivation, respectively.[31] In line with these findings, Gebrehiwot and Veen[38] emphasized on the importance of PMT structures in predicting behavioral intention and motivation of farmers toward farm-level risk reduction measures.

Considering the applicability of PMT in predicting SCPBs in this study, it can be concluded that PMT may be considered as an alternate methodological choice while designing educational interventions aiming at SCPBs promotion among rural farmers.

▶ Limitation

As data collection method in the present study was based on self-report by farmers, recall bias is warranted. Also, measurement of economic status by asking respondents to rate their economic status into good, fair, or weak may be somewhat subjective. What is considered as "good" to some people may not be similar to other people. Another limitation may be the gender-specific nature design of the study which was explained in the "Methods" section. Thus, it is recommended for future studies to include female farmers in the study as well.

▶ Conclusion

It was concluded that PMT was a useful model in predicting cognitive determinants of SCPBs among rural farmers. The mean score for all PMT constructs and SCPBs among rural farmers in Chaldoran County were low. Therefore, conducting educational intervention efforts aiming at SCPB promotion and, consequently, skin cancer prevention among farmers are recommended. Health care providers and community health nurses in rural areas should pay much more attention toward skin cancer prevention among farmers and plan to design specific health educational program for this population applying promising health education theories like PMT. Perceived susceptibility should be paid great attention while designing such interventions. Skin-cancer-related health literacy in rural areas is another priority for future research in this area.

▶ References

1. Siegel R, Naishadham D, Jemal A (2012) Cancer statistics, 2012. *CA Cancer J Clin* 62(1):10–29.
2. Ministry of Health and Medical Education (2004) National report; Registered Cancer cases. Tehran, Diseases Management Center, Non Infectious Section, Cancer Office [Persian].
3. Lomas A, Leonardi-Bee J, Bath-Hextall F (2012) A systematic review of worldwide incidence of nonmelanoma skin cancer. *Br J Dermatol* 166.5:1069–1080.
4. WHO (2015) Skin Cancers. How common is skin cancer? Available at: www.WHO.int/uv/faq/skincancer/en. Accessed 12 Oct 2015.
5. Mahmoodabad SS, Noorbala MT, Mohammadi M, Rahaei Z, Ehrampush MH (2011) Knowledge, attitude, and performance of students toward skin cancer in Yazd, 2009. *Int J Dermatol* 50(10): 1262–1265.
6. Ministry of Health and Medical Education (2008) *National Cancer Registry Report*. Tehran, Deputy for Health Directory, CDC Cancer Office [Persian].
7. Tazval J, Ghaffari M, Robati R (2013) Threat appraisal for skin cancer among rural farmers in Ilam, Iran. *Iran J Dermatol* 16(4): 121–127.

8. Armstrong BK (2004) How sun exposure causes skin cancer: an epidemiological perspective. In *Prevention of skin cancer* (pp. 89–116). Springer, Netherlands.

9. WHO (2012) Skin cancers. Available from: http://www.who.int/uv/faq/skincancer/en/index1.html. Accessed 10 Mar 2012.

10. Reis LAG, Eisner MP, Kosary CL, Hankey B F, Miller BA, Clegg L, Mariotto EJF, Edwards BK (2005) *SEER cancer statistics review, 1975–2002.* National Cancer Institute, Bethesda, MD, 6.

11. Glanz K, Buller DB, Saraiya M (2007) Reducing ultraviolet radiation exposure among outdoor workers: state of the evidence and recommendations. *Environ Health* 6(22):1–11.

12. Halevy DH. the Sun and the Skin. In: Shai A, Maibach HI, Baran R (2001) *Handbook of cosmetic skin care.* London: Martin Dunitz.

13. Rigel DS, Carucci JA (2000) Malignant melanoma: prevention early detection and treatment in the 21 century. *CA Cancer J Clin* 50(4):215–236.

14. Weinhold I, Gurtner S (2014) Understanding shortages of sufficient health care in rural areas. *Health Policy* 118(2):201–214.

15. Gamm L, Linnae H, Bellamy G, Dabney BJ (2002) Rural Healthy People 2010: identifying rural health priorities and models for practice. *J Rural Health* 18(1):9–14.

16. Kronfol NM (2012) Access and barriers to health care delivery in Arab countries: a review. *East Mediterr Health J* 18(12):1239.

17. Yuan F, Qian D, Huang C, Tian M, Xiang Y, He Z, Feng Z (2015) Analysis of awareness of health knowledge among rural residents in Western China. *BMC Public Health* 15(1):1.

18. Ahmadi G, Asadi-Lari M, Amani S, Solaymani-Dodaran M (2015) Survival from skin cancer and its associated factors in Kurdistan province of Iran. *Med J Islam Repub Iran* 29:277.

19. Michie S, Abraham C (2004) Interventions to change health behaviors: evidence-based or evidence-inspired? *Psychol Health* 19(1): 29–49.

20. Norman P, Boer H, Seydel ER (2005) Protection motivation theory. In: Conner M, Norman P, (Eds.), *Predicting Health Behaviour: Research and Practice with Social Cognition Models.* Open University Press, Maidenhead, pp 81–126.

21. Milne S, Sheeran P, Orbell S (2000) Prediction and intervention in health-related behavior: a meta-analytic review of protection motivation theory. *J Appl Soc Psychol* 30(1):106–143.

22. Plotnikoff RC, Trinh L, Courneya KS, Karunamuni N, Sigal RJ (2009) Predictors of aerobic physical activity and resistance training among Canadian adults with type 2 diabetes: an application of the Protection Motivation Theory. *Psychol Sport Exerc* 10(3):320–328.

23. Gochman DS (2013) Handbook of health behavior research II: provider determinants. Springer Science & Business Media.

24. Floyd DL, Prentice-Dunn S, Rogers RW (2000) A meta-analysis of research on protection motivation theory. *J Appl Soc Psychol* 30(2): 407–429.

25. McClendon BT, Prentice-Dunn S (2001) Reducing skin cancer risk: an intervention based on protection motivation theory. *J Health Psychol* 6(3): 321–328.

26. Carley A, Stratman E (2015) Skin cancer beliefs, knowledge, and prevention practices: a comparison of farmers and nonfarmers in a Midwestern Population. *J Agromedicine* 20(2):85–94.

27. Gould M, Farrar R, Berry JL, Mughal MZ, Bundy C, Vail A et al (2015) Sunlight exposure and photoprotection behaviour of white Caucasian adolescents in the UK. *J Eur Acad Dermatol Venereol* 29(4):732–737.

28. Morowatisharifabad M, Bonyadi F, EbrahimzadehArdakani M, Falahzadeh H, Malekzadeh E (2015) Study of sun protective behaviors for skin cancer prevention and its barriers among Kazeroon Farmers. *TB* 13(5):68–82.

29. Zare Sakhvidi MJ, Zare M, Mostaghaci M, Mehrparvar AH, Morowatisharifabad MA, Naghshineh E (2015) Psychosocial predictors for cancer prevention behaviors in workplace using protection motivation theory. *Adv Prev Med* 2015:467498. doi:10. 1155/2015/467498.

30. Mohammadi S, Baghiani Moghadam MH, Noorbala MT, Mazloomi SS, Fallahzadeh H, Daya A (2010) Survey about the role of appearance concern with skin cancer prevention behavior based on protection motivation theory. *Dermatol Cosmet* 1(2):70–77.

31. Baghianimoghaddam MH, Mohammadi S, Norbala MT, Mazloomi SS (2010) The study of factors relevant to skin cancer preventive behavior in female high school students in Yazd based on protection motivation theory. *Knowl Health* 5(1):10–15.

32. Vakili M, Rahaei Z, Nadrian H, YarMohammadi P (2011) Determinants of oral health behaviors among high school students in Shahrekord, Iran based on Health Promotion Model. *Am Dent Hygienists Assoc* 85(1):39–48.

33. Sarkar U, Fisher L, Schillinger D (2006) Is self-efficacy associated with diabetes self-management across race/ethnicity and health literacy? *Diabetes Care* 29(4):823–829.

34. Grembowski D, Patrick D, Diehr P, Durham M, Beresford S, Kay E, Hecht J (1993) Self-efficacy and health behavior among older adults. *J Health Soc Behav* 89–104.

35. Rahaei Z, Ghofranipour F, Morowatisharifabad MA, Mohammadi E (2015) Determinants of cancer early detection behaviors: application of protection motivation theory. *Health Promot Perspect* 5(2):138.

36. Buller DB, Andersen P, Walkosz BJ, Scott MD, Cutter GR, Dignan MB, Zarlengo EM, Voeks JH, Giese AJ (2005) Randomized trial testing a worksite sun protection program in an outdoor recreation industry. *Health Educ Behav* 32:514–535.

37. Morowatisharifabad M A, Momeni SM, Barkhordari FA, Fallahzadeh H (2012) Predictors of unsafe driving in Yazd City, Based on protection motivation theory in 2010. *The Horizon of Medical Sciences* 17(4):49–59.

38. Gebrehiwot T, van der Veen A (2015) Farmers prone to drought risk: why some farmers undertake farm-level risk-reduction measures while others not? *Environ Manag* 55(3):588–602.

THEORY IN ACTION—ARTICLE QUESTIONS

1. How threatening do the farmers perceive skin cancer to be, that is, what are their views on the severity/seriousness of skin cancer, their own vulnerability to it, and the rewards associated with their behavior?

2. Now use the farmers' coping appraisal to explain their skin protective behaviors.

3. Based on the PMT constructs of threat and coping appraisal, what suggestions did the authors make regarding the focus of interventions to reduce skin cancer prevalence?

4. In what ways, if any, were your threat and/or coping appraisal responses the same as those of the farmers? Do you think the suggested intervention foci would be effective?

▶ Chapter References

Ashida, S., Heaney, C., Kmet, J., & Wilkins, J. R. (2011). Using protection motivation theory and formative research to guide an injury prevention intervention increasing adherence to the North American guidelines for children's agricultural tasks. *Health Promotion Practice, 12*(3), 396–405. doi:10.1177/15248399910362034

Beirens, T. M. J., Brug, J., vanBeek, E. F., Dekker, R., den Hertog, P., & Raat, H. (2008). Assessing psychosocial correlates of parental safety behavior using protection motivation theory: Star gate presence and use among parents of toddlers. *Health Education Research, 23*(4), 723–731. doi:10.1093/her/cym058

Bish, A., Yardley, L., Nicoll, A., & Michie, S. (2011). Factors associated with uptake of vaccination against pandemic influenza: A systematic review. *Vaccine, 29*, 6472–6484. doi:10.1016/j .vaccine.2011.06.107

Calder, N., & Aitken, R. (2008). An exploratory study of the influences that compromise the sun protection of young adults. *International Journal of Consumer Studies, 32*, 579–587. doi:10.1111/j.1470-6431.2008.00699.x

Cathcart, R. L., & Glendon, A. I. (2016). Judged effectiveness of threat and coping appraisal anti-speeding messages. *Accident Analysis and Prevention, 96*, 237–248. doi:10.1016/j.aap.2016.08.005

Chambers, R., Tingey, L., Mullany, B., Parker, S., Lee, A., & Barlow, A. (2016). Exploring sexual risk taking among American Indian adolescents through protection motivation theory. *AIDS Care, 28*(9), 1089–1096. doi:10.1080/09540121.206.1164289

Ch'ng, J. W., & Glendon, A. I. (2014). Predicting sun protection behaviors using protection motivation variables. *Journal of Behavioral Medicine, 37*, 245–256. doi:10.1007/s10865-012-982-5

Cismaru, M., Deshpande, S., Thurmeier, R., Lavack, A. M., & Agrey, N. (2010). Preventing fetal alcohol spectrum disorders: The role of protection motivation theory. *Health Marketing Quarterly, 27*, 66–85. doi:10.1080/7359680903519776

Floyd, D. L., Prentice-Dunn, S., & Rogers, R. W. (2000). A meta-analysis if research on protection motivation theory. *Journal of Applied Social Psychology, 30*(2), 407–429.

Glendon, A. I., & Walker, B. L. (2013). Can anti-speeding messages based on protection motivation theory influence reported speeding intentions? *Accident Analysis and Prevention, 57*, 67–79. doi:10.1016/j.aap.2013.04.004.

Johnson & Johnson Consumer, Inc. (2016). Get relief responsibly. Retrieved May 3, 2017, from https://www.tylenol.com/safety-dosing/overview/get-relief.

Keshavarz, M., & Karami, E. (2016). Farmer's pro-environmental behavior under drought: Application of protection motivation theory. *Journal of Arid Environments, 127*, 128–136. doi:10.1016/j.aridenv.2015.11.010

Maddux, J. E., & Rogers, R. W. (1983). Protection motivation and self-efficacy: A revised theory of fear appeals and attitude change. *Journal of Experimental Social Psychology, 19*, 469–479.

Mullan, B., Allom, V., Saunsbury, K., & Monds, L. (2016). Determining motivation to engage in safe food handling behavior. *Food Control, 61*, 47–56. doi:10.1016/j.foodcont.2015.09.025

Munson, K. (2015). Drivers chuckle at funny highway message signs. *Des Moines Register*. Retrieved May 3, 2017, from http://www.desmoinesregister.com/story/news/local/kyle-munson/2015/10/05 /iowa-department-of-transportation-digital-message-sign-humor-zero-fatalities/73231720

National Institute on Alcohol Abuse and Alcoholism. (2006). Drinking and your pregnancy. Retrieved February 9, 2017, from https://pubs.niaaa.noh.gov/publiations/DrinkingPregnancy_HTML/p

Rogers, R. W. (1975). A protection motivation theory of fear appeals and attitude change. *The Journal of Psychology, 91*, 93–114.

Rogers, R. W., & Deckner, W. C. (1975). Effects of fear appeals and psychological arousal upon emotion, attitudes, and cigarette smoking. *Journal of Personality and Social Psychology, 32*, 222–230. doi:10.1037/0022-3514.32.2.222

Ruiter, R. A. C., Kessels, L. T. E., Peters, G. J. Y., & Kok, G. (2014). Sixty years of fear appeal research: Current state of the evidence. *International Journal of Psychology, 49*(2), 63–70. doi:10.1002iijop.12042

Sawant, R. V., Goyal, R. K., Rajan, S. S., Patel, H. K., Essien, E. J., & Sansgiry, S. S. (2016). Factors associated with intention to engage in self-protective behavior: The case of over the counter acetaminophen products. *Research in Social and Administrative Pharmacy, 12*, 327–335. doi:10.1016/j.sapharm.2015.06.005

Tingey, L., Chambers, R., Rosenstock, S., Lee, A., Goklish, N., & Larzelere, F. (2017). The impact of a sexual reproductive health intervention for American Indian Adolescents on predictors of condom use intention. *Journal of Adolescent Health, 60*, 284–291. doi:10.1016/j .jadohealth.2016.08.025

U.S. Department of Health and Human Services, Food & Drug Administration. (2016). *CDER takes steps to end prescription pain medicine misuse, abuse, and addiction.* Retrieved August 22, 2017, from https://www.fda.gov/Drugs/ResourcesForYou/SpecialFeatures/ucm263505.htm

CHAPTER 8
Social Cognitive Theory

STUDENT LEARNING OUTCOMES

After reading this chapter the student will be able to:

- Explain the concept of reciprocal determinism.
- Differentiate among the many constructs of the Social Cognitive Theory.
- Explain how each of the constructs influences health behavior.
- Use the theory to analyze at least one behavior.

SOCIAL COGNITIVE THEORY ESSENCE SENTENCE

Behavior, personal factors, and environmental factors interact with each other, and changing one changes them all.

Constructs

Self-efficacy: Personal belief in one's own ability to successfully do something

Expectations: Anticipated outcomes of a particular behavior

Expectancies: Values assigned to the outcomes of a particular behavior

Self-regulation: Controlling behavior based on personal standards

Observational learning (modeling): Learning by watching others

Reinforcement: Rewards or punishments for doing something

Behavioral capability: The knowledge and skills needed to engage in a particular behavior

Locus of control: Personal belief in one's own power over life events

▶ In the Beginning

Social Cognitive Theory (SCT) has its roots in Albert Bandura's research on observation, social learning, and aggressive behavior dating back to the late 1950s. During this time, the prevailing theory about behavior acquisition was rooted in behaviorism, or the view that behavior results from environmental stimuli, consequences, rewards, and punishments (Pajares, 2004).

In keeping with this, Bandura's early research explored the influence of observation and modeling on behavior acquisition, that is, people learn by watching and copying others. Looking at aggressive behavior in boys through this lens, he found boys were aggressive even when they were from homes in which aggressive behavior was not condoned (not rewarded). Although this type of behavior was unacceptable in the home, the parents of these boys nonetheless expected their sons to be tough and settle disputes with other children physically (aggressively), if necessary. He found the parents themselves were aggressive toward the school system and toward other children they felt were giving their sons a hard time. From this Bandura concluded that the boys learned aggressive behavior by copying or modeling their parents—thus demonstrating the power of observational learning (Bandura & Walters, 1959; Pajares, 2004).

Bandura and his colleagues continued researching the impact of modeling on social behavior in 1961 with the now famous Bobo doll experiments. (The Bobo doll was a 5-foot-tall inflated clown.) Children were separated into groups, with one group observing an adult (model) playing with toys in a room ignoring the Bobo doll in the corner. The other group watched as the adult (model) began playing with toys in the room, then start hitting and beating on the Bobo doll. The children from both groups were then individually left alone with the Bobo doll and other toys. Children who observed the aggressive adult model imitated almost identically much of the physical and verbal aggression they witnessed. In contrast, the children who saw the nonaggressive adult model only rarely interacted with the Bobo doll in an aggressive manner (Bandura, Ross, & Ross, 1961). With modeling and observational learning (environmental factors) as the foundation, research continued into personal factors that contribute to behavior including self-reward, self-regulation, self-efficacy, self-directedness, and self-reflection. Identification of these furthered the idea that behavior is not just the result of the consequences of one's actions (Pajares, 2004), but rather the result of an interplay between environmental factors, personal factors, and behavior—the underlying concept of the SCT (Grusec, 1992).

▶ Theory Concept

SCT is based on the concept of *reciprocal determinism* or the dynamic interplay among personal factors, the environment, and behavior (Bandura, 1977). The way in which people interpret their environment and their personal factors affect their behavior (Parjares, 2004); their behavior affects their personal factors, which can affect their environment, and so on. For example, in a school setting a teacher can work with students to improve their personal factors—self-confidence, knowledge, and cognitive skills—their behavior by improving their studying skills and the environment by altering the classroom structures to enhance rather than undermine student success (Parjares, 2004). The point being that changing one of the three factors changes all of them and, therefore, changes behavior.

An example of this interaction is evident when we look at bottled water use. It is impossible to walk on a campus today and not see both students and faculty toting water bottles. They are ubiquitous. However, the plastic disposable bottles have quickly become an environmental problem in addition to a potential health hazard from the leaching of plastic chemicals into the water. Armed with this information (personal factor—knowledge) campuses across the country have installed water stations or hydration stations (environment). These new and improved "water fountains" filter the water and are constructed purposely for refilling reusable water bottles. Students fill up their reusable bottles (behavior) rather than buying bottles of water, thus helping to eliminate pollution.

▶ Theory Constructs

The factors of reciprocal determinism—personal, environmental, and behavioral— are affected by the many constructs of SCT. These include self-efficacy, expectations, expectancies, self-regulation, observational learning, emotional arousal, behavioral capability, reinforcement, and locus of control. Among the most often used to explain and change behavior are self-efficacy, expectations, expectancies, self-regulation, observational learning (modeling), and reinforcement.

Self-efficacy ~slide #1~

Of all the constructs of SCT, self-efficacy is probably the single most important determinant of behavior because people will only do what they believe they can do. Even when they have the skills and knowledge to accomplish a task, it's still their belief in their own ability to do it that makes the difference between them trying or not (Bandura, 1993). Self-efficacy influences our goals and aspirations. The stronger our belief in ourselves, the greater goals we set for ourselves and the stronger the commitment we make to attaining them (Bandura, 2004). This is the same construct that forms the basis of Self-Efficacy Theory and plays a role in both the Health Belief Model and the Transtheoretical Model. When long-haul truck drivers feel confident they can add more fruit and vegetables to their diets, they eat more of them (Hamilton, Vayro, & Schwarzer, 2015). Severely obese individuals increase their fruit and vegetable intake when they have strong self-efficacy beliefs in their ability to control their unhealthy eating (Annesi, 2011).

The lack of self-efficacy for overcoming barriers to exercising is the greatest stumbling block for parents who wanted to increase their activity levels. The barrier most frequently reported is that of time, or the lack thereof. Armed with this information, interventions aimed at increasing exercise among parents need to focus on improving parental self-efficacy in their ability to overcome the barrier of time (Mailey, Philips, Dlugonski, & Conroy, 2016) because for this population, it's a time management issue rather than a lack of desire, motivation, or knowledge about the benefits of exercise.

Improving self-efficacy for overcoming barriers should also be the focus of interventions aimed at increasing breastfeeding among African-American women. Enhancing breastfeeding self-efficacy can be accomplished, for example, by having new moms practice breastfeeding in steps or stages so they gain mastery of each skill in the process (Eastin & Sharma, 2015) or by having them join a support group with moms who successfully breastfed. This approach enhances self-efficacy through vicarious learning (watching others like themselves successfully breastfeeding) and verbal persuasion (having the other moms cheering them on).

Expectations

Behavior is influenced by expectations. This construct suggests that people behave in certain ways because they anticipate or expect a certain result. A man uses a condom because he expects to be protected from sexually transmitted infections and fatherhood. An overweight woman begins exercising because she expects to lose weight. Students drink because they expect to be accepted as part of the group.

Our expectations of the outcome of a behavior can also cause us to avoid the behavior. For example, women who worry that cancer will be found if they have a mammogram tend not to have mammograms (Rawl, Champion, Menon, & Foster, 2000). People who expect to get sick from the flu vaccine don't get vaccinated. Men who expect to be embarrassed by having a digital rectal exam for prostate cancer probably won't go for the screening (Shelton, Weinrich, & Reynolds, 1999).

Our expectations of outcomes are influenced by any number of things, including our past experiences in similar situations, observing others or hearing about others in a similar situation, and by the emotional or physical response that occurs as a result of the behavior. For example, because of my past experience playing badminton, there is an expectation that I can play tennis. Because the women's figure skating champions are the same age as me, there is an expectation that I can also skate. Because quitting smoking increases appetite, I expect to gain weight.

Expectations for middle school students are predictors of smoking behavior. Given this, addressing expectations for *not* smoking in prevention programs would be beneficial. For example, emphasizing that *not* smoking might result in having more money, more friends, better health, and fresher breath (Miller, Sharma, Brown, & Shahbazi, 2015).

Expectancies

While expectations are the anticipated or expected outcomes of a particular behavior, *expectancies* are the values we place on those outcomes. People tend to do what is likely to produce a positive or good outcome and generally avoid doing things that have negative or unrewarding outcomes (Bandura, 2001). To make it easier to understand, outcomes expectancies are sometimes referred to as "if...then" statements (Connor, Gullo, Feeney, Kavangh, & Young, 2013). Using mammograms as an example, *if* a woman expects that a mammogram will show she has cancer and she doesn't want to know, *then* the expectancy or value she places on the outcome of a mammogram is negative or undesirable and there is a good chance she'll avoid the behavior (going for a mammogram). On the other hand, *if* a woman views early diagnosis of breast cancer as something that would increase her chance of cure (positive expectancy), *then* she will have an annual mammogram.

For Hispanic male college students, positive expectancies of physical activity are potent predictors of their participation in physical activity. Their expectancies of physical activity include improved body image, reduced stress, and enhanced competitive advantage (Magoc, Tomaka, Shamaley, & Bridges, 2016), all positive outcomes. Given this, it makes sense then for campus programs aimed at increasing physical activity among this population to use these outcomes to promote the programs rather than healthy lifestyle, reduced risk of heart disease, and diabetes, for example. Similarly, reduced depression and anxiety are expectancies related to physical activity among young Hispanics in general, whereas expectancies of reduced cardiovascular disease and type 2 diabetes are not (Ryan, 2005).

With older adults, positive expectancies of more immediate, affective results (those that address mood or emotions) are more predictive of exercise behavior than are physical health benefits, which tend to be more long term (Gellert, Ziegelmann, & Schwarzer, 2012). In this population, focusing health messages on expectancies related to immediate changes in feelings or mood rather than the physical health benefits leads to better results.

Another situation where expectancies play a large role in behavior is in marijuana use. As is logical, if the expectancy is positive—I have more confidence when I smoke—then it's more likely the person will smoke. On the other hand, if the expectancy is negative—smoking makes me confused—then it's unlikely the person will smoke or will smoke less (Connor et al., 2013).

The same is true for alcohol use. When socially anxious college students don't believe they have the ability to avoid heavy drinking in social situations (i.e., they have low self-efficacy) and also have positive expectancies for alcohol use (feeling comfortable in the social situation) they drink more than other socially anxious students. However, students with *low* social anxiety who also have positive alcohol expectancies drink almost as much as their socially anxious peers (Gilles, Turk, & Fresco, 2006).

Self-regulation

Self-regulation refers to controlling our behavior based on our own adopted personal standards (Bandura, 2005). It is Bandura's (1991) contention that if this internal mechanism of control didn't exist, and people behaved solely as the result of external forces, they would be like weather vanes shifting constantly in an effort to conform to whatever social expectation they confronted. Rather, this internal control does exist and comes from the beliefs we form about what we can do, the likely outcome of our actions, the goals we set and the plan of action we take that results in the outcomes we expect (Bandura, 1991). Logically, those outcomes provide self-satisfaction and positive self-worth rather than dissatisfaction and negative self-worth (Bandura, 2004).

Self-regulation or self-control, as it is sometimes called, is one of the predictors for male university student human papilloma virus (HPV) vaccine intention. If they are sure they can plan to get vaccinated, and that they can reward themselves with something they like for getting vaccinated, then they are likely to get vaccinated. Knowing this can be very helpful when planning a campus program to increase HPV vaccination among the male students. For example, the goal of getting vaccinated can be broken down into smaller steps such as offering students a number of different dates and times they can get the first dose, offering them a variety of ways to schedule their appointment—email, calling, or in-person (Priest, Knowlden, & Sharma, 2015)—and giving them some control over the process.

Self-regulation is one of the best predictors of healthy eating habits. People who plan and track their eating, plan different strategies to increase fruit, vegetable, and fiber consumption, and decrease fat, have healthier diets (Anderson, Winett, & Wojcik, 2007).

Self-regulation can also be used to implement a health promotion intervention, as it was in the *Cooking with Kids* nutrition program. The paraprofessionals at university extension centers responsible for teaching the curriculum in fourth grade classrooms used self-regulation to set goals for implementation at 1 month, 4 months, and 8 months (Diker et al., 2013).

Self-control is a useful construct for smoking prevention programs aimed at middle school students. For example, helping students set goals for not smoking, having them develop plans for what they can do in situations where there is the temptation to initiate smoking, and rewarding them for refusing to smoke are all examples of self-regulation/control strategies (Miller et al., 2015).

Observational Learning

Observational learning (or modeling) is learning by watching others and copying their behavior. Think back to when you were a child. How did you learn to brush your teeth, tie your shoes, ride a bike, color within the lines, bake cookies, hammer a nail, and get dressed? In addition to learning basic life skills through observation, we adopt observed mannerisms, interpersonal communication style, leadership style, and health practices, to name a few. So much of our behavior results from observational learning that the list might be endless.

As a result, the construct of observational learning can be very useful in explaining why people behave the way they do. Unfortunately, it does not always lead to healthy behaviors. For example, we have known for some time that if a parent (role model) smokes, it is more likely that the child will also smoke. Children learn and do what they see.

The strength of observational learning depends on how much attention is given to the person who is modeling the behavior. This degree of attention is influenced by a number of things, among them the power and attractiveness of the model, the circumstances under which the model is being observed, what is motivating the person to learn the behavior, how important it is that the behavior be learned, and the complexity of the behavior (Bandura, 1977, 1986; Grusec, 1992).

Observational learning is enhanced when the model is someone the observer "connects with" in some way. For example, a parent, a respected teacher, a friend, or a sports figure. This is why companies use celebrity endorsements to sell their products. Think of the athlete who makes it onto the cereal box. Having this person's picture on the box implies that the athlete eats the cereal in the box. If the child eats the cereal, he or she will be like this athlete. The child's desire to do as the model does may be one explanation for why he or she eats the cereal, which is what the food company hopes.

This is the premise for a nutrition DVD intervention, *Food Dudes,* that aims to increase fruit and vegetable intake in 4–11 year olds. In this DVD, cartoon models are shown enjoying fruits and vegetables. Children who copy the behavior by tasting the fruits and vegetables the Food Dudes eat, get rewarded with stickers. This approach significantly increases the fruit and vegetable intake of kids (Staiano, Marker, Frelier, Hsia, & Martin, 2016).

We pay more attention to a model when we need to learn the behavior and when the behavior is complex. For example, people newly diagnosed with diabetes may need to learn how to inject insulin, test their blood glucose levels, and adjust their diets. People are likely to be more attentive when observing how to inject insulin than when observing how to measure a cup of food.

While the incidence of diabetes is on the rise in general, it disproportionately affects low-income, minority, and medically underserved people. Research to identify factors associated with management of diabetes in this population found that those most successful in controlling it had diabetic family members. Observing a family member with diabetes helped them understand the disease, take it seriously, and ultimately manage their own diabetes better (Madden et al., 2011).

Observational learning is the basis of an online physical activity intervention for sedentary adults. Viewers learn by watching videos in which different physical activities (Pilates, resistance training, step aerobics, and yoga) are demonstrated (Carr et al., 2012). The down side to this is the lack of "correction" for incorrect copying. In yoga, for example, doing the poses (asanas) and doing them correctly with proper body alignment are two different things. During an in-person yoga class with a qualified instructor, this situation is addressed.

Observational learning happens all of the time, whether we are aware of it or not. We learn by watching others in person, online, on TV, and in the movies. It is a powerful behavior changing tool.

Reinforcement

Reinforcement is a construct in the SCT with which you may be familiar; it is also the basis for operant conditioning and behavior modification. In general, reinforcement is a system of rewards (positive reinforcement) and punishments (negative reinforcements) in response to behavior. Based on this premise, behavior occurs because people either want the reward or want to avoid the punishment (Bandura, 1977).

A common example of this can be found with children. If a child eats all of the vegetables on his plate, he is rewarded with a favorite dessert; thus, the behavior (eating vegetables) is repeated so the reward (dessert) can be obtained again.

Positive reinforcement might be discontinuing medication for type 2 diabetes because dietary changes and exercise have it under control. Reward might also come in the form of praise from family members for following a healthier diet and keeping diabetes under control or having them change their eating habits, too (Pollard, Zachary, Wingert, Booker, & Surkan, 2014).

Positive reinforcement comes from a variety of sources. Pregnant women in a program aimed at helping them adopt healthier lifestyle behaviors get positive reinforcement from the other women in their support group, their healthcare providers, and through self-reinforcement from keeping a diary of their changes and seeing progress (Smith et al., 2010). In *ProSafe,* an injury prevention program for teens pursuing careers in the food service industry, positive reinforcement for using safety skills in the workplace that were taught in the classroom is positive teacher and supervisor evaluations (Ward et al., 2010).

Unfortunately, not all positive reinforcement rewards "good" behavior. A case in point is bullying. Children who bully others do it because they believe they will be rewarded in some way. It may be parental praise and acceptance of bullying or increased social status among the others kids on the playground (Swearer, Wang, Berry, & Myers, 2014). Just as long as there is positive reinforcement for

bullying behavior, it will continue. This is why one approach to bullying prevention *(Bullying Prevention in Positive Behavior Support)* teaches children the skills
they need to minimize or remove the social rewards for bullying (Ross & Horner,
2009).

Positive reinforcement could be new clothes in a smaller size because of weight
loss, "runner's high" after exercising, or no cavities at a dental check-up because of
flossing every day. All of these are rewards or positive reinforcements that would
likely support continuation of the new behavior. What would a positive reinforcement be for you? (See **FIGURE 8.1**).

Behavior change also results from negative reinforcement or punishment. In this
case, the goal is to stop the behavior from being repeated, rather than encouraging it
to continue. A child who refuses to eat her vegetables is denied dessert and watches
as everyone else eats theirs. To avoid this punishment, she eats her vegetables the
next time, unless, of course, she doesn't like what is being served for dessert. To
avoid being arrested again for driving under the influence, a group of friends desig-
nate a driver when they go out drinking. Antabuse, a medication that causes severe
nausea and vomiting if taken with alcohol, is a negative reinforcement meant to help
those with alcoholism stay sober.

FIGURE 8.1 Positive reinforcement supports continuation of new behavior.
© Warren Goldswain/Shutterstock

However, in the case of "doping"—the use of substances or medical interventions for the primary purpose of improving performance (Johnson, 2012)—punishments are not effective in stopping the behavior and increasing no-doping compliance (Miller & Rollnick, 2002), because the rewards of doping are so powerful—such as a gold medal or a multi million dollar contract. Rewards for not doping, rather than punishment for doping, is more likely to reduce the undesirable behavior (Johnson, 2012).

Behavioral Capability

The construct of behavioral capability tells us that before people can perform a certain behavior, they must have knowledge of the behavior and the skills to perform it. Simply put, before doing something you have to know what it is you're going to do and know how to do it.

When we look at the 2020 Dietary Guidelines for Americans, the recommendations include eating foods low in added sugars, saturated fats, and sodium (U.S. Department of Health and Human Services & U.S. Department of Agriculture, 2015). In order to do this, people have to know how to read food labels to find out which foods in their diets are high in saturated fats, and they need to know the lower in saturated fat options. The same is true of added sugars. In order to comply with this recommendation, people have to know what added sugar means and know how to read a food label in order to choose those with no or limited added sugar. If they do not know this information, they don't have the behavioral capability to make better choices (**FIGURE 8.2**).

Improving the dietary intake of underserved populations is one of many public health goals. To achieve this among low income Mexican-Americans, behavioral capability is key. Behavioral capability in this situation means health literacy or the ability to obtain, process, and understand health information and use it to make health decisions. As it turns out, greater health literacy increases self-efficacy and the two combined improve fruit and vegetable intake and support adoption of healthier behaviors (Guntzviller, King, Jensen, & Davis, 2017).

FIGURE 8.2 Knowledge and skills are needed to make better choices.
© Diego Cervo/Shutterstock

The combination of self-efficacy and behavioral capability also contributes to effective worksite wellness. A case in point is the *Wellsteps Wellness Program.* This program was developed specifically to build behavioral capability and self-efficacy. It accomplishes this by providing skills and tools employees can use immediately, such as a guide for making healthier fast food choices, and strategies to help them maintain rather than gain weight (LeCheminant & Merrill, 2012).

Locus of Control

Although most of the constructs in the SCT explain behavior by the influence of external or social forces, the construct of locus of control is a bit different. This construct explains behavior based on the idea that people have varying degrees of belief in their ability to control what happens to them. This belief in the extent of personal control has an impact on health decisions, and thus on health behavior.

Locus of control works on a continuum from internal to external. Internally controlled people believe that everything that happens to them is a result of their own decisions and behaviors. They believe they have control over all aspects of their lives and their destiny. Externally controlled people believe that forces outside of their control, such as fate, God's will, or important or powerful others, govern all aspects of their lives (Levenson, 1974).

Internality or externality has a strong influence on our health decision making. In the case of breast cancer, for example, women who are more externally controlled are not likely to have mammograms unless their physicians (important or powerful others) tell them to have one. In contrast, women who are more internally controlled will have mammograms regardless of whether their physicians recommend them or not (Borrayo & Guarnaccia, 2002).

Not only does locus of control influence early detection behaviors for breast cancer, it also influences how women cope with a diagnosis of breast cancer. Women with breast cancer who have a greater internal locus of control have a better quality of life, lower anxiety, and less depression. So, the application of this would be in developing interventions that help move women from an external locus to an internal locus as a way to improve their quality of life and lessen their depression and anxiety (Sharif, 2017).

In young adults, internality is associated with greater odds of engaging in healthy behaviors, specifically eating fiber, exercising, and low salt and fat consumption (Steptoe & Wardle, 2001). This isn't only true for young adults. Older urban Taiwanese have a greater internal locus and better nutritional status than their rural counterparts with a higher external locus of control (Chen, Cheng, Chuang, Shao, 2014). Where people fall on the continuum of internality and externality may change depending upon the situation. Some people are very internal when it comes to changing unhealthy behaviors, such as weight loss or stress management, for example. Yet these same people do not wear seatbelts, because "What will be, will be" or "If it's my time to go, there is nothing I can do about it" or "if I die, it's God's will."

In circumstances where externality is related to a "God" locus of control, the belief is that behavior is under God's control. This view among college students influences alcohol use and sexual behavior with greater external "God" locus of control linked to abstinence from alcohol and sex (Moore, 2014), perhaps so as to please God. Whereas students with greater internal locus of control drink more and engage in more sexually risky behaviors (Burnett et al., 2013).

The influence of religion or God on locus of control is found in other populations; only curiously, its influence does not yield the same results. Rather than being associated with an external locus, healthier behaviors are instead related to unhealthy or negative health behaviors and internal locus of control associated with more positive or healthy behaviors (Abraido-Lanza et al., 2007). However, Latinas rely on both God (external) and themselves (internal) to manage their health. In this population, religiosity promotes health seeking behavior because the belief is that God gives us health, but says we have to help ourselves, too (De Jesus, 2016). In summary, according to SCT, personal factors, the environment, and behavior interact with each other; therefore, changing one of them changes all of them (**FIGURE 8.3**).

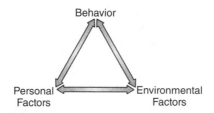

FIGURE 8.3 Social cognitive theory.

Pajares, F. (2002). Overview of social cognitive theory and of self-efficacy. Retrieved from http://www.emory.edu/EDUCATION/mfp/eff .html. Reprinted with permission.

THEORY IN ACTION—CLASS ACTIVITY

In small groups, discuss your experiences with bullying. It could be your personal experiences or those of a friend, family member, neighbor, or classmate.

1. What are the commonalities you notice among your experiences?
2. What are the common characteristics of the bully?
3. Using SCT explain the basis for bullying behavior.
4. Brainstorm how SCT might be used as the basis of a prevention intervention.

    Now, read the following article and answer the questions at the end.

Chapter 8 Article: Reducing Bullying: Application of Social Cognitive Theory[1]

Susan M. Swearer*, Cixin Wang, Brandi Berry, Zachary R. Myers

Susan M. Swearer is a professor of Educational Psychology at the University of Nebraska-Lincoln, 40 Teachers College Hall, Lincoln, NE 68588; Cixin Wang is an assistant professor in the Graduate School of Education at the University of California, Riverside; Brandi Berry is a doctoral candidate in Educational Psychology at the University of Nebraska-Lincoln; and Zachary R. Myers is a doctoral student in Educational Psychology at the University of Nebraska-Lincoln.

Social cognitive theory (SCT) is an important heuristic for understanding the complexity of bullying behaviors and the social nature of involvement in bullying. Bullying has been heralded as a social relationship problem, and the interplay between the individual and his or her social environment supports this conceptualization. SCT has been used to help guide the development of an individualized intervention for bully perpetrators, which will be described in this article. Intervening directly with those who bully others helps understand individual variation in bullying, as well as teaches bully perpetrators alternative, prosocial ways of interacting with others. Students who bully others exhibit a complex array of psychological, cognitive, and social characteristics. In this article, we argue that to truly reduce bullying, interventions must address these psychological, cognitive, and social contributing factors. Only when interventions target these constructs will individuals be able to transform their bullying behaviors into prosocial interactions.

▶ Prevalence of Bullying Involvement

Over the past 2 decades, attention to bullying has exponentially increased among educational, psychological, and legal scholars and practitioners, as well as among youth and adults worldwide. With the recent events between players on the Miami Dolphins football team and allegations of bullying, harassment, and intimidation, bullying has become a major topic in the news and now in locker rooms across the country. However, despite this increased attention to the bullying phenomenon, bullying does not appear to be significantly declining.

Studies have found that 10% to 33% of students report being victimized (Kessel Schneider, O'Donnell, Stueve, & Coulter, 2012; Perkins, Craig, & Perkins, 2011); 1% to 11.5% report both bullying others and being bullied (i.e., bully-victims; Dulmus, Sowers, & Theriot, 2006; Nansel et al., 2001); and 5% to 13% report bullying others (Perkins et al., 2011; Seals & Young, 2003; Solberg & Olweus, 2003). Although lower rates of self-reported bullying behaviors could stem from reluctance to self-report negative behavior, the disparity between the

1   Reproduced from Swearer, S., Wang, C., Berry, B., Myers, Z.R. (2014). Reducing bullying: Application of social cognitive theory. Theory Into Practice, 53, 271-277.
    doi: 10.1080/00405841.2014.947221

* Corresponding author.

number of individuals bullying versus being bullied is consistent with research on various delinquent and criminal activities, which finds that a small number of individuals perpetrate the majority of crimes (Hamparian, Schuster, Dinitz, & Conrad, 1978). Bullying is a significant problem that needs to be reduced, and one way to do this is by intervening directly with the bully perpetrators with the goal to help these individuals change their cognitive and social behaviors that underlie their bullying perpetration.

▶ Influence of Social Cognitive Theory on Bullying Intervention

Bandura's (1977, 1986) social cognitive theory is an updated and expanded version of social learning theory, developed by Miller and Dollard (1941). Social learning theory proposed that individuals learn not only through direct instruction but also by observing others' behaviors and the consequences that follow (Bandura, 1977). For learning to occur, individuals must (a) attend to the observed behavior, (b) encode images of the observed behavior, (c) reproduce those images, and (d) be motivated to perform the behavior. The motivational component is tied to the consequences that follow certain behaviors; specifically, individuals are more likely to engage in a behavior they have learned that the consequences are valued and rewarding (i.e., reinforced). Likewise, if the consequences of a particular behavior are more punishing and less reinforcing, individuals will be motivated to refrain from engaging in that behavior.

Social cognitive theory hinges on the same basic principles as social learning theory (Bandura, 1986). However, social cognitive theory emphasizes the role of cognitions in determining individuals' behaviors (Bandura, 1986). Specifically, social cognitive theory proposes that there is a continuous interaction between the social environment (e.g., witnessing others' behaviors), internal stimuli (e.g., cognitions and feelings), and behaviors. This triadic interaction (i.e., social environment, internal stimuli, and behaviors) is referred to as reciprocal determinism (Bussey & Bandura, 1999; Orpinas & Horne, 2006). Thus, this triadic reciprocal determinism occurs when individuals make cognitive evaluations of the behaviors of individuals in their social environments and the consequences that follow those behaviors (Bussey & Bandura, 1999).

Social cognitive theory has been used to explain aggressive behaviors (Bandura, 1978; Bandura, Ross, & Ross, 1961) and can be applied to the study of bullying by explaining how individuals learn to bully (i.e., via observational learning and reinforcement). Cognitions regarding support for bullying and beliefs regarding the likelihood of positive versus negative consequences affect the likelihood that youths will bully others. Many studies demonstrate a link between observing bullying and other aggressive behaviors and perpetration of bullying behaviors among youth. For example, youth who are exposed to domestic violence in their homes are significantly more likely to bully others than those who are not exposed to domestic violence (Baldry, 2003; Bowes et al., 2009). Children and adolescents who socialize with aggressive peers are more likely to perpetrate acts of aggression than youths who do not associate with aggressive peers (Mouttapa, Valente, Gallaher, Rohrbach, & Unger, 2004). Evidence suggests that youth who live in neighborhoods judged to be less safe (i.e., characterized by more violent behaviors) are more likely than those who live in safer neighborhoods to engage in bullying behaviors (Espelage, Bosworth, & Simon, 2000; Youngblade et al., 2007). Although there are many possible explanations for the correlation between exposure to bullying and other aggressive behaviors and perpetration of bullying behaviors, social cognitive theory asserts that this link happens as a result of observational learning. Consistent with this assertion, some research has found that observational factors are the most strongly related to bullying behaviors (Curtner-Smith, 2000).

Youth have numerous opportunities to learn to bully via observational learning. However, not all youths who are exposed to bullying and aggression will emulate those behaviors. This is where the critical roles of cognition and reinforcement come into play. In terms of cognitions, evidence suggests that youth are less likely to engage in bullying behaviors if they think these behaviors are unacceptable. Research suggests that cognitions surrounding bullying are generally combined with emotions supportive of bullying, and tendencies to engage in bullying reflect this bidirectional relationship. Studies suggest that students holding antibullying attitudes are significantly less likely than those holding probullying attitudes to perpetrate bullying behaviors (Boulton, Trueman, & Flemington, 2002; Poteat, Kimmel, & Wilchins, 2010; Salmivalli & Voeten, 2004; Williams & Guerra, 2007). Thus, research consistently demonstrates that attitudes toward bullying explain (Boulton et al., 2002) and predict (Poteat et al., 2010; Salmivalli & Voeten, 2004) bullying behaviors. Therefore, although many children and adolescents may learn to bully via observational learning, only those who hold probullying attitudes will be likely to actually engage in bullying behaviors. However, it is important to note that attitudes contain cognitive, affective, and behavioral components and reflect a mental state of readiness that influences the likelihood that one will engage in a given behavior in the future (Allport, 1935; Fazio & Olson, 2007). Therefore, probullying attitudes do not always lead to bullying behaviors. Additionally psychological and cognitive factors may affect the likelihood that youth will engage in bullying behaviors, one of which is the perception of positive versus negative consequences.

According to social cognitive theory, children and adolescents tend to avoid behaviors that they believe will be punished and, instead, engage in behaviors that they believe will be rewarded (Bandura, 1977). Thus, according to theory, youth who perpetrate bullying believe that they will be rewarded in some way (e.g., increased social status, access to resources). Further, for the bullying behaviors to be maintained and repeated over time, individuals must receive reinforcement as a result of their bullying behaviors. Consistent with social cognitive theory, family members, adults (Bandura, 1978), and peers (Craig & Pepler, 1995; Mouttapa et al., 2004; O'Connell, Pepler, & Craig, 1999) may reinforce individuals' bullying behaviors (e.g., via praise or acceptance). In fact, one study found that students who bullied on the playground were reinforced by their peers for the bullying behaviors in the majority (i.e., 81%) of incidents (Craig & Pepler, 1995). Therefore, the significant individuals in youths' lives, particularly family members and peers, impact whether youths believe that bullying is acceptable or not and whether it will be rewarded or punished.

Based on the evidence, it appears as though children and adolescents who are most likely to engage in bullying are those who: (a) are exposed to bullying and other aggressive behaviors, (b) endorse probullying attitudes, and (c) interact with individuals who overtly or covertly indicate that bullying is acceptable and reinforce the bullying behaviors of these youths. Clearly, exposure to bullying, supportive attitudes toward bullying, and the expressed attitudes and behaviors of family members, peers, and other individuals are interrelated. For example, parents who condone aggressive and coercive behaviors may model those behaviors for their children (Patterson, 1982), indicate that they support bullying, and reinforce their children's bullying behaviors, all of which are likely to encourage their children to feel and think positively about bullying.

▶ Cognitive-Behavioral Interventions for Aggression and Bullying

Cognitive-behavioral interventions (CBI) are influenced by SCT and, given that bullying has been conceptualized as a cognitive-behavioral phenomenon (Doll et al., 2012), may be an ideal approach to reducing bullying. CBI focuses on how one's thoughts and beliefs affect behavior (DiGiuseppe, 2009). According to CBI, modifying one's dysfunctional beliefs will have a positive impact on thoughts and behavior. In terms of internal stimuli, cognitive distortions, especially those that justify aggression (Barriga, Landau, Stinson, Liau, & Gibbs, 2000; Lardén, Melin, Holst, & Långström, 2006), are associated with bullying perpetration. Furthermore, bullying attitudes (i.e., cognitions and emotions surrounding and tendencies toward bullying) are predictive of students' bullying behaviors in that students endorsing probullying attitudes are more likely to bully others compared with students who endorse antibullying attitudes (Poteat et al., 2010; Salmivalli & Voeten, 2004). Taken together, it appears as though there is much evidence to support the application of social cognitive theory to bullying behaviors and, thus, CBI as an appropriate intervention for students who bully.

Some CBIs have been found to decrease students' bullying behaviors (McLaughlin, Laux, & Pescara-Kovach, 2006). The Coping Power Program (CPP; Lochman & Wells, 2002), a social cognitive intervention that targets children's cognitive processes and parental behaviors, was found to reduce participants' aggressive, delinquent (e.g., substance abuse), and disruptive (e.g., hyperactive) behaviors (Boxmeyer, Lochman, Powell, Yaros, & Wojnaroski, 2007; Jurecska, Hamilton, & Peterson, 2011; Lochman & Wells, 2002, 2004); the best results being associated with use of the full program (i.e., both child and parent components). Problem-Solving Skills Training (PSST) has been found to lead to a decrease in children's aggressive and delinquent behaviors (Kazdin, Bass, Siegel, & Thomas, 1989; Kazdin, EsveldtDawson, French, & Unis, 1987), both used alone and combined with Parent Management Training (PMT; Kazdin, Siegel, & Bass, 1992) and combined with both PMT and parent problem solving (PPS; Kazdin & Whitley, 2003). Aggression Replacement Training (Goldstein, Glick, & Gibbs, 1998) is a three-part multicomponent approach including Skillstreaming, which teaches youths appropriate behaviors, anger control training that targets emotional regulation, and moral reasoning, which has been found to show long-term effects in decreasing aggressive behaviors among youth (Barnoski, 2004). Thus, CBIs, whether used in isolation, paired with other components such as parent training, and/or utilized in the context of a formalized intervention, appears to be effective in decreasing aggressive and disruptive behaviors in youth.

▶ The Target Bullying Intervention Program

Research on cognitive-behavioral programs designed to reduce aggression and impulsive behavior suggests that individualized, cognitive-behavioral approaches can effectively reduce aggression and impulsivity. The Target Bullying Intervention Program (T-BIP; Swearer & Givens, 2006) provides schools with a CBI designed using research on what works in bullying and aggression reduction interventions. The T-BIP is a one-on-one cognitive-behavioral intervention for bully perpetrators. Parents are also involved in the intervention by attending a follow-up meeting, during which time the T-BIP treatment report based on the data from the intervention is reviewed and specific recommendations are discussed. Each component of the T-BIP is supported by research, which offers a higher likelihood of success. For example, one study has shown that the number of students' office referrals decreased significantly after attending the T-BIP intervention, t (60) D 2.5, p D .02 (Swearer, Wang, Collins, Strawhun, & Fluke, 2014).

A critical component that is missing from many extant bullying interventions is a comprehensive assessment of bullying and related problems (Diamanduros, Downs, & Jenkins, 2008; Hilton, Anngela-Cole, & Wakita, 2010; Swearer, Espelage, & Napolitano, 2009). A unique component of the T-BIP is the cognitive-behavioral assessment phase, which helps to identify the cognitive processes and mental health factors associated with bullying. In this phase, the interventionist assesses constructs related to engagement in bullying (i.e., depression, anxiety, cognitive distortions, self-concept, perceptions of school climate, bullying involvement, and treatment acceptability).

▶ Conclusion

Consistent with the principles of social cognitive theory, in which individuals attend to, encode, and model the behaviors they observe contingent on their motivation to attend to the behavior (Bandura, 1977), studies have found that youths who witness aggressive behaviors are more likely to bully others. Youth who witness domestic abuse (Baldry, 2003; Bowes et al., 2009), live in unsafe neighborhoods (Youngblade et al., 2007), and associate with aggressive peers (Mouttapa et al., 2004) are more likely to perpetrate bullying. Students' social environments may also reinforce bullying through procurement of social status (Craig & Pepler, 1995; Mouttapa et al., 2004; O'Connell et al., 1999). Thus, theory and research support the notion that students have opportunities to learn bullying behaviors via observational learning and may be motivated to bully others as a result of reinforcement for these behaviors. CBIs are tailored to an individual's unique cognitions, emotions, and behaviors. Such individualization is a necessary component for effective bullying intervention given that bullying is a complex phenomenon and multiple factors are involved in the causation and maintenance of the bullying behaviors (Doll & Swearer, 2006; Sugimura & Rudolph, 2012).

Bullying prevention and intervention programs should teach students skills that promote effective problem solving strategies and prosocial behaviors. It is important to utilize school counselors, school psychologists, and other community referral systems to provide evidence-based treatment to students involved in bullying. Social cognitive theory suggests that interventions focused on cognitive and social functioning are important for breaking the cycle of bullying involvement.

▶ # References

1. Allport, G. W. (1935). Attitudes. In C. Murchison (Ed.), *Handbook of social psychology* (pp. 798–844). Worcester, MA: Clark University Press.
2. Baldry, A. C. (2003). Bullying in schools and exposure to domestic violence. *Child Abuse & Neglect, 27*, 713–732. doi: 10.1016/S0145-2134(03)00114-5.
3. Bandura, A. (1977). *Social learning theory*. Oxford, England: Prentice-Hall.
4. Bandura, A. (1978). Social learning theory of aggression. *Journal of Communication, 28*, 12–29. doi: 10.1111/j.1460-2466.1978.tb01621.x.
5. Bandura, A. (1986). Social foundations of thought and action: A social cognitive theory. Englewood Cliffs, NJ: Prentice-Hall.
6. Bandura, A., Ross, D., & Ross, S. A. (1961). Transmission of aggression through imitation of aggressive models. *Journal of Abnormal and Social Psychology, 63*, 575–583. doi: 10.1037/h0045925.
7. Barnoski, R. (2004). Outcome evaluation of Washington State's research-based program for juvenile offenders. Olympia, WA: Washington State Institute for Public Policy.
8. Barriga, A. Q., Landau, J. R., Stinson, B. L., Liau, A. K., & Gibbs, J. C. (2000). Cognitive distortions and problem behaviors in adolescents. *Criminal Justice and Behavior, 27*, 36–56. doi: 10.1177/0093854800027001003.
9. Boulton, M. J., Trueman, M., & Flemington, I. (2002). Associations between secondary school pupils' definitions of bullying, attitudes towards bullying, and tendencies to engage in bullying: Age and sex differences. *Educational Studies, 28*, 353–370. doi: 10.1080/0305569022000042390.
10. Bowes, L., Arseneault, L., Maughan, B., Taylor, A., Caspi, A., & Moffitt, T. E. (2009). School, neighborhood, and family factors are associated with children's bullying involvement: A nationally representative longitudinal study. *Journal of the American Academy of Child Adolescent Psychiatry, 48*, 545–553. doi: 10.1097/CHI.0b013e31819cb017.
11. Boxmeyer, C. L., Lochman, J. E., Powell, N., Yaros, A., & Wojnaroski, M. (2007). A case study of the Coping Power Program with aggressive youth. *Journal of Contemporary Psychotherapy, 37*, 165–174. doi: 10.1007/s10879-007-9051-3.
12. Bussey, K., & Bandura, A. (1999). Social cognitive theory of gender development and differentiation. *Psychological Review, 106*, 676–713. doi: 10.1037/0033-295X.106.4.676.
13. Craig, W. M., & Pepler, D. (1995). Observations of bullying in the playground and in the classroom. *School Psychology International, 21*, 22–36. doi: 10.1177/0143034300211002.
14. Curtner-Smith, M. E. (2000). Mechanisms by which family processes contribute to school-age boy's bullying. *Child Study Journal, 30*, 169–186. Retrieved from http://eric.ed.gov/?idDEJ626921.
15. Diamanduros, T., Downs, E., & Jenkins, S. J. (2008). The role of school psychologists in the assessment, prevention, and intervention of cyberbullying. *Psychology in the Schools, 45*, 693–704. doi: 10.1002/ pits.20335.
16. DiGiuseppe, R. (2009). An introduction to cognitive behavior therapies. In A. Akin-Little, S. G. Little, M. A. Bray, & T. J. Kehle (Eds.), *Behavioral interventions in schools: Evidence-based positive strategies* (95–100). Washington, DC: American Psychological Association.
17. Doll, B., & Swearer, S. (2006). Cognitive-behavioral interventions for participants in bullying and coercion. In R. Mennuti, A. Freeman, & R. Christner (Eds.), *Cognitive behavioral interventions in educational settings: A handbook for practice* (pp. 183–201). New York, NY: Brunner-Routledge.
18. Doll, B., Swearer, S. M., Collins, A. M., Chadwell, M. R., Dooley, K., & Chapla, B. A. (2012). Bullying and coercion: School-based cognitivebehavioral interventions. In R. B. Mennuti, R. W. Christner, & A. Freeman (Eds.), *Cognitive behavioral interventions in educational settings: A handbook for practice* (pp. 339–379). New York, NY: Routledge.
19. Dulmus, C., Sowers, K., & Theriot, M. (2006). Prevalence and bullying experiences of victims and victims who become bullies (bully-victims) at rural schools. *Victims & Offenders, 1*, 15–31. doi: 10.1080/15564880500498945.
20. Espelage, D. L, Bosworth, K., & Simon, T. R. (2000). Examining the social context of bullying behaviors in early adolescence. *Journal of Counseling and Development, 78*, 326–333. doi: 10.1002/j.1556-6676.2000.tb01914.x.

21. Fazio, R. H., & Olson, M. A. (2007). Attitudes: Foundations, functions, and consequences. In M. A. Hogg & J. Cooper (Eds.), *The sage handbook of social psychology* (pp. 123–145). London, England: Sage.

22. Goldstein, A. P., Glick, B., & Gibbs, J. C. (1998). *Aggression replacement training* (Rev. ed.). Champaign, IL: Research Press.

23. Hamparian, D. M., Schuster, R., Dinitz, S., & Conrad, J. P. (1978). *Violent few: A study of dangerous juvenile offenders.* New York, NY: Lexington Books.

24. Hilton, J. M., Anngela-Cole, L., & Wakita, J. (2010). A cross-cultural comparison of factors associated with school bullying. *Family Journal, 18,* 413–422. doi: 10.1177/1066480710372919.

25. Jurecska, D. E., Hamilton, E. B., & Peterson, M. A. (2011). Effectiveness of the coping power program in middle-school children with disruptive behaviours and hyperactivity difficulties. *Support for Learning, 26,* 168–172. doi: 10.1111/j.1467-9604.2011.01499.x.

26. Kazdin, A. E., Bass, D., Siegel, T., & Thomas, C. (1989). Cognitive-behavioral therapy and relationship therapy in the treatment of children referred for antisocial behavior. *Journal of Consulting and Clinical Psychology, 57,* 522–535. doi: 10.1037/0022-006X.57.4.522.

27. Kazdin, A. E., Esveldt-Dawson, French, N. H., & Unis, A. S. (1987). Problem-solving skills training and relationship therapy in the treatment of antisocial child behavior. *Journal of Consulting and Clinical Psychology, 55,* 76–85. doi: 10.1037/0022-006X.55.1.76.

28. Kazdin, A. E., Siegel, T. C., & Bass, D. (1992). Cognitive problem-solving skills training and parent management training in the treatment of antisocial behavior in children. *Journal of Consulting and Clinical Psychology, 60,* 733–747. doi: 10.1037/0022-006X.60.5.733.

29. Kazdin, A. E., & Whitley, M. K. (2003). Treatment of parental stress to enhance therapeutic change among children referred for aggressive and antisocial behavior. *Journal of Consulting and Clinical Psychology, 71,* 504–515. doi: 10.1037/0022-006X.71.3.504.

30. Kessel Schneider, S., O'Donnell, L., Stueve, A., & Coulter, R. S. (2012). Cyberbullying, school bullying, and psychological distress: A regional census of high school students. *American Journal of Public Health, 102,* 171–177. doi: 10.2105/AJPH.2011.300308.

31. Lardén, M., Melin, L., Holst, U., & Långström, N. (2006). Moral judgment, cognitive distortions and empathy in incarcerated delinquent and community control adolescents. *Psychology, Crime & Law, 12,* 453–462. doi: 10.1080/10683160500036855.

32. Lochman, J. E., & Wells, K. C. (2002). The Coping Power Program at the middle school transition: Universal and indicated prevention effects. *Psychology of Addictive Behaviors, 16,* S40–S54. doi: 10.1037/0893-164X.16.4S.S40.

33. Lochman, J. E., & Wells, K. C. (2004). The Coping Power Program for preadolescent aggressive boys and their parents: Outcome effects of the 1-year follow-up. *Journal of Consulting and Clinical Psychology, 72,* 571–578. doi: 10.1037/0022-006X.72.4.571.

34. McLaughlin, L., Laux, J. M., & Pescara-Kovach, L. (2006). Using multimedia to reduce bullying and victimization in third-grade urban schools. *Professional School Counseling, 10,* 153–160. Retrieved from http://schoolcounselor.metapress.com.

35. Miller, N. E., & Dollard, J. (1941). *Social learning and imitation.* New Haven, CT: Yale University Press.

36. Mouttapa, M., Valente, T., Gallaher, P., Rohrbach, L. A., & Unger, J. B. (2004). Social network predictors of bullying and victimization. *Adolescence, 39,* 315–335. Retrieved from http://www.ncbi.nlm. nih.gov/pubmed/15563041.

37. Nansel, T. R., Overpeck, M., Pilla, R. S., Ruan, W. J., Simmons-Morton, B., & Scheidt, P. (2001). Bullying behaviors among US youth: Prevalence and association with psychosocial adjustment. *Journal of the American Medical Association, 285,* 2094–2100. doi: 10.1001/jama.285.16.2094.

38. O'Connell, P., Pepler, D., & Craig, W. (1999). Peer involvement in bullying: Insights and challenges for intervention. *Adolescence, 22,* 437–452. doi: 10.1006/jado/1999.0238.

39. Orpinas, P., & Horne, A. M. (2006). Bullying prevention: Creating a positive school climate and developing social competence. Washington, DC: American Psychological Association.

40. Patterson, G. R. (1982). *Coercive family process.* Eugene, OR: Castalia.

41. Perkins, H. W., Craig, D. W., & Perkins, J. M. (2011). Using social norms to reduce bullying: A research intervention in five middle schools. *Group Processes Intergroup Relations, 14,* 703–722. doi: 10.1177/1368430210398004.

42. Poteat, V. P., Kimmel, M. S., & Wilchins, R. (2010). The moderating effect of support for violence beliefs on masculine norms, aggressions, and homophobic behavior during adolescence. *Journal of Research on Adolescence, 21,* 434–447. doi: 10.1111/j.1532-7795.2010.00682.x.

43. Salmivalli, C., & Voeten, M. (2004). Connections between attitudes, group norms, and behaviour in bullying situations. *International Journal of Behavioral Development, 28,* 246–258. doi: 10.1080/01650250344000488.

44. Seals, D. & Young, J. (2003). Bullying and victimization: Prevalence and relationship to gender, grade level, ethnicity, self-esteem, and depression. *Adolescence, 38,* 735–747. Retrieved from http://europepmc.org/abstract/MED/15053498/reloadD0;jsessionidDQu1O M0xuuxrjUoOkwuKj.18.

45. Solberg, M., & Olweus, D. (2003). Prevalence estimation of school bullying with the Olweus Bully/Victim Questionnaire. *Aggressive Behavior, 29,* 239–268. doi: 10.1002/ab.10047.

46. Sugimura, N., & Rudolph, K. D. (2012). Temperamental differences in children's reactions to peer victimization. *Journal of Clinical Child & Adolescent Psychology, 41,* 314–328. doi: 10.1080/15374416.2012.656555.

47. Swearer, S. M., Espelage, D. L., & Napolitano, S. A. (2009). *Bullying prevention and intervention: Realistic strategies for schools.* New York, NY: Guilford Press.

48. Swearer, S. M., & Givens, J. E. (2006, March). *Designing an alternative to suspension for middle school bullies.* Paper presented at the annual convention of the National Association of School Psychologists, Anaheim, CA.

49. Swearer, S. M., Wang, C., Collins, A., Strawhun, J., & Fluke, S. (2014). Bullying: A school mental health perspective. In M. D. Weist, N. A. Lever, C. P. Bradshaw, & J. S. Owens (Eds.), *Handbook of school mental health: Research, training, practice, and policy* (2nd ed., pp. 341–354). New York, NY: Springer.

50. Williams, K., & Guerra, N. (2007). Prevalence and predictors of Internet bullying. *Journal of Adolescent Health* [Supplement], *41* S14–S21. doi: 10.1016/j. jadohealth.2007.08.018.

51. Youngblade, L. M., Theokas, C., Schulenberg, J., Curry, L., Huang, I., & Novak, M. (2007). Risk and promotive factors in families, schools, and communities: A contextual model of positive youth development in adolescence. *Pediatrics, 119,* S47–53. doi: 10.1542/peds .2006-2089H.

THEORY IN ACTION—ARTICLE QUESTIONS

1. Using the constructs of SCT, how is bullying behavior learned?
2. Using the concept of reciprocal determinism as the basis, what are the environmental and personal factors that contribute to bullying behavior?
3. What suggestions are given for the development of effective bullying prevention interventions?
4. How did your explanation for bullying behavior compare to the one presented in the article?
5. How did your ideas for a prevention intervention compare with the suggestions in the article?

▶ Chapter References

Abraido-Lanza, A. F., Viladrich, A., Florez, K. R., Cespedes, A., Aguirre, A. N., & DrLaCruz, A. A. (2007). Commentary: Fatalism reconsidered: A cautionary note for health-related research and practices with Latino populations. *Ethnicity & Disease, 17*, 153–158.

Anderson, E. S., Winett, R. A., & Wojkcik, J. R. (2007). Self-regulation, self-efficacy, outcome expectations, and social support: Social cognitive theory and nutrition behavior. *Annals of Behavioral Medicine, 34*(3), 304–312.

Annesi, J. (2011). Self-regulatory skills usage strengthens the relations of self-efficacy for improved eating, exercise and weigh in severely obese: Toward an explanatory model. *Behavioral Medicine, 37*, 71–76. doi:10.1080/08964289.2011.579643

Bandura, A. (1977). *Social learning theory.* Englewood Cliffs, NJ: Prentice-Hall.

Bandura, A. (1986). *Social foundations of thought and action: A social cognitive theory.* Englewood Cliffs, NJ: Prentice-Hall.

Bandura, A. (1991). Social cognitive theory of self-regulation. *Organizational Behavior, 50*, 248–287.

Bandura, A. (1993). Perceived self-efficacy in cognitive development and functioning. *Educational Psychologist, 28*(2), 117–148.

Bandura, A. (2001). Social cognitive theory: An agentic perspective. *Annual Review of Psychology, 52*, 1–26.

Bandura, A. (2004). Health promotion by social cognitive means. *Health Education and Behavior, 31*(2), 143–164. doi:10.1177/1090198104263660

Bandura, A. (2005). The evolution of social cognitive theory. In K. G. Smith & M. A. Hitt (Eds.), *Great minds in management* (pp. 9–35). Oxford, UK: Oxford University Press.

Bandura, A., Ross, D., & Ross, S. A. (1961). Transmission of aggression through imitation of aggressive models. *The Journal of Abnormal and Social Psychology, 63*(3), 575–582.

Bandura, A., & Walters, R. H. (1959). *Adolescent aggression.* New York, NY: Ronald Press.

Borrayo, E. A., & Guarnaccia, C. A. (2002). Differences in Mexican-born and U.S.-born women of Mexican descent regarding factors related to breast cancer screening behaviors. *Health Care for Women International, 21*(7), 599–614.

Burnett, A. J., Sabato, T. M., Walter, K. O., Kerr, D. L., Wagner, L., & Smith, A. (2013). The influence of attributional style on substance use and risky sexual behavior among college students. *College Student Journal, 47*, 122–136.

Carr, L. J., Dunsiger, S. I., Lewis, B., Ciccolo, J. T., Hartman, S., Bock, B., … Marcus, B. H. (2013). Randomized controlled trial testing an internet physical activity intervention for sedentary adults. *Health Psychology, 32*(3), 328–336. doi:10.1037/a0028962

Chen, S. H., Cheng, H. Y., Chuang, Y. H., & Shao, J. H. (2015). Nutritional status and its health-related factors among older adults in rural and urban areas. *Journal of Advanced Nursing, 71*(1), 42–53. doi:10.1111/jan.12462

Connor, J. P., Gullo, M. J., Feeney, G. F. X., Kavanagh, D. J., & Young, R. M. (2013). The relationship between cannabis outcome expectancies and cannabis refusal self-efficacy in a treatment population. *Addiction Research Report, 109*, 111–119. doi:10.1111/add.12366

De Jesus, M. (2016). How religiosity shapes health perceptions and behaviors of Latina immigrants: Is it an enabling or prohibitive factor? *Psychology, Health & Medicine, 21*(1), 128–133. doi:10.1080/13548506.205.1040031

Diker, A., Cunningham-Sabo, L., Bachman, K., Stacey, J. E., Walters, L. M., & Wells, L. (2013). Nutrition educator adoption and implementation of an experiential foods curriculum. *Journal of Nutrition Education and Behavior, 45*(6), 499–509. doi:10.1016/j.jneb.2013.07.001

Eastin, A., & Sharma, M. (2015). Using social cognitive theory to predict breastfeeding in African-American women. *American Journal of Health Studies, 30*(4), 196–202.

Gellert, P., Ziegelmann, J. P., & Schwarzer, R. (2012). Affective and health-related outcome expectancies for physical activity in older adults. *Psychology and Health, 27*(7), 816–828.

Gilles, D. M., Turk, C. L., & Fresco, D. M. Social anxiety, alcohol expectancies, and self-efficacy as predictors of heavy drinking in college students. *Addictive Behaviors, 31*, 388–398. doi:10.1016/j.addbeh.2005.05.020

Grusec, J. E. (1992). Social learning theory and developmental psychology: The legacies of Robert Sears and Albert Bandura. *Developmental Psychology, 28*(5), 776–786.

Guntzviller, L. M., King, A. J., Jensen, J. D., & Davis, L. A. (2017). Self-efficacy, health literacy, and nutrition and exercise behaviors in a low income, Hispanic population. *Journal of Immigrant Minority Health, 19*, 489–493. doi:10.1007/s10903-016-0384-4

Hamilton, K., Vayro, C., & Schwarzer, R. (2015). Social cognitive antecedents of fruits and vegetable consumption in truck drivers: A sequential mediation analysis. *Journal of Nutrition Education and Behavior, 47*(4), 379–384. doi:10.1016/j.jneb.2015.04.325

Johnson, M. B. (2012). A systemic social-cognitive perspective on doping. *Psychology of Sport and Exercise, 13*, 317–323. doi:10.1016/j.psychspot.2011.12.007

LeCheminant, J. D., & Merrill, R. M. (2012). Improved health behaviors persist over two years for employees in a worksite wellness program. *Population Health Management, 15*(5), 261–266. doi:10.1089/pop.2011.0083

Levenson, H. (1974). Activism and powerful others: Distinctions within the concept of internal–external control. *Journal of Personality Assessment, 38*, 377–383.

Madden, M. H., Tomsik, P., Terchek, J., Navacruz, L., Reichsman, A., Clark, T.C., ... Werner, J. J. (2011). Keys to successful diabetes self-management for uninsured patients: Social support, observational learning, and turning points: A safety net providers' strategic alliance study. *Journal of the American Medical Association, 103*(3), 257–261.

Magoc, D., Tomaka, J., Shamaley, A. G., & Bridges, A. (2016). Gender differences in physical activity and related beliefs among Hispanic college students. *Hispanic Journal of Behavioral Sciences, 38*(2), 279–290. doi:10.1177/0739986316637355

Mailey, E. L., Philips, S. M., Dlugonski, D., & Conroy, D. E. (2016). Overcoming barriers to exercise among parents: A social cognitive theory perspective. *Journal of Behavioral Medicine, 39*, 599–609. doi:10.1007/s10865-016-9744-8

Miller, G., Sharma, M., Brown, D., & Shahbazi, M. (2015). Using social cognitive theory to predict intention to smoke in middle school students. *American Journal of Health Studies, 30*(2), 59–65.

Moore, E. W. (2014). Assessing God locus of control as a factor in college students' alcohol use and sexual behavior. *Journal of American College Health, 68*(8), 578–587. doi:10.1080/07448481.2014.947994

Pajares, F. (2004). Overview of social cognitive theory and of self-efficacy. Retrieved November 16, 2016, from https://www.uky.edu/~eushe2/Pajares/eff.html

Pollard, S. L., Zachary, D. A., Wingert, K., Booker, S. S., & Surkan, P. J. (2014). Family and community influences on diabetes-related dietary change in a low-income urban neighborhood. *The Diabetes Educator, 40*(4), 462–469. doi:10.1177/0145721714527520

Priest, H. M., Knowlden, A. P., & Sharma, M. (2015). Social cognitive theory predictors of human papillomavirus vaccination intentions of college men at a southern university. *International Quarterly of Community Health Education, 35*(4), 371–385. doi:10.1177/0272684X15583289

Rawl, S. M., Champion, V. L., Menon, U., & Foster, J. L. (2000). The impact of age and race on mammography practices. *Health Care for Women International, 21*(7), 583–598.

Ross, S. W., & Horner, R. H. (2009). Bully prevention in positive behavior support. *Journal of Applied Behavior Analysis, 42*(4), 747–759.

Ryan, M. P. (2005). Physical activity levels in young adult Hispanics and whites: Social cognitive theory determinants. *Psychology and Health, 20*(6), 709–727.

Sharif, S. P. (2017). Locus of control, quality of life, anxiety, and depression among Malaysian breast cancer patients: The mediating role of uncertainty. *European Journal of Oncology Nursing, 27*, 28–35. doi:10.1016/j.ejon.2017.01.005

Shelton, P., Weinrich, S., & Reynolds, W. A. (1999). Barriers to prostate cancer screening in African-American men. *Journal of National Black Nurses Association, 10*(2), 14–28.

Smith, D. M., Whitworth, M., Sibley, C., Taylor, W., Gething, J., Chmiel, C., & Lavender, T. (2010). The design of a community lifestyle program to improve the physical and psychological well-being of pregnant women with a BMI of 30 kg/m^2 or more. *BMC Public Health, 10*(284), 1–10. doi:10.1186/1471-2458-10-284

Staiano, A. E., Marker, A. M., Frelier, J. M., Hsia, D. S., & Martin, C. K. (2016). Influence of screen-based peer modeling on preschool children's vegetable consumption and preferences. *Journal of Nutrition Education and Behavior, 48*(5), 331–335. doi:10.1016/j.jneb.2016.02.005

Steptoe, A., & Wardle, J. (2001). Locus of control and health behaviour revisited: A multivariate analysis of young adults from 18 countries. *British Journal of Psychology, 92*, 659–672.

Swearer, S., Wang, C., Berry, B., & Myers, Z. R. (2014). Reducing bullying: Application of social cognitive theory. *Theory into Practice, 53*, 271–277. doi:10.1080/00405841.2014.947221

Ward, J., DeCastro, A. B., Tsai, J. H., Linker, D., Hildahl, L., & Miller, M. E. (2010). An injury prevention strategy for teen restaurant workers. *American Association of Occupational Health Nurses Journal, 58*(2), 57–65. doi:10.3928/08910162-20100127-01

U.S. Department of Health and Human Services and U.S. Department of Agriculture. (2015, December). *2015–2020 Dietary Guidelines for Americans* (8th ed.). Retrieved from http://health.gov/dietaryguidelines/2015/guidelines

CHAPTER 9
Diffusion of Innovation

STUDENT LEARNING OUTCOMES

After reading this chapter the student will be able to:

- Explain the concept of Diffusion of Innovation.
- Discuss the characteristics of an innovation.
- Discuss time relative to innovation adoption.
- Identify communication channels used in diffusion.
- Identify social systems through which innovations diffuse.
- Use the theory to explain the adoption of one health behavior.

DIFFUSION OF INNOVATION ESSENCE SENTENCE

Behavior changes as innovations are adopted.

Constructs

Innovation: The new idea, product, process, or thing
Communication channels: How an innovation is made known to members of the social system
Social system: The group structure into which an innovation is introduced
Time: How long it takes different segments of a social system to adopt an innovation

▶ In the Beginning

Diffusion of innovation is a communication theory rooted in ruralsociology (Valente & Rogers, 1995). In the 1920s, research supported by the U.S. Department of Agriculture was conducted to determine the effectiveness of the different methods used to inform farmers of new (innovative) farming practices (Wilson, 1927). This type of research continued into the 1930s with studies on how a variety of other innovations (postage stamps, limits on municipal taxation rates, and compulsory school laws) were shared and eventually accepted (Pemberton, 1936; Valente & Rogers, 1995).

Building on this, research done in 1943 on the diffusion of hybrid corn seed by Ryan and Gross (1943) laid the foundation for an understanding of how new practices (innovation) were spread into society; that is, how innovation diffuses. What prompted Ryan and Gross's research was the unexpected reaction of farmers to hybrid corn seed. Since the hybrid seed increased crop yield and produced hardier, drought-resistant corn, farmers were expected to quickly switch to the new seed. However, this isn't what happened. Instead, it took seven years on average for a farmer to go from trying the hybrid seed to planting 100% of his land with it. Obviously, something other than economics was at the root of this seemingly irrational behavior (Rogers, 2004; Ryan & Gross, 1943). What Ryan and Gross (1943; Valente & Rogers, 1995) found was that the spread of the hybrid corn innovation was a *social* process that resulted from interpersonal communication—that is, one farmer tried it because another farmer told him he had already tried it and liked it. Diffusion of innovation provided the explanation for the farmers' slow adoption of the new type of seed. From this research came four main aspects of diffusion: the innovation-decision process, the role and source of the communication channel, the normal distribution curve or the rate of adoption, and the characteristics of people who adopt an innovation at the various rates (Valente & Rogers, 1995).

▶ Theory Concept

Diffusion of innovation is the process by which new ideas (innovations) are disseminated (diffused) and adopted by a society. As new ideas are adopted and integrated into the society—that is, they become the norm—behavior changes.

▶ Theory Constructs

How a new idea spreads through a society, and why some become part of the social fabric and others do not, can be explained by the four main constructs of this theory: the innovation, the channels through which it is communicated, time, and the social system. Diffusion is the process by which this takes place (Rogers, 2003).

Innovation

An innovation is something new or novel, whether it is a device, a practice, or an idea. Diffusion and ultimate adoption (or rejection) of an innovation is affected by certain characteristics of the innovation itself. These characteristics include having an advantage over what is already available, compatibility with social norms and values, trial on a limited basis, ease of use, and having observable results. Innovations with these characteristics are adopted more rapidly than those without them (Rogers, 2003; Rogers & Scott, 1997) (**FIGURE 9.1**). Pedometers, contact lenses, *in vitro* fertilization, sun screen, nicotine patches, MRIs, stents, and hearing aides are all examples of things that started out as innovations and ended up being part of our everyday lives.

FIGURE 9.1 Innovation.
© Mastertasso/Shutterstock

Relative Advantage

An innovation has a greater chance of adoption if it is better than what is already out there or if it fills a void where nothing else similar exists. In either case, the innovation has a relative advantage over what is currently available.

Although the toothbrush has been around for years, the electric toothbrush is an innovation with a number of advantages. It removes more plaque, is easier to use for people with poor or limited dexterity, is gentler on gums and tooth enamel (because less pressure is applied than is with a manual toothbrush), and because it usually has a timer, it encourages brushing for the recommended 2 minutes.

Another example is "candy" calcium supplements. Standard calcium supplements are relatively large pills that are taken, on average, two to three times a day. Changing the calcium delivery system from a large pill to a candy-like formulation was an innovation with a relative advantage. Eating a piece of chocolate "candy" twice a day is much more appealing than swallowing a bunch of large pills.

While restaurants serving locally grown foods would not have been viewed as an innovation 100 years ago, this is an innovation today. The advantages of using locally grown foods over foods sourced from large-scale agri-businesses include better taste, freshness, variety, and sometimes price (Inwood, Sharp, Moore, & Stinner, 2009).

With so much attention being given to the adoption of environmentally sustainable practices, the advantages to adoption of these has not been lost on the hotel and resort industry. While the relative advantage may not always be directly related to health, anything that supports good environmental stewardship is welcomed. In this case, the relative advantage of environmental sustainable practices is avoidance of regulatory penalties. Hotels are required to follow practices that minimize negative environmental impact. The fines associated with not following these regulations are expected to increase in the years to come; thus adoption of environmentally sustainable practices would go a long way in avoiding these (Smerecnik & Andersen, 2011).

In 1996 when the Pharmacy-based Vaccination Program began, it was an innovation. By 2009, every state in the country allowed pharmacists to vaccinate (Chun, Sautter, Patterson, & McGhan, 2016). Think about the relative advantage of this innovation. Prior to this, influenza vaccination was only available at a healthcare provider's office or a clinic. It required an appointment and a special trip to the facility. Being able to get vaccinated at a local pharmacy or at the pharmacy in a large grocery store, without an appointment, were advantages over what was previously available. Convenience is the advantage.

An interesting innovation that has not taken hold to the extent it should or could have, even though at first look it seems to have a relative advantage, is entomophagy, or insect eating. Insects are a good source of protein. They don't take much land, water, or labor to grow. They also don't take much in terms of feed compared to the amount of edible protein we can get from them (Costa-Neto, 2013).

Since entomophagy can be considered a "failed innovation" let's look at why from the perspective of relative advantage. First, it fares poorly when compared to existing food technology. It is not associated with a position of status, and in fact in countries and cultures where insects are eaten, it is usually looked down upon and seen as something for the rural poor or primitive (Costa-Neto, 2013).

Another major disadvantage of this innovation is a lack of availability. Insects are not on the supermarket shelf. People who do eat them often buy them at a pet store, fish bait shop, or order them online (Meyer-Rochow & Chakravorty, 2013). Can you think of other reasons why this innovation hasn't "taken off?"

Trialability

It is advantageous if an innovation can be used on a trial basis or limited scale. If people can try something new without making a major commitment to it in terms of time, money, or effort there is a better chance of it being adopted. This is why companies make trial sizes of new products and offer coupons.

Take vision correction, for example. If you decide to switch from glasses to contact lenses, there is a trial period before you make a commitment to using them and buy a year's supply. Even then, you can switch back and forth between the contacts and glasses. On the other hand, you can't try Lasik vision correction because Lasik is corrective surgery that permanently changes the shape of the cornea (Food and Drug Administration [FDA], 2004).

A classic example of trialability is the practice of pharmaceutical companies giving physicians free samples. Free samples promote physician adoption of medication, and when samples are given to patients, it promotes their adoption as well (Kane & Mittman, 2002).

Food companies use this all of the time to get you to try their products by giving away free samples. The next time you're in a grocery store, be aware of the "free samples" being offered. Most times, it's for a new processed food product; rarely is it for fresh fruits and vegetables.

Looking at the pharmacist vaccination innovation again, trialability of this is obvious. People can easily try it once and if they don't like it, they can go to their healthcare provider's office or clinic the following year.

Complexity

An innovation's complexity will also affect its likelihood of adoption. The more complex it is to understand and use, the less likely it is to be adopted or even tried. A prime example of this is the female condom. They are not easy to use the first time (Piot, 1998). They require proper placement before and during sex and careful removal afterwards. Unless a woman feels she can insert the condom, keep it in place, and remove it correctly, the odds of her using it after the first time are not good, nor are the chances of it being adopted (Hollander, 2004).

In contrast, the nicotine patch is relatively simple to use. Choose an area of skin on the upper body that is free from hair, intact, and dry. Open the package, peel the protective covering off the patch, and apply it to the skin. Pretty simple.

In 2007, the Centers for Disease Control and Prevention encouraged people to adopt an innovative technique to reduce disease transmission through droplet infection from sneezing or coughing. It calls for people to sneeze and cough into their upper sleeve instead of into their hands or into the air (Centers for Disease Control and Prevention [CDC], 2007; Lounsbury, 2006). This is not a complex innovation. It requires no special training, equipment, or practice. Anyone can use it.

Adoption of sustainable practices at hotels and ski resorts is predicated on their ease of implementation. In fact, ease of implementing sustainable practices is the most significantly related variable in the prediction of their adoption (Smerecnik & Andersen, 2011). The easier it is for resorts to put an innovation in place, the greater the likelihood they will (**FIGURE 9.2**).

A peer HIV education intervention addressed innovation complexity by providing opportunities for peer educators to practice making dental dams from condoms (Winter, 2013). This helped them convey the message to other students that it was easy to do and enabled them to demonstrate how easy it was.

FIGURE 9.2 Complexity affects adoption.
© doglikehorse/Shutterstock

Sometimes there can be a misperception about how complex a group of people might judge an innovation to be. When a home telecare system was implemented in the Netherlands approximately 10 years ago, there was concern about how well it would be accepted, given that it was intended for the elderly and chronically ill. Home telecare is an audio-visual connection between a person living at home and a healthcare provider using communication technology (Peeters, DeVeer, van der Hoek, & Francke, 2012).

Interestingly, even though older people are not generally computer savvy or technologically adept, those using the home telecare system did not find it complicated. When asked to rate their agreement with four statements about the complexity of home telecare, they had an average score of 4.06 on a 1–5 scale of agreement, with 1 being disagree and 5 being agree. The statements were: It's easy for me to use the technology, I can easily make contact with the home telecare system, I can clearly see the home telecare nurses, I can clearly hear the home telecare nurses (Peeters et al., 2012). The lesson learned here is that complexity is in the mind of the user!

Compatibility

To be adopted, an innovation needs to be compatible with the existing values and needs of the people, culture, or social environment (Rogers, 2003). Certainly in the case of the female condom, its adoption would not likely occur among women whose culture considers touching one's own genitals taboo or whose religious beliefs prohibit contraception.

Incompatibility with social norms was one of the issues at the heart of HIV/AIDS prevention in Tanzania, a country with one of the highest rates of AIDS in the world. Although most infections were transmitted horizontally (adult to adult) through heterosexual intercourse, a substantial number of infants were infected through vertical transmission (from infected mother to child). Consequently, one of the interventions tried was aimed at preventing transmission of HIV through breast milk (Burke, 2004; Israel-Ballard et al., 2005).

Although the solution to this problem seems obvious—just have mothers use formula—it wasn't that easy. The majority of Tanzanian women breastfed their children until 2 years of age because it was expected of them. Even HIV-positive women were expected to breastfeed. Consequently, women who did not breastfeed were stigmatized. However, there was a way to reduce the risk of HIV transmission in breast milk; namely, by heat treating. Heat treating destroys HIV in breast milk without significantly changing its nutrient content (Burke, 2004; Israel-Ballard et al., 2005). But heat treating breast milk requires the mother to express her milk and then heat it using one of two simple methods. Although heat treating is effective, simple to do, and still allows the mother to feed her child breast milk, expressing breast milk was taboo and incompatible with local practices and beliefs (Burke, 2004).

Although originally introduced in the 1980s, hand sanitizers were not considered socially acceptable at the time. If a business provided them for its customers, questions were raised about the cleanliness of the establishment. Times have changed, and people are now more germ phobic. Today, if a business offers hand sanitizers, customers are grateful (Yee, 2007). Hand sanitizers are now available in a host of places—from supermarkets (to wipe off cart handles) to fast-food restaurants and children's playgrounds. People carry personal-sized containers of sanitizer in their purses, briefcases, and backpacks. It is almost to the point now where *not* using a hand sanitizer is socially unacceptable.

An interesting situation of innovation compatibility was discovered in regard to the adoption of transportation cycling—bicycling as a mode of transportation rather than solely as a form of exercise. As it turns out, women see cycling for transportation as a "male" behavior, and less socially acceptable for them (Nehme, Perez, Ranjit, Amick, & Kohl, 2016).

Observability

If the results of using an innovation can be seen by other people, it is more likely to be adopted. Think about the rate of adoption of breast augmentation, tattoos, and body piercing. Observability may explain why these have become so widely adopted. Observability drives the diet industry. People try new diets because if they work, the results are noticeable.

Observability has affected health care as well. Early on, chiropractic care was something novel, an innovation. It was a different way to treat illness. Its adoption was largely based on word of mouth and improvement observed by others (McCarthy & Milus, 2000). The same situation occurred with acupuncture. While it was first seen as something novel (although it dates back 2500 years in China), it is now an accepted treatment option, especially for chronic pain management. Its results are observable (Eshkevari & Heath, 2005) in that many people who had limited mobility prior to treatment are active after.

Observability was key for an intervention aimed at increasing student participation in an existing school breakfast program. The innovations included changing the breakfast menu to include grab-n-go items, moving the location of the breakfast service to the school entry way, and allowing students to eat in the hallways. As a result, lines of students formed at the main entrance of the school which increased visibility and participation (Haesly, Nanney, Coulter, Fong, & Pratt, 2014).

Communication Channel

Diffusion is the active sharing or communication of information among people. It is a social process: people talking to one another about a new idea, product, tool, food, and so on (Haider & Kreps, 2004; Rogers, 2003). The communication channel is how word of an innovation spreads.

The most effective and rapid means of communicating something new is through mass media—television, newspapers, radio, and online. Mass media is a one way communication channel that can reach a huge audience very quickly, making a large portion of a society readily aware of a new product or idea.

As appealing as this method is to get the message out, it is often not the best means of ensuring adoption of an innovation. Sometimes, one-on-one conversation is more effective. For example, one person tries a new product, and she talks with a friend about it, who then talks to another friend, and so on. This is demonstrative of diffusion as a social process that relies on interpersonal communication (Rogers, 2003). Today, social media plays an integral role in spreading the message about something new from person to person.

Interpersonal communication and the transfer of information about ideas occur most frequently between two people who are the same, or *homophilius*, meaning they share the same beliefs, education level, or socioeconomic level, to name but a few characteristics (Rogers, 2003). A friend talking to friends would have a greater impact on the latter trying something new that the former has already tried (**FIGURE 9.3**). Thus, the likelihood of an innovation being adopted also depends on how people find out about it, and from whom.

Restaurants implementing the "innovation" of local food sourcing utilize the wait staff as an integral component of the communication channel. They are the ones who interact with consumers and can educate them, one-on-one, about the restaurant's use of local foods and can encourage them to try meals prepared with the ingredients (Inwood et al., 2009).

A program in Zambia aimed at reducing the incidence of malaria among children attending one particular school identified community health workers as the primary communication channel to get the word out about using long-lasting insecticide treated mosquito nets (LLINs) on beds. After a two week training, the Zambian community health workers went into the school to teach the children about malaria prevention using the bed nets and gave them to the children to bring home. The children then became the communication channel through which the parents were made aware of bed nets (Steury, 2013).

Multiple communication channels were used to disseminate an innovative set of nursing practice guidelines aimed at preventing multidrug resistant tuberculosis in hospitals. They included half day workshops, individual and group discussions, and follow-up visits. Conferences, practices sessions, seminars, journal publications, and targeted mailings are other possible channels that could also have been used (Anowar, Petchetchian, Isaramalai, & Klainin-Yobas, 2013).

FIGURE 9.3 Friends talking with friends is an effective means of diffusing information about an innovation.

© Phil Date/Shutterstock

Time

How long it takes different segments of a social system to adopt or reject an innovation is the result of the innovation-decision process. This process takes time because it follows a sequence of steps that includes knowledge, persuasion, decision, implementation, and confirmation (Rogers, 2003).

The Innovation-Decision Process

Knowledge. Common sense tells us that before people can adopt an innovation, they have to know it exists. Knowledge of an innovation is where the communication channels come into play, as discussed previously. Think about how the general public was made aware of the pharmaceutical innovation for erectile dysfunction. Advertisements in magazines, newspapers, TV, direct mail, and disclosure by well-known public figures were all used to inform us about a pharmaceutical innovation to treat a problem many people did not even know existed.

This same thing is happening now with Pseudobulbar Affect or PBA, a neurological condition that happens after a stroke or other type of brain injury. Symptoms of PBA are typically uncontrolled laughing or crying—which is often confused with depression (National Stroke Association, 2016). While this is not a new aliment, pharmaceutical treatment for it is being advertised on mass media, so the general population is now becoming aware of it.

In 2006, a vaccine against human papillomavirus (HPV) that protects against cervical cancer was introduced for girls and young women aged 9 to 26. Prior to its release, the pharmaceutical company that developed the vaccine began a multimedia "Tell Someone" disease awareness campaign. The campaign was designed to raise awareness of the relationship between HPV and cervical cancer, preparing the U.S. market for the vaccine's release (O'Malley, 2006). Once parents, teens, and young women were aware of the vaccine's availability, they were able to decide if they would adopt the innovation, that is, be vaccinated. (Unfortunately, the campaign failed to mention that HPV is a sexually transmitted infection and that there are other ways to prevent or reduce infection (O'Malley, 2006).)

Although the effects of global warming are being felt by everyone across the globe, Africa is particularly vulnerable. In the next few years, it's predicted that usable land for crops will diminish, growing seasons will change, and the yield of rain fed crops will decline. The innovation needed to address this issue and change behavior is adoption of the scientific fact of global warming. Even though a study of the population in one particular area of South Africa found that many were aware of global warming and how they contribute to it, some had inaccurate information and others didn't know the actions they could take to mitigate it. To support adoption of the innovation, targeted mass media messages were developed to correct the inaccuracies and increase knowledge (Santos, 2012).

Persuasion. During the persuasion stage, people develop an attitude (either positive or negative) about the innovation (Haider & Kreps, 2004; Rogers, 2003). This comes from having knowledge of or information about the innovation and then mentally applying it to a present or future situation. It is a thought process people go through that helps them formulate a perception of the innovation (Rogers, 2003). It's like trying the innovation on, so to speak.

A positive attitude was characteristic of the non governmental Canadian health agencies and food retailers that partnered with and adopted Health Canada's Eating Well Campaign. This innovation used a social media approach to address childhood obesity. Health organizations with reserve attitudes toward Health Canada and limited exposure to the social media channels used to diffuse the campaign (Fernandez et al., 2016) were not as readily persuaded to adopt it. Understanding what influences or persuades an organization, a group of people, or an individual to adopt an innovation can go a long way in supporting its successful diffusion.

During the persuasion stage of adopting bicycling as a means of transportation, people think about riding to a destination, but haven't actually done it. They are still in the process of forming attitudes toward biking as transportation rather than for exercise or as a leisure time activity. Given that women tend to view bike transportation as less compatible with who they are (e.g., I'm not the kind of person that rides a bike for transportation) and see it as a male behavior, their attitudes would be less favorable toward innovation adoption (Nehme et al., 2016).

Persuasion was used when a hospital administration wanted to implement an innovative screening program for domestic violence in a postpartum clinic. The clinic staff had to be persuaded of the benefits and appropriateness of the program. They had to be given information that would help them develop a positive attitude toward asking new mothers questions about domestic violence right after they delivered their babies. This was accomplished by having staff engage in training activities that made domestic violence real to them through dialogue with survivors, sharing their own stories, and clinical storytelling (Janssen, Holt, & Sugg, 2002).Sometimes, opinion leaders are the ones who need to be persuaded about the benefits of an innovation in order to gain access to the people who would be helped most by the innovation. This is what happened in rural Haiti when HIV/AIDS education was first introduced. The trusted, influential opinion leaders were voodoo practitioners. They had to be persuaded that preventing HIV/AIDS was easier than trying to cure it. Once these influential people adopted the idea of prevention, they made people in the rural villages accessible, and the message of HIV/AIDS prevention was passed along. (Unfortunately, funding for this project was terminated because "the U.S. government objected to the involvement of voodoo practitioners in the project" (Barker, 2004, p. 133).)

Decision. Once people have knowledge of an innovation and have developed an attitude toward it, they engage in activities that result in their decision to adopt or reject the innovation (Rogers, 2003). This is similar to decisional balance in the Transtheoretical Model.

To support adoption of the postpartum violence program discussed earlier, the program developers provided opportunities for the staff to observe assessments being conducted. Watching new mothers respond in a positive, nonjudgmental way to questions about domestic violence (Janssen et al., 2002) helped the staff decide to adopt the violence assessment.

Let's look at "candy" calcium supplements. Before this method of delivery can be adopted, people need to know about this innovative way to take a mineral supplement and they need a good attitude about eating candy. Trying the supplements would be the activity that would result in the decision to adopt or reject the innovation.

Sometimes, however, even if people decide that an innovation is a good idea, they still decide not to adopt it. Reasons for rejection of an innovation that clearly is beneficial might be cost, conflict with values and beliefs, logistics, or lack of skill needed to use the innovation. For example, even though taking calcium in candy form might be seen as a terrific idea, especially after trying it, it still may not be adopted because it is much more expensive than taking calcium in pill form.

Implementation. The implementation stage occurs when the innovation is tried. Obviously, before people adopt something new, they have to try it to see if they like it. You may have decided that a hybrid car is a terrific innovation, and that you'd like one. But, before you buy a hybrid, you'll take one for a test drive. Your test drive will result in you either buying the car (adoption), not buying the car (rejection), or adding or changing some of the options on the car (reinvention).

In supporting adoption of bicycling as a mode of transportation, having people take a social ride to a neighborhood event is the test drive, or trial. If the experience is pleasant, it could lead to them using a bike for transportation to a destination (Nehme et al., 2016). But this doesn't necessarily mean they'll bike commute to work. It may mean they'll ride to a local store or to the coffee shop to meet friends, which is an improvement over taking the car. If the trial experience was not a good one, it may mean they put their bikes back into storage or sell them.

Sometimes, even though people decide an innovation is good, they don't try it and consequently don't adopt it. For example, Internet-based cardiac recovery (rehabilitation) interventions are a new way to serve the needs of those who cannot, or who choose not to attend in-person programs. However, some cardiac clients will not try it, even though they may have decided the idea is good. The reasons are many, including lack of access to a computer, inability to operate a keyboard, and inadequate health literacy (Nguygen, Carrieri-Kohlman, Rankin, Slaughter, & Stubarg, 2004).

While the potential is great to prevent Fetal Alcohol Spectrum Disorders by identifying at risk pregnant women in primary care offices, healthcare providers often don't recognize substance abuse problems or intervene appropriately when they do (Zoorob, Aliyu, & Hayes, 2010). To address this, a brief alcohol intervention (BAI) was developed for use with all women receiving Women, Infant and Children (WIC) services at two Illinois health departments. The intervention consists of two questionnaires, one to identify at-risk and problem drinking, the other to explore tolerance to alcohol and lifetime issues with alcohol or other addiction (Moise, Green, Toth, & Muhall, 2014).

The intervention evaluation showed staff perceptions at both health departments were favorable. However, it also showed that the screening questions made them feel uncomfortable when responses to the initial questions established there was no at-risk drinking problems, but they were still required to continue with the reminder of the questions. Consequently, the screening questionnaire was revised, a feedback mechanism was developed to address staff concerns, and training, technical assistance, and implementation adjustments were made to take into account the diversity of the health departments and their needs (Moise et al., 2014). If the trial implementation results in unacceptable outcomes or the innovation is too costly, culturally inconsistent, or logistically not feasible, it will be rejected. In the example of HIV/AIDS in rural Haiti discussed earlier, if the voodoo practitioners had not been persuaded that preventing was easier than curing, then promoting HIV/AIDS prevention in the villages would not have been possible.

When implementing online health promotion programs that require registering on a site, privacy concerns have to be addressed. This is especially important with a young adult intervention population (Carter, Corneille, Hall-Byers, Clark, & Younge, 2015.) If privacy is not addressed, it could well result in rejection that has nothing to do with the innovation itself, but rather a technical issue. Nonetheless, the decision would be non adoption.

Confirmation. Sometimes the innovation-decision process is completed once the decision is made to either adopt or reject the innovation. Other times, when the decision is made to adopt, people need reinforcement or confirmation from others that it was a good decision. Conflicting messages about the goodness of their decision causes dissonance, or an uncomfortable state of mind (Rogers, 2003) that comes from having made a decision that continues to be questioned or evaluated. We have all done this at one time or another; we make a decision and then continue to question ourselves and others as to whether the decision was a good one or not.

There are times when the decision to adopt is not supported by others, leading to discontinuance or rejection of the innovation. People also discontinue the use of something that was previously adopted when a better "something" comes along to replace it, or if they are dissatisfied with its performance or outcome (Rogers, 2003). Sometimes, instead of discontinuing use of the innovation in these situations, the innovation is reinvented or modified.

A prime example of discontinuance or rejection of a previously adopted innovation is Project DARE (Drug Abuse Resistance Education). Project DARE was developed in 1983 as a joint effort between the Los Angeles Police Department and the Los Angeles school district as a way to decrease or eliminate drug use among children and adolescents. Its innovation was having uniformed police officers teach children about the perils of drug use. The program focused on resistance, skill training, self-esteem building, information about gangs, and legal issues related to drug use (Singh et al., 2011). There was tremendous interest in and adoption of this way to address a growing drug problem. In fact, by the end of 1999, it had been implemented in at least 75% of school districts in the United States and in 44 other countries (Griffith, 1999). Unfortunately, the program was not effective (Dukes, Stein, & Ullman, 1997; Dukes, Ullman, & Stein, 1996; Lynam et al., 1999; West & O'Neal, 2004).

To address this, DARE was revised (reinvented) in 2003 to focus on the decision making process and factors known to support resiliency in students at-risk for drug abuse. Preliminary results of the new program provided evidence that it is influencing normative beliefs and attitudes toward substance abuse and adoption of refusal skills to resist substance abuse (Singh et al., 2011).

Adoption Curve

In addition to the innovation-decision process, adoption occurs at different rates by different segments of the population. The rate of adoption follows an adoption curve, a bell-shaped curve that sorts people into the following five categories or segments: innovators, early adopters, early majority, late majority, and laggards (**FIGURE 9.4**). These segments reflect the amount of time it takes people to adopt an innovation. Placement on the curve depends on a number of characteristics,

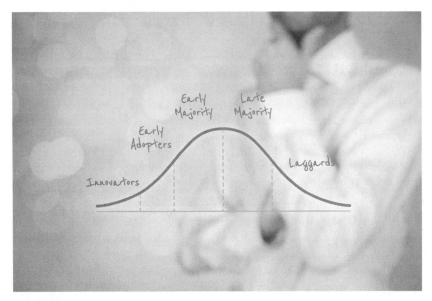

FIGURE 9.4 Adoption of innovation curve.
© Jirsak/Shutterstock

such as comfort with risk taking, socioeconomic status, extent of social networks, and leadership. Where one falls on the adoption curve may differ depending on the innovation.

Innovators

People in the first segment on the curve are the innovators. Innovators represent that small fraction of the population who like to take chances. Innovators are risk takers. They have the financial resources to absorb possible loss from an unprofitable innovation. They are technologically savvy in that they understand and can apply complex technical knowledge, and they can cope with the unpredictability of an innovation (Rogers, 2003).

Innovators are the people who try everything as soon as it is available. They were the first ones to buy an iPod and plasma screen TV, to drive a hybrid, have acupuncture, use solar power, recycle, and eat organic. Innovators tend to be independent, change-oriented risk takers who are inclined to interact with others like themselves rather than a broad cross section of the population. In fact, going back to the Lasik example used earlier, people who are risk takers are considered good candidates for this procedure (FDA, 2004).

Sometimes the innovators are unexpected people. In the case of restaurant use of locally produced food, the innovators were celebrity chefs. They started using locally grown foods in their own restaurants and because of their notoriety, greatly influenced others in the culinary community to follow their lead (Inwood et al., 2009).

In Zambian communities, the township chief is the innovator. If the chief accepts the innovation, then the community members will, too (Steury, 2013).

Knowing this, it makes sense then to initially focus innovation adoption efforts at the chiefs rather than the community members.

Early Adopters

Early adopters make up the next segment on the adoption curve. They represent a slightly larger portion of the population than do the innovators. Early adopters tend to be the opinion leaders in a community. They are well respected and are often seen as role models. They have a powerful influence over others because they are often the people others like to emulate. They usually have high self-esteem and complex communication networks. They talk to and know a lot of different people and therefore have a broad influence in the community (Rogers, 2003) and credibility (Winter, 2013).

Early Majority

The early majority represents one of the largest segments of the population. On the bell curve, they are part of the inclining side of the bell. They are greatly influenced by opinion leaders and mass media. Although they do adopt new things, they do it over time. But, given their sheer number, when they begin to adopt, the innovation becomes mainstream (Rogers, 2003).

Late Majority

The late majority is on the downward side of the bell curve. These people tend to question change and wait until an innovation is an established norm or a social or economic necessity. They tend to have more modest financial resources and to be greatly influenced by their peers (Rogers, 2003). In some societies, the late majority are the social outcasts, the homeless, or those without families (Steury, 2013).

Laggards

The last group on the curve is the laggards. Laggards tend to be conservative and traditional, suspicious of innovation, and risk adverse, with lower self-esteem and less education. They also tend to be geographically mobile and detached from the social environment. Laggards wait a long time before adopting an innovation, even when it's obvious that the innovation is advantageous (Rogers, 2003). These would be the people who just bought their first computer.

Social System

The fourth construct in diffusion of innovation is the social system. A social system can be a number of entities from a few individuals or an informal or formal group of people, to organizations that are interrelated and engaged in solving a joint problem to accomplish a goal (Backer & Rogers, 1998; Rogers, 2003). Examples of social systems are the physicians in a hospital, the families in a community, or consumers in the United States. All units in a social system, whether they are individuals (such as the physicians in the hospital) or a collective entity (such as each family in a community), cooperate with each other to reach a common goal. It is the common goal that holds them together. Social systems are essentially different groupings of people.

As such, they also include the norms, values, beliefs, attitudes, and other common characteristics of the people who comprise the system. Diffusion takes place within these social systems (Rogers, 2003).

Diffusion of an innovation through a social system is exemplified by the CDC's Business Responds to AIDS (BRTA) program. BRTA was a way to bring HIV/AIDS prevention education to the workplace and through this effort, prevent discrimination against people with HIV/AIDS at work. The social system through which this program was diffused included all private companies in the United States (Backer & Rogers, 1998).

The malaria prevention program in Zambia was diffused through the social system of local churches and schools. Trained community health workers educated parents in the local churches and children in the schools (Steury, 2013). The Kitchen Garden Project in the South Central Asian country of Nepal is another example of diffusion of an innovation through a social system. The social system used here was neighborhoods. The project was implemented to combat the country's high infant and maternal mortality rates, which were due mostly to inadequate vitamin A intake. The innovation was to have individual households in neighborhoods plant gardens to grow their own high vitamin A—containing fruits and vegetables (Barker, 2004).

In summary, according to Diffusion of Innovation, the characteristics of an innovation—how it is made known, how long it takes for a decision to be made about it, and the group structure into which it is being introduced—all affect its adoption and, therefore, behavior (**FIGURE 9.5**).

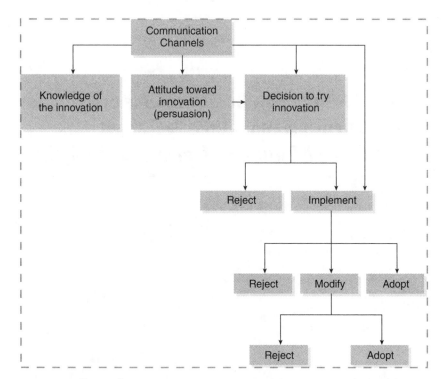

FIGURE 9.5 Diffusion of innovation.

Modified from Rogers, E. (1962). *Diffusion of Innovation*, Fifth Edition. Free Press, Simon & Schuster Adult Publishing Group.

THEORY IN ACTION—CLASS ACTIVITY

Imagine upon graduation, you are hired by a large urban hospital as part of a team responsible for implementing a new telemedicine program for low income, medically underserved African American and Latino communities in the hospital's service area. Part of your job is to market the program to these communities.

Since "telemedicine" is an innovative way to deliver specialty medical care to the underserved communities, you decide to base marketing materials on the Diffusion of Innovation, specifically the characteristics of an innovation.

Telemedicine at your hospital uses telecommunication equipment (video conferencing) and computer technology at specific telemedicine clinics throughout the community to provide specialty care without an in-person visit. The clinics are staffed by physicians' assistants who examine the patients and identify the medical specialist needed to diagnose and treat the problem. The medical specialist is contacted via video conferencing and examinations are done using scopes with cameras, when appropriate.

1.   What information would you include in your marketing materials about:
     Relative advantage
     Complexity
     Trialability
     Compatibility
     Observability
2.   Do you think it would be necessary to develop two sets of marketing materials, one for African-Americans and one for Latinos? Why or why not?

Now, read the following article and answer the questions at the end.

Chapter 9 Article: How Do Low-Income Urban African Americans and Latinos Feel about Telemedicine? A Diffusion of Innovation Analysis[1]

Sheba George,[1] Alison Hamilton,[2] and Richard S. Baker[3]

[1] Center for Biomedical Informatics, Charles R. Drew University of Medicine and Science, 2594 Industry Way, Lynwood, CA 90262, USA
[2] Department of Psychiatry, UCLA and VA Greater Los Angeles Healthcare System, 11301 Wilshire Boulevard, Los Angeles, CA 90073, USA
[3] College of Medicine, Charles R. Drew University of Medicine and Science, 1731 E. 120th Street, Los Angeles, CA 90059, USA

1   Reproduced from George, S., Hamilton, A. & Baker, R. S. (2012). How do low-income urban African-Americans and Latinos feel about telemedicine?: A diffusion of innovation analysis. *International Journal of Telemedicine and Applications*, 2012. doi: 10.1155/2012/715194.

Introduction. Telemedicine is promoted as a means to increase access to specialty medical care among the urban underserved, yet little is known about its acceptability among these populations. We used components of a diffusion of innovation conceptual framework to analyze preexperience perceptions about telemedicine to assess its appeal among urban underserved African Americans and Latinos. *Methods.* Ten focus groups were conducted with African American ($n = 43$) and Latino participants ($n = 44$) in both English and Spanish and analyzed for key themes. *Results.* Both groups perceived increased and immediate access to multiple medical opinions and reduced wait time as relative advantages of telemedicine. However, African Americans expressed more concerns than Latinos about confidentiality, privacy, and the physical absence of the specialist. This difference may reflect lower levels of trust in new health care innovations among African Americans resulting from a legacy of past abuses in the US medical system as compared to immigrant Latinos who do not have this particular historical backdrop. *Conclusions.* These findings have implications for important issues such as adoption of telemedicine, patient satisfaction, doctor-patient interactions, and the development and tailoring of strategies targeted to each of these populations for the introduction, marketing, and implementation of telemedicine.

▶ 1. Introduction

Telemedicine involves using computer information and telecommunication technologies to provide health care when the provider and care recipient are in separate geographic locations. It has been promoted as a vehicle to increase access to specialty care among the urban underserved minorities, yet little is known about its acceptability among such populations. The literature on the adoption and diffusion of new technology, such as telemedicine, suggests that stakeholders' perceptions about a new innovation and the extent to which they see it as a "relative advantage" are central to the rate of diffusion and adoption.[1] The objective of this study is to explore perceptions regarding telemedicine among African Americans and Latinos in South Central Los Angeles.

It is well documented that racial/ethnic minorities and socioeconomically disadvantaged individuals face significant barriers to receiving basic health care.[2-6] African Americans and Latinos make up the largest proportion of minority populations who experience the most severe and concentrated types of health disparities. Much of this disparity in health is thought to be due to lack of timely access to appropriate health care.[3] Medically underserved populations experiencing health disparities tend to be concentrated in either inner city or rural areas. These areas are plagued by low physician-to-population ratios, limited specialty care, and health care facilities that suffer from overcrowding, inadequate infrastructure, and inefficient organizational structures.[2-5, 7-11] Given that the Institute of Medicine's report on quality of health care has already identified illiteracy and distrust of technology as potential barriers to the delivery of telemedicine in urban underserved settings, it is important to assess community perceptions of this technology.[8] South Central Los Angeles serves as a prime example of such an inner city setting, making it an excellent location for a case study.

Telemedicine has been promoted as an innovative approach to bridging the health care delivery gap by increasing access to services for medically underserved communities. The role of telemedicine in facilitating increased access to care has traditionally been framed in terms of its ability to mitigate geographic barriers. Accordingly, remote rural communities have been the primary beneficiaries of telemedicine implementation.[12] However, limited access to appropriate medical care, particularly specialty care, is a major challenge for inner city communities as well.

Although telemedicine has the potential of redressing the health care delivery problems of the inner city, there is little in the existing literature on telemedicine or health care in general that sheds light on perceptions about telemedicine among the general population and, more specifically, the urban underserved population.[9, 10, 13, 14] It is important to examine the concurrence (or divergence) between the medical aims that drive such solutions and "on-the-ground" perceptions of those receiving care, particularly among inner city African American and Latino populations. In a study of an urban urgent care dermatology clinic, while patients generally reported high levels of satisfaction, 36% of the study sample expressed self-consciousness around the camera and 17% were uncomfortable having facial pictures taken.[15] In terms of outcomes, the Informatics for Diabetes Education and Telemedicine (IDEATel) project[5] found that African American and Hispanic American participants were less adherent to the diabetes self-care intervention than white participants, suggesting the need for culturally tailored interventions.[16, 17] The issue of community acceptance of such new techniques has yet to be resolved.

Diffusion of innovation (DOI) theory is useful in understanding the importance of assessing perceptions about a new technology such as telemedicine among a population before its introduction in order to promote likelihood of adoption. Though there are several components to DOI theory, here we focus on its applicability to characteristics of the innovation itself, that is, how an innovation spreads from innovators to others within a social system. Rogers' classic DOI model points to five factors that shape the rate of diffusion of new innovations among stakeholders: (a) the perception of relative advantages, (b) the compatibility with past experiences and existing values, (c) the complexity of the innovation, (d) observability of benefits, and (e) trialability of the innovation on a limited basis. For example, according to this framework, if patients perceive the relative advantages of using telemedicine to be greater than existing options with regard to savings in time/money, increases in comfort, social status, and so forth, they will be more likely to adopt telemedicine. The compatibility factor points to the importance of consistency of telemedicine use with "past experiences, existing values and needs of potential adopters."[18] Whereas the first two factors focus on the stakeholders' needs, experiences, and values, the latter three factors (complexity, observability of benefits, and trialability) focus on aspects of the innovation. It seems important to understand which of these factors maybe most relevant at baseline for specific type of populations within particular geographical contexts vis-à-vis a new innovation in order to best promote the diffusion of the innovation.

Most of the studies that examine patient perceptions about telemedicine tend to question participants on their past experiences of receiving health care through telemedicine.[19, 20] However, preexperience perceptions are important to the success of telemedicine adoption since they shape a patient's initial decision to (a) sample a telemedicine service and (b) use the service on a continual basis.[21] There is scant research on viewpoints about telemedicine among the target population before the introduction of telemedicine. Some exceptions include studies by Bashshur,[22] Brick et al.[23] and Turner et al.[21] The first two studies found that patients do not perceive telemedicine as preferable to seeing a doctor in person, even though they appreciated the usefulness of telemedicine for emergency situations and minor problems. Turner and colleagues found that the greater the perceived relative advantage and the greater the perceived compatibility of the innovation, the greater the intent to adopt it with varying levels of openness depending on the task situation (e.g., their respondents were more open to telemedicine care in emergency situations than for specialist care). However, none of these studies examines the perceptions of urban inner-city populations regarding telemedicine and the specificities of their care contexts.

Given that there is little research on the perceptions about telemedicine among African American and Latino underserved populations, we examined the pretelememedicine perceptions of these groups and the differences between them. In addition to our focus on these two populations, we were interested in identifying the differences between elders in these groups (over 65) and younger adults (parents of school-aged children) since these are the two groups most likely to utilize and benefit from telemedicine services with a clear source of health care reimbursement. We hypothesized that the elderly would be less amenable to the idea of new technology and parents would be more willing to consider trying the technology to meet the needs of their children.

▶ 2. Methods

2.1 Setting: South Central Los Angeles

The research was conducted in South Central Los Angeles, which is home to more than 1.4 million individuals, most of whom are racial/ethnic minorities (62.7% Hispanic, 33.4% African American). South Central is the most socioeconomically disadvantaged community in Los Angeles, with 28% of the population living below the federal poverty level.[24] The population faces several barriers to receiving timely care: in 2005, 40.2% reported that they could not afford to see a physician when needed and 27.5% of adults reported transportation problems as a barrier that kept them from obtaining needed medical care.[25]

2.2 Procedures

Focus group methodology was utilized to explore the range of individual opinions within relatively homogeneous groups (described below), using a standardized set of questions.[26–29] The research team consisted of the authors and two research associates who assisted with the recruitment and moderation of the focus groups.

Community-based recruiting efforts were used to develop a sample population for the focus groups. Flyers about the focus groups were posted in community centers and public housing complexes. Interested individuals called the number on the flyer. When 8–10 individuals from the priority populations (African American and Latino parents of school-aged children and seniors) responded to these efforts, focus groups were assembled (see **TABLE A.1** for group composition). The focus groups took place in community and senior centers. Informed consent was obtained

TABLE A.1 Focus group composition.

	African Americans $N = 43$		Latinos $N = 44$	
	Groups	N	Groups	N
Seniors, $N = 37$ (average age = 67; range 61–83 years)	1	9	6	10
	2	8	7	10
Parents, $N = 50$ (average age = 34; range 21–55 years)	3	7	8	8
	4	9	9	9
	5	10	10	7

Sheba George, Alison Hamilton, and Richard S. Baker, "How Do Low-Income Urban African Americans and Latinos Feel about Telemedicine? A Diffusion of Innovation Analysis," *International Journal of Telemedicine and Applications*, vol. 2012, Article ID 715194, 9 pages, 2012. doi:10.1155/2012/715194

from all participants. All participants completed a background questionnaire and were paid $20 at the end of the focus group.

After introductions, participants were asked for their definitions of the word "telemedicine." After a short discussion, a brief video presentation—a dramatization of a patient, receiving care for ear pain at a telemedicine clinic—was shown to focus group participants. Groups that were Spanish speaking (5 of the 10 groups) were shown a Spanish version of the video. In the video, the patient's ear pain is assessed by a physician's assistant (PA) who contacts an ear, nose and throat (ENT) specialist using videoconferencing. This ENT specialist is depicted as being distant from the clinic; he examines the patient using an otoscope with a camera at the end, which transmits images of the patient's ear to the specialist. All parties (patient, specialist, PA) are able to see each other through videoconferencing technology.

The video was followed by a focus group discussion about participants' reactions to and perceptions about receiving medical care through telemedicine. The moderator used a semistructured interview script that covered reactions to the video, perceived advantages and disadvantages of telemedicine, diagnoses/health conditions for which telemedicine would be appropriate, and general experiences in receiving health care services (**TABLE A.2**).

2.3 Data Analysis

All interviews were audio- and videotaped and transcribed, and all Spanish-language transcripts were translated into English by a professional transcription and translation agency. Atlas, it was used for data analysis. The transcripts were analyzed using the constant comparative method of data analysis.[30] Transcripts were initially deductively coded by the second author with questions from the interview script guiding the predominant themes. These themes were summarized and discussed by the research team, and then the data underwent another level of more inductive coding

TABLE A.2 Focus group script—interview themes and examples of questions*.	
Broad themes	**Example questions**
A telemedicine clinic in your community	(i) How do you feel about it? (ii) How did you form this impression? (iii) From what particular experiences?
Perceived advantages and disadvantages of telemedicine	(i) What are specific benefits? (ii) What are potential challenges? (iii) Would telemedicine address any specific gaps/issues you have with your present form of health care?
Ideal recipients of telemedicine care	(i) Would you use telemedicine yourself? (ii) Would you recommend it to a friend? (iii) Would it be particularly suitable for older people/young children?
Conditions and context of use	(i) For what types of health conditions would you be most comfortable using telemedicine? (ii) How often and under what conditions (e.g., weekends only) would you want to use such a clinic?

* These are examples of only some of the initiating questions used. Other more probing questions were asked of participants depending on what their responses were in order to gain more in-depth information.

Sheba George, Alison Hamilton, and Richard S. Baker, "How Do Low-Income Urban African Americans and Latinos Feel about Telemedicine? A Diffusion of Innovation Analysis," *International Journal of Telemedicine and Applications,* vol. 2012, Article ID 715194, 9 pages, 2012. doi:10.1155/2012/715194.

to explicate the range of issues that were raised in response to each question and to compare across categorical groupings (parents versus elders, African American participants versus Latino participants). Through an iterative process of immersion in the data and refining the categories, key themes and DOI theoretical insights were identified and interpreted collaboratively by the authors.

▶ 3. Results

Participants emphasized two DOI factors: relative advantages and compatibility with experiences and existing values. There were some differences between African Americans and Latinos in how they viewed these factors. While the two groups had similar perceptions of the relative advantages of telemedicine, they had differing perceptions of the compatibility of telemedicine with their experiences and existing values, resulting in different types of concerns (see **TABLE A.3**). Participants were understandably less prone to raise innovation-focused factors that are important to rate of adoption (complexity, observability of benefits, and trialability) because they were not familiar with telemedicine. We did not identify consistent discernible differences by age.

TABLE A.3 Advantages and concerns about telemedicine for African American and Latino participants.

	Advantages	Concerns
African Americans	(1) Reduced waiting time (2) Immediate feedback (3) Increased access to specialists (4) Increased access to multiple medical opinions (5) Convenience for children and the elderly	(1) The physical absence of the physician specialist (2) Ability to monitor the specialist's qualifications (3) Privacy/confidentiality issues related to the presence of personal information on the Internet (4) Adequacy of telemedicine scopes to make accurate diagnoses
Latinos	(1) Reduced waiting time (2) Immediate feedback (3) Increased access to specialists (4) Increased access to multiple medical opinions (5) Convenience for children and the elderly (6) Greater accuracy of diagnoses due to precision of computers (7) Avoiding poverty-related embarrassment and in-person physician interaction	(1) Privacy/confidentiality issues related to the presence of personal information on the internet, to a lesser extent (2) Adequacy of telemedicine scopes to make accurate diagnoses, to a lesser extent (3) Concerns about whether telemedicine would be available to uninsured/ undocumented

Sheba George, Alison Hamilton, and Richard S. Baker, "How Do Low-Income Urban African Americans and Latinos Feel about Telemedicine? A Diffusion of Innovation Analysis," *International Journal of Telemedicine and Applications*, vol. 2012, Article ID 715194, 9 pages, 2012. doi:10.1155/2012/715194

3.1 Relative Advantages

For both African Americans and Latinos, there were several relative advantages to telemedicine as compared to their usual modes of health care. The main advantages noted in all of the focus groups were: (1) reduced waiting time, (2) immediate feedback as to diagnosis and course of action, (3) increased access to specialists, and (4) increased access to multiple medical opinions. It is important to note that these perceived advantages are not necessarily correct perceptions of how telemedicine operates, but they do illustrate the values that participants associated with this type of system.

With regard to speed and accuracy of diagnosis, one Latino participant said that telemedicine would be a "novelty" because "it can give you the diagnosis right away cause they' re consulting the specialist so you can get your diagnosis instantly. I think that's good." Another Latino participant in another group said: "Science is more advanced and you will be able to see everything through the Internet ... It will be like having the doctor in front of you but you won't have to go to his office. The laboratory won't take a lot of time and you will really know what you have."

Telemedicine's potential convenience in terms of these issues and in terms of logistics (such as location) was perceived to be very appealing. The African American participants felt that telemedicine would be particularly beneficial for children and the elderly. For example, one participant said, "I can see it going places. I can see where people will like it. Young people will love it. Their families, I can see my children, you know, loving it for their children, you know, in many cases. First, because they do not have enough time to do whatever, you know, because they are so busy all the time. So that helps to get an immediate feedback and to give a diagnosis and a solution to a problem."

While the same four major advantages were discussed in all of the groups, Latino participants also noted several additional advantages and seemed, overall, more positive and enthusiastic about the prospect of telemedicine. They felt that telemedicine could potentially cut down on misdiagnoses, particularly because the computer gives "exact data." This idea of the precision of computers was raised in three of the Latino focus groups. One group felt that telemedicine might result in more choice over which doctor is assessing you and might provide better doctors. One group pointed out that telemedicine would result in more jobs for nurses.

The location and convenience of the clinics were also discussed more extensively in the Latino focus groups, because they felt that the clinics would be easier with children and with transportation. For example, "I would love something like this to open as soon as possible, because we need it. We need it for all of our children, because sometimes we take them all in when one has an appointment. You save time seeing the specialist that one of your children needs, or if another specialist is needed, you don't waste any time, you save time and see the doctor you want to see and it would be great if Medi-care would pay for these services."

3.1.1 Concerns about Compatibility with Past Experiences and Existing Values

African Americans and Latinos had very different perceptions about the compatibility of this innovation with their experiences and existing values. Participants' main concerns about telemedicine were confidentiality/privacy (considering the use of the Internet for the transmission of personal information) and the process of diagnosis (considering the use of scopes rather than actual clinical observation, i.e., physician's physical presence). Overall, African Americans were more concerned about these issues, and were especially concerned about the physical absence of the physician and the perceived inability to monitor the (distant) specialist's qualifications and level of attention. Latino participants were substantially less concerned about these issues and in some cases felt very differently about them. They did, however, express concerns about whether telemedicine would be made accessible to uninsured and undocumented individuals.

3.1.2 Technology Issues: Confidentiality and Privacy

For both African American and Latino participants, the technology critical to telemedicine posed some problems. On a technical level, some participants in both sets of groups discussed the possibility that the computer could go down or the system could fail. More important than this concern, however, was that personal information could be obtained by individuals other than those involved in the telemedicine encounter. For example, there was discussion among African American participants that one's identity could be stolen and that one's pictures would be "floating around." The Internet was perceived as "insecure" and "for anybody." One African American participant noted, "Internet is the Internet. So that means your name is out there and whatever your problem is, it's on the Internet. And you know, records are supposed to be a personal thing between you and your doctor, but if it's going to be on the Internet, then it's for anybody." In one group, participants discussed how they did not even like the idea of Internet banking due to the possibility of a breach in privacy. In another group, a participant imagined that children would be able to see medical images on the computer: "The kids, you know, they go to the library and they say, "mamma, guess what I see?" Now if I'm sick and there's something wrong with me, I don't want the Internet to know, too. No, no, then the whole world will see."

In contrast to the African American participants, Latino participants seemed more confident that privacy would be protected, and they were not as concerned that privacy could not be guaranteed. One participant said that the "standard ordinary person" would not even be interested in "anything scientific, and less still related to health." These participants, for the most part, expressed that maintenance of confidentiality was the physician's responsibility, and that the physician would not risk his license with a questionable system: "I don't think [the doctor] would risk his degree to give out the files of all the patients that are in the computer because he would be responsible." In another group, participants discussed asking for confidentiality, and they felt that by asking, confidentiality would be assured: "If you tell the person who's going to carry out the treatment that you want confidentiality in your case, I don't think there would be any problem. But you must ask for it. It won't come on its own." For some Latino participants, the technology assured more privacy. One Latino participant stated, "I feel there's more privacy. I really like the idea because the computer gives you exact data. It makes me feel better, you know? "Cause the fact that you're being looked at through the computer, it removes the self-consciousness, shame, or whatever of talking openly to a doctor. Like this, without being face to face, I can say whatever I wanted." There was some concern about identity theft, but, overall, Latino participants felt confident that transmitted information would remain confidential. As noted above, even for those who were not convinced of the confidentiality, there was typically little concern. One Latino participant said, "It doesn't matter to me that people should see me because the whole world has to know what science is doing."

3.1.3 Diagnosis and the Physical Absence of the Specialist

One of the main topics addressed in the focus groups was the physical absence of the specialist, which is one of the main distinguishing features of telemedicine. Discussions on this topic revealed the complexity of the doctor-patient interaction, illustrated by the multiple layers of meaning that participants attach to such interactions. Because of the richness of this set of findings, our results regarding the importance of physical presence and touch in telemedicine for these populations will be elaborated upon in a separated publication and here we will provide a summary of the findings. In general, the participants associated the physical presence or absence of the specialist to their (1) satisfaction with a medical encounter, (2) level of assurance that appropriate information was being conveyed, and (3) ability to accurately gauge the reactions of the specialist and monitor the latter's activities.

Several of the African American participants' concerns about not being physically with the specialist seemed related to sensory experiences of vision and touch, that is, being unable to "see" the specialist in person and/or not having the specialist touch the patient. For example, the physical absence of the physician was related to concerns about being able to assess if "the truth" was being told to the patient. For others, it was about being able to monitor the activities of the specialist (e.g., "How do I know that the doctor ain't on the other side and he's getting high?"). The importance of the physical presence of the specialist, particularly sight and touch, was often related to the specialist's capacity to make accurate diagnoses.

The Latino participants seemed less concerned about the physical absence of the physician in the telemedicine clinic. Having the doctor physically present did not equate with better care for these participants, as expressed in such statements as, "It makes no difference having the doctor in front of you." Participants expressed that even when the doctor is present, they tend to "only ask questions," whereas it is the nurse who provides care. The doctor "bases his opinions on what the nurse tells him," so diagnosis could take place just as well from a distance.

Interestingly, some Latino participants expressed a preference for telemedicine because of the physical absence of the physician. The reasons for this preference seemed to be centered on embarrassment about gender, age, and class differences between the provider and patient. As one participant explained, she preferred gynecological exams by telemedicine because it would help her avoid in-person interactions with "young, attractive" (male) gynecologists.

3.1.4 Qualifications and Qualities of the Physicians

As noted above, some African American participants were concerned that the telemedicine physician would not be giving the patient his/her undivided attention. This relates to an issue that came up in several of the focus groups, which is how do you trust in the physician who is not in the room with you? How do you know he is qualified and certified?

One African American participant wondered how experienced the telemedicine physicians would be: "How many years of experience have they had? You know, some of them might not even have but six months, some might not even have a year. So you have to take all that into consideration because I myself don't want anything that hasn't been in medicine over a year to be looking at me ... I still prefer an experienced doctor, whether he's on telemedicine or I see him in person." There was suspicion that the physician might not be who s/he claims to be, as expressed by an African American participant in the following question: "What is the reassurance that we have that this so-called specialist that's on the screen really is what he's supposed to be?"

Latino participants had more discussions about how they know the qualifications of any physicians, telemedicine or not. Most often, knowledge of a physician's quality and qualifications came from the success of the treatment, the physician's interpersonal qualities, or other people's recommendations. For example, "I have been seeing my current doctor for more than seven years, and he gives you the medicine and so you don't have to come back. And that's how we would know if they are good doctors or not." Another participant responded, "If I go to my doctor, I'm not 100% sure if he is a doctor or not. In terms of whether or not a doctor is good, well, you try him and see. I like the way I was treated."

In two Latino focus groups, participants agreed that one knows of a doctor's quality because "the medicines he gives you do you good." The participants said that the telemedicine personnel would be responsible for assuring the quality of the physicians: "We are trusting in you like we trust in the clinics we go to. We trust that the doctor we are going to see is really a certified doctor who has gone to school and who knows medicine. I think you must take that risk, for it's the responsibility of those who are in charge of the clinic." Latino participants also discussed seeking information on their own as to the qualifications of physicians, for example, by looking on the Internet: "All you do is go to a website and all you have to do is fill in the doctor's name and the clinics you've been to. There are many doctors that have done bad things and they are in jail, and their names are not on the list and that's another way to find out if a doctor is good or not." In general, while both African American and Latino participants shared concerns about the qualifications of the telemedicine physician providing care, the latter tended to think that the risks were not necessarily greater for telemedicine-based physicians as compared to physicians seen in person, and they expressed more trust that the quality of the physicians would have to be acceptable.

▶ 4. Discussion

Telemedicine has been promoted as an innovative approach to bridging the health care delivery gap particularly for underserved communities. While inner-city minority communities could potentially benefit from this innovation, there is little in the existing literature that speaks to the acceptability of such a solution among minority populations. To the best of our knowledge, this is the first study that explicitly examines perceptions about telemedicine among urban underserved minority populations, although some studies on telemedicine have included minority cultural groups[31] and studies of minority perceptions of health care in general have been done.[32]

Both African American and Latino focus group participants emphasized two DOI factors that shape the rate of diffusion of an innovation: relative advantage and compatibility with past experience. Participants were less likely to discuss complexity, observability of benefits, and trialability of telemedicine, likely because these factors focus on features of the innovation, with which the study participants were not very familiar. We contend that they were more likely to talk about telemedicine's relative advantages and compatibility since these factors were salient to their current concerns about their health care needs, lived experiences, and existing values, and they could be discussed despite their lack of first-hand experience with telemedicine.

The advantages of any health care innovation are usually assessed by potential users relative to their current experiences of receiving care. This was true regarding telemedicine for the focus group participants. Given their underserved inner-city location, the study participants overwhelmingly identified timely access to care as one of the greatest relative advantages of telemedicine. Telemedicine appears to provide some relatively efficient solutions to issues such as the challenge of transportation to get to specialist care, lack of timely access to specialists, the lack of timely diagnoses and feedback, and the lack of multiple opinions in a specialist-scarce zone.

However, the two groups had different concerns about health care received through telemedicine, reflecting differences in the compatibility of their lived experiences and values with the perceived nature of telemedicine-based care. For African Americans, their experiences as a community with a history of slavery and continuing racism in many aspects of their lives, particularly with health care, may affect their views on new and innovative medical care.[33, 34] The legacy of past abuses such as medical experimentation on slaves and the Tuskegee syphilis experiment and other types of continuing racism in health care contribute to lower levels of trust and a higher level of suspicion.[34–37]

A related issue that has been studied in more detail is the attitude of minorities toward enrollment in medical research, where similar findings have been reported about African American attitudes towards research.[38–46] Among African Americans, mistrust is frequently associated with the perception that research will benefit whites or the research institution and not people of color. Furthermore, mistrust of the health care system was a primary barrier that prevented African Americans from participating in medical research.[38]

For the African American participants in this study, the emphatic need to "see" and "touch" the physician seemed related to similar issues of trust. The physical absence of the physician, the instability of technology, and the inability to monitor the specialist's qualifications were all highlighted as concerns with telemedicine for the African American participants. All these concerns reflect a sense of vulnerability when placing trust in a medical system that historically has been unreliable and not trustworthy. African American participants expressed a need to be vigilant and monitor physicians to make sure that they would get quality care, particularly when telemedicine appeared to present greater opportunities for care to be compromised. This concern about quality of care is consistent with literature that indicates African Americans' less than satisfying interactions with physicians.[47, 48]

With regard to technology, there were many levels of concern. First, there was concern about whether the scopes used in telemedicine would perform adequately to allow physicians to make accurate diagnoses. Second, there was some concern about the computer system failing. However, the bulk of the apprehension among African Americans regarding technology was about the insecurity of transmitting personal data and images over the Internet when using telemedicine. A third issue of trust reiterated by African American participants was that of being able to trust the qualifications and qualities of the physician who is not in the room. There was concern about the level of experience of the physician, suggesting that these participants were concerned that telemedicine might be a way to unload inexperienced or second-rate doctors on them.

In contrast, the Latino participants had distinctly different responses to telemedicine, which may be explained partly by their different vantage points and lived experiences. Latinos, across age groups, appeared to have a significantly more trusting attitude towards the health care system in general and telemedicine in particular. This difference was reflected in their very different attitudes towards the telemedicine-related issues identified as problematic by African Americans, namely, the physician's virtual presence, the usage of technology, and the qualifications and qualities of physicians. The Latino participants' relative lack of concern about the physical absence of the physician points to the possibility that physical exams and the touch of the physician in time-pressured primary care visits are becoming less frequent[49] and consequently telemedicine is not that different from their expected standards of care.

Latino participants tended to equate the use of technology with access to scientific advances and expressed faith in the appropriate authorities to maintain confidentiality. Technology was seen by many Latinos as assuring greater accuracy (more exact data). Such optimism and openness towards technological innovations among Latinos was markedly different from the attitude found among African American participants. Despite the fact that both groups may experience what is commonly called the "digital divide," they had noticeably different opinions about technology in general.

Latino participants also differed from African Americans in that they trusted the administrators of both telemedicine and non-telemedicine clinics to be responsible for hiring qualified doctors. Finally, the knowledge of the quality and qualifications of the physicians was determined by the success of the treatment, whether telemedicine or nontelemedicine based.

The qualitative racial/ethnic differences in attitudes about telemedicine-based health care among Latinos and African Americans point to differences in their lived experiences and values. The point of reference for many African Americans is the history of racism and medical experimentation and abuse they have experienced collectively in the United States. In contrast, immigrant Latinos encounter the US medical system without this particular historical backdrop and their point of reference maybe less than optimal health care in their home countries, along with a generally positive perception of the American health care and medical education systems. For many of the immigrant Latinos, access to American health care and especially telemedicine-based care that is perceived as scientifically and technologically cutting edge also seems to be seen as a positive improvement. Thus, in terms of the DOI framework, there appears to be good compatibility between the needs, lived experiences, and values of Latinos with the structure and delivery of telemedicine-based care.

4.1 Implications for Telemedicine

Our findings of differences in attitudes toward telemedicine suggest that it will be necessary to tailor approaches to the introduction, marketing, and implementation of telemedicine among these different populations. It is critical to gather this information before the extensive introduction of telemedicine clinics in innercity communities for at least three reasons.

First, this information can be important for determining the best manner in which to introduce and market telemedicine among these two groups. Based on the findings from this study, it is important to identify the gaps in knowledge or the misinformation that can lead to distrust of new technology or the overestimation about the benefits of new technology and false expectations. The information gathered from this study can be used to help lower the barriers to acceptance of telemedicine by developing educational materials that address misinformation and gaps in knowledge. Marketing information could be tailored to address the specific concerns voiced by the two racial/ethnic groups, such as clearly informing African Americans about the medical qualifications of the specialists and the security procedures for maintaining confidentiality and level of diagnostic accuracy using telemedicine equipment.

Second, this information can be important in selecting the optimal ways in which to implement new telemedicine clinics. For example, for African Americans, having an initial in-person meeting with a physician may be important in helping establish trust and better preparing the patient for future virtual appointments. For real-time telemedicine consultations, cameras could be set up to make the specialist's activities especially transparent to the patients. Physicians' assistants or the nurses in the clinics and the specialists involved in telemedicine could be better informed about the concerns of each of these groups so that they can address these concerns (such as reassurances about confidentiality), even if the patients do not voice them.

Third, this data can also serve as a baseline point of comparison for studies that will examine changes in patient perceptions over time. As telemedicine becomes implemented in urban settings and becomes more familiar to African American and Latino populations, it will be important to have an understanding of their baseline pre-experience perceptions regarding telemedicine to gauge the changes in attitudes towards telemedicine as it spreads into different communities.

4.2 Limitation

There are several important limitations to our data and study findings. First, we have a relatively small convenience sample and our participants are not statistically representative of the wider population in inner-city settings. However, as is common to qualitative methods, they represent information-rich cases, homogenously stratified across race and age, to allow in-depth understanding of the perceptions about telemedicine among these groups. Another limitation is that for the majority of our participants, the only information about telemedicine came from the video they saw at the beginning of the focus group. While telemedicine was portrayed in a typical setting with a typical health problem, our participants' understanding and consequent reactions to telemedicine were clearly influenced by what we were able to show them in a short video. For example, we represented telemedicine primarily as a diagnostic interaction with a specialist and did not address its other potential uses, such as in the long-term management of chronic diseases. Our finding of no age group differences may be a reflection of the limitations of our study design. We may have needed a more sensitive interview protocol that would have more finely delineated the nuances of age differences in our sample.

▶ 5. Conclusion

Using the DOI framework regarding features of an innovation, this study contributes to an underresearched area by exploring the pre-experience perceptions of telemedicine among urban, underserved African Americans and Latinos. Despite reservations, many participants indicated that they would take advantage of telemedicine clinics.

Through this study, we were able to identify components of the DOI framework that spoke to the experiences of the two minority groups—particularly with regards to compatibility with past experiences and existing values. It will be important to develop larger studies in different geographical regions with different populations to further understand the importance of these factors for the introduction/marketing, implementation, and eventual adoption of telemedicine among diverse populations.

▶ Acknowledgments

The authors acknowledge the National Center for Research Resources (NCRR) Research Centers in Minority Institutes (RCMI) Grant G12-RR03026 at Charles Drew University; the Agency for Health Care Research and Quality (AHRQ) Grant 1R24-HS014022-01A1; the NIH-NIMHDGrant U54MD007598 (formerly U54RR026138); and the Community Technology Foundation Grant (2004-TT-002) for support during the research and writing of this paper.

▶ References

1. T. Greenhalgh, G. Robert, F. Macfarlane, P. Bate, and O. Kyriakidou, "Diffusion of innovations in service organizations: systematic review and recommendations," *Milbank Quarterly*, vol. 82, no. 4, pp. 581–629, 2004.

2. B. L. Chang, S. Bakken, S. S. Brown et al., "Bridging the digital divide: reaching vulnerable populations," *Journal of the American Medical Informatics Association*, vol. 11, no. 6, pp. 448–457, 2004.

3. A. Nelson, "Unequal treatment: confronting racial and ethnic disparities in health care," *Journal of the National Medical Association*, vol. 94, no. 8, pp. 666–668, 2002.

4. K. A. Phillips, M. L. Mayer, and L. A. Aday, "Barriers to care among racial/ethnic groups under managed care," *Health Affairs*, vol. 19, no. 4, pp. 65–75, 2000.

5. S. Shea, J. Starren, R. S. Weinstock et al., "Columbia University's Informatics for Diabetes Education and Telemedicine (IDEATel) Project: rationale and design," *Journal of the American Medical Informatics Association*, vol. 9, no. 1, pp. 49–62, 2002.

6. D. R. Williams, "Race, socioeconomic status, and health the added effects of racism and discrimination," *Annals of the New York Academy of Sciences*, vol. 896, pp. 173–188, 1999.

7. D. S. Puskin, "Opportunities and challenges to telemedicine in rural America," *Journal of Medical Systems*, vol. 19, no. 1, pp. 59–67, 1995.

8. W. C. Richardson, *Crossing the Quality Chasm: A New Health System for the 21st Century*, Institute of Medicine, Washington, DC, USA, 2001.

9. P. S. Whitten, F. S. Mair, A. Haycox, C. R. May, T. L. Williams, and S. Hellmich, "Systematic review of cost effectiveness studies of telemedicine interventions," *British Medical Journal*, vol. 324, no. 7351, pp. 1434–1437, 2002.

10. W. R. Hersh et al., *Telemedicine for the Medicare Population: Update*, Agency for Healthcare Research and Quality, Rockville, Md, USA, 2006.

11. R. S. Baker, N. L. Watkins, M. R. Wilson, M. Bazargan, and C. W. Flowers, "Demographic and clinical characteristics of patients with diabetes presenting to an urban public hospital ophthalmology clinic," *Ophthalmology*, vol. 105, no. 8, pp. 1373–1379, 1998.

12. T. S. Nesbitt, D. M. Hilty, C. A. Kuenneth, and A. Siefkin, "Development of a telemedicine program," *Western Journal of Medicine*, vol. 173, no. 3, pp. 169–174, 2000.

13. E. L. Carter, G. Nunlee-Bland, and C. Callender, "A patientcentric, provider-assisted diabetes telehealth self-management intervention for urban minorities," Perspectives in Health Information Management/AHIMA, American Health Information Management Association, 2011.

14. K. Shahid, A. M. Kolomeyer, N. V. Nayak et al., "Ocular telehealth screenings in an urban community," *Telemedicine and e-Health*, vol. 18, no. 2, pp. 95–100, 2012.

15. N. Scheinfeld, M. Fisher, P. Genis, and H. Long, "Evaluating patient acceptance of a teledermatology link of an urban urgent-care dermatology clinic run by residents with board certified dermatologists," *SKINmed Journal*, vol. 2, no. 3, pp. 159–162, 2003.

16. P. M. Trief, R. Izquierdo, J. P. Eimicke et al., "Adherence to diabetes self care for white, African-American andHispanic American telemedicine participants: 5 year results from the IDEATel project," *Ethnicity & Health*. In press.

17. R. S. Weinstock, J. A. Teresi, R. Goland et al., "Glycemic control and health disparities in older ethnically diverse underserved adults with diabetes: five-year results from the Informatics for Diabetes Education and Telemedicine (IDEATel) study," *Diabetes Care*, vol. 34, no. 2, pp. 274–279, 2011.

18. E. M. Rogers, *Diffusion of Innovations*, Free Press, 1995.

19. A. Allen and J. Hayes, "Patient satisfaction with teleoncology: a pilot study," *Telemedicine Journal*, vol. 1, no. 1, pp. 41–46, 1995.

20. H. Mekhjian, J. W. Turner, M. Gailiun, and T. A. McCain, "Patient satisfaction with telemedicine in a prison environment," *Journal of Telemedicine and Telecare*, vol. 5, no. 1, pp. 55–61, 1999.

21. J. W. Turner, R. J. Thomas, and N. L. Reinsch Jr., "Willingness to try a new communication technology: perceptual factors and task situations in a health care context," *Journal of Business Communication*, vol. 41, no. 1, pp. 5–26, 2004.

22. R. L. Bashshur, "Public acceptance of telemedicine in a rural community," *Bioscience Communications*, vol. 4, pp. 17–38, 1978.

23. J. E. Brick, R. L. Bashshur, J. F. Brick, and R. M. D'Alessandri, "Public knowledge, perception, and expressed choice of telemedicine in rural West Virginia," *Telemedicine Journal*, vol. 3, no. 2, pp. 159–171, 1997.

24. Department of Health Services, L.A.C., *The Health of the Residents in South Service Planning Area of Los Angeles County*, Los Angeles County Department of Health Services, 2007.

25. Department of Health, *Los Angeles County Health Survey*, Department of Health, Los Angeles, Calif, USA, 2005.

26. M. Agar and J. MacDonald, "Focus Groups and ethnography," *Human Organization*, vol. 54, no. 1, pp. 78–86, 1995.

27. R. A. Krueger and M. A. Casey, *Focus Groups: A Practical Guide for Applied Research*, Sage Publications, 2000.

28. D. L. Morgan, *Focus Groups as Qualitative Research*, Sage Publications, 1997.

29. D. W. Stewart, P. N. Shamdasani, and D. W. Rook, *Focus Groups: Theory and Practice*, Sage, 2007.

30. A. L. Strauss, *Qualitative Analysis for Social Scientists*, Cambridge University Press, 1987.

31. D. C. Alverson, B. Holtz, J. D'Iorio, M. Devany, S. Simmons, and R. K. Poropatich, "One size doesn't fit all: bringing telehealth services to special populations," *Telemedicine and e-Health*, vol. 14, no. 9, pp. 957–963, 2008.

32. M. Lillie-Blanton, M. Brodie, D. Rowland, D. Altman, and M. McIntosh, "Race, ethnicity, and the health care system: public perceptions and experiences," *Medical Care Research and Review*, vol. 57, no. 1, pp. 218–235, 2000.

33. W. D. King, "Examining African Americans' mistrust of the health care system: expanding the research question," *Public Health Reports*, vol. 118, no. 4, pp. 366–367, 2003.

34. T. A. LaVeist, K. J. Nickerson, and J. V. Bowie, "Attitudes about racism, medical mistrust, and satisfaction with care among African American and white cardiac patients," *Medical Care Research and Review*, vol. 57, no. 1, pp. 146–161, 2000.

35. L. E. Boulware, L. A. Cooper, L. E. Ratner, T. A. LaVeist, and N. R. Powe, "Race and trust in the health care system," *Public Health Reports*, vol. 118, no. 4, pp. 358–365, 2003.

36. V. N. Gamble, "Under the Shadow of Tuskegee: African Americans and Health Care," *American Journal of Public Health*, vol. 87, no. 11, pp. 1773–1778, 1997.

37. S. B. Thomas and S. C. Quinn, "Public health then and now: the Tuskegee Syphilis Study, 1932 to 1972: implications for HIV education and AIDS risk education programs in the black community," *American Journal of Public Health*, vol. 81, no. 11, pp. 1498–1504, 1991.

38. D. P. Scharf, K. J. Mathews, P. Jackson, J. Hofsuemmer, E. Martin, and D. Edwards, "More than Tuskegee: understanding mistrust about research participation," *Journal of Health Care for the Poor and Underserved*, vol. 21, no. 3, pp. 879–897, 2010.

39. R. BeLue, K. D. Taylor-Richardson, J. Lin, A. T. Rivera, and D. Grandison, "African Americans and participation in clinical trials: differences in beliefs and attitudes by gender," *Contemporary Clinical Trials*, vol. 27, no. 6, pp. 498–505, 2006.

40. D. F. Farmer, S. A. Jackson, F. Camacho, and M. A. Hall, "Attitudes of African American and low socioeconomic status white women toward medical research," *Journal of Health Care for the Poor and Underserved*, vol. 18, no. 1, pp. 85–99, 2007.

41. C. A. Gadegbeku, P. K. Stillman, M. D. Huffman, J. S. Jackson, J. W. Kusek, and K. A. Jamerson, "Factors associated with enrollment of African Americans into a clinical trial: results from the African American study of kidney disease and hypertension," *Contemporary Clinical Trials*, vol. 29, no. 6, pp. 837–842, 2008.

42. P. Herring, S. Montgomery, A. K. Yancey, D. Williams, and G. Fraser, "Understanding the challenges in recruiting blacks to a longitudinal cohort study: the adventist health study," *Ethnicity and Disease*, vol. 14, no. 3, pp. 423–430, 2004.

43. V. A. Johnson, K. A. Edwards, S. L. Sherman et al., "Decisions to participate in fragile X and other genomics-related research: native American and African American voices," *Journal of Cultural Diversity*, vol. 16, no. 3, pp. 127–135, 2009.

44. H. M. Linden, L. M. Reisch, A. Hart et al., "Attitudes toward participation in breast cancer randomized clinical trials in the African American community: a focus group study," *Cancer Nursing*, vol. 30, no. 4, pp. 261–269, 2007.

45. Y. R. Smith, A. M. Johnson, L. A. Newman, A. Greene, T. R. B. Johnson, and J. L. Rogers, "Perceptions of clinical research participation among African American women," *Journal of Women's Health*, vol. 16, no. 3, pp. 423–428, 2007.

46. S. B. Wyatt, N. Diekelmann, F. Henderson et al., "A community-driven model of research participation: the Jackson Hearth Study participant recruitment and retention study," *Ethnicity and Disease*, vol. 13, no. 4, pp. 438–455, 2003.

47. M. P. Doescher, B. G. Saver, P. Franks, and K. Fiscella, "Racial and ethnic disparities in perceptions of physician style and trust," *Archives of Family Medicine*, vol. 9, no. 10, pp. 1156–1163, 2000.

48. R. L. Johnson, S. Saha, J. J. Arbelaez, M. C. Beach, and L. A. Cooper, "Racial and ethnic differences in patient perceptions of bias and cultural competence in health care," *Journal of General Internal Medicine*, vol. 19, no. 2, pp. 101–110, 2004.

49. S. Saha, J. J. Arbelaez, and L. A. Cooper, "Patient-physician relationships and racial disparities in the quality of health care," *American Journal of Public Health*, vol. 93, no. 10, pp. 1713–1719, 2003.

THEORY IN ACTION—ARTICLE QUESTIONS

1. What advantages were identified by all focus group participants?
2. What additional advantages were identified by Latinos?
3. How compatible is the innovation with existing values?
4. Although not specifically addressed in the article, what might be implied about the perceived complexity of the innovation?
5. What might be implied about trailability?
6. What might be implied about observability?
7. Based on the information provided in the article, what would you change in your marketing materials?
8. What do the authors recommend for marketing the program given the feedback from the two groups, and how does this compare to your recommendation?

▶ Chapter References

Anowar, M. N., Petpichetchian, W., Isaralalai, S., & Klamim-Yobas, P. (2013). Using nursing practice guidelines for the prevention of multidrug-resistant tuberculosis among hospitalized adult patients in Bangladesh. *International Journal of Nursing Practice, 19*(Suppl 3), 81–88.

Backer, T. E., & Rogers, E. M. (1998). Diffusion of innovation theory and work-site AIDS programs. *Journal of Health Communication, 3*, 17–28.

Barker, K. (2004). Diffusion of innovations: A world tour. *Journal of Health Communication, 9,* 131–137.

Burke, J. (2004). Infant HIV infection: Acceptability of preventive strategies on Tanzania. *AIDS Education and Prevention, 16*(5), 415–425.

Carter, L., Corneille, M., Hall-Byers, N. M, Clark, T., & Younge, S. N. (2015). Exploring user acceptance of a text-message based health intervention among young African-Americans. *Transactions on Human-Computer Interaction, 7*(3), 110–124.

Centers for Disease Control and Prevention. (2007). Cover your cough. Retrieved March 30, 2013, from http://cdc.gov/flu/protect/covercough.htm

Chun, G. J., Sautter, J. M., Patterson, B. J., & McGhan, W. F. (2016). Diffusion of pharmacy based influenza vaccination over time in the United States. *American Journal of Public Health, 106*(6), 1099–1100.

Costa-Neto, E. M. (2013). Insects as human food: An overview. *Amazonica—Revista de Antropologia, 5*(3), 562–582. (online)

Dukes, R. L., Stein, J. A., & Ullman, J. B. (1997). Long-term impact of Drug Abuse Resistance Education (D.A.R.E.). *Evaluation Review, 21,* 483–500.

Dukes, R. L., Ullman, J. B., & Stein, J. A. (1996). A three-year follow-up of Drug Abuse Resistance Education (D.A.R.E.). *Evaluation Review, 20,* 49–66.

Eshkevari, L., & Heath, J. (2005). Use of acupuncture for chronic pain. *Holistic Nursing Practice, 19*(5), 217–221.

Fernandez, M. A., Desroches, S., Turcotte, M., Marquis, M., Dufour, J., & Provencher, V. (2016). Factors influencing the adoption of a healthy eating campaign by federal cross-sector partners: A qualitative study. *BMC Public Health, 16,* 1–12. doi:10.1186/s12889-016-3523-x

Food and Drug Administration. (2004). Lasik eye surgery. Retrieved April 1, 2013, from http://www.fda.gov/MedicalDevices/ProductsandMedicalProcedures/SurgeryandLifeSupport/LASIK/default.htm

Griffith, J. S. (1999). Daring to be different? A drug prevention and life skills education program for primary schools. *Early Child Development and Care, 158,* 95–105. doi:10.1080/0300443991580108.

Haesly, B., Nanney, M. S., Coulter, S., Fong, S., & Pratt, R. J. (2014). Impact on staff of improving access to the school breakfast program: A qualitative study. *American School Health Association, 84*(4), 267–274. doi:10.1111/josh.12142

Haider, M., & Kreps, G. (2004). Forty years of diffusion of innovations: Utility and value in public health. *Journal of Health Communication, 9,* 3–11.

Hollander, D. (2004). Long-term use of female condom may hinge partly on depth of instruction. *International Family Planning Perspectives, 30*(1). Retrieved December 8, 2004, from http://www.agi-usa.org/pubs/journals/3004904b.html

Inwood, S. M., Sharp, J. S., Moore, R. H., & Stinner, D. H. (2009). Restaurants, chefs and local foods: Insights drawn from application of a diffusion of innovation framework. *Agriculture and Human Values, 26,* 177–191.

Israel-Ballard, K., Chantry, C., Dewey, K., Lonnerdal, B., Sheppard, H., Donovan, R., …. Abrams, B. (2005). Viral, nutritional, and bacterialsafety of flash-heated and pretoria-pasteurized breast milk to prevent mother-to-child transmission of HIV in resource-poor countries: A pilot study. *Journal of Acquired Immune Deficiency Syndromes, 40*(2), 175–181.

Janssen, P. A., Holt, V. L., & Sugg, N. K. (2002). Introducing domestic violence assessment in a postpartum clinical setting. *Maternal and Child Health Journal, 6*(3), 195–203.

Kane, M., & Mittman, R. (2002). *Diffusion of innovation in health care.* Oakland: California HealthCare Foundation. Retrieved April 1, 2013, from http://www.chcf.org/publications/2002/05/diffusion-of-innovation-in-health-care

Lounsbury, B. (2006). Why don't we do it in our sleeves? Retrieved March 17, 2007, from http://www.coughsafe.com/index.html

Lynam, D. R., Milich, R., Zimmerman, R., Novak, S. P., Logan, T. K., Martin, C., … Clayton, R. (1999). Project DARE: No effects at ten year follow-up. *Journal of Consulting and Clinical Psychology, 67*(4), 590–593.

McCarthy, K. A., & Milus, T. (2000). Patient education viewed through the lens of diffusion of innovations research. *Topics in Clinical Chiropractic, 7*(4), 15–24.

Meyer-Rochow, V. B., & Chakravortry, J. (2013). Notes on entomophagy generally and information on the situation in India in particular. *Applied Entomology and Zoololgy, 48*(2), 105–112.

Moise, I. K., Green, D., Toth, J., & Muhall, P. (2014). Evaluation of an authority innovation-decision: Brief alcohol intervention for pregnant women receiving Women, Infants and Children services at two Illinois Health Departments. *Substance Use and Misuse, 49*, 804–812. doi:10.3109.1082 6084.2014.880484

National Stroke Association. (2016). *Pseudobulbar affect—PBA*. Retrieved November 30, 2016, from http://www.stroke.org/we-can-help/survivors/stroke-recovery/post-stroke-conditions/emotional /pba

Nehme, E. K., Perez, A., Ranjit, N., Amick, B. C., & Kohl, H. W. (2016). Behavioral theory and transportation cycling research: Application of the diffusion of innovations. *Journal of Transport & Health, 3*, 346–356. doi:10.1016/j.th.2016.05.127

Nguygen, H. Q., Carrieri-Kohlman, V., Rankin, S. H., Slaughter, R., & Stubarg, M. S. (2004). Supporting cardiac recovery through health technology. *Journal of Cardiac Nursing, 19*, 200–208.

O'Malley, K. (2006, June 13). Merck & Co: The marketing machine behind Gardasil. *Pharmaceutical Business Review*. Retrieved May 25, 2007, from http://www.pharmaceutical-business-review .com/article_feature.asp?guid=463AB18E-B911-4CC6-BD44-FB9CC69C6561

Peeters, J. M., deVeer, A. J. E., van der Hoek, L., & Francke, A. L. (2012). Factors influencing the adoption of home telecare by elderly or chronically ill people: A national survey. *Journal of Clinical Nursing, 21*, 3183–3193. doi:10.1111/j.1365.2702.2012.04173.x

Pemberton, H. E. (1936). The curve of culture diffusion rate. *American Sociological Review, 1*(4), 547–556.

Piot, P. (1998). *The female condom and AIDS: UNAIDS point of view*. Geneva, Switzerland: UNAIDS. Retrieved April 1, 2013, from http://www.unaids.org/en/media/unaids/contentassets /dataimport/publications/irc-pub03/fcondompv_en.pdf

Rogers, E. M. (2003). *Diffusion of innovation*. New York, NY: Free Press.

Rogers, E. M. (2004). A prospective and retrospective look at the diffusion model. *Journal of Health Communication, 9*, 13–19.

Rogers, E. M., & Scott, K. L. (1997). The diffusion of innovations model and outreach from the National Network of Libraries of Medicine to Native American communities. Retrieved October 30, 2004, from http://nnlm.gov/pnr/eval/rogers.html

Ryan, B., & Gross, N. (1943). The diffusion of hybrid seed corn in two Iowa communities. *Rural Sociology, 8*, 15–24.

Santos, M. A. O. (2012). Investigating consumer knowledge of global warming based on Roger' knowledge stage of the innovation decision process. *International Journal of Consumer Studies, 36*, 385–393. doi:10.1111/j.1470-6431.2011.01069.x

Singh, R. D., Jimerson, S. R., Renshaw, T., Saeki, E., Hart, S. R., Earhart, J., & Stewart, K. (2011). A summary and synthesis of contemporary empirical evidence regarding the drug abuse resistance education program (D.A.R.E.). *Contemporary School Psychology, 15*, 93–102.

Smerecnik, K. R., & Andersen, P. A. (2011). The diffusion of environmental sustainability innovations in North American hotels and ski resorts. *Journal of Sustainable Tourism, 19*(2), 171–196.

Steury, E. E. (2013). Malaria prevention in Zambia: A practical application of the diffusion of innovations model. *Journal of Transcultural Nursing, 24*(2), 189–194. doi:10.1177/104365961247201

Valente, T. W., & Rogers, E. M. (1995). The origins and development of the diffusion of innovation paradigm as an example of scientific growth. *Science Communication, 16*(3), 243–273.

West, S. L., & O'Neal, K. K. (2004). Project D.A.R.E. outcome effectiveness revisited. *American Journal of Public Health, 94*, 1027–1029. doi:10.2105/APHA.94.6.1027

Wilson, M. C. (1927). Influence of bulletins news stories and circular letters upon farm practice adoption with particular reference to methods of bulletin distribution. Washington, DC: U.S. Department of Agriculture, Federal Extension Circular No. 57.

Winter, V. R. (2013). Diffusion of innovations theory: A unifying framework for HIV peer education. *American Journal of Sexuality Education, 8*, 228–245. doi:10.1080/15546128.2013.838512

Yee, D. (2007). Hand sanitizers becoming popular. Retrieved March 17, 2007, from http:// www.abqtrib.com/news/2007/jan/05/hand-sanitizer-becoming-popular

Zoorob, R., Aliyu, M. H., & Hayes, C. (2010). Fetal alcohol syndrome: Knowledge and attitudes of family medicine clerkship and residency directors. *Alcohol, 44*(4), 379–385. doi:10.1016 /j.alcohol.2009.10.012

CHAPTER 10

Social Ecological Model

STUDENT LEARNING OUTCOMES

After reading this chapter the student will be able to:

- Discuss the different levels of factors used in the Social Ecological Model.
- Give an example of factors at each level of the Social Ecological Model.
- Use the Social Ecological Model to explain one of their health behaviors.

SOCIAL ECOLOGICAL MODEL ESSENCE SENTENCE

Factors at many levels influence health behavior.

Levels

Intrapersonal level factors: Characteristics within the person
Interpersonal level factors: Relationships between people
Institutional level factors: Rules, regulations, and policies at the workplace
Community level factors: Social network norms and environmental conditions
Societal level factors: Cultural norms, economic, and other policies

▶ In the Beginning

Explaining behavior from an ecological perspective has its origins in Germany in the 1870s, when two researchers, Schwabe and Bartholomai, studied how neighborhoods affected the development of the children who live in them (Bronfenbrenner, 1974, 1994). However, it wasn't until the mid-1970s when Urie Bronfenbrenner, a developmental psychologist, put this approach on the map, so to speak (Bronfenbrenner, 1974). From Bronfenbrenner's extensive review of the literature, he found that the context in which child development research was conducted—in unfamiliar surroundings, with people the child didn't know, for a short period of time without any of the things or people the child is used to—provided a partial picture because there was a stark contrast between the research environment and the reality in which the child lived. Thus, an often used quote of his is "American developmental psychology is the science of behavior of children in strange situations with strange adults" (Bronfenbrenner, 1974, p. 3).

To address this, Bronfenbrenner (1974, 1994) developed a theoretical model based on two propositions. The first is that human development occurs through a process of complex back-and-forth interactions between things in a person's immediate environment and that in order for these interactions to effect development, they must occur fairly regularly over time. He called these proximal or close processes. Examples of these processes are found in the parent–child relationship, child–child relationships, and group or solitary play. The second proposition is that the effect of these back-and-forth interactions vary depending on the personal characteristics of the child, the environment in which they take place, and the developmental outcome being studied (Bronfenbrenner, 1974, 1994).

Additionally, the Social Ecological Model (SEM) viewed the environment as a critical component of behavior and differentiated it into a set of concentric systems or levels. Each level of the environment is inside the other—like nesting dolls—starting with the one in which relationships are closest to the person (family, school, and friends) to the one in which the relationships are most distant (the effects of time). The different concentric organizations of the environment, originally labeled microsystem, mesosystem, exosystem, macrosystems, and chronosystems, each has its own characteristics and interactions with the others which affect human development and behavior (Bronfenbrenner, 1994).

▶ Theory Concept

There are many ways in which health behavior can be explained. But for the most part, theories and models explain it based on one of two types of factors: internal—such as beliefs, attitudes, skills, perceptions, and expectations or external in the social environment, such as social supports, significant others, models, and rewards or consequences. Similarly, the SEM also explains behavior using these factors but differs in that it uses *both* internal and external factors, rather than one or the other. In addition, the external environment is seen as being composed of both the social and physical environments (Sallis & Owen, 1997). Therefore, when the SEM is used in health promotion, the intent is to change the environment (social or physical), since changes in the environment change individual behavior (McLeroy, Bibeau, Steckler, & Glanz, 1988).

▶ Theory Levels

Unlike the other theories and models, the SEM is a point of view or perspective, and as such it does not have constructs per se (Sallis & Owen, 2002). The internal and external factors that underpin behavior are presented as levels (McLeroy et al., 1988). Perceptually, these levels are like concentric circles (**FIGURE 10.1**), with the

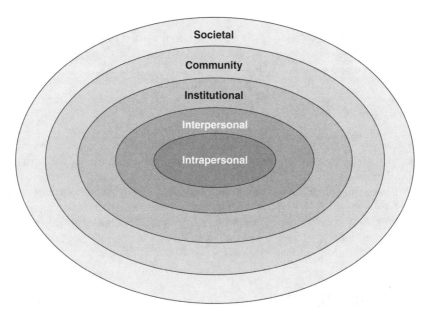

FIGURE 10.1 An ecological model.

Modified with permission from World Health Organization original article entitled "The ecological framework": http://www.who.int/violenceprevention/approach/ecology/en/#.Wa8UgiblTzU.email. Accessed September 5th, 2017.

smallest at the center representing the internal or intra personal level; then moving to the external levels, which include the interpersonal level; and widening to the community, institutional, and finally the societal level. The basis of the SEM is recognition of the dynamic interplay among the various factors at different levels that affect behavior (Stokols, 1992). Because of this interplay between and among the many levels of influence, changing one can have an impact on them all (Spence & Lee, 2003). This concept is similar to reciprocal determinism in the Social Cognitive Theory.

Although this multilevel perspective is consistent in all ecological models, the specific terms used to describe the levels or factors may differ slightly. The level designations presented here are those commonly used in health education and health promotion.

Intrapersonal Level

The SEM recognizes the contribution intrapersonal-level factors make to health behavior. The impact of intrapersonal-level factors cannot be understated. In fact, historically they have been the foundation for explaining health behavior and the basis for health promotion interventions (Novilla, Barnes, DeLaCruz, Williams, & Rogers, 2006). Intrapersonal-level factors include knowledge, attitudes, beliefs, personality traits (McLeroy et al., 1988), skills, perceptions (Novilla et al., 2006), personal-history (World Health Organization [WHO], 2006), self-efficacy, and perceptions (Sallis & Owen, 1999), to name but a few of the more common ones.

An example of intrapersonal factors and health behavior is seen in the results of a 50-city study of alcohol use. The personal characteristics or intrapersonal factors of those who drank more included age, gender, education level, employment status, income, marital status, impulsivity, risky driving, and being born inside the United States. Further, those who drank more frequently were older, white, and male with greater incomes and less than full time employment (Gruenewald, Remer, & LaScala, 2013).

Health literacy is another example of how personal characteristics affect health behavior. Factors such as health knowledge, attitudes, beliefs, perception of disease risk, and preference regarding level of personal involvement in health, all impact health literacy (McCormack, Thomas, Lewis, & Rudd, 2017), and by extension, health behavior. Interestingly, the intrapersonal factor of perception of efficacy played a role in the H1N1 (swine flu) vaccination rates in 2009. People who perceived the vaccine as effective in preventing swine flu were more likely to be vaccinated. Surprisingly, the perception of susceptibility *to* swine flu infection was not a factor contributing to vaccination (Kumar et al., 2012).

Interpersonal Level

The next set of factors in the SEM is at the interpersonal level. These are external factors included in the relationships we have with our relatives, friends, and peers. These people provide our social identity, make up our support systems, and define our role within the social structure (McLeroy et al., 1988; WHO, 2006).

Our relationships with others at this level influence our health behavior (see **FIGURE 10.2A–B**). For example, in the case of smoking, the strongest predictor of this behavior is having parents, siblings, or peers who smoke. Thus, if your friends and parents smoke, it is more likely that you will too (von Bothmer, Mattsson, & Fridlund, 2002). The same is true of drug-taking behavior. The peer group and family have a major influence on whether or not someone will engage in this behavior (Eddy, Donahue, Webster, & Bjornstad, 2002).

Bullying behavior is a complex and unique type of interpersonal aggression that is a consequence of not only individual characteristics, but the child's relationships with peers, family, teachers, neighbors, and society. Specifically at the interpersonal level, family characteristics play a role in the perpetration of bullying behavior including family member gang involvement, lack of parental supervision, emotional support and communication, authoritarian parenting style, parental abuse, and parental and/or domestic conflict (Swearer & Hymel, 2015).

Another important relationship at the interpersonal level is the one people have with their healthcare providers. When we look at HIV/AIDS prevention among older adults through the lens of these relationships, we see how they can have a profound effect on health behavior. Typically, physicians are less likely to discuss sexual health matters (including safer sex) with patients over 50. However, not discussing safer sex may be interpreted as it not being an issue for older adults, which may in turn lead to unsafe sexual practices that expose people to infection (Jacobson, 2011). Evidence of this very outcome is found in the CDC 2014 HIV Surveillance Report which indicates that in 2013, adults age 55 and older accounted for 26% of people living with HIV and in 2014, people 50 and older accounted for 17% of new HIV diagnoses (CDC, 2015).

A

B

FIGURE 10.2 Our relationships influence our behavior for better or worse.

Another example of how interpersonal factors related to healthcare professionals influence behavior is with colorectal cancer screening. In a demonstration project developed by the Louisiana Comprehensive Cancer Control Program, patient
navigators were the healthcare professionals in the interpersonal sphere of influence.
They educated patients on the importance of colorectal cancer screening, explained

how to complete and return the preliminary screening test (fecal immunochemical test), contacted the patients with the results, and assisted with any needed follow-up (Nuss, Williams, Hayden, & Huard, 2012). Each interaction with the navigator reinforced positive health behaviors.

Relationships with people who are physically active enable people to connect to one another and support each other in being physically active. For example, parents of young children can support one another by providing child care for each other, people who already have a personal trainer can provide access to one for someone who doesn't (McNeil, Kreuter, & Subramanian, 2006), and someone who belongs to a health club can bring a friend as a guest. Think about this in the context of your own interpersonal relationships on campus. If your friends use the recreation facilities on campus, isn't there a better likelihood that you will too?

Also important is that when people engage in physical activity with others in their social network, physical activity can be established as a social norm (Stahl et al., 2001). When a behavior becomes a social norm, it is acceptable and often expected that members of the social network engage in the behavior. If the behavior is a health enhancing one, everyone benefits.

Institutional Level

In the SEM, factors at the institutional or organizational level can promote or constrain behaviors. These are the rules, regulations, and policies of informal structures (Eddy et al., 2002; McLeroy et al., 1988) that are often associated with the workplace environment. Examples of institutional level factors include policies providing flex time to enable employees to attend health programs, healthy food selections in the cafeteria (Eddy et al., 2002), corporate sponsorship of health initiatives, incentives for participation in health activities, use of worksite communication networks to share information about health initiatives (Watt, Donahue, Eddy, & Wallace, 2001), and recommendations from the medical establishment (Kumar et al., 2012).

Institutional factors in a school setting can affect bullying behavior. Bullying is greater in schools where there is an unfavorable environment and low academic performance expectations (Barboza et al., 2009), poor teacher–student relationships (Bacchini, Esposito, & Affuso, 2009), and support (Barbozoa et al., 2009).

Institutional factors, in the form of recommendations from healthcare providers, were significant for people who chose to receive the H1N1 vaccine in 2009. There was a greater chance of people getting vaccinated if they received information from healthcare providers about the vaccine and if they believed the healthcare providers wanted them to be vaccinated (Kumar et al., 2012).

Organizational factors affect the success of screening programs, as in the case of screening for colorectal cancer. Among the factors are access to screening equipment to handle the patient load and a referral systems for patients needing follow-up treatment (Nuss et al., 2012).

To promote physical activity among Latino populations, the church is often a partner in health promotion. Organizational factors such as allowing announcements about the physical activity schedule at mass and ministry meetings, including class and activity schedules in the church bulletin, permitting presentations at church events, and allotting space for classes and other activities (Haughton, Ayala, Elder, & Arredondo, 2015).

Community Level

At the community level, factors influencing behavior include social networks, norms, or standards of behavior that exist formally or informally among individuals, groups, or organizations (Eddy et al., 2002; McLeroy et al., 1988; WHO, 2006). The norms of the community are associated with specific behaviors, some health enhancing and some not. For instance, they might include involvement in health initiatives such as the Great American Smoke-out (Watt et al., 2001), participation in organized sports, volunteering at the local fire department, not cutting your lawn on Sunday morning, driving children to school rather than letting them to walk, or allowing underage youngsters to drink in your home.

Looking at violent behavior, associated factors at this level include high population density, people frequently moving in and out, and great diversity relative to age and income. These factors result in a community with little social glue holding it together. Violence is more likely to occur in a community with these characteristics. It is also more likely in communities where there is drug trafficking, a high level of unemployment, and where people do not know their neighbors and are not involved in local community activities (WHO, 2006).

Similarly, we see a greater likelihood of bullying behavior in children exposed to dangerous or violent neighborhoods. These are neighborhoods where there is robbery, fighting and the risk of harassment by a stranger. In fact, children who are bullies or who have both bullied and been the victims of bullying are more likely to have experienced neighborhood violence like this, than are children who are always the victims of bullying (Bacchini et al., 2009).

Other factors, such as access to full-service supermarkets and fresh fruits and vegetables affect behavior relative to dietary intake (see **FIGURE 10.3**). If the only food available in a community is poor quality and high calorie—think fast food—then it is only logical for the people in that community to have diets predominately composed of those foods.

FIGURE 10.3 Community-level factors influence health behavior.
© Lisa S./Shutterstock

Societal Level

At the societal level we find broader factors that encourage or discourage specific behaviors. These include economics, social policies, social or cultural norms of behavior, and attitudes. Going back to the violence example, factors at the societal level that encourage this behavior would be cultural acceptability of conflict resolution through violent means, parental rights overriding child welfare, and male dominance over women and children (WHO, 2006).

If we look at smoking behavior from the societal level, laws are now in effect in many states banning indoor smoking in public places and making the sale of cigarettes to minors illegal. These laws affect behavior and ultimately health.

Another example is the 2012 changes in the standards for the national school lunch and breakfast program which required schools to increase availability of fruits and vegetables, whole grains, fat-free or low-fat milk and reduce sodium, saturated and trans fats, within children's calorie requirements (Nutrition Standards in the National School Lunch and Breakfast Program, 2012). With this one policy change the dietary intake of every child in the country who eats breakfast or lunch at school changed!

The 2012 ban on sugary drinks of more than 16 oz. in NYC is an example of a society-level change in policy that was an attempt to change the behavior of everyone who lives, works, or visits NYC! While its intention was noble, it was challenged in the courts and ruled illegal in 2014.

Think of all the other societal standards affecting health behavior—seat belt laws, driving age, drinking age, age of consent, vaccination requirements for school attendance, and Medicare enrollment at age 65, to name a few.

In summary, the SEM explains behavior as the result of an interplay between internal and external factors.

THEORY IN ACTION—CLASS ACTIVITY

In the African country of Zimbabwe, married couples and those in long-term relationships are at greatest risk for HIV, a situation not expected given that marriage or a stable long-term relationship is usually associated with safer sex behavior.

Based on your knowledge of HIV/AIDS risk reduction behaviors (safer sex) but not knowing anything else about the culture of this country, in small groups:

1. Identify safer sex behaviors.
2. Brainstorm possible factors at the personal, interpersonal, and community level that may account for the high rates of HIV among those married or in long-term relationships.
3. Brainstorm how these factors might be used to develop intervention to reduce the risk of HIV among married persons.

Then, read the following article and answer the questions at the end.

Chapter 10 Article: Understanding barriers to safer sex practice in Zimbabwean marriages: implications for future HIV prevention interventions[1]

Esther Mugweni[1*], Mayeh Omar[2] and Stephen Pearson[2]

[1]Department of Infection and Population Health, University College London, Mortimer Market Centre off Capper Street, London WC1E 6JB, UK and
[2]Nuffield Centre for International Health and Development, University of Leeds, 101 Clarendon Road, Leeds LS2 9LJ, UK

Abstract

Against the backdrop of high human immunodeficiency virus (HIV) prevalence in stable relationships in Southern Africa, our study presents sociocultural barriers to safer sex practice in Zimbabwean marriages. We conducted 36 in-depth interviews and four focus group discussions with married men and women in Zimbabwe in 2008. Our aim was to identify barriers faced by married women when negotiating for safer sex. Participants identified individual, relational and community-level barriers. Individual level barriers made women voiceless to negotiate for safer sex. Being voiceless emanated from lack sexual decision-making power, economic dependence, low self-efficacy or fear of actual or perceived consequences of negotiating for safer sex. Relational barriers included trust and self-disclosure. At the community level, extended family members and religious leaders were said to explicitly or implicitly discourage women's safer sex negotiation. Given the complexity and multi-levelled nature of barriers affecting sexual behaviour in marriage, our findings suggest that HIV prevention interventions targeted at married women would benefit from empowering individual women, couples and also addressing the wider community.

▶ Introduction

More than 80% of new human immunodeficiency virus (HIV) infections in women in Africa are estimated to occur in marriage or long-term relationships, yet very few HIV prevention interventions exist to empower women in such relationships to negotiate for safer sex.[1, 2] Couples in stable long-term relationships or marriages in Africa are the largest HIV risk group.[3–6] This is also the case in Zimbabwe where

---

1 Reproduced from Mugweni, E., Omar, M. & Pearson, S. (2015). Understanding barriers to safer sex practice in Zimbabwean marriages: Implications for future HIV prevention interventions. *Health Education Research*, *30*(3), 388–399. doi: 10.1093/her/cyu073.

* Corresponding author.

heterosexual intercourse is the main mode of HIV transmission among married or cohabiting couples.[7] (The term sex in this article refers to heterosexual intercourse.)

According to the Zimbabwe Demographic Health Survey, HIV prevalence among men and women aged between 15 and 49 years tested between 2010 and 2011 was highest among widows (56%) and widowers (61%).[7] HIV, being the leading cause of death among adults in this region, is consequently the major cause of widowhood.[8, 9] Quantitative research from rural Zimbabwe suggests that high prevalence of HIV during widowhood is a result of infections acquired before becoming widowed.[10]

Preventing HIV infection in married or stable relationships is now an international HIV prevention priority.[8] Marriage is near universal in Zimbabwe; the proportion of never-married women declines from 74% in the 15–19 years age group to 2% in the 45–49 years age group.[7] Previous research in Zimbabwe indicates that persons in marriages or long-term cohabiting unions have a higher risk of acquiring HIV infection than never married people due to increased frequency of sex and low condom use.[11]

Safer sex strategies represent a principle objective of global HIV prevention interventions that address sexual transmission of HIV.[1] Our study contributes to an emerging body of literature that highlights the complexities of adopting safer sex practice in stable relationships.[3–5, 12, 13] Safer sex negotiation involves communicating and persuading a partner to support one's view on safer sex or achieving a mutually agreeable view on safer sex. Safer sex strategies include abstinence, mutual monogamy, correct and consistent condom use, male circumcision, voluntary counselling and testing (VCT) for HIV, open communication on sexual issues and treatment of sexually transmitted infections.[1, 14, 15]

In Zimbabwe, safer sex practice within marriage remains low and little is known about the sociocultural context of sexuality in marriage or how this affects practice of safer sex by married women.[11, 16] This article aims to elucidate the personal, social and cultural barriers to safer sex practice faced by women in Zimbabwean marriage. Our working definition of 'marriage' matches the common understanding of marriage in Zimbabwean society. A couple may become married through the event of a customary, court or church wedding or if they have been cohabiting or living together as husband and wife. This definition is also used in the Zimbabwe Demographic Health Survey.[10]

▶ The current study

Overall our study aimed to develop interventions to empower married Zimbabwean women to negotiate for safer sex. This article reports on findings related to one of the research objectives, that is, to describe and explain sociocultural barriers faced by married women when negotiating for safer sex. Ethical approval was obtained from the Leeds Institute of Health Sciences Ethical Committee and the Medical Research Council of Zimbabwe (MRCZ/A/1493).

▶ Method

The study methodology has been well described elsewhere[17] hence we only provide a summary of the methodology in this section. We used a qualitative research design for this exploratory study. While some studies involve only one episode of fieldwork, repeat cross-sectional or panel studies may be done to capture a full picture on a subject.[18]

Phased studies are also used if each cross sectional study influences instrument design for subsequent studies.[19, 20] To this end, our study was conducted in three phases.

We began data collection with program implementers to overview current HIV prevention programs for married people and possible interventions. Issues for further investigation such as the need for interventions were confirmed in Phase 1 and became part of the Phase 2 interview schedule. Phase 2 researched sources and solutions to powerlessness to negotiate for safer sex based on the findings of Phase 1. As indicated in similar studies, powerless populations may not have the capacity to carry out the interventions they suggest.[21, 22] This necessitated a Phase 3 where we engaged program implementers in interviews based on the Phase 2 results. We collected data to understand the organizational or sociocultural feasibility of implementing some of the suggested interventions.

This article is based on the second phase of the study; conducted between October and December 2008. Thirty-six in-depth interviews and four focus group discussions were conducted with married men and women in Harare. Participants were recruited into the study using intensity sampling and snowball sampling. Intensity sampling was from three organizations working in HIV prevention services: a faith-based organization that provides marital counselling; an anti-domestic violence NGO and a NGO that supports HIV positive couples. We recruited participants that were not married to each other due to the sensitive and taboo nature of discussing sexuality in the research setting. Previous research indicates that this approach may allow participants to be more open about sensitive issues because of anonymity and reduced fear that their spouse may get to know their responses.[23] Furthermore, this approach meant that the potential threat of physical violence on participants and researcher was minimized. However, this meant that we did not have each spouse's understanding of barriers to safer sex experienced as a couple.

All interviews were transcribed verbatim into a computer, with NVivo used to manage the data. Data analysis used framework analysis.[24, 25] We started by familiarization with the data, from which a coding system was developed and applied. Next, we sorted data so that material with similar content was located together.[24, 26] The first author did the coding of the data. Finally we used anonymized quotations to illustrate descriptive and explanatory findings.[24, 26]

▶ Results

Thirty-three men and 31 women participated in Phase 2 of the study (**TABLE A.1**). The majority of the participants (43.8%) were between 35 and 44 years old. There was a mix of employment status; most women (48.4%) were informally employed. All men were employed with an almost equal mix of informal and formal employment. Participants had been married for a wide range of time with most participants reporting between 6 and 15 years in marriage. Most of the participants were educated to secondary level and a few had tertiary education.

Analysis of the data indicated that married women faced barriers to safer sex at individual, relational and community levels (**FIGURE A.1**). Individual barriers were a direct product of a person's social status. Relational barriers were a direct product of interpersonal dynamics within the marital relationship. We also identify community-level barrier which other authors refer to as structural barriers.[27, 28] Structural barriers include social, economic, cultural or organizational factors that

TABLE A.1 Sociodemographic characteristics of interview and focus group discussion participants.[17]

	Men (%) $n=33$	Women (%) $n=31$
Age group		
20–24 years		9.7
25–34 years	33.3	32.3
35–44 years	48.5	38.7
>45 years	18.2	19.3
Employment status		
Informal	51.5	48.4
Formal	48.5	25.8
Unemployed		25.8
Number of years married		
<6 years	36.4	38.7
6–15 years	45.5	32.3
>15 years	18.2	22.6
Educational status		
Primary education	0.1	3.6
Secondary education	60.6	70.6
Tertiary education	30.3	25.8

Reproduced from Mugweni, E., Omar, M. & Pearson, S. (2015). Understanding barriers to safer sex practice in Zimbabwean marriages: Implications for future HIV prevention interventions. *Health Education Research, 30*(3), 388–399. doi: 10.1093/her/cyu073.

constrain individual uptake of safer sex.[27] As we have described barriers pertaining to masculinity and femininity elsewhere, they are not repeated in this article.[17] Although we have made a distinction between the barriers, we must point out that sometimes an overlap existed between the various barriers.

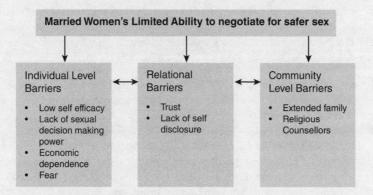

FIG. A.1 Barriers to safer sex practice faced by married women. We begin this section by describing the individual barriers, and then we describe relational barriers. We complete this section with a description of community-level barriers.

Reproduced from Mugweni, E., Omar, M. & Pearson, S. (2015). Understanding barriers to safer sex practice in Zimbabwean marriages: Implications for future HIV prevention interventions. *Health Education Research, 30*(3), 388-399. doi: 10.1093/her/cyu073.

▶ Individual barriers

I ask my friends, 'If you caught your husband with a girlfriend would you ask him to use a condom'. They say it's difficult for us women .... (Tinofiramukati) Most times we suffer silently ... We just die silently.

(Female, Interview respondent, Aged 31)

In participants' reports on married women's limited ability to negotiate for safer sex, several male and female participants used phrases such as, 'lack of voice'; 'voiceless'; 'can't stand up for herself' or 'dying silently'. On the basis of these narratives, we define this concept of voicelessness as an inability to express one's opinion about safer sex needs. It also refers to a lack of being heard or listened to when one gives their opinion on uptake of safer sex. This concept has been described in other studies in the United States and Zimbabwe examining women's limited ability to negotiate for safer sex.[21, 29] We now discuss the four themes participants cited to explain their voicelessness: (i) lack of sexual decision-making power, (ii) fear, (iii) low self-efficacy and (iv) economic dependence.

(a) Lack of sexual decision-making power

In some narratives by both men and women, it was implicitly as well as explicitly indicated that married women's voicelessness emanated from an inferior social position that required women to be quiet, listen to their husbands and not make suggestions about their sexual lives. Their silence was described as a feminine sign of respect. Consequently these women were voiceless to negotiate for safer sex.

Other participants indicated that women were not silent about their sexual lives. However, they faced another manifestation of voicelessness. When these women suggested condom use or refused unprotected sex, this was met with sexual violence or vehement refusal to use condoms from their partner. John, for example, thought that his wife had no basis for asking him to use a condom, because she 'belonged to him':

> JOHN: My wife will be saying, '... Ah what about wearing some condoms?' As you look at me do you think I can wear protection on my wife?
> INTERVIEWER: Condoms?
> JOHN: Yes. It's not possible?! If she is mine, she is mine. Even if I may go and do other things out there, if she is mine, she is mine ... She may talk but as a man I have a final say. Because I can say to her, 'Why do you want me to wear a condom are we prostitutes?' I, as her husband, I have the say ... whether to put on or not to put on the protection.

(John, Interview Respondent, Aged 35)

As far as John was concerned, as the man, he made the final decision on whether or not to use condoms with her. Refusal to use condoms was functional—it showed male sexual decision-making power. In other qualitative research in Africa on gender relations in heterosexual relationships, such refusal is identified as both a mark of hegemony and a successful claim to power.[30, 31]

It is imperative to understand how sexual decision-making power in Zimbabwean marriage is constructed, as this may explain the experiences of men like John. In the extract, John objectified his wife. Although this was not universal in the dataset, some men thought they had overall sexual decision making power because of bride price. Bride price is part of the formal marriage in many African cultures and involves payment in the form of cattle or money from the groom to the bride's father and his family.[29, 32–34]

There is evidence to suggest that representations of the hegemonic masculinity are changing in Southern Africa.[31, 35, 36] Themes in the data indicate that the traditional voicelessness of married women is being challenged and shifting. Indeed, some men in this study acknowledged that their wives had a 'voice' in their sexual lives but not necessarily the power to make firm decisions about safer sex. Change was also reflected in women who reported being able to successfully negotiate mutual monogamy or the occasional condom use.

(b) Fear

The second representation of voicelessness was a fear of the likely consequences of asking for safer sex. Actual and perceived consequences reported by participants included rejection, abandonment, physical, sexual or emotional abuse or general deterioration of the marital relationship. Women negotiating for safer sex feared their actions would be misinterpreted sometimes as condoning an affair, as Clive noted:

> You find that if women negotiate for safer sex, it's almost like licensing the affair. Where you say ... If you want us to have safer sex, you are aware and not only are you aware but you are by implication, ok with my affair. You really know that I am having sex with someone else. So this affair shouldn't be an issue to you.

(Clive, Interview respondent, Aged 45)

Clive explained that by negotiating for safer sex, a wife indirectly gave her husband permission to have extramarital sexual relations. It was as if asking for condoms or abstinence removed a husband's obligation to monogamy. Therefore, voicelessness was interpreted as a silent way of communicating to the husband that having affairs was unacceptable. The need to negotiate for mutual monogamy was portrayed as being more important to women than negotiating other forms of safer sex strategies such as condoms.

In other narratives from women, persistent negotiation of abstinence or condoms was described as generating fear that husbands may seek other sexual partners. This in turn created the fear of separation or divorce. Avoiding divorce and practising safer sex became competing interests and in some women's narratives, preserving the marriage was more important than practising safer sex.

(c) Low self-efficacy

Both male and female participants also explained some womens' voicelessness as a product of low self-efficacy. In the context of this study, participants described this concept as an inability to persuade a husband to use condoms or to go for VCT. Alternative working definitions of self-efficacy have been offered by other researchers.[21]

Some participants associated low self-efficacy with femininity characterized by a sexual passivity. Unsafe sex was 'done to women' and they were unable to refuse. One woman explained low self-efficacy as a product of sexual desire. When she was sexually aroused, she was unable to convince the husband to use condoms. Similar issues were raised in one of the female focus group discussions:

EMELIA: When our husbands go out to girlfriends; the husbands are touched in some ways that wives are not allowed ...

CHIDO: Because of all that he is getting from girlfriends, he will not give you any sex. You actually will be envying chickens or dogs that will be mating, saying 'If only I was the one mating'.

(OTHERS LAUGH)

JANET: When the man is unfaithful, the wife is hungry for sex. Today he comes home and he says he is tired and tomorrow he comes home and says he is tired. When he finally touches the wife, she is so hungry she will do it with no condom so that she can finish 'hukasha' (sexual desire) that has been kept for a year.

The above discussion corresponds with other scholars' views that negotiation may not be an appropriate concept for safer sex as it does not demonstrate and capture the view that sex can be a highly charged and emotive experience.[37] This above discussion highlights that the highly charged nature of some sexual encounters reduced self-efficacy in the practice of safer sex.

Nevertheless, there were other stories of self-efficacy with regards to safer sex. Women in a different focus group discussion narrated refusing unprotected sex and abstaining from sex for several months if the husband refused condom use. These women were not passive participants in sex but were actively decided what happened. They had a voice in their sexual lives. However, some men in the focus group discussions suggested women were largely inconsistent about safer sex. It was reported that some women insisted on safer sex for a while but reverted to unprotected sex after their anger about affairs had subsided; as documented in a similar study in Nigeria.[13]

(d) Economic dependence

Women's voicelessness was also explained as a product of economic dependence on their husbands. This dependence made some women afraid to ask for condoms or VCT because they feared that divorce could result. Even though divorce would reduce the risk of HIV infection, it had undesirable financial implications. In the harsh economic climate of Zimbabwe, when data were collected (October–December 2008), the fear of losing financial support cannot be underestimated. Economic dependence has been associated with inability to negotiate for safer sex in other studies that have investigated women's vulnerability to HIV in Southern Africa.[38, 39]

Only one woman in this study reported being able to consistently practice safer sex. At the time of the interview, Charity, a successful medical professional had been married for 15 years to James, an equally successful medical professional. In the third year of their marriage James admitted having an affair with a work colleague. When Charity first asked that they use condoms, James categorically refused. As the final authority in the marriage, he continued to have unprotected sex with Charity.

In the interview, Charity explained weighing the possible consequences of persistently asking James for condoms:

> INTERVIEWER: How did you manage to convince your husband to use condoms? How did you handle the situation?
> CHARITY: It's either condoms or no sex. You just get to a place where you are prepared to maybe lose your marriage. Because, he might say, 'No, I will not do that with you so you are actually giving me a leeway to leave you. Because you are not giving me what is my right (unprotected sex)'. So, by the time that I demanded condoms, I was prepared for anything. I felt so wronged that if he chose to go then I said to myself it was not meant to be (taps the table several times to show emphasis). Because how can you wrong me and expect me to take you as you are and share the risk? It takes a very daring wife ... very daring wife to ask for a condom.

After initial powerlessness, Charity managed to get James to use condoms. Unlike some of the other women she was prepared to lose the marriage, the house and social status to protect herself from the risk of HIV infection.

We must point out that her success in adopting safer sex did not occur overnight. Furthermore, Charity was a little different from other women in the study who failed to practice safer sex consistently. Some of the latter group were poor and had little education. Even for those who had some education; finding gainful employment would be more difficult for them than for Charity, a medical professional in a country of acute medical personnel shortages. Furthermore, Charity had the option of leaving her husband if he refused to practice safer sex knowing full well that she was economically empowered with more life choices available. Other married women's economic dependence on their husbands made making such ultimatums unlikely.

Having said this, none of the women whose husband was having affairs highlighted that they did not leave the husband because they were unable to take care of themselves without him. On the contrary, some women had started small business projects (such as selling fish) because of the additional financial cost of supporting a second household or partner. Yet these women did not divorce or ask for condom use. We speculate that the relationship between poverty and ability to negotiate for safer sex is much more complex than just assuming that poverty means inability to negotiate for safer sex.

▶ Relational barriers

Relational barriers concern how interpersonal relationships are constructed.[40] In the narratives, trust and lack of self-disclosure were two prominent and complex relational barriers that were faced by some married women when they negotiated for safer sex.

(a) Trust

In this study, trust was described by male and female participants as an assumption that a spouse was behaving benevolently towards their husband or wife. This description of trust has also been documented in a qualitative study on condom use in Southern Africa.[41] Male and female participants reported that a spouse was deemed trustworthy if their behaviour showed no indication of involvement with other sexual partners. Some of the assumed indications of extramarital sexual activity included persistent disinterest in sex, phone calls or text messages from (presumably) other sexual partners or persistently coming home late. In the absence of these indications, trust prevailed and some women assumed that mutual monogamy was their safer sex strategy. As such, requesting condom use was deemed unnecessary. In reality, however, trust was sometimes misplaced. Some men spoke of their discretion when they had affairs and ensuring any incriminating indicators were concealed.

Hannah, for example, reported that in the twenty years of marriage she had never suspected her husband of having an affair. Consequently, she had not negotiated for other safer sex strategies (such as condom use) because she assumed they were mutually monogamous and she trusted her husband. It was a great shock to get an HIV-positive result after a bout of unexplained fever. Her trust had limited her ability to negotiate for other safer sex strategies.

Having said this, several female participants voluntarily reported that they did not trust their husbands to be monogamous. However, similar to a study in Nigeria,[13] this mistrust did not result in condom or VCT uptake. Again this shows how multiple barriers may operate concurrently to prevent women from negotiating for safer sex.

(b) Lack of self-disclosure

In several US studies, close relationships (such as marriage), were viewed as forums for engaging in self-disclosure.[42-44] However, cultures vary significantly in how this is experienced in marriage. Without a spouse extensively disclosing their sexual history, wives reported underestimating the risk of contracting HIV from them. This was the case for Jane, who accidentally came across her husband Martin's tuberculosis treatment cards as she cleaned their home. In 3 months that they had been married he had never mentioned tuberculosis or his HIV positive status. Lacking this information, Jane had assumed that as long as they were mutually monogamous, HIV infection was unlikely:

> My husband has infected me with HIV. He says that he is sorry but that does not help me! It does not reverse my status. It will not make me HIV negative. I got married to a man who never told me he was living with HIV/AIDS. He was a person who was hiding from me what he knows. When we started living together, I saw his hospital cards when he was treated for TB and I thought to go for testing in July this year, and I tested positive.
>
> (Female, Interview Respondent, Aged 24).

Contrastingly, Melody's husband disclosed his affair with a woman who had died of AIDS. Even with this information, Melody had unprotected sex with him. Again, the point is made that barriers were experienced differently by participants.

▶ Community-level barriers

Powerlessness to negotiate for safer sex was sometimes a product of factors beyond the individual or relational level. We discuss community-level barriers below:

(a) Extended family

Marriage in Zimbabwe involves the families of the bride and groom becoming related and forming part of the extended family of the couple. In this study, the extended family was sometimes accused of making safer sex negotiation in the form of divorce difficult for women. The extended family members were said to sometimes insist that women persevere in risky marriages, as Sharon explained:

> The relatives say, 'You stay there for the children! What do you think is so important about you? All of us this is how our mothers lived. Don't you know this is what men do?!' And so for you to walk out it's like you are a weak woman. How come you can't do what all the other women are doing? What is so special about you?
>
> (Female, Interview Respondent, Aged 27)

Previous research indicates that senior extended family members may discourage women from divorcing due to the resulting social stigmatization.[45, 46] In participants' narratives, divorce was seen as a failure in emphasized femininity. This is because in the African patriarchal system, a woman's social status is measured by her success in marriage.[47] The Shona word for 'divorced' (*kurambwa*) translates as 'rejected'. Thus, rejection was not just from the husband but from the extended family and the community, as Maureen clarified:

> MAUREEN: It's unacceptable in our culture to divorce (*kurambwa*). So a person would rather be bruised and wounded and torn up as long as they are Mrs so and so.
> INTERVIEWER: So it is unacceptable to whom?
> MAUREEN: To society, to relatives, to friends. It's stigmatized. People reject you and say, 'Even her husband left her'. It's almost like you are an outcast.

(Female, interview respondent, Aged 31)

Some contrary narratives included women obtaining support from their extended family to practice other forms of safer sex such as treatment of STIs, VCT or condom use. For example, after Simone's husband was caught having sex with a girlfriend at work, his wife went to his grandfather to petition for help in getting him to go for VCT. As a traditional authority figure in the family, the grandfather had the power to tell his grandson to attend VCT which enabled Simone to practice safer sex.

(b) Religious counsellors

In this study, respondents talked spontaneously about how central religion was to marriage through beliefs, doctrines, prayer, faith or church attendance. Given this background, religious leaders and counsellors played a significant role in the lives of some women. In the doctrine of some churches, messages preached directly prohibited divorce. Women whose husbands were having affairs were sometimes advised to pray and 'have faith' that their husbands would stop having affairs. One participant who counsels women in difficult marriages explained how the HIV epidemic had prompted changes in the religious counsel given to women:

> INTERVIEWER: Why hasn't she walked out of the marriage?
> ALICE: I will be honest, I think the main thing is this whole Christian thing that, 'Believe God. It's going to work out. You can't divorce etc'. Although there has been a change in Christian counseling that if you are at risk of infection and you can't negotiate safer sex and the man is turning violent and things like that really you have to think of divorce as an option.

(Female, Interview Respondent, Aged 28)

▶ Discussion

In this article, we described and explained individual, relational and community-level barriers to safer sex by married women. A limitation of our study is that we did not interview couples. This could have given a fuller picture of relational barriers as they are experienced by couples and this may be an area for future research. Another limitation is that we present only women's experience of barriers. We acknowledge that men in Southern Africa also face barriers when negotiating for safer sex with their wives.[48, 49] Finally, on reflection we would have investigated further how barriers to safer sex practice are affected by the length of marriage or a spouse's educational level. We think this is an important area for future research and would be useful for HIV prevention program implementers in developing targeted interventions.

Despite these limitations, our study highlights new information on the 'voice-lessness' faced by some women when negotiating for safer sex in marriage. This voicelessness was reported as emanating from a lack of sexual decision-making power, economic dependence, low self-efficacy or fear. Sometimes more than one of these factors operated in a single sexual encounter forming a complex myriad of barriers to overcome in order to succeed at safer sex. This complexity implies that empowering married women to negotiate for safer sex calls for complex interventions, with various components to address the different barriers simultaneously.

Lack of sexual decision-making power was reported as a product of women's inferior social position. This association is well documented in the literature from Zimbabwe.[29, 50] Other participants attributed women's lack of sexual decisionmaking power to the bride price practice; which was sometimes interpreted as comodification of women and a basis for objectifying wives in our study and in other previous research.[4, 29, 51, 52]

Because asking for safer sex was sometimes seen as licensing an affair, some women preferred not to confront their husbands about infidelity. This preference represents an almost non verbal negotiation for mutual monogamy. An underlying assumption from public health practitioners is that when risk of HIV infection is known, married women would want to use condoms or abstain from sex.[31, 53] However, in our study, this approach was sometimes seen as condoning extramarital affairs and thus undesirable. HIV program implementers may view such a strategy as insufficient or futile. However this strategy may be conceivable for women given the emotional, social and economic security of married life. There is need for sensitivity to this local context in HIV prevention.

Our study brings to light the negative social, emotional and financial implications of safer sex negotiation, as highlighted by previous studies.[54-56] Our study affirms that these financial implications may limit what may be envisaged as a safer sex option. However, this finding is contrary to previous studies in Malawi and Mozambique that indicate women are able to divorce when at risk of HIV.[31, 53] It is possible that interventions that address the social stigma of divorce as well as interventions that strengthen laws to protect the rights of divorcing women in Zimbabwe, may go a long way in empowering women to leave marriages that put them at risk of contracting HIV.

Besides voicelessness, trust was a relational barrier to safer sex negotiation as noted in other literature.[41, 46, 57] This creates real dilemmas in the construction of HIV prevention interventions. How can married people assess monogamy in their spouse? Do we design interventions that tell people to disregard trust? We have no clear cut answers to these complex questions and broad statements on this issue are unlikely to be useful. Interpersonal interventions such as couple counselling may be more useful in addressing this issue and can be explored in relation to couple counselling for HIV.[58-60]

At the community level, contradictory narratives were given on the role of extended family members in safer sex negotiation. In some narratives extended family members exacerbated the vulnerability of women by insisting that they persevere in marriage, even when HIV infection was known to be a significant risk. This social pressure has been documented in other studies.[46, 61] There is need to develop interventions targeted at the community that married women live in, which socially reward women for preserving in difficult and sometimes hazardous marriages.

On the other hand, and as documented elsewhere,[31] some women obtained support to practice safer sex with their husbands from respected family members who were knowledgeable about HIV. HIV prevention information should therefore not narrowly target married people but also influential older members of the community who are often seen as 'fountains of knowledge' in the Zimbabwean culture. They may be able to provide a supportive environment for practising safer sex. It is equally important to also target religious leaders who were said to prohibit divorce among congregation members. It is possible that partnering with religious leaders to provide HIV education would enable them to give women more effective and appropriate counselling facing the risk of HIV from a husband.

▶ Conclusion

This research addresses the gap in the HIV prevention strategies for married women. The results indicate that safer sex in marriage is negotiated in a wider sociocultural context. Effective prevention strategies must address this sociocultural context by targeting married women, married couples and community members to strengthen women's ability to negotiate for safer sex.

▶ Acknowledgements

We would like to thank all the women, men and organizations that participated in this study. We would also like to thank Prof. James Hakim, Rangarirai Tigere, Thomasina Muchakwana and Alice Thole for their support during the data collection. Finally, we express our gratitude to the independent reviewers for their invaluable input and support.

▶ Funding

University of Leeds Tetley Lupton Scholarship (to E.M.).

▶ References

1.   UNAIDS. AIDS Epidemic Update. Joint United Nations Programme on HIV/AIDS (UNAIDS) and World Health Organization. Geneva: WHO, 2010.
2.   UNFPA. State of the World Population 2005. Geneva: United Nations Population Fund, 2005.
3.   Coma JC. When the group encourages extramarital sex: difficulties in HIV/AIDS prevention in rural Malawi. Demogr Res 2013; 28: 849–79.

4. Mkandawire-Valhmu L, Wendland C, Stevens P et al. Marriage as a risk factor for HIV: learning from the experiences of HIV-infected women in Malawi. Glob Public Health 2013; 8: 187–201.

5. Tenkorang EY. Negotiating safer sex among married women in Ghana. Arch Sex Behav 2012; 41: 1353–62.

6. Coates TJ, Richter L, Caceres C. HIV prevention 3 behavioural strategies to reduce HIV transmission: how to make them work better. Lancet 2008; 372: 669–84.

7. Zimbabwe Demographic Health Survey (ZDHS). Central Statistical Office. Harare, MA: Macro International, 2011.

8. UNAIDS. AIDS Epidemic Update. Joint United Nations Programme on HIV/AIDS (UNAIDS) and World Health Organization. Geneva: WHO, 2009.

9. WHO. Global Burden of Disease. Geneva: World Health Organisation, 2002b.

10. Lopman BA, Nyamukapa C, Hallett T et al. Role of widows in the heterosexual transmission of HIV in Manicaland, Zimbabwe, 1998–2003. Sex Transm Infect 2009; 85: I41–8.

11. Hageman KM, Dube HM, Mugurungi O et al. Beyond monogamy: opportunities to further reduce risk for HIV infection among married zimbabwean women with only one lifetime partner. Aids Behav 2010; 14: 113–24.

12. Thege B. Rural black women's agency within partnerships amid the South African HIV epidemic. Afr J AIDS Res 2009; 8: 455–64.

13. Smith D. Modern marriage, men's extramarital sex, and HIV risk in southeastern Nigeria. Am J Public Health 2007; 97: 997–1005.

14. Shelton JD, Halperin DT, Nantulya V et al. Partner reduction is crucial for balanced "ABC" approach to HIV prevention. Br Med J 2004; 328: 891–3.

15. WHO. Preventing HIV/AIDS in young people: a systematic review of the evidence from developing countries in WHO Technical Report Series D. In: Ross DA, Dick B, Ferguson J, WHO (eds). UNAIDS-Interagency Task Team on Young People. Geneva: World Health Organisation, 2006b, 43–78.

16. Callegari L, Harper CC, van der Straten A et al. Consistent condom use in married Zimbabwean women after a condom intervention. Sex Transm Dis 2008; 35: 624–30.

17. Mugweni E, Pearson S, Omar M. Traditional gender roles, forced sex and HIV in Zimbabwean marriages. Culture Health Sex 2012; 14: 577–90; www.tandfonline.com.

18. Lewis J, Ritchie J. Generalising from qualitative research. In: Ritchie J, Lewis J (eds). Qualitative Research Practice : A Guide for Social Science Students and Researchers. London: SAGE Publications, 2003.

19. Russell S, Seeley J. The transition to living with HIV as a chronic condition in rural Uganda: working to create order and control when on antiretroviral therapy. Soc Sci Med 2010; 70: 375–82.

20. Uys LR, Holzemer WL, Chirwa ML et al. The development and validation of the HIV/AIDS Stigma Instrument Nurse (HASI-N). Aids Care 2009; 21: 150–9.

21. Romero L, Wallerstein N, Lucero J et al. Woman to woman: coming together for positive change-using empowerment and popular education to prevent HIV in women. Aids Educ Prev 2006; 18: 390–405.

22. Wallerstein N. Powerlessness, empowerment and health: implications for health promotion programs. Am J Health Promot 1992; 6: 197–205.

23. Morrow S. Honor and respect: feminist collaborative research with sexually abused women in qualitative research methods for psychologists. Fischer C (ed). London: Elsevier, 2006.

24. Ritchie J, Spencer J, O'Connor W. Carrying out qualitative analysis. In: Ritchie J, Lewis J (eds). Qualitative Research Practice: A Guide for Social Science Students and Researchers. London: Sage Publications, 2003, 220–63.

25. Bazeley P. Qualitative Data Analysis with NVivo. London: Sage Publications, 2007.

26. Miles M, Huberman M. Qualitative Data Analysis: An Expanded Source Book. 2nd edn. London: Sage, 1994.

27. Gupta GR, Parkhurst JO, Ogden JA et al. HIV prevention 4 Structural approaches to HIV prevention. Lancet 2008; 372: 764–75.

28. Rotheram-Borus MJ, Swendeman D, Flannery D et al. Common factors in effective HIV prevention programs. Aids Behav 2009b; 13: 399–408.

29. Duffy L. Culture and context of HIV prevention in rural Zimbabwe: the influence of gender inequality. J Transcult Nurs 2005; 16: 23–31.

30. Silberschmidt M. Male Sexuality in the context of socioeconomic change in rural and urban East Africa. In: Sexuality in Africa Magazine. Nigeria: Africa Regional Sexuality Resource Centre Lagos, 2005, 5–8.

31. Bandali S. Norms and practices within marriage which shape gender roles, HIV/AIDS risk and risk reduction strategies in Cabo Delgado, Mozambique. Aids Care 2011; 23: 1171–6.

32. Wendo C. African women denounce bride price. Lancet 2004; 363: 716.

33. Esen UI. African women, bride price, and AIDS. Lancet 2004; 363: 1734.

34. Marindo R, Pearson S, Casterline JB. Condom Use and Abstinence among Unmarried Young People in Zimbabwe: Which Strategy, Whose Agenda? In: Council P (ed). Population Council, 2003.

35. Jobson G. Changing masculinities: land-use, family communication and prospects for working with older men towards gender equality in a livelihoods intervention. Cult Health Sex 2010; 12: 233–46.

36. Pearson S, Makadzange P. Help-seeking behaviour for sexual health concerns: a qualitative study of men in Zimbabwe. Cult Health Sex 2008; 10: 361–76.

37. Edgar T, Noar S, Freimuth V (eds). Communication Perspectives on HIV/AIDS for the 21st Century. London: Lawrence Erlbaum Associates Taylor and Francis Group, 2008.

38. Kim J, MacPherson E, Pronyk P et al. Ford Foundation: Global Review of Good Practices on the Intersections Between HIV/AIDS and Economic Empowerment. London: London School of Hygiene and Tropical Medicine, 2009.

39. Pronyk P, Hargreaves J, Kim J et al. Effect of a structural intervention for the prevention of intimate-partner violence and HIV in rural South Africa: a cluster randomised trial. Lancet 2006; 368: 1973–83.

40. Emmers-Sommer T, Allen M. Safer sex in personal relationships: the role of sexual scripts in HIV infection and prevention. In: Duck S (ed). Lawrence Erlbaum Associates Series on Personal Relationships. Mahwah New Jersey: Lawrence Erlbaum Associates, 2005.

41. PSI. Evaluating the Trusted Partner Campaign in Four Sub-Saharan African Countries. Washington, DC: Population Services International, 2008.

42. Cantor N, Malley J. Life tasks, personal needs and close relationships in Cognition in close relationships. In: Fletcher G, Fincham F (eds). Hillsdale: Lawrence Erlbaum Associates, 1991.

43. Rempel J, Holmes J, Zanna M. Trust in close relationships. J Pers Soc Psychol 1985; 49: 95–112.

44. Marston PJ, Hecht ML, Manke M et al. The subjective experience of intimacy, passion, and commitment in heterosexual loving relationships. Pers Relationsh 1998; 5: 15–30.

45. Stephan W, Ngige L. Families in Sub-Saharan Africa in Families in Global and multicultural persperctives. In: Ingoldsby B, Smith S (eds). London: Sage Publications, 2006, 247–73.

46. Chingandu L. Multiple Concurrent Partnerships: The story of ZimbabweAre small houses a key driver? Southern African HIV and AIDS Information Dissemination Service Harare, 2007.

47. Boonzaier F. If the man says you must sit, then you must sit': The relational construction of woman abuse: Gender, subjectivity and violence. Fem Psychol 2008; 18: 183–206.

48. Simpson A. Sons and fathers/boys to men in the time of AIDS: Learning masculinity in Zambia. J South Afr Stud 2005; 31: 569–86.

49. Reniers G. Marital strategies for regulating exposure to HIV. Demography 2008; 45: 417–38.

50. Njovana E, Watts C. Gender violence in Zimbabwe: a need for collaborative action. Reprod Health Matters 1996; 7: 46–55.

51. Feldman R, Maposhere C. Safer sex and reproductive choice: findings from "positive women: voices and choices in Zimbabwe. Reprod Health Matters 2003; 11: 162–73.

52. Kesby M. Participatory diagramming as a means to improve communication about sex in rural Zimbabwe: a pilot study. Soc Sci Med 2000; 50: 1723–41.

53. Schatz E. 'Take your mat and go'! Rural Malawian women's strategies in the HIV/AIDS era. Cult Health Sex 2005; 7: 479–92.

54. Hirsch J, Wardlow H, Smith DJ, Phinney HM, Parikh S, Nathanson CA. The secret: love, marriage, and HIV. In: Wardlow H (ed). Nashville, TN: Vanderbilt University Press, 2009.

55. Bassett M, Mhloyi M. Women and AIDS in Zimbabwe: the making of an epidemic. Int J Health Serv 1991; 21: 143–56.

56. Mhloyi M. Perceptions on Communication and Sexuality in Marriage in Zimbabwe. Women Therapy 1990; 10: 61–73.

57. Emmers-Sommer, Crowell T, Allen M. Safer sex in marriage. In: Emmers-Sommer T, Allen M. (eds). Safer Sex in Personal Relationships: The Role of Sexual Scripts in HIV infection and Prevention. London: Lawrence Erlbaum Associates, 2005.

58. Larsson EC, Thorson A, Nsabagasani X et al. Mistrust in marriage-Reasons why men do not accept couple HIV testing during antenatal carea qualitative study in eastern Uganda. Bmc Public Health 2010; 10: 769.

59. Musheke M, Bond V, Merten S. Couple experiences of provider-initiated couple HIV testing in an antenatal clinic in Lusaka, Zambia: lessons for policy and practice. Bmc Health Serv Res 2013; 13: 97.

60. Tabana H, Doherty T, Rubenson B et al. Testing together challenges the relationship: consequences of HIV testing as a couple in a high HIV prevalence setting in rural South Africa. Plos One 2013; 8: e66390.

61. Taruberekera N, Kaljee LM, Mushayi W et al. Concurrent heterosexual partnerships, HIV risk and related determinants among the general population in Zimbabwe. Washington, DC: Population Services International, 2009.

THEORY IN ACTION—ARTICLE QUESTIONS

1. According to the authors, what practices are considered "safer sex"?
2. What factors at the intrapersonal level contribute to the high rates of HIV/AIDS among married persons and those in long-term relationships?
3. What factors at the interpersonal or relationship level contribute to the high rates of HIV/AIDS?
4. What factors at the community level contribute to the high rates of HIV/AIDS?
5. How do the authors suggest factors contributing to the high rates of HIV in this population might be used to develop culturally appropriate interventions?
6. How did your brainstorming of factors associated with HIV risk among married persons compare with the content of the article?
7. How similar/difference were your suggestions for interventions compared to those made by the authors?

▶ Chapter References

Bacchini, D., Espotito, G., & Affuso, G. (2009). Social experience and school bullying. *Journal of Community & Applied Social Psychology, 19*, 17–32. doi:10.1002/casp.975

Barboza, G. E., Schiamberg, L. B., Oehmke, J., Korzeniewski, S. J., Post, L. A., & Heraux, C. G. (2009). Individual characteristics and multiple contexts of adolescent bullying: An ecological perspective. *Journal of Youth and Adolescence, 38*, 101–121. doi:10.1007/s10964-008-9271-1

Bronfenbrenner, U. (1974). Developmental research, public policy, and the ecology of childhood. *Child Development, 45*, 1–5.

Bronfenbrenner, U. (1994). Ecological models of human development. In *International encyclopedia of education* (2nd ed., Vol. 3, pp. 1643–1647). Oxford, UK: Elsevier Sciences Ltd.

Centers for Disease Control and Prevention. (2015). HIV Surveillance Report, 2014. Retrieved May 1, 2017, from http://www.cdc.gove/hiv/library/reports/suveillance

Eddy, J. M., Donahue, R. E., Webster, R. D., & Bjornstad, E. (2002). Application of an ecological perspective in worksite health promotion: A review. *American Journal of Health Studies, 17*(4), 197–202.

Gruenewald, P. J., Remer, L. G., & LaScala, E. A. (2013). Testing a social ecological model of alcohol use: The California 50 city study. *Addiction, 109*, 736–745. doi:10.1111/add.12438

Haughton, J., Ayala, G. X., Burke, K. H., Elder, J. P., Montanez, J., & Arredondo, E. (2015). Community health workers promoting physical activity. *Journal of Ambulatory Care Management, 38*(4), 309–320. doi:10.1097/JAC.0000000000000108

Jacobson, S. (2011). HIV/AIDS interventions in an aging U.S. population. *Health & Social Work, 36*(2), 149–156.

Kumar, S., Quinn, S. C., Kim, K. H., Musa, D., Hilyard, K. M., & Freimuth, V. S. (2012). The social ecological model as a framework for determinants of the 2009 H1N1 influenza vaccine uptake in the United States. *Health Education and Behavior, 39*(2), 229–243.

McCormack, L., Thomas, V., Lewis, M. A., & Rudd, R. (2017). Improving low literacy and patient engagement: A social ecological approach. *Patient Education and Counseling, 100*(1), 8–13. doi:10.1016/j.pec.2016.07.007

McLeroy, K. R., Bibeau, D., Steckler, A., & Glanz, K. (1988). An ecological perspective on health promotion programs. *Health Education Quarterly, 15*, 351–377.

McNeil, L. H., Kreuter, M., & Subramanian, S. V. (2006). Social environment and physical activity: A review of concepts and evidence. *Social Science & Medicine, 63*, 1011–1022.

National School Lunch and Breakfast Program, 77 Federal Register, 4088 (2012) (to be codified at 7 C.F.R. pts 210 and 220). Retrieved December 21, 2016 from https://www.gpo.gov/fdsys/pkg/FR-2012-01-26/pdf/2012-1010.pdf

Novilla, M. L. B., Barnes, M. D., DeLaCruz, N. G., Williams, P. N., & Rogers, J. (2006). Public health perspectives on the family: An ecological approach to promoting health in the family and community. *Family and Community Health, 29*(1), 28–42.

Nuss, H. J., Williams, D. L., Hayden, J., & Huard, C. R. (2012). Applying the social ecological model to evaluate a demonstration colorectal cancer screening program in Louisiana. *Journal of Health Care for the Poor & Underserved, 23*(3), 1026–1035.

Sallis, J. F., & Owen, N. (1997). Ecological models of health behavior. In K. Glanz, B. K. Rimer, & F. M. Lewis (Eds.), *Health behavior and health education* (2nd ed., pp. 403–424). San Francisco, CA: Jossey-Bass.

Sallis, J. F., & Owen, N. (1999). *Physical activity and behavioral medicine.* Thousand Oaks, CA: Sage Publications.

Sallis, J. F., & Owen, N. (2002). Ecological models of health behavior. In K. Glanz, B. K. Rimer, & F. M. Lewis (Eds.), *Health behavior and health education* (3rd ed., pp. 462–484). San Francisco, CA: Jossey-Bass.

Spence, J. C., & Lee, R. E. (2003). Toward a comprehensive model of physical activity. *Psychology of Sport and Exercise, 4*, 7–24.

Stahl, T., Rutten, A., Nutbeam, D., Bauman, A., Kannas, L., Abel, T., … van der Zee, J. (2001). The importance of social environment for physically active lifestyle results from an international study. *Social Science and Medicine, 52*(1), 1–10.

Stokols, D. (1992). Establishing and maintaining healthy environments: Toward a social ecology of health promotion. *American Psychologist, 47*(1), 6–22.

Swearer, S. M., & Hymel, S. (2015). Understanding the psychology of bullying. *American Psychologist, 70*(4), 344–353. doi:10.1037/a0038929

von Bothmer, M. I. K., Mattsson, B., & Fridlund, B. (2002). Influences on adolescent smoking behaviour: Siblings' smoking and norms in the social environment do matter. *Health and Social Care in the Community, 10*(4), 213–220

Watt, G. F., Donahue, R. E., Eddy, J. M., & Wallace, E. V. (2001). Use of an ecological approach to worksite health promotion. *American Journal of Health Studies, 17*(3), 144–147.

World Health Organization. (2006). Ecological framework. Retrieved January 2, 2017, from http://www.who.int/violenceprevention/approach/ecology/en.

CHAPTER 11

Social Capital Theory

SOCIAL CAPITAL THEORY ESSENCE SENTENCE

Behavior is influenced by who we know and how we know them.

Constructs

Networks: The connections or associations we have with other people and, through them, the connections with the people in their networks

Relationships: The strength of the association with other people

▶ In the Beginning

Although not called "social capital" at the time, the underlying concept of social capital was used in the 1970s to challenge the equal opportunity and affirmative action policies of the 1960s. These were based on the belief that if everyone with the same ability is given the same opportunity, they will all rise to their potential and achieve. The argument against this was that affirmative action and equal opportunity ignore the whole social context that influences achievement or success regardless of ability or potential (Loury, 1976).

The term "social capital" was introduced in the 1980s by the French sociologist Pierre Bourdieu. Social capital, as Bourdieu saw it, was made up of social obligations or relationships that can be converted into economic capital (money) in certain situations (Bourdieu, 1986). Stated another way, being part of a group gives each individual in the group access to the resources (social capital) of all the other people in the group (Bourdieu, 1986; Portes, 1998) and in this way affects behavior.

Social capital, then, is the type and extent of personal and institutional relationships in a community (Woolcock, 1998) consisting of all the networks, norms, and structures that support interactions between people with access to them (Paldam, 2000). It can be confusing, though, because it is sometimes viewed as a feature of the community or social structure external to the individual, as in community resources (Bolin, Kindgren, Lindstrom, & Nystedt, 2003; Lin, 1999; Lochner, Kawachi, & Kennedy, 1999), and other times as a personal or individual characteristic, as in ones' own network of friends, colleagues, and social supports (Lin, 1999; Lochner et al., 1999).

Regardless of which view of social capital is used, communities with high levels of social capital have high levels of civic engagement, social interaction, trust among community members, and social structures that support it (Putnam, 1993), all of which generally have a positive effect on health outcomes (Murayama, Fujiwara, & Kawachi, 2012). This may be due to the role social capital plays in the diffusion of knowledge through a community or group of people, how it exerts informal controls that support the maintenance of healthy behavioral norms, or how it promotes access to community services and supports mutual respect between people (Kawachi & Berkman, 2000).

Given all of this, it's important to keep in mind that social capital doesn't "just happen" in a community. It builds from community characteristics such as historical patterns of mobility or stability of the residents, municipal investment in housing, local infrastructure, services, and policies (Kawachi, Subramanian, & Kim, 2008).

▶ Theory Concept

From a public health or community perspective, the concept of *social capital* refers to the networks, relationships, norms, and trust people need to cooperate with each other, in a reciprocal fashion, for the benefit of all (Putnam, 2000; Putnam, Leonardi, & Nanetti, 1993). Social capital includes the resources (monetary and otherwise) we have available to us by virtue of our connections with others.

▶ Theory Constructs

The constructs of Social Capital Theory are networks and relationships. The extent (or amount, if you will) of our social capital depends on the "richness" of the people we know in terms of their connections and their resources (money, education, clout, and so on) (Carpiano, 2006) and our relationship with them.

Networks

Networks are the connections or associations we have *with* other people, and *through* them the connections with the people in their networks. However, before network resources (i.e., the social capital) can be used or accessed, there must be trust and reciprocity between the members of the social network (Carpiano, 2006). Trust and reciprocity are at the very core of Social Capital Theory. They lead to the expectations and obligations that come with being part of a particular network (Hawe & Shiell,

2000). Without trust and reciprocity, there is no social capital. Perhaps it is in this way that social capital influences health behavior.

The networks of social capital are diverse; they are what make up our social environment. They may be whole societies, communities, neighborhoods, civic associations, organizations, schools, religious affiliations, or families, to name but a few. Think of all the groups to which you belong and the resources (connections, clout, money, and jobs) available to you as a result of your relationships with the people in these networks.

Social capital can also include one's social skills or ability to negotiate and work with others to find solutions to common problems. It may refer to styles and forms of leadership, structure of service delivery, and social unity among communities (Szreter & Woolcock, 2004).

As you can see, social capital can be many things. Consequently, it is often used as an umbrella term that takes into account social cohesion (which includes trust and reciprocity), support, and integration or participation (Almedon, 2005) in social networks. It is the connectedness that people have to the people around them (Carpiano, 2006). When people feel connected to each other, they develop behaviors and attitudes that benefit themselves and their society as a whole (Putnam, 2000).

When people are excluded from a social network and don't have access to its social capital, it can have a negative effect on behavior. Unless people can be "named, blamed and shamed" (Rose, 2000, p. 1407) for unacceptable behavior (health or otherwise), there is little incentive for them to conform or behave in acceptable ways (Wakefield & Poland, 2005).

A community in which people are more connected to each other, where everyone knows everyone else and they each watch out for each other, is better able to support positive health behaviors and dissuade negative ones (Berkman & Kawachi, 2000; Ross & Jang, 2000), organize itself, and positioned to fight with one voice in one direction (Veenstra et al., 2005). In this type of neighborhood, there may be lower tolerance for illegal behavior, drug use, or crime (**FIGURE 11.1**) (Berkman & Kawachi, 2000; Ross & Jang, 2000); improved child development and adolescent well-being; better mental health and less youth delinquency; overall reduced mortality; lower susceptibility to binge drinking, depression, and loneliness; and higher perceptions of well-being and health (Szreter & Woolcock, 2004).

A specific example of how social capital and its networks contribute to health is seen in the case of mothers' groups for women with young children. Mothers' groups provide an opportunity for new moms to learn from other moms about childcare, develop a support network, kindle friendships, and foster connections with the community (Strange, Fischer, Howat, & Wood, 2014). Participation in these groups, which support the development of social networks, positively affects mental well-being (Strange, Bremmer, Fisher, Howat, & Wood, 2016), possibly by reducing anxiety from learning that other moms' went through similar things, which normalizes the experiences (Strange et al., 2014).

While social networks can and do provide for social capital, it takes a high degree of trust in the social network in order for this to happen. In communities or neighborhoods where there is high social capital there will also be high levels of trust between people in the network, and frequent swapping of favors. People help each other trusting that the favor will be returned (Fujiwara, Yamaoka, & Kawachi, 2016).

FIGURE 11.1 Neighbors watching out for each other.
© carolyn brule/ShutterStock

Trust and social networks in the community are key factors associated with infant/child abuse. In communities where there is trust among neighbors and supportive social networks, there is less infant abuse and neglect. A reason for this might be lower stress levels among mothers living in neighborhoods or communities with high social capital because of the strong relationships and knowledge that there is help in an emergency. Another reason could be that healthy parenting practices are quickly conveyed between the network members; for example, effective, safe ways to deal with an infant in distress. Further, social networks with their cohesive members help to enforce healthy child-rearing practices, but can also mobilize resources and make timely referrals to social agencies in cases of abuse (Fujiwara et al., 2016).

Unfortunately, the number of Americans living in communities where neighbors socialize and trust each other has steadily declined (Putnam, 1995). This does not bode well for the health of a community or the health of the people living in it. In neighborhoods and communities with few networks and little trust, there are higher rates of stress, isolation, and lower rates of child well-being, ability to respond to environmental health hazards, and likelihood of receiving effective health interventions (Szreter & Woolcock, 2004).

It is important to remember that social networks need to be nurtured. Networks, once developed, do not remain in place forever unless they are attended too. The connections with people in the network have to be maintained through social interaction if the benefits of social capital are to remain intact (Bolin et al., 2003).

This is no different than the social network of friends you're developing and nurturing during your years at college. Once you graduate, unless you all "keep in touch" with one another, the strength of the network you are developing now will weaken and the amount of social capital it provides will diminish.

However, strong networks in a community don't guarantee better living condition or better health. For example, with drug use, it is the network of users and dealers that keep the unhealthy behavior going.

Relationships

The more people you know, the more relationships you have, the more connected you are to a variety of others in a number of ways, the more resources you have at your disposal (see **FIGURE 11.2**). This is akin to the old saying, "It's not what you know, but who you know that counts." In the case of social capital, it's also *how* you know them, too.

There are three different types of relationships that affect social capital, each defined by the strength of the association between the people who make up the social network. They are bonding, bridging, and linking social capital.

Bonding Social Capital

Bonding social capital refers to those relationships between people who see themselves as being similar in terms of their shared social identity (Szreter, 2002;

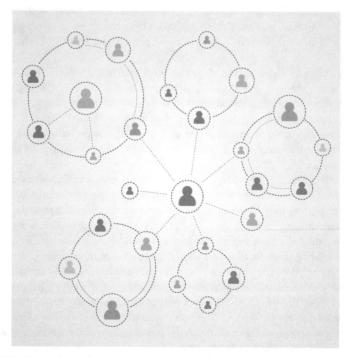

FIGURE 11.2 Networks are the connections we have with other people and their connections.
© Mert Toker/Shutterstock

Szreter & Woolcock, 2004; Woolcock, 2001), origin, status, or position in society (Szreter, 2002). An example of this is the network of ties that holds families and groups together (Wakefield & Poland, 2005). Think about the behaviors, attitudes, expectations, and obligations that come with being part of your family. How do these things impact your health behavior?

Social networks, in general, facilitate and support bonding between people. This support may directly or indirectly positively or negatively affect health. This occurs directly by their impact on self-esteem, exercise, sexual activity, the utilization of health services, or stress levels (Berkman, Glass, Brissette, & Seeman, 2000). To cope with the stress of an HIV/AIDS diagnosis, people in rural Canada use the social capital of their bonding relationships. The people with whom they have close, trusting ties are the ones to whom they disclose their diagnosis and the ones from whom they obtain emotional support (Veinat, 2010).

Strong ties between family members or close friends can encourage adoption of healthy behaviors. In rural China, for example, these bonds lead to support for group exercising, limiting salt in the diet, and sharing information about cardiovascular disease and diabetes (Zhang et al., 2016), all health promoting behaviors.

Korean immigrants in the United States who have strong bonding relationships share information and norms of behavior with each other, which results in significantly lower rates of depression (Kim, Auh, Lee, & Ahn, 2013). It's not surprising that having close ties to others like yourself who are facing or have faced the same issues and challenges as you, lessens isolation and depression.

Bonding relationships also influence health more indirectly through their effects on the larger social, economic, political, and environmental determinants of health (Berkman et al., 2000). They may affect the types of jobs and housing available in a neighborhood, as well as neighborhood wealth (Veenstra et al., 2005).

But bonding social capital doesn't always contribute to health in a positive way. Take for example stress among household decision makers in high poverty, minority, inner city neighborhoods. While you would think strong relationships between people struggling with similar economic and environmental stressors would serve to reduce their stress, the exact opposite sometimes happens. Bonding relationships can cause more stress because of the added obligations they create (Mitchell & LaGory, 2002).

Another example of when conforming to the group norms does not result in positive health outcomes is when group norms support unhealthy or inappropriate behaviors. Take the case of a woman enduring sexual harassment in the workplace. She may be reluctant to report it for fear of being blacklisted within the network, thus losing her job and ending up unemployable (Wakefield & Poland, 2005). Similarly, in cultures where spousal abuse is considered the norm, women tolerate repeated beatings because it is the norm of the group not to complain about such treatment. Complaining may result in a divorce. Although bringing relief from the beatings, a divorce may also mean losing her children to her ex-husband and his family and being an outcast in her society. Keep in mind that when people don't or can't conform to the group norms of their bonding relationships, they are excluded from the social network and barred from accessing its social capital (Wakefield & Poland, 2005).

Bridging Social Capital

Bridging social capital refers to networks of people who come together as acquaintances. They are from different social groups and differ in some sociodemographic sense, be it age, ethnicity, education, or self-esteem (Wakefield & Poland, 2005). People become part of these networks to engage in an activity with mutually beneficial outcomes that are not possible within their bonded relationships. Examples of bridging relationships are those among sports team members, a choir, people working on a group project, students in a class, and tenants in an apartment building (Szreter, 2002). These relationships may affect health behavior by virtue of a desire to do what the group does, or to be a "team player," in order to have access to the resources of the group.

When students participate in a community or service organization, they develop bridging relationships with other members of the group. These relationships tend to decrease the likelihood of alcohol abuse or risky drinking behaviors (Theall et al., 2009). On the other hand, the bridging relationships formed within a sorority or fraternity often have the exact opposite effect.

For Brazilian adolescents, bridging social capital affords them access to resources they would not normally have available to them by allowing the development of relationships with people from different social classes in a society with inherent socioeconomic inequities. Building these relationships has a positive effect on self-rated health. Whereas adolescents who do not have these relationships, don't know or interact with people from different social classes or participate in community projects, have poor or very poor self-reported health (Borges, Campos, Vargas, Ferreria, & Kawachi, 2010).

The positive health effects of bridging social capital are sometimes tied to demographics. In one such example, bridging relationships were found to improve stress among White community members, but worsen it among Blacks (Beaudoin, 2009). Similarly, bridging social capital is inversely associated with self-rated health among Japanese women, but either not as strongly associated or not significantly associated among men. Further, high bridging social capital among Japanese women is also associated with reduced odds of poor health (Iwase et al., 2012).

Linking Social Capital

The weakest social capital relationships are *linking* relationships. In these, we have norms of respect and networks of trusting relationships, but they are between people who interact across power or authority gradients representing formal institutions (see **FIGURE 11.3**). These are the relationships between teacher and student, police officer and crime victim, or physician and patient (Szreter & Woolcock, 2004).

For rural Canadians living with HIV/AIDS, linking relationships with their healthcare providers help them cope with stress and stigmatization in addition to coping with their disease. These network relationships provide much needed information about their health status and treatment (Veinat, 2010), thereby affecting their health decisions and health behavior.

Linking social capital also impacts health protective behaviors, such as those associated with influenza prevention. For example, when people trust the government

FIGURE 11.3 Relationship across power gradient.
© Blend Images/Shutterstock

they are more likely to comply with prevention recommendations during a flu outbreak, such as getting vaccinated and frequent handwashing (Chuang, Huang, Tseng, Yen, & Yang, 2015).

Linking social capital takes on much greater importance in economically disadvantaged communities, where the relationships between people in positions of power with greater social capital and those with lesser of both must be built on trust and mutual respect in order for health needs to be met and outcomes to improve (Stretzer & Woolcock, 2004). In one particular situation with migrant workers, linking social capital was used as the foundation for a triage system implemented by community health nurses to connect them to voluntary agencies and humanitarian groups for services. The effectiveness of the program was the result of the trusting relationships the nurses built with the people who needed care (Mason, 2016).

When there is a lack of linking social capital (that is little trust between individuals and institutions), can negatively affect health behaviors, as is the case with drug abuse. Men who live in neighborhoods with low linking social capital are at greater risk of drug abuse than are those living in neighborhoods with high levels of linking social capital, perhaps because they are less integrated with societal norms and values (Sundquist et al., 2016).

These same outcomes have been found with both mental health issues and coronary heart disease. Specifically, depression rates are greatest in neighborhoods with low levels of social capital, as are the rates of psychosis (Lofors & Sundquist, 2007) and risk of coronary artery disease (Sundquist, Johansson, Yang, & Sundquist, 2006).

Linking social capital, that sense of trust and connectedness to institutions and people of power, seems to have a significant effect on health—but why? Perhaps it's the sense of being part of a bigger whole rather than having to go it alone, or the comfort in trusting that others in more powerful positions are there to help you.

Whatever it is, the extent of linking social capital in our neighborhoods, communities, and society as a whole, impacts our health.

In summary, social capital in all its forms maybe a useful framework as a starting point for identifying what health promoting environments look like and may be a useful tool for achieving them (Erikson, 2011). However, it's important to remember that trust is at the very heart of it all; impacting norms, expectations, relationships and, therefore, behavior (see **FIGURE 11.4**).

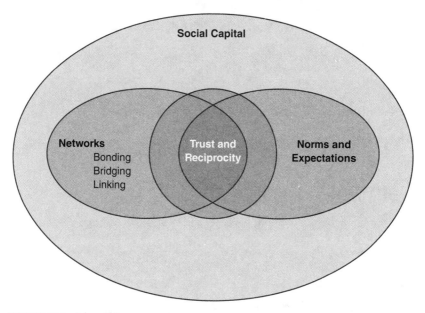

FIGURE 11.4 Social capital.

THEORY IN ACTION—CLASS ACTIVITY

Take a moment to think about all the relationships you have—those with your family and friends, teachers and classmates, sorority and fraternity sisters and brothers, church members, neighbors, healthcare providers, etc.

Make a list of as many of your relationships as you can.

Then, categorize them by the strength of the relationship—bonding, linking or bridging.

Pick one or two from each category and think about how each of the relationships came about—what allowed them to happen?

How do your relations contribute to your health?

When you have completed this portion of the activity, share your results with your classmates.

Next, read the following article and answer the questions at the end.

Chapter 11 Article: Building social capital as a pathway to success: community development practices of an early childhood intervention program in Canada[1]

Hongxia Shan[1,2], Nazeem Muhajarine[1,3*], Kristjana Loptson[1,4] and Bonnie Jeffery[1,5]

[1]The Saskatchewan Population Health and Evaluation Research Unit, Saskatchewan, Canada
[2]Department of Educational Studies, University of British Columbia, Vancouver, British Columbia, Canada
[3]Department of Community Health and Epidemiology, University of Saskatchewan, Saskatoon, Saskatchewan, Canada
[4]Department of Political Sciences, University of Alberta, Edmonton, Alberta, Canada and
[5]Department of Social Work, University of Regina, Regina, Saskatchewan, Canada

▶ SUMMARY

In the last three decades, various concepts and strategies have been developed to address social determinants of health. This paper brings together the different focuses of health promotion, and demonstrates that effective health intervention programs need to be conducted at multiple levels and fronts. Specifically, based on the evaluation of *KidsFirst*, an early childhood intervention program in Saskatchewan, Canada, this paper presents the program practices effective in enhancing the social capital and social cohesion at the community and institutional levels. The findings fall into three interconnected areas: strengthening community fabric; building institutional social capital and bonding, linking and bridging. *KidsFirst* has brought the community together through conducting broad and targeted community consultations, and developing partnerships and collaborative relationships in an open and transparent manner. It has also developed institutional social capital through hiring locally and encouraging staff to deepen connections with the communities. Additionally, it has endeavoured to create conditions that enable vulnerable families to enhance connectedness among themselves, link them to services and integrate them to the larger community. The program's success, however, depends not only on the program's local practices, but also on the government's central policy framework and commitment. In particular, the program's focus on children's healthy development easily resonated with local communities. Its endorsement of local

---

1 Reproduced from Shan, H., Muhajarine, N., Loptson, K., & Jeffery, B. (2012). Building social capital as a pathway to success: Community development practices of an early childhood intervention program in Canada. *Health Promotion International*, 29(2), 244–255. doi: 10.1093/heapro/das063.

* Corresponding author.

and intersectoral leadership has facilitated mobilizing community resources and knowledge. Further, its commitment to local ownership of the program and structural flexibility has also determined the extent to which the program could fit into the histories of local communities.

Keywords: community development; social capital; evaluation research; intervention program

▶ **Introduction**

Following the Ottawa Charter for Health Promotion, various community-based concepts and strategies have been developed in population health to address social determinants of health (e.g., Ziglio et al., 2000; Wise and Signal, 2000; Labonte, 2004). Concomitant with the traditional community concepts, such as community development, community empowerment and community capacity, there have emerged a number of social concepts including social capital, social cohesion and social inclusion/exclusion. If the community-based notions have shifted the focus of health promotion from individuals to the community environments, the social concepts may have been instrumental in directing attention to the higher orders of political systems and perhaps give us another reason to attend to the community (Labonte, 2004). Corresponding to the conceptual expansion, the past three decades have witnessed the emergence of ever more proactive health promotion strategies, ranging from community capacity building (e.g. Crisp et al., 2000; Laverack, 2003) to building alliances and intersectoral partnerships (e.g. Gillies, 1998; Jones and Barry, 2011), as well as advocacy (Carlisle, 2000). Specific to the Aboriginal people, a most vulnerable population, whose health is disproportionately impacted by cultural disruption, institutionalized racism, colonialism and long-term social marginalization (St Denis, 2007; King, 2009), decolonizing approaches (Mundel and Chapman, 2010) have also been proposed to promote health in culturally relevant manners. Echoing the expansive interests of health promotion practices, the Global Health Promotion Conference in Nairobi 2009 (Lin et al., 2009) also proposed that health promotion strategy should address not only individual empowerment, but also community empowerment, health systems strengthening, intersectoral action, as well as building institutional and organizational capacity for health promotion.

This paper demonstrates that effective health intervention needs to be conducted at multiple institutional and societal levels and fronts. Specifically, it presents a range of effective health promotion practices reported in our evaluation of *Kids-First*, an early childhood intervention program serving vulnerable families in targeted areas in Saskatchewan, Canada. In the study, research participants repeatedly emphasized 'relationship building' as a fundamental pathway for the program to evolve and thrive. With this observation, we organize our findings as they are related to enhancing social capital building at both the institutional and community levels. The rest of the paper is divided into five sections. The first section focuses on the conception of social capital that informed our data analysis. The second and third sections introduce the *KidsFirst* program and the evaluation methods, respectively. The fourth section presents the research findings and the last is a discussion of the limitations and implications of the findings.

▶ Social Capital as a Determinant of Health

Social capital is a notion that has recently been introduced to population health (Kawachi and Berkman, 2003; Szreter and Woolcock, 2004). It is a multilevel and multi-component concept generally defined as a relational resource, such as personal and community networks, sense of belonging, civic engagement, norms of reciprocity and trust, which determines the quality of life, including our well-being and good health (e.g. Coleman, 1988; Putnam, 2000; Lin, 2001; Szreter and Woolcock, 2004). While the term, social capital, became well known through Coleman and Putnam's work much earlier, our paper is directly informed by the writings of Wakefield and Poland (Wakefield and Poland, 2005) and Mignone and O'Neil (Mignone and O'Neil, 2005).

Wakefield and Poland (Wakefield and Poland, 2005) have argued that social capital cannot be conceived in isolation from social, economic and political struc-turing of inequality. They have identified three constructs of social capital. The first, communitarian social capital, which follows Putnam's tradition, refers to the norms and social trust and ties that facilitate cooperation for mutual benefits (Putnam, 2000). The second is institutional social capital. Woolcock and Narayan (2000) referred to institutional social capital as the quality of formal institutions, including their 'internal coherence, credibility competence and external account-ability to civil society'. Wakefield and Poland (Wakefield and Poland, 2005) further emphasized the importance of 'scaling up' individual social ties program staff pos-sess and use these for organizational and community development purposes. The third is Bourdieu's critical construct (Bourdieu, 1979, 1986), which sees social capi-tal as resources accrued to the socially and economically privileged individuals and groups. According to Bourdieu, differences in access to and control of social capital may explain why the same amount of economic and cultural capital may mean dif-ferent degrees of profit, powers and influence for different actors. Wakefield and Poland (Wakefield and Poland, 2005) thus suggest that community developers con-sider the duality (inclusivity and exclusivity) of social capital and consciously engage in transformative practices.

Building on Woolcock and Narayan's work (2000), Mignone and O'Neil (Mignone and O'Neil, 2005) see three dimensions to social capital that are particularly relevant to Aboriginal communities: bridging, bonding and linkage. The notions of bonding and bridging originated with Putnam (2000), who maintained that among all of the dimensions of social capital, the distinction between bridging and bond-ing is the most important. Bonding refers to the inward-looking social ties that reinforce and strengthen group identity and bridging to the outward-looking ties that overcome social cleavages. Woolcock and Narayan (2000) further pointed out that any entity, be it organizations, communities or state institutions, alone do not possess all of the resources for change; therefore, it is important for these entities to be linked and synergized. For Aboriginal people, Mignone and O'Neil (Mignone and O'Neil, 2005) define bonding as relations within individual Aboriginal com-munities, bridging as the horizontal links between Aboriginal communities and other communities, and linkage as the connections between Aboriginal communi-ties and state institutions and private/public corporations.

The above review shows that social capital is a relational resource within and between groups that can be cultivated, mobilized and transformed for the wellbeing of a community. As well, social capital is not solely about shared values and norms; it is also about social and economic privileges and entitlements that are often unevenly distributed. Further, social institutions play an important role in mediating the distribution and production of social capital. With this understanding of social capital in place, we now turn to the *KidsFirst* program.

KidsFirst

KidsFirst is a provincial government initiated, community-based early childhood intervention program implemented in nine sites with high community needs in Saskatchewan, Canada. The vision of the program is that vulnerable children enjoy a good start in life and be nurtured and supported by caring families and communities. The aim of the program is to enhance existing services, fill service gaps and support front-line staff working with high risk families (Saskatchewan Education, Health, Intergovernmental and Aboriginal Affairs & Social Services, 2001).

At its inception, each site formed a program management committee with senior-level representatives from human service sectors such as the health region, school divisions, social services and Aboriginal or Métis organizations. For each site, a community accountable partner, usually the health region or the school board, was designated. The program management committee and the community partner then hired a program manager to coordinate the development of the program in each site. Working with the management committee, program managers consulted with individuals and organizations to identify community needs and service gaps. They then formed partnerships with other organizations, particularly service providers, by funding and supplementing existing services for vulnerable families, such as home visitation, mental health and addictions counselling and early learning and childcare.

Home visitation is the core component of *KidsFirst*. Home visitors support families by meeting their basic needs, sharing prenatal and parenting knowledge with them and linking them to services and to their communities. Most home visitors are hired from the local community, and many are mothers who have at one time faced similar struggles as *KidsFirst* parents. All home visitors undergo standard program training, which is facilitated by the Provincial Early Childhood Development Unit (ECDU) of the Ministry of Education, the government unit overseeing the program.

KidsFirst is a voluntary program for parents with children from prenatal to age 5. Program participants are primarily identified through in-hospital birth screenings. Some are referred by existing *KidsFirst* parents or social service providers. Program eligibility is assessed based on the presence of risk factors, including low maternal education level, maternal substance abuse, mental health issues, low infant birth weight and financial or social instability. The program targets at-risk families of all cultural backgrounds, including women with Aboriginal heritage. Aboriginal people share with the general population some common determinants of health, such as income, education, employment, social support and access to health services. Owing to colonialism and long-term marginalization, they also face some Aboriginal specific health factors (Kendall, 2001; St Denis, 2007; King, 2009). Among others, the residential school system in Canada, has not only disrupted family and community lives, but also led to the loss of Aboriginal languages, knowledge and traditions as well as devaluation of Aboriginal identities (Kirmayer et al., 2003; Aboriginal Healing Foundation, 2012). As a result, compared with other populations, Aboriginal families and children may be more likely to suffer from serious health issues that are challenging to redress.

▶ Research Methods

Mixed methods research was conducted to determine how the program has met its goals and objectives (see Muhajarine et al., 2007); the quantitative study was conducted to measure the short-term impacts *KidsFirst* has had on participating parents and children, while the qualitative study was designed to capture the program impacts that could not be captured by numbers, and identify ways in which the program has taken effect. Research questions were derived from the Evaluation Framework (see Muhajarine et al., 2007), which the research team developed collaboratively with the program staff and policy makers. Specifically, the qualitative study asked what impacts the program has had on parents, children and the communities, and what program policies and practices contributed to the program outcomes (Muhajarine et al., 2010).

For the field research, researchers travelled to all nine sites between May and October 2009 to conduct interviews and focus groups, make observations and take field notes. As shown in Table 10.1, semi-structured interviews were conducted with 28 home visitors, 15 home visitor supervisors, each of the 9 program managers, 34 *KidsFirst* clients and 1 Aboriginal Elder who worked with the program. Additionally, 10 staff focus groups were conducted with home visitors, supervisors and supporting staff, 7 with management committees and 2 with a combination of management committee and supporting agencies. A focus group was also conducted with members of ECDU. Focus groups not only enabled us to learn about the program from the perspectives of various stakeholders efficiently, but also allowed us to observe the dynamics of different groups across sites. All research participants

TABLE A.1 Interview and focus group participants.

Interviews	Focus groups
9 Program Manager interviews	10 staff focus groups (2 in the North) consisting of home visitors, home visitor supervisors and support staff
31 parent interviews	7 supporting agency focus groups
1 Aboriginal Elder interview	7 management committee focus groups
15 home visitor supervisor interviews	2 combined supporting agency/ management committee focus groups
28 home visitor interviews	1 Early Childhood Development Unit (ECDU) focus group
Total number of interviews: 84	Total number of focus groups: 27
Total number of interview participants: 87	Total number of focus group participants: 155

had been involved in the program for at least 6 months at the time of the interviews. With the exception of the ECDU focus group, research participants were identified from a contact list provided by program managers.

In the study, research participants were asked to relay their experiences with the program, and potential areas for program improvement, and to identify changes in parenting practices and community collaboration that have come about as a result of the program. A separate interview guide was used for *KidsFirst* parents, home visitors, home visitor supervisors and program managers. A separate focus group guide was used for *KidsFirst* staff, management committees, supporting agencies and ECDU (see Muhajarine et al., 2010). The diversity of our study participants allowed us to capture different experiences and perspectives as well as to enhance the reliability of the research findings.

Interviews and focus group discussions were tape recorded, transcribed verbatim and sent back to the research participants for checking. For data analysis, we adopted a basic interpretive qualitative approach, which is descriptive and inferential in nature, focusing on uncovering meaning from research participants' views (Merriam, 2002). With a basic interpretive qualitative approach, data were 'inductively analyzed to identify the recurring patterns or common themes that cut across the data' (Merriam, 2002). ATLAS.ti, a qualitative data analysis tool, was used for coding and analysis purposes.

Building social capital as a pathway to success: community development practices

In this section, from the lens of social capital building, we present *KidsFirst* policies and practices that the research participants reported to be effective in improving the life circumstances of children. These practices are thematically summarized including strengthening the community fabric, building institutional social capital and bonding, linking and bridging. We also highlight the overall program framework and policy commitments that are essential to the success of the program, including the program's goals to advance children's health and wellbeing, intersectoral leadership and the program's commitment to community planning and structural flexibility.

Strengthening the community fabric

By strengthening the community fabric, we mean that *KidsFirst* has brought the community together, cultivated communitarian social capital and improved institutional and service environments. In this respect, the program has benefited from broad and targeted community consultation, and building partnership and collaborative relationship through transparent communications.

Conducting community consultation both broadly and in a targeted manner. To develop the program, *KidsFirst* has reached out to service agencies and other organizational and institutional bodies, as well as individual community members, which, to a certain extent, has served to bridge cleavages between *KidsFirst* families and other social groups across occupations, organizations and class lines. Through broad outreach, *KidsFirst* made the program known to the public, and raised the awareness of the community with regard to children's health; it has also gained support from different organizations such as local fire departments, doctor's offices, pharmaceutical manufacturers and business owners. These organizations pooled their efforts with *KidsFirst* by organizing fundraising events, donating medications, providing free services and spreading health information.

KidsFirst also conducted targeted outreach. For instance, in some sites, it was able to build on existing interagency work where different service agencies had worked together to identify community needs. Reportedly, where the program succeeded in building on community momentum, it has benefited from the synergy, leadership, knowledge, trust and relationships that had been cultivated over the years within the community.

> *KidsFirst* came to the tables [of the interagency group] looking for resources . . . everybody knew what the gaps were and . . . It is the process we have gone through to build trust amongst the agencies, . . . that had brought us to where [the program is].
>
> (Management Committee Member)

Targeted outreach also refers to focused community consultation that *KidsFirst* conducted in some sites around particular issues.

> I called together people in the community who were experts in [specific areas]. . . when we were talking about mental health, I had mental health folks in the community come together and provide us some advice about what kind of model we wanted and [which organization] we might want to take that. And when we did the home visiting piece we had huge groups, . . . thirty people sitting around a table talking about what were our challenges and what were our strengths, and what might we do. And . . . we had families at those tables.
>
> (Program Manager)

In focused community consultation, different stakeholders were involved in discussing specific issues and services. This practice has helped *KidsFirst* identify community needs and effective service delivery models, and reorient existing services by educating service providers about the needs of the community. For instance, some agencies were initially critical of *KidsFirst* parents for not keeping their appointments. When they learned from home visitors and/or family members the different factors inhibiting families from accessing services, they started to understand that the ways in which they provided services might be part of the problem. With this insight, some organizations changed their service delivery methods. In one site, an agency began transporting families to and from their appointments. In some other sites, community agencies have started providing childcare, food and transportation during their evening events and have since noted an increase in family attendance in their programs.

Building partnerships and collaborative relationships. To bridge gaps in services, *KidsFirst* forms partnerships and works collaboratively with service agencies, which may have helped improve the quality of institutional and service environments. One barrier obstructing inter-agency collaboration is territorialism (see Altman et al., 1991). Some study participants suggested that service organizations may become territorial when they are put in a position to compete for the same pool of funding or when the policies, procedures and mandates of different institutions conflict.

With regard to partnership formation, the study shows, when *KidsFirst* selects its service partners in a transparent manner, it reduces conflict and competition among service organizations. Below are some effective practices reported in one particular site:

> We picked our partners like an interview process. So they came to the table and we had sort of a little community panel and they presented what they thought they could bring to the program and the families, and that was how we made our decisions. It was very transparent in the community. We had very good agencies say things like '. . . I know exactly what you're looking for. You've been transparent about that. We are not a good fit but those folks that are applying are a good fit'. We didn't have fallout from the decisions.
>
> (Program Manager)

Of note, while interviewing typically accentuates power differences between the interviewer and the interviewees, and necessarily encourages competition, by using the format of a community panel, the program created an opportunity for *KidsFirst* and the community agencies to mutually assess needs and fits in an open and transparent manner. As a result, the program was able to reach partnerships with selected agencies, without hurting its community bases or relationship with other stakeholders.

Territorialism is an issue when *KidsFirst* staff worked together with other agencies and organizations whose institutional mandates conflicted with those of *KidsFirst*, as demonstrated in the following example:

> [Their services were] butting up against ours and vice versa, and I've met with them and said 'Look our programs are designed to be in conflict with each other so this is not a personality issues, it's a policy and procedural' . . . for example we encourage moms to spend that time after they have a baby to do the bonding and the attachment whereas [their] piece is they need to be moving forward . . . back into work or education at three months. We are designed to be in conflict.
>
> (Program Manager)

In order to work through mistrust and conflicts due to institutional differences, *KidsFirst* in this particular site convened community organizations to discuss issues and to produce common protocols. We noted that dialogue and open communications helped draw healthy work boundaries for different organizations, and foster mutual understanding among individual workers, which enabled them to work across institutional constraints.

Building institutional social capital. To integrate the program into local communities, *KidsFirst* puts great value on staff's personal ties with both parents and other organizations within the community. Staff's individual relationships with other members in their respective communities constitute a form of institutional social capital, an essential element for the success of the program.

Scaling up individual ties. Relationship building, according to many research participants, is crucial to the success of the program. Parent respondents especially valued their relationships with home visitors. Some referred to home visitors as 'friends', and some saw them as family members. Some parents indicated emotional investment when they decided to let in home visitors. One parent, for instance, felt hurt when she had to change home visitors.

> I kinda got shuffled around from three different home visitors the first while which was a little difficult 'cause you start opening up to one person, get used to her and then you gotta start opening up again with the next person.
> (Parent)

Home visitors are the program ambassadors who work directly with vulnerable families. To engage and retain parents, *KidsFirst* has made a point to match families with home visitors with whom they can connect at a personal level. It has also hired home visitors from the local communities; many of the home visitors had similar backgrounds as those of the parents on the program. Some sites also intentionally hired Cree speakers and elders to work with Aboriginal parents.

While the relationships and connections home visitors establish with parents are scaled up into institutional social capital, in the process, home visitors may run the risk of experiencing burnout. It is not uncommon for *KidsFirst* families to call home visitors and show up at their homes for help outside of their working hours, which was reported to be a problem for a number of home visitors. As well, given the relational and emotional work home visitors conduct, and the extremely difficult circumstances they witness, some home visitors have also had traumatic experiences.

Another aspect of home visitors' relational work is to develop formal and informal social relations with other service providers while linking families to services. Through establishing these relationships, home visitors sometimes are able to make changes in how other service providers deliver services.

It should be noted that it is not only home visitors, but also *KidsFirst* staff at all levels who engage in relationship building within the community. In sites where the program is reported to be a success, research participants described good relationships between *KidsFirst* and other service organizations, and researchers observed rapport and healthy dynamics among the program staff who participated in focus group discussions.

Hiring staff locally and community development. When *KidsFirst* expands its institutional social capital through hiring staff locally, it directly contributes to community development. In particular, it opens up employment and other life opportunities for the hired staff.

> Well . . . one of the things that we didn't expect to happen . . . was [that] we've had a huge impact on our home visitors and their families . . . As they're being trained, they're learning all kinds of new information. So I think we're seeing a ripple [effect], which is very good . . . Many of the

home visitors come from the neighbourhoods that we're [serving], ... from a community development perspective, that's been a really unanticipated goodie. Many of our home visitors who leave the program are leaving to go back to school. We've got several in faculty of education, [and] in faculty of social work ...

(Program Manager)

While the program provides personal growth opportunities to its staff, the day-to-day work does not come without challenge for the home visitors, especially those without formal training in social services. For instance, some home visitors reported difficulty in filling out paper work and entering information on the computerized information management system. Some also found it a challenge to deal with extremely high-risk families. These findings call for additional customized training programs to better meet the needs of the staff.

Bonding, linking and bridging. Families play a central role in shaping children's development. Parents' access to services, social networks and opportunities for social and community participation are all key determinants of health (e.g. Lynch, 2000). *KidsFirst* has provided families with assistance ranging from meeting their basic needs, to a greater degree of integration within the community. From the perspective of social capital development, the program has played a significant role in creating bonding relationships among the families, linking them to services and bridging them more broadly to the community at large. While creating bonding, linking and bridging conditions is important for all *KidsFirst* families, it may be particularly relevant for the Aboriginal families whose 'stock' of social capital has been negatively affected by social, cultural, and political marginalization and economic deprivation throughout history (e.g. Mignone and O'Neil, 2005).

Creating bonding opportunities. *KidsFirst* across sites has created opportunities for the families to develop relationships and support networks with other families. One parent said:

KidsFirst also gave us ... another social network because there were other families in the program that you went with your children ... now these families are people who are friends of ours.

(Parent)

When engaging Aboriginal families, *KidsFirst* has also provided culturally relevant programs and services. For instance, in *KidsFirst* North, which serves a predominantly Aboriginal population, the program has been working to reestablish the parenting knowledge lost due to the residential school system. It has organized cultural activities such as retreats for parents and families where elders reconnect the young parents with land and lake-based activities. During these gatherings, parents learn traditional and holistic approaches to family life and parenting. Great-grandparents who have witnessed the disruption of language transmission to their grandchildren teach Cree and Dené at these events and within their extended family homes. In other sites, the program has also made conscious efforts to integrate culturally specific programming to make *KidsFirst* more relevant to clients with Aboriginal backgrounds. One home visitor reported using Aboriginal prenatal calendars when working with Aboriginal women. In some communities, home visitation services are also offered in Cree or Dene´, which has helped a number of families overcome language barriers, and supported the use of these languages in the community. Through such activities, the program works to encourage cultural continuity for Aboriginal people, which may strengthen their cultural identity and sense of community.

Linking families to services. The study revealed that many *KidsFirst* parents do not trust state institutions and lack the means, knowledge and confidence to seek out help on their own. *KidsFirst* has played a central role in linking parents with health and other services. It has provided referrals and arranged transportation and childcare so that parents can keep their appointments. Home visitors also accompanied parents when they accessed services and modelled ways of self-advocacy vis-à-vis institutions. This is the type of support that Vygotsky termed as 'scaffolding' (Vygotsky, 1978), where home visitors support families to use different services and then, when parents feel more confident using services on their own, gradually withdraw support. A parent described the support she received this way:

> I [didn't] trust doctors with me . . . [then] my home visitor came with me and held my hand through it all. I'm able to go on my own now.
> (Parent)

While linking families to services brings us back to the reality that *KidsFirst*, a government-funded project, represents a state apparatus after all, the ways in which *KidsFirst* builds linkages between the individual and the institutional suggests an orientation towards community development. Instead of subjecting families to institutional management, the program strives to develop families' confidence to independently use, navigate and negotiate within the service system.

> [The home visitor has helped me stand up for myself] . . . [I]f I ever had to take my daughter [to the doctor's], . . . and I knew there was something wrong, . . . [If I was told], '. . . there's nothing wrong', I [would] just stick to [my] guns and make sure things [get] checked out.
> (Parent)

On the other hand, *KidsFirst* has also combated social marginalization through advocating for the families within governmental institutions. The program has influenced the ways in which other services agencies work with the families through informing, if not educating, them of the reality of *KidsFirst* families. In some other cases, the program has directly influenced the policies and practices of governmental departments. For instance, housing safety was identified as a concern for families. In response, in one site, *KidsFirst* brought housing concerns to the local municipality's attention. At another site, involvement from *KidsFirst* and other local agencies led to the development of a bylaw to regulate property standards within the local municipality. Such advocacy work is significant in challenging the structural exclusion that parents may experience.

Bridging families to the community life. Given long-term poverty, social isolation and in some instances, mental health and addiction issues, as well as associated low self-confidence and self-efficacy, many *KidsFirst* families do not participate in community activities and affairs. *KidsFirst* has contributed to breaking this cycle by enabling their voices, and expanding their social opportunities in the community.

In some sites, it has systematically involved families in program development, which has enabled them to participate in the decision making process within the community.

> With the community development work . . . there's [a] focus . . . on . . . strategizing and thinking about tapping into the voice of actual community members; of families who've been [an] influence for their children, to be that voice . . . [We use] focus groups, and we use a model called Developmental Assets, which is a positive framework for families in communities to look at how children are thriving in your community. And it's strength-based.
>
> (Management Committee Member)

KidsFirst not only involves families in the initial program consultation process, but also encourages them to be part of the program in many other capacities. For instance, in one site, some families were invited to sit on hiring committees. In another site, some families were involved in streamlining services. In yet another site, because the program has been open and welcoming to families' voices, some family members have reportedly developed a sense of ownership over the program.

> They're phoning . . . to make a suggestion, . . . they phone with 'Have you ever thought' and . . . it's because we've provided that kind of welcoming . . . 'It's your program' right . . . so 'What kind of program will work for you?' We've had families who've actually influenced some of our practice.
>
> (Program Manager)

While what is presented here is from the management perspective, it does suggest that the management recognizes the significance of having parents driving the development of the program.

While encouraging voices from participating families in the community, *KidsFirst* has also worked to bridge families to the community beyond the program. For instance, through measures such as providing transportation, it has encouraged and enabled *KidsFirst* families to join family-centred and community-based social activities where they had new opportunities to socialize and connect. Through participating in these activities, some families were able to expand their own social networks. Some also started giving back to the community by volunteering in different programs. A few even took on leadership roles within their community. In some cases, *KidsFirst* has also played an instrumental role in helping parents return to school and to the labour market. What needs to be emphasized is that expanding the social capital at the community level is not a one-way street. Instead, the program in some sites has also undertaken community education and cultural training to break down racial stereotypes about Aboriginal populations, and to explore some underlying causes of poverty and poor health associated with these populations.

Program framework and policy commitment. The success of *KidsFirst* depends not only on the program's local practices, but also on the overall program framework and policy commitment. The study showed that the program's focus on children's health, its intersectoral leadership framework, and its commitment to local planning and flexibility constituted structural conditions for the success of the program.

Community development programs planned and implemented from above often encounter resistance because they may conflict with agendas and interests of the community (Carlisle, 2010). *KidsFirst* staff across sites reported that it was easy to find allies within the community because partners could easily support the program's focus on children's wellbeing. Intersectoral leadership was also emphasized as an important success factor; it facilitated *KidsFirst* tapping into and mobilizing the expertise and resources from key sectors within the community. In sites where management staff from different organizations are involved in *KidsFirst*'s management committee, reportedly, information and messages from *KidsFirst* get communicated efficiently to other organizations, and this could lead to relatively quick feedback, actions and changes. One drawback of intersectoral leadership, however, as some of the research participants mentioned, is that it may have added layers of accountability that at times unnecessarily prolonged the decision-making process for the program.

Policy commitment to local planning and flexibility in program structure also determines the extent to which *KidsFirst* integrates into the history and realities of local communities. Many research participants believed that the strength of the program is that while the government sets the major guidelines, it has left open the opportunity for communities to shape their program to suit their local histories and contexts. As a result, the program has evolved differently from site to site, which reflects the particular needs, local resources, history and leadership in different communities.

It needs to be raised that the program framework may not always be facilitative of the development of the program locally. Prior to the launching of *KidsFirst*, collective inter-agency work had existed in some sites. Reportedly, when the program framework was aligned with the existing capacity, infrastructure and community momentum in particular sites, it gained a strong head start in program implementation. In contrast, where the program mandate contradicted what the local community believed to be the most effective strategies, it had a hard time gathering community support, and the establishment of the program was delayed. For example, in one site, the local community was planning to build additional facilities to serve all families. This measure did not fit within the *KidsFirst* framework, which does not typically allow stand-alone projects independent of existing services. In this case, the local people involved in the program planning process felt that their priorities were not taken into account, and as a result, lost interest in engaging further with *KidsFirst*. It took the program a long time to remedy the damage done.

▶ Conclusion, Limitations, and Implications

Through the lens of social capital building, in this paper, we presented a set of effective community development policies and practices reported by the research participants in our evaluation of *KidsFirst*. The notion of social capital was not in the original evaluation framework. Yet, in the study, 'relationship building' was a recurring theme in the interview data collected. Program staff believed that relationship building with parents, with community organizations and with community members at large was most challenging, and yet it was an essential pathway to the success of the program. While some *KidsFirst* participants joined the program for tangible benefits such as food coupons and free transportation, many highly cherished the personal relationship they were able to build through the program. Further, although the evaluation focused on the short-term impacts of *KidsFirst*, particularly in relation to children's developmental outcomes, we would suggest that the long-term impact of the program is contingent on how the program is able to enhance social capital at the individual, community and institutional levels.

The findings presented are not without their limitations. First, not all the practices illustrated are evident across all nine *KidsFirst* sites. We elicited best practices from the research participants, but did not explore if the same practices were employed across sites, or if there was consensus among research participants regarding the effectiveness of particular practices. Secondly, given that this paper focuses on the program policies and practices, *KidsFirst* staff who provided us with detailed descriptions of the program have had more of a presence and voice than the parents. Despite the limitations, this paper has significant implications for health promotion programs in other settings. To start with, echoing WHO's call for multidimensional action, we suggest that effective health promotional practices need to be implemented at different levels and fronts. In the study, effective practices are not only about empowering individual parents in vulnerable families, they are also about building social cohesion among the community members, building partnerships and intersectoral collaboration at the institutional levels, advocating for the disempowered, as well as providing culturally relevant services. These health promotion strategies are not parallel or discrete practices. Rather, they interconnect and coalesce around building capacity and social capital among individuals, institutions and communities. We therefore hope to sensitize community developers and researchers to the significance of the everyday activity of relationship and social capital building.

To enable the vulnerable individuals to develop social capital, it is important for health promotion programs to recognize both their basic needs and their needs for social connection and space. Further, when programs help enlarge the social space for marginalized populations, they embark on a project that is not solely about social cohesion. Given the uneven distribution of social capital, which often serves to exclude, health promotion programs may also need to tackle fundamental inequalities in people's access to information, resources, services and community membership. Should the programs manage to advocate for the marginalized and engage the larger community in this project, they would be working to enhance the social capital at the community level, and contributing to the common well-being of the community. To build social capital in communities where Aboriginal people are involved, it is also important for the program to be culturally relevant and to explicitly take on a decolonizing approach. In the case of *KidsFirst*, conscious efforts have been made to re-engage and reconnect Aboriginal families with Aboriginal languages and traditions, which may have helped affirm the cultural identities of these families.

The study also notes that for a community-based program directed from above, building institutional social capital through scaling up individual staff's local connections may be instrumental for the program's success and longer term sustainability in the local community. Hiring local community members and encouraging all staff to develop relationships in the community therefore are of strategic importance. Management, however, needs to recognize that additional workload and worker burnout may result due to the blurring of private and public lives for the staff. Specialized training may need to be provided to effectively support staff. Finally, we reiterate that social capital is a crucial determinant as well as mediator of health that can be addressed through multi-pronged health intervention programs. We consider this paper one among many that are needed to deepen our understanding of community-based interventions to promote health equity through enhancing social capital at multiple and intersecting levels—individual, institutional and community.

▶ Acknowledgements

We acknowledge the insights, as well as the financial contributions, provided by the Early Childhood Development Unit (Gail Russell, Gary Shepherd, Rob Gates, Wendy Moellenbeck and Murray Skulmoski) and each of the nine *KidsFirst* program sites. We also thank the *KidsFirst* program managers, the staff at all sites and all those who participated in the interviews and focus groups for providing the stories and experiences which formed the substance of this study. This study was developed with the guidance, support and contributions of the many members of the *KidsFirst* Evaluation Team. This includes the following *KidsFirst* investigators: Nazeem Muhajarine (PI, nazeem.muhajarine@usask.ca for inquiries about the study), Angela Bowen, Jody Glacken, Kathryn Green, Bonnie Jeffery, Thomas McIntosh, David Rosenbluth, Nazmi Sari as well as the following research staff: Darren Nickel, Taban Leggett, Fleur Macqueen Smith, Hongxia Shan and Robert Nesdole. Additionally, we recognize the work of Julia Hardy, Jillian Lunn, Karen Smith, Hayley Turnbull, Kristjana Loptson, Kathleen McMullin and Taban Taban Leggett in the process of data collection for this study.

▶ Funding

This project was supported in part by funding received from the Canadian Population Health Initiative-Canadian Institute for Health Information and the Government of Saskatchewan. All errors and interpretations are the responsibility of the authors and are not necessarily the views of the funding agencies.

▶ References

1. Aboriginal Healing Foundation. (2012) *Speaking My Truth: Reflections on Reconciliation & Residential School.* Aboriginal Health Foundation, Ontario, Ottawa.
2. Altman, D. J., Endres, J., Linzer, J., Lorig, K., Howard-Pitney, B. and Rogers, T. (1991) Obstacles to and future goals of ten comprehensive community health promotion projects. *Journal of Community Health, 16,* 299–314.
3. Bourdieu, P. (1979) Distinction: A Social Critique of the Judgement of Taste. Trans. R. Nice. Routledge, London.

4.   Bourdieu, P. (1986) The forms of capital. In Richardson, J. G. (ed.), *Handbook of Theory and Research for the Sociology of Education*. Greenwood Press, New York.

5.   Carlisle, S. (2000) Health promotion, advocacy and health inequalities: a conceptual framework. *Health Promotion International, 15*, 369–376.

6.   Carlisle, S. (2010) Tackling health inequalities and social exclusion through partnership and community engagement? A reality check for policy and practice aspirations from a social inclusion partnership in Scotland. *Critical Public Health, 20*, 117–27.

7.   Coleman, J. S. (1988) Social capital in the creation of human capital. *American Journal of Sociology, 94*(Supplement), S95–S120.

8.   Crisp, B. R., Swerissen, H. and Duckett, S. J. (2000) Four approaches to capacity building in health: consequences for measurement and accountability. *Health Promotion International, 15*, 99–107.

9.   Gillies, P. (1998) The effectiveness of alliances and partnerships for health promotion. *Health Promotion International, 13*, 1–21.

10. Jones, J. and Barry, M. M. (2011) Exploring the relationship between synergy and partnership functioning factors in health promotion partnerships. *Health Promotion International, 26*, 408–20.

11. Kawachi, I. and Berkman, L. (2003) *Neighborhoods and Health*. Oxford University Press, New York, NY.

12. Kendall, J. (2001) Circles of disadvantage: Aboriginal poverty and underdevelopment in Canada. *American Review of Canadian Studies, 31*, 43–59.

13. King, M. (2009) Aboriginal health. Part 2: the underlying causes of health gap. *Lancet, 374*, 76–85.

14. Kirmayer, L. J., Simpson, C. and Cargo, M. (2003) Healing traditions: culture, community and mental health promotion with Canadian Aboriginal people. *Australasian Psychiatry, 11*(Suppl. 1), S15–23.

15. Labonte, R. (2004) Social inclusion/exclusion: dancing the dialectic. *Health Promotion International, 19*, 115–121.

16. Laverack, G. (2003) Building capable communities: experiences in a rural Fijian context. *Health Promotion International, 18*, 99–106.

17. Lin, N. (2001) Building a network theory of social capital. In Lin, N., Cook, K. and Burt, R. S. (eds), *Social Capital: Theory and Research*. Aldine de Gruyter, New York, pp. 3–29.

18. Lin, V., Pettersson, B., Brink, E., David, A. and Agarwal, S. (2009) A primer for mainstreaming health promotion. *Prepared for the 7th Global Conference for Health Promotion*. http://gchp7 .info/resources/downloads/primer.pdf (11 February 2012, date last accessed).

19. Lynch, J. (2000) Income inequality and health: expanding the debate. *Social Science and Medicine, 51*, 1001–05.

20. Merriam, S. (2002) *Introduction to Qualitative Research*. Jossey-Bass, San Francisco.

21. Mignone, J. and O'Neil, J. (2005) Conceptual understanding of social capital in first Nations Communities: an illustrative description. *Pimatisiwin: A Journal of Aboriginal and Indigenous Community Health, 3*, 8–44.

22. Muhajarine, N., Glacken, J., Cammer, A. and Green, K. (2007) KidsFirst program evaluation phase I: Evaluation framework: Saskatchewan Population Health Evaluation and Research Unit. http://www.kidskan.ca/node/174 (16 March 2010, date last accessed).

23. Muhajarine, N., Loptson, K., Shan, H., Turnbull, H., Premji, S., Leggett, T., McMulliin, K. and the Evaluation Research Team. (2010) Saskachewan KidsFirst Program Evaluation: Report of the Qualitative Study. http://www.kidskan.ca/node/279 (16 March 2010, date last accessed).

24. Mundel, E. and Chapman, G. E. (2010) A decolonizing approach to health promotion: the case of the Urban Aboriginal Community Kitchen Garden Project. *Health Promotion International, 25*, 166–173.

25. Putnam, R. D. (2000) *The Collapse and Revival of American Community*. Simon and Schuster, New York. Saskatchewan Education, Health, Intergovernmental and Aboriginal Affairs & Social Services. (2002) KidsFirst Program Manual, Regina, Saskatchewan: Government of Saskatchewan.

26. St Denis, V. (2007) Aboriginal education and anti-racist education: building alliances across cultural and racial identity. *Canadian Journal of Education, 30*, 1068–1092.

27. Szreter, S. and Woolcock, M. (2004) Health by association? Social capital, social theory and the political economy of public health. *International Journal of Epidemiology, 33,* 650–667.

28. Vygotsky, L. S. (1978) Interaction between learning and development. In Cole, M. (ed.), *Mind in Society: The Development of Higher Psychological Processes.* Harvard University Press, Cambridge, MA, pp. 79–91.

29. Wakefield, S. and Poland, B. (2005) "Family, friend or foe?" Critical reflections on the relevance and role of social capital in health promotion and community development. *Social Science and Medicine, 60,* 2819–2832.

30. Wise, M. and Signal, L. (2000) Health promotion development in Australia and New Zealand. Health Promotion International, 15, 237–248.

31. Woolcock, M and Narayan, D. (2000) Social capital: implications for development theory, research, and policy. *World Bank Res Obs, 15,* 225–249.

32. Ziglio, E., Hagard, S. and Griffiths, J. (2000) Health promotion development in Europe: achievements and challenges. *Health Promotion International, 15,* 210–265.

THEORY IN ACTION—ARTICLE QUESTIONS

1. What was the vision of the *KidsFirst* program?
2. What were the program eligibility criteria?
3. How did the program support the development of bonding social capital?
4. How might bonding relationships contribute to the health of the children?
5. Why was it so important for the program to support the development of linking social capital?
6. How did the program support linking social capital?
7. In what ways might these linking relationships contribute to the health of the children?
8. What factors hindered *KidsFirst* families from developing their own bridging social capital relationships?
9. In what ways did the *KidsFirst* program support development of bridging social capital for the families?
10. In what ways would bridging relationships contribute to the health of the children?

▶ Chapter References

Almedon, A. (2005). Social capital and mental health: An interdisciplinary review of primary evidence. *Social Science & Medicine, 61*(5), 943–964.

Beaudoin, E. C. (2009). Bonding and bridging neighborhoodliness: An individual-level study in the context of health. *Social Science & Medicine, 68*(12), 2129–2136. doi:10.1016 /j.socscimed.2009.04.015

Berkman, L., Glass, T., Brissette, I., & Seeman, T. (2000). From social integration to health: Durkheim in the new millennium. *Social Science & Medicine, 51,* 843–857.

Berkman, L., & Kawachi, I. (2000). *Social Epidemiology.* New York, NY: Oxford University Press.

Bolin, K., Lindgren, B., Lindstrom, M., & Nystedt, P. (2003). Investments in social-capital— Implications of social interactions for the production of health. *Social Science & Medicine, 56*(12), 2379–2390.

Borges, C. M., Campos, A. C. V., Vargas, A. D., Ferreira, E. F., & Kawachi, I. (2010). Social capital and self-rated health among adolescents in Brazil: An exploratory study. *BMC Research Notes, 3*, 338–346. doi:10.1186/1756-0500-3-338

Bourdieu, P. (1986). The forms of capital. In J. G. Richardson (Ed.), *Handbook of theory and research for the sociology of education* (pp. 241–258). New York, NY: Greenwood.

Carpiano, R. M. (2006). Toward a neighborhood resource-based theory of social capital for health: Can Bourdieu and sociology help? *Social Science and Medicine, 62*, 165–175.

Chuang, Y., Huang, Y., Tseng, K., Yen, C., & Yang, L. (2015). Social capital and health-protective behavior intentions in an influenza pandemic. *PLoS ONE, 10*(4), 1–14. doi:10.1371/journal.pone.0122970

Erikson, M. (2011). Social capital and health-implications for health promotion. *Global Health Action, 4*, 5611. doi:10.3402/gha.v4i0.5611

Fujiwara, T., Yamaoka, Y., & Kawachi, I. (2016). Neighborhood social capital and infant physical abuse: A population-based study in Japan. *International Journal of Mental Health Systems, 10*, 1–7. doi:10.1186/s13033-016-0047-9

Hawe, P., & Shiell, A. (2000). Social capital and health promotion. A review. *Social Science & Medicine, 51*, 871–885.

Iwase, T., Suzuki, E., Fujiwara, T., Takao, S., Doi, H., & Kawachi, I. (2012). Do bonding and bridging social capital have differential effects on self-rated health? A community based study in Japan. *Journal of Epidemiology and Community Health, 66*(6), 557–562. doi:10.1136/jech.2010.115592.

Kawachi, I., & Berkman, L. F. (2000). Social cohesion, social capital and health. In L. F. Berkman & I. Kawachi (Eds.), *Social epidemiology* (pp. 174–190). New York, NY: Oxford Press.

Kawachi, I., Subramanian, S. V., & Kim, D. (2008). Social capital and health: A decade of progress and beyond. In I. Kawachi, S. V. Subramanian, & D. Kim (Eds.), *Social capital and health* (pp. 1–26). New York, NY: Springer.

Kim, B. J., Auh, E., Lee, Y. J., & Ahn, J. (2013). The impact of social capital on depression among older Chinese and Korean immigrants: Similarities and differences. *Aging and Mental Health, 17*(7), 844–852. doi:10.1080/13607863.2013.805399

Lin, N. (1999). Building a network theory of social capital. *Connections, 22*, 28–51. Retrieved January 24, 2017, from www.insna.org/pdf/keynote/1999.pdf

Lochner, K., Kawachi, I., & Kennedy, B. P. (1999). Social capital: A guide to its measurement. *Health & Place, 5*(4), 259–270.

Lofors, J., & Sindquist, K. (2007). Low-linking social capital as a predictor of mental disorders: A cohort study of 4.5 million Swedes. *Social Science & Medicine, 64*, 21–34. doi:10.1016/j.socscimed.2006.08.024

Loury, G. C. (1976). A dynamic theory of racial income differences (Discussion Paper No. 225). Retrieved July 20, 2012, from http://www.kellogg.northwestern.edu/research/math/papers/225.pdf

Mason, D. M. (2016). Caring for the unseen: Using linking social capital to improve healthcare access to irregular migrants in Spain. *Journal of Nursing Scholarship, 48*(5), 448–455. doi:10.111/jnu.12228

Mitchell, C. U., & LaGory, M. (2002). Social capital and mental distress in an impoverished community. *City & Community, 1*, 199–223.

Murayama, H., Fujiwara, Y., & Kawachi, I. (2012). Social capital and health: A review of prospective multilevel studies. *Journal of Epidemiology, 22*(3), 179–187. doi:10.2188/jea.JE20110128

Portes, A. (1998). Social capital: Its origins and applications in modern sociology. *Annual Review of Sociology, 24*(1), 1–24.

Putnam, R. D. (1993). What makes democracy work? *National Civic Review, 8*(2), 101–107. doi:10.1002/ncr.4100820204

Putnam, R. D. (1995). Bowling alone: America's declining social capital. *Journal of Democracy, 6*(1), 65–78.

Putnam, R. D. (2000). Bowling alone: The collapse and revival of American community. New York, NY: Simon and Schuster.

Putnam, R. D., Leonardi, R., & Nanetti, R. Y. (1993). *Making democracy work: Civic traditions in modern Italy*. Princeton, NJ: Princeton University Press.

Rose, N. (2000). Citizenship and the third way. *American Behavioral Scientist, 43*, 1395–1411.

Ross, C. E., & Jang, S. J. (2000). Neighborhood disorder, fear, and mistrust: The buffering role of social ties with neighbors. *American Journal of Community Psychology, 28*(4), 401–420.

Strange, C., Bremner, A., Fisher, C., Howat, P., & Wood, L. (2016). Mothers' group participation: Association with social capital, social support and mental well-being. *Journal of Advanced Nursing, 72*(1), 85–98. doi:10.1111/jan.12809

Strange, C., Fischer, C., Howat, P., & Wood, L. (2014). Fostering supportive community connections through mothers' groups and playgroups. *Journal of Advanced Nursing, 70*(12), 2835–2846. doi:10.1111/jan.12435

Sundquist, J., Johansson, S., Yang, M., & Sundquist, K. (2006). Low linking social capital as a predictor of coronary heart disease in Sweden: A cohort study of 2.8 million people. *Social Science & Medicine, 62*, 954–963. doi:10.1016/j.socscimed.2005.06.49

Sundquist, J., Sjostedt, C., Winkleby, M., Li, X., Kendler, K. S., & Sundquist, J. (2016). Neighborhood linking social capital as a predictor of drug abuse: A Swedish national cohort study. *Addictive Behaviors, 63*, 37–44. doi:10.1016/j.addbeh.2016.07.002

Szreter, S. (2002). The state of social capital: Bringing back in power, politics, and history. *Theory and Society, 31*(2), 573–621.

Szreter, S., & Woolcock, M. (2004). Health by association? Social capital, social theory and the political economy of public health. *International Journal of Epidemiology, 33*(4), 650–667.

Theall, K. R., DeJong, W., Scribner, R., Mason, K., Schneider, S. K., & Simonsen, N. (2009). Social capital in the college setting: The impact of participation in campus activities on drinking and alcohol related harms. *Journal of American College Health, 58*(1), 15–23.

Veenstra, G., Luginaah, L., Wakefield, S., Birch, S., Eyles, J., & Elliott, S. (2005). Who you know, where you live: Social capital, neighborhood and health. *Social Science & Medicine, 60*, 2799–2818.

Veinat, T. (2010). A multi-level model of HIV/AIDS information/help network development. *Journal of Documentation, 66*(6), 85–905.

Wakefield, S. E. L., & Poland, B. (2005). Family, friend or foe? Critical reflections on the relevance and role of social capital in health promotion and community development. *Social Science & Medicine, 60*, 2819–2832.

Woolcock, M. (1998). Social capital and economic development: Toward a theoretical synthesis and policy framework. *Theory and Society, 27*, 151–208.

Woolcock, M. (2001). The place of social capital in understanding social and economic outcomes. *Canadian Journal of Policy Research, 2*(1), 1–17.

Zhang, Y., Ma, D., Cui, R., Hilawe, E. H., Chiang, C., Hirakawa, Y., … Aoyama, A. (2016). Facilitators and barriers of adopting healthy lifestyle in rural China: A qualitative analysis through social capital perspectives. *Nagoya Journal of Medical Science, 78*(2), 163–173. Retrieved January 24, 2017, from https://www.ncbi.nlm.nih.gov/pmc/articles/PMC4885816

CHAPTER 12

Choosing a Theory

STUDENT LEARNING OUTCOMES

After reading this chapter the student will be able to:

- Explain how theory is used in practice.
- Use a set of guidelines to choose a theory.
- Determine whether a chosen theory is appropriate for the given situation.

▶ Guidelines for Choosing a Theory

Knowing some of the many different theories and models that can be used to explain health behavior is one thing—knowing which theory to use when is another. Unfortunately, because there are no right or wrong theories, there is no magic formula or chart to tell you which theory is just right for a given situation. Some may work better than others in a particular situation, with a certain population, to address a specific health problem, or to produce a desired result.

With this said, the following guidelines may help you narrow down the choices:

1. Identify the health issue and the intervention population.
2. Gather information about the health issue in the intervention population.
3. Identify possible causes for the issue in the intervention population.
4. Identify the level of interaction (intrapersonal, interpersonal, or community) under which the causes most logically fit.
5. Identify the theory or theories that best match the level and the causes.

Identify the Health Issue and the Intervention Population

The first and most logical step in identifying a theory is to identify the health issue you are going to address and the population in which it will be addressed. Is the issue alcohol use at the high school, a head lice outbreak at the local day care center, or falls among the elderly? Each problem and population may require a different theory. The same problem in different populations may also require different theories.

Be as specific as possible when determining the population (Nigg & Durand, 2016). What are the population's characteristics—gender, ethnicity, culture, age, socioeconomic status, and education level? For example, if the problem is underage drinking, is it middle school students or high school? Boys, girls or both? Students on the sports teams or those not involved in sports? Where does the population live—rural or urban setting, senior complex, apartments/condos, or in sprawling suburban neighborhoods? Continuing with the underage drinking example, is the problem in a particular housing development, apartment complex, neighborhood, or part of town?

Gather Information

Next, do a literature search to learn what others have found from research and done in terms of interventions about the issue in the particular population. A literature search is not limited to a search of the Internet (**FIGURE 12.1**). You need to search the professional literature using an appropriate database. Ones commonly used for health education and health promotion include the following:

- CINAHL (Cumulative Index to Nursing and Allied Health Literature): Available through a university or college library or a public library
- Academic Search Complete: Accessed through a university or college library

FIGURE 12.1 Conduct a literature search.
© lightpoet/Shutterstock

- PubMed: Maintained by the National Library of Medicine and National Institutes of Health; accessed directly at http://www.pubmed.gov
- ERIC (Education Resource Information Center): The database for school health information; accessed directly at http://www.eric.ed.gov

Identify Possible Causes for the Health Issue

Third, take the information you found in the literature and combine it with the other information you have gathered about your population. This will enable you to identify possible causes for the issue; that is, to answer the question "Why does this issue exist?" What are the behaviors contributing to or causing the issue? Be specific about the behaviors. Remember, theories help explain the *why* of health behavior; that is, why people do what they do. Why is it that some people fall, use alcohol, get head lice, go for mammograms, or drive too fast, and others do not?

Identify the Level of Interaction

Once you determine possible causes for the health issue, it is time to determine under which level of interaction these causes fall—intrapersonal, interpersonal, community, or all three. Identifying the level helps you narrow down which theories would most likely explain the behavior and therefore, would best serve as the basis for change. For example, in the underage alcohol use scenario, the level of interaction might well be interpersonal; that is, peer pressure, but intrapersonal factors might also play a role as well. Think about which ones they might be.

Identify the Theory or Theories That Match Best

Use the Theory Chart in this chapter to help you identify which theories would most likely explain the behavior and enable you to plan an intervention to change the behaviors you have identified. Remember, for a theory to be most effective, all of it should be used (Hochbaum, Sorenson, & Lorig, 1992), although sometimes constructs from different theories are mixed in the same intervention.

If you end up with more than one possible theory to use, narrow it down by asking yourself the following questions:

- What (behavior) has this theory explained in the past?
- How much evidence is there in the literature to support using this theory to address the issue?
- What are the theory's weaknesses?

While two theories might be equally as good in predicting a particular outcome, in choosing between them it's also important to know the underlying reason why each predicts the outcome and in which target populations (Schwarzer, 2014).

Say the health issue is a high rate of influenza among the elderly in your community. After assessing the situation, you find the causes for this are poor compliance with influenza vaccination, lack of transportation to the health department to be vaccinated, and inadequate parking facilities. Anecological approach would be appropriate in this situation to explain the poor compliance behavior, but transportation issues and poor parking might be explained by the perceived barriers construct of the Health Belief Model. When you think you have determined which theory would fit best, see how it answers the next set of questions (National Cancer Institute [NCI], 2003):

- Is it logical given the situation I am trying to address?
- Is it similar to the theories others have used successfully in similar situations I found in the literature?
- Is it supported by research?

Choosing a theory is a lot like choosing your clothes. All of your clothes do the same thing—they cover your body—but they do it in different ways. You choose which clothes to wear depending on a host of factors, such as time of day, climate, occasion, and what your friends are wearing. For example, you wouldn't wear a bathing suit to shovel snow. Once you decide which clothes to wear, you need to try them on to see if they fit.

Theories, just like clothes, all do the same thing. They all help explain why people do what they do, but they do it in different ways. You choose a theory depending on a host of factors, such as behavioral causes of the health issue or problem, the level of interaction (intrapersonal, interpersonal, or community), the population, and the desired outcomes or change. Once you decide on which theory to use, you need to apply it to see if it fits (**TABLE 12.1**).

TABLE 12.1 Theory Chart

Level	Theory	Construct
Intrapersonal	*Self-Efficacy Theory:* People will only try to do what they think they can do, and people won't try what they think they can't do	Mastery experience
		Vicarious experience
		Verbal persuasion
		Emotional state
	Theory of Reasoned Action and Theory of Planned Behavior: Health behavior results from intention influenced by attitude, norms, and control	Attitudes
		Subjective norms
		Behavioral control
		Volitional control
	Health Belief Model: Personal beliefs influence health behavior	Perceived seriousness
		Perceived susceptibility
		Perceived benefits
		Perceived barriers
		Cues to action
		Modifying variables
		Self-efficacy

	Attribution Theory: There is a cause or explanation for things that happen	Locus of control
		Stability
		Controllability
	Transtheoretical Model or Stages of Change: Behavior change is a process that occurs in stages	Stages of change
		Processes of change
		Self-efficacy
	Protection Motivation theory: Fear triggers threat and coping appraisals which motivate people to change attitudes and behaviors	Threat severity
		Threat probability
		Response efficacy
		Self-efficacy expectancy
		Response cost
Interpersonal	*Social Cognitive Theory:* Behavior, personal factors, and environmental factors interact with each other, and changing one changes them all	Self-efficacy
		Observational learning
		Expectations
		Expectancies
		Emotional arousal
		Behavioral capability
		Reinforcement
		Locus of control
Community	*Diffusion of Innovation:* Behavior changes as innovations are adopted	Innovation
		Communication channels
		Time
		Social system
	Ecological Models: Factors at many levels influence health behavior	Intrapersonal level
		Interpersonal level
		Community level
		Institution level
		Societal level
	Social Capital Theory: Behavior is influenced by who we know and how we know them	Bonding relationships
		Bridging relationships
		Linking relationships

It's important to identify a theory that *explains* why people engage in a particular unhealthy behavior, but equally as important to use it when developing interventions. Consequently, there should be evidence of the theory's effectiveness in changing the underlying causes or determinants of the unhealthy behavior, evidence that by changing them the unhealthy behavior can be changed to a healthier one, and evidence that the intervention techniques are effective in changing the theoretical construct domain (Michie, Johnson, Francis, Hardeman, & Eccles, 2008) (see **TABLE 12.2**). Construct domains are the underlying focus of the construct, such as ability, beliefs in self-efficacy, and social influences in subjective norms.

The techniques provided in **TABLE 12.3** are not meant to be exhaustive, but rather a starting point.

TABLE 12.2 Constructs and Domains			
Level	**Theory**	**Construct**	**Construct Domain**
Intrapersonal	*Self-Efficacy Theory:* People will only try to do what they think they can do, and people won't try what they think they can't do	Mastery experience	Skill
		Vicarious experience	Skills
		Verbal persuasion	Ability beliefs, skills
		Emotional state	Emotions
	Theory of Reasoned Action and Theory of Planned Behavior: Health behavior results from intention influenced by attitude, norms, and control	Attitudes	Emotions
		Subjective norms	Social influence
		Behavioral control	Ability beliefs
		Volitional control	Ability beliefs
	Health Belief Model: Personal beliefs influence health behavior	Perceived seriousness	Consequence beliefs
		Perceived susceptibility	Consequence beliefs
		Perceived benefits	Consequence beliefs
		Perceived barriers	Consequence beliefs
		Cues to action	Social influence, decision process
		Modifying variables	Motivation
		Self-efficacy	
			Ability beliefs

	Attribution Theory: There is a cause or explanation for things that happen	Locus of control	Ability beliefs, social influences
		Stability	Emotions, coping skills
		Controllability	Ability beliefs, social influences
	Transtheoretical Model or Stages of Change: Behavior change is a process that occurs in stages	Stages of change	Action plans
		Processes of change	Decision process
		Self-efficacy	Ability beliefs
	Protection Motivation theory: Fear triggers threat and coping appraisals which motivate people to change attitudes and behaviors	Threat severity	Motivation, knowledge
		Threat probability	Motivation, knowledge
		Response efficacy	Knowledge
		Self-efficacy expectancy	Ability beliefs
		Response cost	Knowledge, social influences
Interpersonal	*Social Cognitive Theory:* Behavior, personal factors, and environmental factors interact with each other, and changing one changes them all	Self-efficacy	Ability beliefs
		Observational learning	Motivation
		Expectations	Consequence beliefs
		Expectancies	Consequence beliefs
		Emotional arousal	Emotions
		Behavioral capability	Skills
		Reinforcement	Social influence
		Locus of control	Ability beliefs, social influence
Community	*Diffusion of Innovation:* Behavior changes as innovations are adopted	Innovation	Social influence
		Communication channels	Motivation
		Time	Social influences
		Social system	Social influences

(continues)

TABLE 12.2 Constructs and Domains (*continued*)

Level	Theory	Construct	Construct Domain
	Ecological Models: Factors at many levels influence health behavior	Intrapersonal level	Ability beliefs, knowledge, skills, emotions, motivation
		Interpersonal level	Social influences, motivation
		Community level	Social influences, action plans
		Institution level	Social influences, motivation
		Societal level	Social influences, action plans
	Social Capital Theory: Behavior is influenced by who we know and how we know them	Bonding relationships	Consequence beliefs, motivation, emotions
		Bridging relationships	Social influences, consequence beliefs, motivation
		Linking relationships	Social influences, consequence beliefs, motivation

THEORY IN ACTION—CLASS ACTIVITY

There is growing concern over the misuse of antibiotics. Since their disbursement is by prescription only, the source of the problem lies squarely with healthcare professionals with prescription powers. Therefore, one way to address the issue is to persuade those individuals to prescribe methods other than antibiotics for the treatment of infections often caused by pathogens other than bacteria; for example upper respiratory infections, ear infections, and sore throats.

Although there is considerable research in the literature on the issue of antibiotic misuse in the treatment of these infections, the problem persists.

In small groups:

1. Brainstorm possible reasons why healthcare professionals continue to prescribe antibiotic treatment for infections that do not warrant them.
2. Using the constructs domain chart (Table 12.2) identify a theory and constructs/construct domains that might explain each of the reasons and be useful as the basis for an intervention.

Next, read the following article and answer the questions at the end.

TABLE 12.3 Construct Domains and Intervention Techniques

Use this Technique	For this Construct Domain								
	Knowledge	Skills	Ability Beliefs	Consequence Beliefs	Motivation	Decision Process	Social Influences	Emotions	Action Plans
Goal/target/outcome		XXX							xxx
Self-monitoring		XXX	Xxx	XXX		xxx			
Contracts									xx
Rewards		Xxx			Xxx				
Graded task, easy to difficult		Xxx	Xxx		Xxx				
Problem solving, decision making	xxx	Xxx	Xxx		Xxx				
Stress management								Xxxx	
Coping skills			Xxx					Xxx	
Planning and implementation						XXXX			Xxx

(continues)

TABLE 12.3 Construct Domains and Intervention Techniques (*continued*)

Use this Technique	For this Construct Domain								
	Knowledge	Skills	Ability Beliefs	Consequence Beliefs	Motivation	Decision Process	Social Influences	Emotions	Action Plans
Prompts, triggers, and cues						Xxx			xxx
Peer pressure or social support			Xxx		Xxx		Xxx		
Persuasive communication				Xxx	Xxx		Xxx		
Modeling, demonstration		Xxx							
Homework	xxx	xxx							
Feedback			Xxx	Xxx					
Positive self-talk			Xxx						
Imagery									xxx
Perform in different settings		Xxx							

Modified from: Michie, S., Johnston, M., Francis, J., Hardeman, W., & Eccles, M. (2008). From theory to intervention: Mapping theoretically derived behavior determinants to behavior change techniques. *Applied Psychology, 57*(4), 660–680. DOI: 10.1111/j.1464-5097.2008.00341.x

Chapter 12 Article: Developing the content of two behavioural interventions: Using theory-based interventions to promote GP management of upper respiratory tract infection without prescribing antibiotics #1[1]

Susan Hrisos[1]*, Martin Eccles[1], Marie Johnston[2], Jill Francis[3], Eileen FS Kaner[1], Nick Steen[1] and Jeremy Grimshaw[4]

[1]Institute of Health and Society, Newcastle University
[2]Department of Psychology, University of Aberdeen
[3]Health Services Research Unit, University of Aberdeen
[4]Clinical Epidemiology Program, Ottawa Health Research Institute and Department of Medicine, University of Ottawa

Abstract

Background: Evidence shows that antibiotics have limited effectiveness in the management of upper respiratory tract infection (URTI) yet GPs continue to prescribe antibiotics. Implementation research does not currently provide a strong evidence base to guide the choice of interventions to promote the uptake of such evidence-based practice by health professionals. While systematic reviews demonstrate that interventions to change clinical practice can be effective, heterogeneity between studies hinders generalisation to routine practice. Psychological models of behaviour change that have been used successfully to predict variation in behaviour in the general population can also predict the clinical behaviour of healthcare professionals. The purpose of this study was to design two theoretically-based interventions to promote the management of upper respiratory tract infection (URTI) without prescribing antibiotics.

Method: Interventions were developed using a systematic, empirically informed approach in which we: selected theoretical frameworks; identified modifiable behavioural antecedents that predicted GPs intended and actual management of URTI; mapped these target antecedents on to evidence-based behaviour change techniques; and operationalised intervention components in a format suitable for delivery by postal questionnaire.

Results: We identified two psychological constructs that predicted GP management of URTI: "Self-efficacy," representing belief in one's capabilities, and "Anticipated

1 Reproduced from Hrisos, S., Eccles, M., Johnston, M., Francis, J., Kaner, E.F.S., et al., (2008). Developing the content of two behavioral interventions: Using theory based interventions to promote GP management of upper respiratory tract infection without prescribing antibiotics. *BMC Health Services Research, 8*(11), 1–8. doi: 10.1186/1472-6963-8-11

* Corresponding author.

consequences," representing beliefs about the consequences of one's actions. Behavioural techniques known to be effective in changing these beliefs were used in the design of two paper-based, interactive interventions. Intervention 1 targeted self-efficacy and required GPs to consider progressively more difficult situations in a "graded task" and to develop an "action plan" of what to do when next presented with one of these situations. Intervention 2 targeted anticipated consequences and required GPs to respond to a "persuasive communication" containing a series of pictures representing the consequences of managing URTI with and without antibiotics.

Conclusion: It is feasible to systematically develop theoretically-based interventions to change professional practice. Two interventions were designed that differentially target generalisable constructs predictive of GP management of URTI. Our detailed and scientific rationale for the choice and design of our interventions will provide a basis for understanding any effects identified in their evaluation.

Trial registration: Clinicaltrials.gov NCT00376142

▶ Background

Despite the considerable resources devoted to promoting the use of new evidence by clinicians, translating clinical and health services research findings into routine clinical practice is an unpredictable and often slow process. This phenomenon is apparent across different healthcare settings, specialties and countries, including the UK,[1-5] other parts of Europe[4] and the USA,[5, 6] with obvious implications for the quality of patient care.

Many systematic reviews of implementation interventions show that various interventions (e.g., reminder systems, interactive educational sessions) can be effective in changing health care professionals' clinical behaviour[7-11] but a consistent message is that these are effective only some and not all of the time. Why interventions have such variable success is difficult to establish as few of the studies reviewed to date provide an underlying theoretical basis to explain how or why an intervention might work.[12] Without such understanding of an intervention's "active ingredients" and what factors modify its effectiveness, there is little to guide the choice of intervention other than intuition or the knowledge that a similar intervention has been empirically successful in a previous study.[9]

Interventions to implement evidence-based practice are often complex. The framework for the investigation of complex interventions suggested by the Medical Research council (MRC)[13] illustrates the current situation with implementation research (**TABLE A.1**). To date most implementation research studies aiming to change clinicians' behaviour have involved trials at the exploratory or definitive randomised controlled trials (RCTs) stages of this framework, with few published studies providing evidence of preceding theoretical or modelling research. We aimed to address this gap in the current evidence-base through the development of a systematic intervention modelling process (IMP) for intervention development and evaluation that corresponds to each of the theoretical, modelling and experimental phases of the MRC Framework.[14]

Incorporating research findings into clinical practice almost invariably necessitates a change in clinical behaviour. Based on the idea that clinical behaviour is a form of human behaviour, we applied psychological models of behaviour change that have been used to predict variation in behaviour in the general population to the clinical behaviour

TABLE A.1 Comparison of the stages in an evaluation of complex interventions to stages of drug evaluation

Evaluation of drugs	Pre-clinical	Phase I	Phase II	Phase III	Phase IV
Evaluation of implementation strategies	Theory	Modelling	Exploratory trial	Definitive RCT	Long-term implementation

Reproduced from Hrisos, S., Eccles, M., Johnston, M., Francis, J., Kaner, E.F.S., et al., (2008). Developing the content of two behavioral interventions: Using theory based interventions to promote GP management of upper respiratory tract infection without prescribing antibiotics. *BMC Health Services Research, 8*(11), 1–8. doi: 10.1186/1472-6963-8-11

of healthcare professionals. There is growing evidence to support the use of such theories in this way.[15–17] Psychological theory also underpins many behaviour change techniques for which there is evidence of effectiveness in changing the behaviour in other settings. Knowledge of the target behaviour or its cognitive antecedents is used to guide the selection of relevant interventions. For example, if individuals' beliefs about their capabilities relevant to a given task predict their behaviour, then their behaviour may be changed if they work through a series of tasks graded in order of increasing difficulty. This technique has been demonstrated to strengthen beliefs about capabilities.

This paper describes the process we used to design two theory-based interventions to promote the evidence-based management of upper respiratory tract infection, by GPs, without prescribing antibiotics. To enable experimental modelling and evaluation of the interventions prior to their use in a definitive RCT—which also forms part of the IMP—the interventions were developed in the context of an "intervention modelling experiment" (IME).[16] In an IME, key elements of an intervention are manipulated in a manner that simulates the "real world" as much as possible, but the measured outcome is an interim, or proxy, endpoint that represents the behaviour, rather than the actual behaviour itself. The evaluation of the interventions described here is reported in our partner paper.[18]

▶ Methods

The process for the choice and development of the interventions was through a series of systematic steps, summarised in **TABLE A.2**.

Specification of the target behaviour/s

The consultation for upper respiratory tract infection (URTI) is one of the most frequent in general practice.[19] Research evidence has shown that antibiotics are of limited effectiveness in treating URTI.[20–22] However, GPs continue to manage patients with uncomplicated URTI by prescribing antibiotics.[23, 24] In specifying our target behaviour, we used the "TACT" principle, a systematic way of defining behaviour in terms of its Target, Action, Context and Time.[25] For the behaviour, "managing patients presenting with uncomplicated URTI without prescribing antibiotics", the target is the patient, the action is managing without prescribing an antibiotic, the context is the clinical condition (uncomplicated URTI) and the time is during a primary care consultation.

TABLE A.2 Steps in developing a theory based behavioural intervention	
1.	Specify target behaviour(s).
2.	Select theoretical framework (for empirical investigation at baseline and to assess process).
3.	Conduct a predictive study with a (preferably representative) sample drawn from the population of interest, to identify modifiable variables that predict the target behaviour(s) and their means/distributions. Based on the findings of this study, choose which variables to target. These variables are the proposed mediators of behaviour change.
4.	Map targeted variables onto behaviour change techniques and select techniques that (a) are likely to change the mediator variables and (b) it is feasible to operationalise.
5.	Choose appropriate method(s) of delivery of the techniques.
6.	Operationalise intervention components (techniques) in appropriate combination and order.

Note: As part of an iterative process, results from the implementation modelling experiment will provide information for feedback loops that address earlier points in this sequence. This feedback loop permits change, development or refinement of the intervention.

Reproduced from Hrisos, S., Eccles, M., Johnston, M., Francis, J., Kaner, E.F.S., et al., (2008). Developing the content of two behavioral interventions: Using theory based interventions to promote GP management of upper respiratory tract infection without prescribing antibiotics. *BMC Health Services Research, 8*(11), 1–8. doi: 10.1186/1472-6963-8-11

Selection of the theoretical framework

Our choice of theoretical framework was guided by the findings of a previous study by the authors which explored the utility of a range of psychological models in identifying provider-level factors predictive of clinical behaviour.[26] This study found that three theories included constructs that predicted GPs' prescribing behaviour for URTI: Theory of Planned Behaviour (TPB),[27] Social Cognitive Theory (SCT)[28, 29] and Operant Learning Theory (OLT).[30] These theories explain behaviour in terms of factors amenable to change (e.g., beliefs, perceived external constraints); and they include non-volitional components that acknowledge that individuals do not always have complete control over their actions. They have also been rigorously evaluated in other settings, providing a sound scientific basis for the development of interventions.

According to the TPB, specific behaviours can be predicted by the strength of an individual's intention to enact that behaviour. Intentions are thus the precursors of behaviour and the stronger the intention, the more likely it is that the behaviour will occur. Intention is, in turn, influenced by the individual's attitudes towards the behaviour; their perceptions of social pressure to perform the behaviour ("subjective norms"); and the extent to which they feel able to perform the behaviour ("perceived behavioural control"). SCT considers self-efficacy (confidence that one is able to perform the behaviour), outcome expectancy (an individual's estimate that a given behaviour will lead to certain outcomes), risk perception and individuals' goals in explaining behaviour, including proximal goals (such as intentions). OLT proposes that behaviours that have contingent consequences for the individual are more likely to be repeated when the individual's "anticipated consequences" of their behaviour are favourable, and will become less frequent if their anticipated consequences are less positive. OLT also proposes that behaviours performed frequently in the same situation are likely to become habitual (automatic).[30]

These theoretical frameworks allow the identification of potential causal pathways underlying behaviour change (i.e., evaluation of thought processes that explain behaviour change). Within any subsequent evaluation of the impact of the intervention being developed, the measurement of potential mediators of behaviour change targeted by an intervention allows an understanding of the causal mechanisms involved in the change. This is one part of a "process evaluation".

Identification of constructs to target for change

In addition to guiding our choice of theoretical framework, we also used the findings of Eccles *et al.*[26] to identify which constructs to target with our interventions. In that study, a random sample of GPs from Scotland were surveyed about their views and experiences of managing patients with uncomplicated URTI. Theory-based cognitions were measured by a single postal questionnaire survey during a 12 month period. Two interim outcome measures of stated intention and behavioural simulation were collected at the same time as the predictor measures. GPs' simulated behaviour was elicited using five clinical scenarios describing patients presenting in primary care with symptoms of an URTI. GPs were asked to decide whether or not they would prescribe an antibiotic and decisions in favour of prescribing an antibiotic were summed to create a total score out of a possible maximum of five. Data on actual prescribing behaviour were also collected from routinely available prescribing data for the same 12 month period. Analyses explored the predictive value of theory based cognitions in explaining variance in the behavioural data (**TABLE A.3**).

In considering the most important constructs to target in this modelling experiment we selected constructs that were significantly correlated with GPs' actual behaviour (rates of prescribing antibiotics). There were five candidate psychological constructs: Intention (TPB); risk perception and self-efficacy (SCT) and anticipated consequences and evidence of habitual behaviour (OLT) (Table A.3). Scores on these constructs were also significantly correlated with behavioural simulation scores. As Intention was also to be a dependent variable in the modelling experiment it was not appropriate to directly target this construct. Habitual behaviour was also not selected as a target variable as it is not a causal determinant but rather an attribute of behaviour, and is modified indirectly by targeting other causal aspects of behaviour. The remaining three constructs: self-efficacy, risk perception and anticipated consequences were the theoretical constructs chosen as targets for our interventions.

Mapping targeted constructs onto behaviour change techniques

In choosing the most appropriate behaviour change techniques for the target constructs, we first mapped the three target constructs onto the theoretical construct domains identified by Michie et al. (2005)[31] (**TABLE A.4**). We then used a recently developed tool which further maps these theoretical construct domains on to behaviour change techniques.[32] This tool documents expert consensus on the use of 35 behaviour change techniques as appropriate interventions to change each construct domain. The techniques are supported by evidence of their effectiveness.[33]

TABLE A.3 Summary of the systematic selection of theoretical constructs to target in the development of the interventions[1]

Theoretical Construct	Intention		Simulated Behaviour		Behaviour		Mapped beliefs that discriminate between GPs who do and do not intend to manage URTI without antibiotics[17]
TPB	Predictor Y/N	r	Predictor Y/N	r	Predictor Y/N	r	
Attitude direct*	Y	0.49	Y	0.32	N	0.07	
Attitude indirect*	Y	0.41	Y	0.21	N	0.02	
Intention	–	–	Y	0.44	Y	0.19*	
PBC direct	Y	−0.28	Y	−0.39	N	−0.04	
PBC indirect	Y	0.60	Y	0.49	N	0.17*	
Subjective norm	N	0.04	N	0.005	N	−0.10	

SCT							
**Risk perception	Y	0.54	Y	0.35	Y	0.17*	■ Prescribing an antibiotic for these patients will reduce their risk of developing minor complications such as otitis media and sinusitis (BB) ■ Because I don't know the cause of these patients' sore throats, I will prescribe an antibiotic so that I don't miss something (CB) ■ In most cases, the patient will finish the course of antibiotics I prescribe (CB)
Outcome expectancy (2 items)	Y	0.41	Y	0.19	N	−0.05	
Outcome expectancy (7 items)	Y	0.21	Y	0.27	N	−0.03	
Self-efficacy	Y	0.56	Y	0.43	Y	0.14*	■ If a patient asks for an antibiotic then I will prescribe one whether it is medically indicated or not (CB) ■ I am more inclined to prescribe an antibiotic for patients of a lower social class (CB) ■ Because I don't know the cause of these patients' sore throats, I will prescribe an antibiotic so that I don't miss something (CB) ■ In most cases, the patient will finish the course of antibiotics I prescribe (CB)

(continues)

TABLE A.3 Summary of the systematic selection of theoretical constructs to target in the development of the interventions[1] *(continued)*

						OLT
**Anticipated consequences	Y	0.54	Y	0.35	0.17*	■ Prescribing an antibiotic for these patients will reduce their risk of developing minor complications such as otitis media and sinusitis (BB) ■ Because I don't know the cause of these patients' sore throats, I will prescribe an antibiotic so that I don't miss something (CB) ■ In most cases, the patient will finish the course of antibiotics I prescribe (CB)
Evidence of habitual behaviour	Y	0.64	Y	0.46	0.23*	Y

1. Data from interim analysis of dataset[25]

* TPB attitudes and PBC constructs can be measured "indirectly" by asking individuals to report their specific beliefs or directly by asking individuals to report at a more general level

**The SCT risk perception questions were also used as a measure of OC anticipated consequences. CB = Control Belief; BB = Behavioural Belief

Reproduced from Hrisos, S., Eccles, M., Johnston, M., Francis, J., Kaner, E.F.S., et al., (2008). Developing the content of two behavioral interventions: Using theory based interventions to promote GP management of upper respiratory tract infection without prescribing antibiotics. *BMC Health Services Research, 8*(11), 1–8. doi: 10.1186/1472-6963-8-11

TABLE A.4 Mapping of target constructs to construct domain & behavioural change techniques

Target Construct	Construct Domain	Behavioural Change Techniques
Self-Efficacy (SCT)	Beliefs about one's capabilities	■ Self-monitoring ■ Graded Task ■ Increasing skills ■ Coping skill ■ Rehearsal ■ Social pressure ■ Feedback ■ Self-talk ■ Motivational interviewing
[1]Risk perception [1]Anticipated consequences	Beliefs about the consequences of one's action	■ Self-monitoring ■ Persuasive communication ■ Information regarding behaviour outcome, connection between the two ■ Feedback

[1] Risk perception & Anticipated consequences are similar constructs and use a shared measure.

Reproduced from Hrisos, S., Eccles, M., Johnston, M., Francis, J., Kaner, E.F.S., et al., (2008). Developing the content of two behavioral interventions: Using theory based interventions to promote GP management of upper respiratory tract infection without prescribing antibiotics. *BMC Health Services Research, 8*(11), 1–8. doi: 10.1186/1472-6963-8-11

Choose an appropriate method of delivery

A paper-based method of delivery of the intervention was chosen because, recognising the geographical spread of the sample, for a subsequent evaluation greater efficiency would be obtained if the experiment could be administered by post.

Operationalising the intervention components

Different ways of operationalising the interventions as paper-based tasks were developed using an iterative process involving the study team members (MJ, JF, SH, EFK & ME). It was important to recognise that a paper-based format might be a relatively passive means of delivering the intervention components. Hence to limit this possibility, the interventions were operationalised to maximise the interactive nature of each intervention component.

▶ Results

Two interventions were developed, directed at changing different constructs. The first intervention targeted the theoretical construct of self-efficacy (from SCT). This construct mapped on to the theoretical construct domain, "beliefs about capabilities". The main behaviour change technique selected was "graded task".[29] The aim of this intervention was to increase GPs' beliefs in their capabilities of managing URTI without prescribing antibiotics. The graded task technique does this by promoting incrementally greater levels of "mastery" by building on existing abilities, demonstrating success at each level. Two further behaviour change techniques, "rehearsal" and "action planning" were additional components of this intervention. The "rehearsal" technique used the generation of alternative strategies as a way of rehearsing alternative actions that could be applied to the clinical situation. The "action planning" technique involved asking the participants to develop a plan of actions they intended to take when confronted by a clinical situation in which a patient presented with an URTI. Interventions are named according to the principle behaviour technique used.

- *Graded Task intervention* (Additional file 1): Recipients were presented with five situations in which GPs would be required to manage a patient presenting with sore throat. The situations were derived from questionnaire items used in the predictive survey[17] and ranked in order of difficulty based on the responses to these questions by GPs. Starting with the easiest, respondents were asked to consider each of these situations in turn, and to indicate if they could confidently manage the patient without prescribing an antibiotic. The response format was "Yes," "Maybe" and "No". Thus the typical pattern of responses would be a series of successes ("yes") before a series of failures ("no") in response to more difficult situations. They were then asked to select the situation that they found the least difficult to achieve from those they had rated as "Maybe" or "No," and write the number of this situation in a box provided. If they had rated all of the situations listed as "Yes," they were asked to write down a related situation that they would find difficult to achieve. Focusing on their selected situation, participants were then instructed to a) generate possible alternative management strategies for that situation and then b) to develop a plan of what they would do to manage this situation in the future.

The second intervention targeted the theoretical constructs of anticipated consequences (from OLT) and risk perception (from SCT). These constructs both mapped on to the theoretical construct domain "beliefs about consequences". The behaviour change technique selected was "persuasive communication." The aim of this intervention was to encourage GPs to consider some potential consequences for themselves, their patients and society of managing URTI with and without prescribing antibiotics. This intervention also incorporated elements of the behaviour change technique, "provide information regarding behaviour, outcome and connection between the two" (Table A.4).

- *Persuasive Communication intervention* (Additional file 2): This intervention presented GPs with two sequences of five pictures illustrating some possible consequences of managing URTIs with or without antibiotics. The consequence illustrated in each fictitious situation depicted was created to reflect the content of questionnaire items used by Eccles *et al.*[26] to ask about risk perception and anticipated consequences; and the discriminant beliefs identified by Walker *et al.*[17] as predictive of GPs who do and do not intend to manage URTI without antibiotics. The first row of pictures represents "Dr A", who manages URTI by prescribing antibiotics and the second row representing "Dr B", who manages URTI without prescribing antibiotics. To highlight the suggested consequences and to help recipients relate these possible consequences to each doctor's prescribing behaviour, questions were placed beneath each picture. Participants were not required to respond to these questions. However, to further enhance the interactive nature of this intervention GPs were asked to indicate on a bi-polar analogue scale a) the extent to which they try to be like Dr A or Dr B (i.e., their "intended" behaviour) and b) the extent to which they are actually like Dr A or Dr B (i.e., their "actual" behaviour).

▶ Discussion

A major problem with implementation research to date has been the limited understanding about what interventions contain and how they are meant to work. Contributing to this is the frequently scant, or absent, reporting of the process of intervention development. In addition, few studies provide a theoretical basis for the choice and design of interventions to change clinical practice. We have developed an intervention modelling process (IMP) that corresponds closely to the theoretical and early modelling phases of the MRC Framework[13]—explicit stages of development that are currently lacking in implementation research. The systematic approach we have used here in the development of the content of two theory-based behavioural interventions forms the initial part of the IMP.

The contents of the interventions were designed to differentially target specific "determinants of behaviour change"—theoretical constructs that were identified in a previous study as predictive of both the behaviour and the intention of GPs to manage URTI without prescribing antibiotics. This was achieved by linking these constructs to appropriate behaviour change techniques. The basis for our choice of target constructs is strengthened by the established predictive utility of the theoretical models we used in this process. Likewise, the behaviour change techniques used are also supported by a substantial evidence base for their effectiveness across a range of settings.[33,34] Thus the final interventions are underpinned by a robust scientific rationale with which to explain "why and how" we expect each intervention to have their effect, and are placed within a sound theoretical framework that guides a process for their evaluation and refinement.

In general, the poor reporting of intervention detail, prevents replication. Such inadequate description of implementation interventions hinders the development of a cumulative science of implementation. We have tried to illustrate here the type of description of intervention components that will make it possible to replicate their essential features. By describing the interventions in terms of discrete and identifiable behaviour change techniques we are clearly differentiating between the key components of the intervention content (the proposed "active ingredients") and the method by which the intervention was delivered (i.e., as a paper-based task). Such differentiation makes it possible to investigate whether the same behaviour change techniques differ in effectiveness across other modes of delivery, whilst also offering the potential to explain differences in effectiveness across different settings. Routine reporting of detailed description—such as we provide here—would greatly enhance the replicability of implementation studies.

The systematic approach used in this study was constrained in two ways. Firstly, the choice of target constructs was limited to those which predicted both simulated and actual prescribing behaviour. We applied this limitation because an evaluation of these interventions will be generalisable to the real clinical context only if there is close correspondence between the measures of intention, simulated behaviour and actual behaviour. However, external validation for our choice of target constructs is provided by Walker et al 2001, as our target constructs are represented in the discriminant beliefs identified by these authors.[17] Secondly, the chosen mode of delivery (paper-based and postal survey) influenced both the choice of behaviour change technique and the construction of the intervention components. A secondary aim of this theory-based approach is to develop methods for "pre-testing" and optimising the potential effect of interventions (implementation modelling experiments) prior to their use at service-level. Hence, a final consideration was the feasibility of using the techniques in both a modelling experiment context and a service-level randomised controlled trial. Our choice of behaviour change techniques was thus further influenced by their adaptability to the real-world setting.

▶ Conclusion

We have demonstrated that it is feasible to develop interventions to change professional practice that are underpinned by a robust, scientific rationale. Theoretical models, empirical data and evidence-based behaviour change techniques were integrated systematically to produce two interventions that aim to change clinical behaviour. This approach is a way forward towards creating a scientific evidence-base relating to the choice, development and delivery of effective interventions to increase evidence-based clinical practice.

▶ Acknowledgements

This study is funded by the European Commission Research Directorate as part of a multi-partner program: Research Based Education and Quality Improvement (ReBEQI): A Framework and tools to develop effective quality improvement programs in European healthcare. (Proposal No: QLRT-2001-00657). Jeremy Grimshaw holds a Canada Research Chair in Health Knowledge Transfer and Uptake. Jill Francis is a member of the Aberdeen Health Psychology Group, funded by the Institute of Applied Health Sciences, and of the Health Services Research Unit, funded by the Chief Scientist Office of the Scottish Executive Department of Health. The views expressed are not necessarily those of the funding bodies.

▶ References

1. Smith TDW, Clayton D: Individual variation between general practitioners in labelling of hypertension. BMJ 1990, 300:74–75.
2. Eccles M, Bradshaw C: Use of secondary prophylaxis against myocardial infarction in the North of England. BMJ 1991, 302:91–92.
3. Ketley D, Woods KL: Impact of clinical trials on clinical practice: example of thrombolysis for acute myocardial infarction. Lancet 1993, 342:891–894.
4. Woods KL, Ketley D, Lowy A, Agusti A, Hagn C, Kala R, Karatzas NB, Leizorowicz A, Reikvam A, Schilling J, Seabra-Gomes R, Vasiliauskas D, Wilhelmsen L: Beta-blockers and antithrombotic treatment for secondary prevention after acute myocardial infarction. Eur Heart J 1998, 19:74–79.
5. Chassin MR, Brook RH, Park RE, Keesey J, Fink A, Kosecoff J, Kahn K, Merrick N, Solomon DH: Variations in the use of medical and surgical services by the Medicare population. N Engl J Med 1986, 314(5):285–290.
6. Winslow CM, Solomon DH, Chassin MR, Kosecoff J, Merrick NJ, Brook RH: The appropriateness of carotid endarterectomy. N Engl J Med 1988, 318(12):721–727.
7. Bero L, Grilli R, Grimshaw JM, Harvey E, Oxman AD, Thomson MA: Closing the gap between research and practice: an overview of systematic reviews of interventions to promote implementation of research findings by health care professionals. BMJ 1998, 317:465–468.

8. Oxman AD, Thomson MA, Davis DA, Haynes RB: No magic bullets: a systematic review of 102 trials of interventions to improve professional practice. CMAJ 1995, 153(10):1423–1431.
9. Grimshaw J, Shirran L, E TR, Mowatt G, Fraser C, Bero L: Changing provider behaviour: an overview of systematic reviews of interventions. Med Care 2001, 39(Suppl 2):II-2-II-45.
10. Ranji SR, Steinman MA, Shojania KG, Sundaram V, Lewis R, Arnold S, Gonzales R: Antibiotic prescribing behavior Vol 4. In Closing the quality gap: a critical analysis of quality improvement strategies Technical Review 9. Edited by: Shojania KG, McDonald KM, Wachter RM, Owens DK. Rockville MD, Agency for Healthcare Research and Quality; 2006:255–261.
11. Shojania KG, Ranji SR, McDonald KM, Grimshaw JM, Sundaram V, Rushakoff RJ, Owens DK: Effects of quality improvement strategies for type 2 diabetes on glycemic control. JAMA 2006, 296(4):427–440.
12. Davies P: The use of psychological theories in clinical guideline implementation research (PhD Thesis). University of Aberdeen; 2003.
13. Medical Research Council: A framework for development and evaluation of RCTs for complex interventions to improve health. 2000.
14. Eccles MP, Johnston M, Hrisos S, Francis J, Grimshaw J, Steen IN, Kaner EF: Translating clinicians' beliefs into implementation interventions (TRACII): a protocol for an intervention modelling experiment to change clinicians' intentions to implement evidence-based practice. Implementation Science 2007, 2(27).
15. Eccles MP, Hrisos S, Francis J, Kaner E, Dickinson HO, Beyer F, Johnston M: Do self-reported intentions predict clinicians' behaviour: a systematic review. Implementation Science 2006, 1:28.
16. Bonetti D, Eccles M, Johnston M, Steen IN, Grimshaw J, Baker R, Walker A, Pitts N: Guiding the design and selection of interventions to influence the implementation of evidence-based practice: an experimental simulation of a complex intervention trial. Soc Sci Med 2005, 60:2135–2147.
17. Walker AE, Grimshaw JM, Armstrong E: Salient beliefs and intentions to prescribe antibiotics for patients with a sore throat. British Journal of Health Psychology 2001, 6:347–360.
18. Hrisos S, Eccles MP, Johnston M, Francis J, Kaner E, Steen IN, Grimshaw J: An intervention modelling experiment to change GPs' intentions to implement evidence-based practice: Using theory-based interventions to promote GP management of upper respiratory tract infection without prescribing antibiotics #2. BMC Health Serv Res 2008, 8(1):10.
19. Butler CC Hood, K, Kinnersley, P, Robling, M, Prout, H, Houston, H, et al.: Predicting the clinical course of suspected acute viral upper respiratory tract infection in children. Fam Pract 2005, 22(1):92–95.
20. Del Mar CB, Glasziou PP, Spinks AB: Antiobiotics for sore throat. Cochrane Database Syst Rev 2004:CD000023.
21. Spurling GK, Del Mar CB, Dooley L, Foxlee R: Delayed antibiotics for symptoms and complications of respiratory infections. Cochrane Database Syst Rev 2004:CD004417.
22. Arroll B, Kenealy T, Kerse N: Do delayed prescriptions reduce antibiotic use in respiratory tract infections? A systematic review. Br J Gen Pract 2003, 53(496):871–877.
23. Ashworth M, Charlton J, Ballard K, Latinovic R, Guilliford M: Variations in antibiotic prescribing and consultation rates for acute respiratory infection in UK general practices 1995–2000. Br J Gen Pract 2005, 55:603–608.
24. Ashworth M, Latinovic R, Charlton J, Cox K, Rowlands G, Gulliford M: Why has antibiotic prescribing for respiratory illness declined in primary care? A longitudinal study using the General Practice Research Database. Journal of Public Health 2004, 26:268–274.
25. Fishbein M: Attitude and the prediction of behavior. In Readings in atttiude theory and measurement. Edited by: Fishbein M. New York, Wiley; 1967:477–492.
26. Eccles MP, Grimshaw JM, Johnston M, Steen N, Pitts NB, Thomas R, Glidewell E, Maclennan G, Bonetti D, Walker A: Applying psychological theories to evidence-based clinical practice: identifying factors predictive of managing upper respiratory tract infections without antibiotics. Implementation Science 2007, 2(August):26.
27. Ajzen I: The theory of planned behaviour. Organizational Behaviour and Human Decision Processes 1991, 50:179–211.
28. Bandura A: Self-efficacy: the exercise of control. New York , Freeman; 1997.

29. Bandura A: Health promotion from the perspective of social cognitive theory. In Understanding and changing Health Behaviour: from Health Beliefs to Self-Regulation. Edited by: Norman P, Abraham C, Conner M. Amsterdam , Harwood; 2000.

30. Blackman D: Operant conditioning: an experimental analysis of behaviour. Edited by: Blackman D. London , Methuen; 1974.

31. Michie S, Johnston M, Abraham C, Lawton R, Parker D, Walker A: 'Psychological Theory' Group. Making psychological theory useful for implementing evidence based practice: a consensus approach. Quality & Safety in Health Care 2005, 14(1):26–33.

32. Francis JJ, Michie S, Johnston M, Hardeman W, Eccles MP: How do behaviour change techniques map on to psychological constructs? Results of a consensus process: Galway, Ireland. Volume 20 Suppl 1. Psychology & Health; 2005:83–84.

33. Bandura A: Self-efficacy: towards a unifying theory of behaviour change. Psychological Review 1977, 84:191–215.

34. Bonetti D, Johnston M, Pitts NB, Deery C, Ricketts I, Bahrami M, Ramsay C, Johnston J: Can psychological models bridge the gap between clinical guidelines and clinicians' behaviour? A randomised controlled trial of an intervention to influence dentists' intention to implement evidence-based practice. Br Dent J 2003, 195(7):403–407.

THEORY IN ACTION—ARTICLE QUESTIONS

1. What do the authors state is their guide for choosing or developing appropriate interventions?
2. What three theories did the authors identify as containing constructs predictive of physician prescription behaviors?
3. How do these theories compare with the theories your group identified?
4. What three constructs from which of the theories discussed in Question 2 were found to most closely predict the prescribing behavior of physicians and chosen as the basis of intervention development?
5. What theory, construct, construct domain, and behavior change techniques were used in the development of the first intervention?
6. What steps did the authors take to develop their interventions?
7. What were the similarities and differences between the results of your brainstorming session and the results presented in the article?

▶ Chapter References

Hochbaum, G. M., Sorenson, J. R., & Lorig, K. (1992). Theory in health education. *Health Education Quarterly, 19*(3), 295–313.

Michie, S., Johnston, M., Francis, J., Hardeman, W., & Eccles, M. (2008). From theory to intervention: Mapping theoretically derived behavior determinants to behavior change techniques. *Applied Psychology, 57*(4), 660–680. doi:10.1111/j.1464-5097.2008.00341.x

National Cancer Institute. (2003). *Theory at a glance: A guide for health promotion practice.* Washington, DC: U.S. Department of Health and Human Services.

Nigg, C. R., & Durand, Z. (2016). The theoretical basis for engagement in physical activity among older adults. *Annual Review of Gerontology and Geriatrics, 36*, 251–271. doi:10.1891/0198-8794.36.251

Schwarzer, R. (2014). Life and death of health behavior theories. *Health Psychology, 8*(1), 53–56. doi:10.1080/17437199.2013.810959

Index

Note: Page numbers followed by *f* and *t* indicate figures and tables, respectively.

A

ability/aptitude, 86
Academic Search Complete, 280
acetaminophen, 146
achievement, 83
action, 116
adopters, early, 204
adoption curve, 202–204, 203*f*
AIDS. *See* human immunodeficiency
    virus (HIV)
alcohol overdose, treatment, 3
American cultural norms, 5
antibiotics, misuse of, 286
attitudes, 36–37
    health behavior and, 6
    intention and, 36
Attribution Theory, 2, 283*t*, 285*t*
    concept, 84
    constructs, 84–90
    controllability, 89–90
    flowchart, 90*f*
    locus of control, 85–86
    stability, 86–89
avoidance behavior, 17, 17*f*

B

babysitting, 13
back-and-forth interactions, 226
Bandura, A., 12, 169–170
behavior change. *See* stages of change
behavioral capability, 177–178, 177*f*
behavioral control, 39–40
beliefs, health behavior and, 6
bonding social capital, 255–256
Bourdieu, Pierre, 251
bovine spongiform encephalitis (BSE), 60
bridging social capital, 257

Bronfenbrenner, Urie, 225–226
BRTA program. *See* Business Responds to
    AIDS (BRTA) program
BSE. *See* bovine spongiform encephalitis
    (BSE)
bullying, 175–176, 228, 230
Business Responds to AIDS (BRTA)
    program, 205

C

cancer prevention, "Sun Protection Is Fun"
    program, 15
Centers for Disease Control and Prevention,
    195
    Business Responds to AIDS (BRTA)
        program, 205
change
    processes, 117–121, 122–124, 122*f*,
        123–124*t*
    stages, 112, 122–124, 122*f*, 123–124*t*, 283*t*
child development research, 225
chronic obstructive pulmonary disease,
    self-liberation, 121
CINAHL (Cumulative Index to Nursing and
    Allied Health Literature), 280
CJD. *See* Creutzfeldt–Jakob disease (CJD)
close processes. *See* proximal processes
cognitive processes of change, 117
colon cancer, 61, 62
colonoscopy, 62
colorectal cancer, 61, 229
communication channel, 197–198
community-level factors, health behavior
    and, 231, 231*f*
community-level theories, 2–3, 283*t*,
    285–286*t*
compatibility, 196–197
complexity, 195–196

N

NAGCAT. *See* North American Guidelines for Children's Agriculture Tasks (NAGCAT)
National Highway Traffic Safety Administration, 5
negative reinforcements, 175, 176
neighborhoods, 253–254, 254*f*
networks, of social capital, 252–255, 255*f*
nicotine patch, 115, 195
North American Guidelines for Children's Agriculture Tasks (NAGCAT), 147

O

obesity, 67
and controllability, 89
observability, 197
observational learning (modeling), 174–175
observations, 4
Orthodox Judaism, 6

P

PBA. *See* Pseudobulbar Affect (PBA)
PBC. *See* perceived behavioral control (PBC)
perceived barriers, 62–63, 63*f*
perceived behavioral control (PBC), 40
perceived benefits, 61–62
perceived seriousness, 59
perceived susceptibility, 59–61
personal attributions, 84
personal perception, 58
persuasion, innovation-decision process, 199–200
PMT. *See* Protection Motivation Theory (PMT)
pneumonia, causes, 6
positive reinforcements, 175–176
pre-contemplation stage, 112–113
pre-thinking stage. *See* pre-contemplation stage
preparation, 115, 115*f*
processes of change, 117–121, 122–124, 122*f*, 123–124*t*
Project DARE (Drug Abuse Resistance Education), 202
ProSafe (injury prevention program), 175

Protection Motivation Theory (PMT), 150*f*, 283*t*, 285*t*
concept, 145–146
constructs, 146–150
coping appraisal, 148–150
threat appraisal, 146–148
proximal/close processes, 226
Pseudobulbar Affect (PBA), 199
psychological readiness, 58
PubMed, 281

Q

qualitative research methods, 4

R

reasoning methods, 3–4
reciprocal determinism, 170
factors of, 171
reciprocity, trust and, 252–253
reinforcement
management, 121
SCT and, 175–177
relationship-level factors, health behavior, 228–230
relationships, 255–259, 258*f*
bonding, 256
bridging, 257
linking, 257–258
relative advantage, 193–194
religion, health behavior and, 6
Respecting the Circle of Life: Mind, Body and Soul, 149
response cost, 149, 150*f*
response self-efficacy, 148–150
risk avoidance, 60*f*
risk-taking behavior, 4
"runner's high" effect, 17

S

safer sex, 38, 59, 62, 149, 228
scientific inquiry, 3
SCT. *See* Social Cognitive Theory (SCT)
self-efficacy expectancy, 145, 148–149
Self-Efficacy Theory, 2, 7, 11–30, 18*f*, 282*t*, 284*t*
behavioral control and, 39
characteristics, 11

U

V

W